CONSUMER DEBT AND SOCIAL EXCLUSION IN EUROPE

Markets and the Law

Series Editor:
Geraint Howells, University of Manchester, UK

Markets and the Law is concerned with the way the law interacts with the market through regulation, self-regulation and the impact of private law regimes. It looks at the impact of regional and international organizations (e.g. EC and WTO) and many of the works adopt a comparative approach and/or appeal to an international audience. Examples of subjects covered include trade laws, intellectual property, sales law, insurance, consumer law, banking, financial markets, labour law, environmental law and social regulation affecting the market as well as competition law. The series includes texts covering a broad area, monographs on focused issues, and collections of essays dealing with particular themes.

Other titles in the series

Codifying Contract Law
International and Consumer Law Perspectives
Edited by Mary Keyes and Therese Wilson, both at Griffith University, Australia
ISBN 978-1-4724-1561-5

The European Unfair Commercial Practices Directive
Impact, Enforcement Strategies and National Legal Systems
Edited by Willem van Boom, Amandine Garde and Orkun Akseli
ISBN 978 1 4724 2340 5

The Law and Economics of Enforcing European Consumer Law
A Comparative Analysis of Package Travel and Misleading Advertising
Franziska Weber
ISBN 978 1 4 7241 7046

The Organizational Contract
From Exchange to Long-Term Network Cooperation in European Contract Law
Edited by Stefan Grundmann, Fabrizio Cafaggi and Giuseppe Vettori
ISBN 978 1 4724 2124 1

Consumer Debt and Social Exclusion in Europe

Edited by

HANS-W. MICKLITZ
European University Institute, Italy

IRINA DOMURATH
University of Copenhagen, Denmark

Routledge
Taylor & Francis Group
LONDON AND NEW YORK

First published 2015 by Ashgate Publishing

Published 2016 by Routledge
2 Park Square, Milton Park, Abingdon, Oxon OX14 4RN
605 Third Avenue, New York, NY 10017

First issued in paperback 2021

Routledge is an imprint of the Taylor & Francis Group, an informa business

British Library Cataloguing in Publication Data
A catalogue record for this book is available from the British Library.

Library of Congress Cataloging-in-Publication Data
Micklitz, Hans-W., author.
Consumer debt and social exclusion in Europe / by Hans-W. Micklitz and Irina Domurath.
pages cm. -- (Markets and the law)
Includes bibliographical references and index.
ISBN 978-1-4724-4903-0 (hardback : alk. paper)
1. Consumer credit--Law and legislation--European Union countries. 2. Debtor and creditor--European Union countries. 3. Consumer protection--Law and legislation--European Union countries. 4. Bankruptcy--European Union countries. 5. Foreclosure--European Union countries. 6. Marginality, Social--European Union countries. I. Domurath, Irina. II. Title.
KJE2150.M53 2015
346.407'7--dc23

2014041037

ISBN 13: 978-1-03-209853-1 (pbk)
ISBN 13: 978-1-4724-4903-0 (hbk)

Contents

List of Figures and Tables

Figures

Tables

Notes on Contributors

Beatrice Andresan-Grigoriu is a teacher at the National Institute of Magistracy in Romania and head of the EU law department. Her teaching focuses on general EU law. She studied law at the University of Bucharest and obtained a Magister and Master of Philosophy in European and Comparative Law from the University of Oxford.

Marta Cantero Gamito is a PhD candidate at the European University Institute. She holds degrees in Law, Business Management, and External Trade & International Relations from the University of Cordoba, as well as an LLM from the European University Institute. She is a member of the Spanish Bar Association and a coordinator of the Working Group European Private Law at the European University Institute, Florence, Italy. Her research focus lies in the area of European (regulatory) private law, consumer and contract law.

Guido Comparato is a postdoctoral researcher at the law department of the European University Institute, Florence, Italy, within the research project 'European Regulatory Private Law'. He obtained his PhD from the University of Amsterdam, the Netherlands, where he was a researcher within the Centre for the Study of European Contract Law. His Bachelor and Master of Laws were awarded from the University of Ferrara, Italy. His main research interests lie in the theory and politics of private law.

Irina Domurath is a PhD candidate at the University of Copenhagen and the University of Iceland. She received her legal formation (Humboldt University) as well as admittance to the Bar in Berlin, Germany. She has published articles and contributions on European consumer law, solidarity, and the EEA Agreement. Her PhD topic and main research interest is consumer credit law, the role of credit in modern market economies, and over-indebtedness.

Catarina Frade is Assistant Professor of the School of Economics at the University of Coimbra-Portugal. She holds a degree in law as well as a Master and PhD in Economics. She is a permanent researcher of the Centre for Social Studies and used to be the executive coordinator of the Observatory of Consumer's Indebtedness (2001–2010). Her current research interests are consumer over-indebtedness and bankruptcy, risk and regulation, and economic law.

Pablo Gutiérrez de Cabiedes is Professor of Procedural Law at the University of Zaragoza, Spain. He received his legal education and PhD at the University of Navarra, Spain. Apart from publishing commentaries and articles on collective action and group actions, he has worked at the implementation of European consumer law for the Spanish government in the area of procedural law. He also researches over-indebtedness of households and bankruptcy law.

Mónika Józon is Associate Professor for European Law at the Sapientia-Hungarian University of Transylvania, Romania, after having held a position as Associate Professor at the Corvinus University in Budapest, Hungary. She obtained a PhD from the Academy of Economy Studies in Bucharest and holds an LL.M in European Business Law of the Amsterdam School of International Relations. Her main research area is comparative and European private law (unfair contract terms law and product liability law) with a focus on the methodology of European private law and the evolving judicial culture at Member State level. She is board member of the International Association of Consumer Law and co-leader of the product liability group within the Trento Common-Core of European Private Law.

Elaine Kempson is Emeritus Professor at the University of Bristol where she was professor of personal finance and social policy research. She is an adviser on consumer protection to the Central Bank of Ireland and a non-executive director of the Financial Ombudsman Service board. Her research concerns various aspects of personal financial services, including banking, saving and investment, insurance, credit and mortgages and pensions, and financial inclusion, over-indebtedness and financial capability. In 2014 she has been working as a consultant to the World Bank Russian Trust Fund on financial literacy and education.

M. Elvira Méndez Pinedo is Professor of European Law (EU and EEA law) at the University of Iceland. She holds a Doctoral Degree in European Law from the University of Alcalá de Henares (Madrid). She has published books in Spanish on European consumer law (*The Protection of Consumers in the European Union: Towards a Common Procedural Consumer Law*) and in English on the nature of EU and EEA law (*EC and EEA Law: A Comparative Study of the Effectiveness of European Law*) and co-authored *The Authority of European Law: Exploring Primacy of EU Law and Effect of EEA Law from European and Icelandic Perspectives*. Her research focuses on European consumer law and European procedural law and encompasses the legality and fairness of Icelandic indexed loans.

Georgios Mentis is Professor of Civil Law at the University of Athens and practising attorney at law before the Supreme Court in Greece. He studied law in Greece and Germany and has published articles on unfair terms, product liability and contract law. He has also co-authored a book on *Unfair Contract Terms in Consumer and Business Contracts* (2000). His main research and professional interests are banking law, company law and contract law, especially the law of agency and distribution contracts, the law of mergers and acquisitions, the law of stock exchange, product liability and environmental law.

Hans-W. Micklitz is Professor for Economic Law at the European University Institute and holds the Jean Monnet Chair of Private Law and European Economic Law at the University of Bamberg, Germany (on leave). He studied law and sociology in Mainz, Lausanne/Geneva (Switzerland), Giessen and Hamburg. He has worked as a consultant for organisations such as the OECD, UNEP, CI (Consumers International), as well as ministries in Austria, Germany, the UK, the European Commission. He holds an ERC Grant 2011–2016 on European Regulatory Private Law. His main field of research and consulting activities concern European law, European private and consumer law.

Madalina Moraru is a PhD candidate in law at the European University Institute (EUI) in Florence, Italy. She has LLM degrees in EU law from Durham University and the European University Institute, and a bachelor degree in law from the University of Bucharest. She participated as country correspondent for Romania, legal expert and project leader in several European projects on different topics such as the protection of EU citizens abroad, fundamental rights of EU citizens and third country nationals, and training of national judges from EU Member States on the due process rights. Besides these issues, her research interests include the judicial cooperation on civil and criminal matters and consumer protection.

Katerina Pantazatou is an Adjunct Junior Lecturer at the University of Luxemburg. She obtained an LLM in Commercial Law from the University of Cambridge and a PhD from the European University Institute with a thesis on European economic integration through 'fiscality'. Her undergraduate law degree was taken at the University of Athens. Her research interests comprise European law, tax law, EU funds, competition law, and EU administrative and constitutional law.

Mariana Pinheiro Almeida is a PhD candidate at the University of Coimbra and a member of the Portuguese law firm Mendes Ferreira. She received a Master in Business and Company Law from the Catholic University of Portugal. Her postgraduate studies focus on contract and consumer law. She has co-authored a book on essential public services.

Iain Ramsay is Professor at Kent Law School. His research interests lie primarily in the two areas of credit and insolvency and the regulation of consumer markets at national, regional and international level. His approach is interdisciplinary, drawing on economic and socio-legal perspectives. He has written extensively on comparative consumer insolvency and is a co-drafter of the World Bank *Report on the Treatment of the Insolvency of Natural Persons*. His current research interests focus on personal insolvency in an age of austerity in Europe and North America. He is an elected member of the American Law Institute.

Akos Rona-Tas is Professor at the University of California, San Diego and is a research associate at Met@risk, INRA, Paris. He is author of the book *Great Surprise of the Small Transformation: Demise of Communism and Rise of the Private Sector in Hungary*, and co-author of *Plastic Money: Constructing Markets of Credit Cards in Eight Postcommunist Countries* with Alya Guseva. He has published several articles in journals including the *American Sociological Review*, *American Journal of Sociology*, *Theory and Society*, *Socio-Economic Review*, *Social Science Research*, *Research on Sociology of Organizations*, *Journal of Comparative Economics*, and various chapters in edited volumes. He is currently working on the problem of rationality and uncertainty in two different global contexts: credit assessment and the use of science in risk management, and also on puzzles of market construction.

Acknowledgements

The idea for this book came in the late autumn of 2013, when we organised a conference entitled 'The over-indebtedness of European consumers after the financial crisis' at the European University Institute in Florence. On that occasion, we invited specialists from six European countries to present results of a commissioned study to an audience of academics, policy makers, and interest groups. It became obvious that while European countries are still grappling with the effects of the financial crisis on the macro-level, adverse developments on the micro-level were rather approached with single responsive measures instead of comprehensive plans. Turning indebtedness into over-indebtedness, the financial crisis has had large-scale social effects in terms of social exclusion that follows default on mortgage instalments, eviction and homelessness.

We thank all contributors for their interest, time, and effort involved in conference and the data collection as well as the writing of the contributions. In addition, we thank the Schufa credit bureau in Germany, without which the conference held in November 2013 and the research presented here would not have been possible. The Schufa funding complemented the ERC Grant by Hans-W. Micklitz on 'European Regulatory Private Law'.

Hans-W. Micklitz
Irina Domurath

PART I
The Framework

Chapter 1
Introduction

Irina Domurath and Hans-W. Micklitz

For several years now social inclusion has been at the top of policy agendas for the EU and its Member States. In its Europe 2020 strategy,[1] the EU established the target of lifting at least 20 million people out of poverty and social exclusion by 2020. This target is inherently connected to the EU goal of social cohesion,[2] which is to be achieved by sharing the benefits of growth and jobs. Consumer credit plays a pivotal role for both growth and social inclusion because it enables citizens to foster economic growth by buying goods and services on the internal market and to fulfil their own consumerist desires and achieve the standard of living to which they aspire. In this context, consumer credit has been increasingly expanded into all layers of society by liberalising access to such credit.

However, six years into the global economic and financial crisis social inclusion is not being achieved in many European countries. Many consumers in Europe struggle with high levels of indebtedness and over-indebtedness, being at the risk of default and eviction from their homes as a result of the profound economic, political, and social repercussions European countries have experienced. Governmental and constitutional crises, high levels of public debt, the adoption of austerity measures, unprecedented high levels of unemployment, and increasing poverty have affected many European societies. As a result, the EU has entered into a process of re-examining the structure and design of the banking system within the internal market, with far-reaching political and institutional consequences. New regulatory mechanisms and private law rules are being designed at the supranational and national level. The focus, however, has been on the impact of the crisis on states and on the banks. State default, sovereign debt and bailouts have made the headlines, while the impact of the economic crisis on consumers, as debtors of consumer credit or as mortgage holders, has raised much less concern.

Knowledge of the concrete issues, problems, and tentative solutions tested in the countries most affected by the crisis is crucial in order to have an informed debate about the effects of policy measures on (over-)indebted consumers as well as financial and social inclusion and exclusion. Therefore the major added value of the contributions presented here is twofold: firstly the attempt to deepen our knowledge on the impact of the economic crisis on over-indebtedness of consumers through empirical analysis and secondly to analyse the knowledge that has been gathered and to put it into the wider theoretical and academic debate on over-indebtedness.

The six empirical studies from the three Euro countries (Greece, Spain and Portugal) and three non-Euro countries (Hungary, Romania and Iceland) provide information on the effects of the financial and monetary crisis in six European countries that have been significantly hit by the

1 Communication from the Commission 'Europe 2020: A strategy for smart, sustainable and inclusive growth', 3 March 2010, COM (2010) 2020 final.

2 See Communication from the Commission to the European Parliament, the Council, the European Economic and Social Committee and the Committee of the Regions 'The European Platform against Poverty and Social Exclusion: A European framework for social and territorial cohesion', 16 December 2010, COM (2010) 758 final.

financial crisis. Consequently, the studies provide insight into the situation of indebted European consumers, the causes of over-indebtedness, and attempts to alleviate debt burdens. What all countries chosen for the case studies have in common is that they have received bailout loans from Eurozone countries and the IMF under the condition of implementing intrusive austerity measures. While the loans were mainly used to improve the financial position of the banks or the economy in general, austerity measures have had an impact on many social issues. For this reason, the country reports focus on the situation of those most affected – namely indebted people with some form of consumer debt or a mortgage on residential property – assessing the effects of a wide range of factors such as the bursting of the housing bubble, the decline in house prices and wages, rising unemployment, and currency depreciation.

The country reports demonstrate that, despite initial signs of cautious macro-economic recovery in 2013,[3] recovery at the micro-economic level remains tentative. This is especially so for consumers with mortgages who are still facing increasing levels of (over-)indebtedness and are struggling with the effects of the crisis, both in financial and social terms. The country reports show a convergence in all countries with regard to the problems and causes of over-indebtedness, especially with regard to the adverse impact of macro-economic 'external shocks', such as the bursting of a housing bubble, unprecedented high levels of unemployment, or the devaluation of the currency, but also provide evidence of divergence concerning the governmental and administrative responses to over-indebtedness with regard to aim, design, and effectiveness. In the three non-Euro countries some specific issues have perhaps aggravated the problems consumers face. For instance, Iceland (participating in the EU internal market framework through the EEA Agreement) was the first country to experience the resignation of a government and new elections in 2009. In Iceland, Hungary, and Romania the vast majority of the loans to private households were connected to foreign currencies with the benefits of lower interest rates and longer maturities but the risk of depreciation of the local currency and subsequent inability of the borrower to repay their foreign currency loans.[4]

All these factors have influenced contractual relations and have brought to the fore the importance of private law and private law litigation, before the highest courts in the countries and the European courts. The *Aziz* decision of the CJEU[5] has had an immense impact both on Spanish procedural law and on the legal orders of other European states with regards to the interpretation

---

3 Recent developments since 2013, cautiously interpreted as the first signs of economic recovery, have been identified on both sides of the Atlantic, see for example in the United States: http://www.economist.com/node/21550256; Portugal: http://www.economist.com/news/europe/21584346-few-crumbs-cheer-count-welcome-good-news-between-bail-outs; Spain: http://www.ft.com/cms/s/0/4a56f51c-2b60–11e3-bfe2–00144feab7de.html#axzz2suJHGJzv, http://www.economist.com/news/europe/21587811-mariano-rajoy-predicts-economic-joy-spain-still-has-long-way-go-worst-may-be-over; and Greece: http://www.economist.com/news/finance-and-economics/21577076-back-source-euro-zone-crisis-daring-hope-fearing-fail.

4 We have to distinguish between foreign-currency loans (loans denominated in foreign currencies), FX-indexed loans (loans indexed to foreign currencies and thus dependent on the exchange rate), and CPI-indexed loans (loans indexed to the consumer price index thus dependent on inflation). See further on the issue P. Yesin, 'Foreign currency loans and systemic risk in Europe', Federal Reserve Bank of St. Louis Review, May/June 2013, 95(3), pp. 219–35, available at http://research.stlouisfed.org/publications/review/13/03/219–236Yesin.pdf.

5 *Mohamed Aziz v. Caixa d'Estalvis de Catalunya, Tarragona i Manresa (Catalunyacaixa)*, C-145/11 (14/3/2013); note H.-W. Micklitz, Unfair Contract Terms – Public Interest Litigation before European Courts Case C-415/11 Mohamed Aziz, in V. Colaert and E. Terryn (eds) Landmark Cases of EU Consumer Law – in Honour of Jules Stuyck, Intersentia, 2013, 615–34.

of unfair contractual terms in mortgage agreements. It can be regarded as a turning point for over-indebted consumers in Europe, as it not only triggered a number of follow-up requests for preliminary rulings from Spanish courts to clarify certain issues but also led to requests from other countries within[6] and outside the EU (albeit after initial reluctance). The Icelandic Supreme Court has declared FX-indexed loans illegal and sought an advisory opinion from the EFTA-Court on the legality of CPI-indexed mortgage loans. Private law is considered to be of utmost importance as a means of last resort for solving over-indebtedness issues resulting from mortgage agreements. Whether and to what extent private litigation contributes to the search for broader political solutions remains to be seen.

The country reports also highlight the shortcomings of EU consumer policy, which is largely based on the image of the reasonably circumspect consumer who is empowered, predominantly through the provision of information and competition in the internal market with the information asymmetry to be addressed by credit registries and credit bureaus. In this regard, the EU suffers from a clear market bias that promotes and requires easy access to consumer and mortgage credit,[7] in line with the Anglo-American vision of 'cheap money' as a means of achieving financial and social inclusion. The 2008 crisis, however, provoked over-indebtedness yielding financial and social exclusion without there being a European policy to counteract such effects.

The rapporteurs were: Georgios Mentis and Ekaterini Pantazatou for Greece, Mónika Józon for Hungary, M. Elvira Méndez Pinedo and Irina Domurath for Iceland, Catarina Frade and Mariana Pinheiro Almeido for Portugal, Beatrice Andresan-Grigoriu and Madalina Moraru for Romania, and Pablo Gutiérrez de Cabiedes Hidalgo and Marta Cantero Gamito for Spain. The country reports are based on a cross-country study collecting information against a factual background of empirical data relating to over-indebtedness. The rapporteurs were required to answer a broad questionnaire with the help of different sources: statistics and empirical sources, legal sources, policy documents and secondary academic sources amongst others. Whenever data collection proved insufficient the rapporteurs were encouraged to collect primary data themselves through interviews with affected parties. Most rapporteurs conducted semi-structured interviews with different parties such as consumers, bank employees or representatives from consumer organisations. Obviously, there are limits to such an approach: comprehensive data collection proved difficult, not least due to the lack of consistent statistics, common parameters for the measurement of concepts or the limited preparedness of the targeted groups to be available for interviews. Despite these limits, the country reports provide an extremely useful basis for analysis.[8]

The book is structured in the following way: Guido Comparato (Chapter 2) opens the larger debate with a deeper analysis of financial and social inclusion. He elaborates on the dichotomy between the promotion of financial inclusion with a view to achieving social inclusion and the actual result of financial exclusion not only through the social repercussions of over-indebtedness

6 The Hungarian Supreme Court raised questions relating to unilateral changes to loan contracts by banks as well as exchange rate margins *Árpád Kásler, Hajnalka Káslerné Rábai v. OTP Jelzálogbank Zrt*, C-26/13, Judgment of 30 April 2014.

7 See OECD Discussion Paper on Information Sharing 'Facilitating Access to Finance', available at http://www.oecd.org/investment/psd/45370071.pdf.

8 The contributions in the book provide for a condensed analysis of the findings only. The complete country reports are accesible via the internet for those who are interested in using the data. Further information on the setup of the research can be found therein, see I. Domurath, G. Comparato and H-W. Micklitz, 'The Over-Indebtedness of European Consumers – a View from Six Countries', EUI Working Paper LAW 2014/10, pp. 15–18.

but also through the regulatory responses that put emphasis on financial stability. He also elicits the role and politics of private law against the background of the inclusion–exclusion dichotomy.

The six country reports form Part II of the book (Chapters 3 to 8), starting with the report from the Euro countries (Greece, Portugal and Spain) and concluding with the non-Euro countries (Hungary, Iceland and Romania). Against this empirical background, the other contributions in this volume analyse the inclusion–exclusion and the over-indebtedness paradigms, both from an *ex ante* viewpoint, concerned with the causes and prevention of over-indebtedness and social exclusion, and from an *ex post* viewpoint, focussing on the measures taken after over-indebtedness has occurred in order to remedy its negative effects.

In Part III, Elaine Kempson (Chapter 9) starts her analysis by painting a broad picture of how the crisis has affected European consumers, ranging from the causes of over-indebtedness to the characteristics of debt. She contends that there are different structural conditions in the countries that have influenced over-indebtedness levels in the European countries: the nature of a country's economy as the economic downturn hit, the state of household finances at that point in time, and the policy measures adopted in the aftermath of the crisis. She arrives at this conclusion drawing from comparative statistics for individual countries as well as information contained in the six country reports.

The prevention of over-indebtedness is the focus of two contributions by Irina Domurath and Akos Rona-Tas. Irina Domurath (Chapter 10) deals with consumer contract law, analysing the tools available in the EU legal framework on consumer credit and mortgage contracts for the prevention of over-indebtedness. She examines the conceptualisation of *responsible lending* and *responsible borrowing*, claiming that the EU legal order starts from a much too narrow understanding too much engrained by the responsible consumer rhetoric. She concludes by suggesting complementary private law tools to strengthen the current framework, especially tools that address 'external shocks' and the increased access to credit. Akos Rona-Tas (Chapter 11) elicits the role of credit bureaus in the contractual design of credit agreements in modern globalised economies. Even though credit bureaus are intended to reduce the risk of over-indebtedness and protect lenders from defaulting borrowers by solving the information asymmetry problem, Akos Rona-Tas calls into question the fulfilment of that purpose based on the contention that credit bureaus have the 'perverse effects' of extending credit to 'worse' borrowers; that their data is socially constructed and, hence, of diminished quality; that they are built on the false assumption that payment depends solely on the debtor who intends to exploit his information advantage, neglecting the relational nature of credit; and that credit scoring can even make it unnecessarily hard for individuals to obtain credit if the information submitted to credit bureaus is too broad.

Iain Ramsay (Chapter 12) looks into the *ex post* measures taken in order to alleviate over-indebtedness. After explaining the responses taken against the background of policy ideas, actors and institutional settings, he goes on to describe the separation of consumer credit as belonging to the economic establishment of the internal market and personal insolvency regulation as part of the social problem of over-indebtedness. He sheds light on the influence of economics on household deleveraging in different countries around the globe, which regards the latter as an economic problem that hampers economic growth, and analyses the emerging EU narrative of promoting entrepreneurialism through personal insolvency. He concludes by remarking that the 'responsibilisation' of personal insolvency becomes a means of addressing financial and social exclusion from the market, while the balance between personal responsibility and the facilitation of re-entry to the market still needs to be found.

In the final remarks Hans-W. Micklitz (Chapter 13) positions the debate on consumer over-indebtedness in the broader framework on financialisation and the possible impact it might have on the future development of a consumer credit law. His main argument is that the *micro* level of over-indebtedness mirrored in the individual harm of consumers has to be linked to the *macro* level of household over-indebtedness. Such a perspective requires deeper investigations into the role and function that private law, and more specifically contract law, might have as a new mode of governance that reaches beyond the privity of contract.

Chapter 2
The Design of Consumer and Mortgage Credit Law in the European System

Guido Comparato

Over the course of the first decade of the 21st century the general level of household indebtedness, including mortgage and consumer credit loans, has generally increased in Europe.[1] The level of indebtedness became a considerable social problem for many individuals in various European countries after the outbreak of the 2007–2008 financial crisis, which had serious ramifications for Europe. These simple observations should be placed in the specific political, economic and social context which has characterised Western societies in recent years in which it is possible to observe an increase in the level of consumption and household debt. It should be noted that the increase in levels of household debt was not solely a casual development rooted in the changing consumption habits of a more and more individualistic society. Rather, this increase was most notably the result of specific economic and political choices which informed the overall economic and legal architecture of several Western countries. Focusing specifically on Europe, the increase in household debt, which was moderate in some states and significant in others in the mid-2000s, can be directly linked to the macroeconomic situation in those countries as well as to other structural factors.[2] In other words, whilst from a purely private law perspective credit is simply the result of a bilateral transaction, in a broader sense the recourse that individuals make to private debt cannot be considered a purely private matter. On the contrary credit is strongly dependent on more general factors which must also be taken into account in any legal analysis. Admitting that a link between increased consumer credit and macroeconomic figures exists,[3] it becomes obvious that the economic crisis would necessarily affect contractual relations, exposing some consumers on the front line to the detrimental effects of poor macroeconomic figures.

When the financial crisis hit Europe a large number of citizens proved to be unable to continue to make payments on their loans which in numerous instances resulted in home repossessions, similar to what thousands of citizens experienced in the United States just a few years earlier. Such developments increased levels of social exclusion, in direct contrast with the initial promise of financial inclusion for an ever-increasing number of citizens. The fact that this development was not limited to the default of a few debtors and the failure of a limited number of contractual agreements, but rather became an extensive social phenomenon, suggests that the reasons behind the crisis are systemic in nature. Levels of over-indebtedness, considering the variations in different European Member States, can therefore be explained also on thc basis of general economic factors.[4] In particular, those countries that witnessed a considerable rise in household debt are

1 Chmelar, 2013, 13, 3.

2 Chmelar, 2013, 3.

3 On the need to consider the interaction between macroeconomics and contract law in this context, *see* Köndgen, 2011, 43.

4 In particular, Elaine Kempson, Chapter 9, this volume, identifies three factors: 'the nature of a country's economy as the economic downturn hit, the state of household finances as the economic downturn

now experiencing over-indebtedness and adverse social effects to such an extent that leads one to wonder not only what occurred in the economy but also – and perhaps more relevant for legal analysts – in the contractual design and legal governance of mortgage and consumer credit. It is suggested that some Member States were made more vulnerable to the economic downturn by a failure to regulate mortgage and consumer credit markets.[5]

The specific focus in this chapter lies in the role and the politics of private law in this context against the background of the inclusion/exclusion dichotomy. It will highlight the role of private law in the more general socio-economic context and the changes that are being made as a result of the economic crisis. At the same time, in a multi-level governance context such as Europe where different measures can be taken for different motives by diverse lawmakers and regulators, the description of the design of consumer law in Europe cannot avoid the question of the distribution of competences between the national and the supranational levels, a topic which also appears to be decisive in this area. This chapter therefore attempts to examine the design of the consumer credit system in the multi-level system of the European Union in a broad sense both before and during the crisis. Subsequently, this chapter will consider how the design of this system relates to the idea of financial and social inclusion. In doing so the chapter firstly examines the political and economic considerations which were aimed at extending the market and promoting financial inclusion, which underpin the legal and institutional framework for mortgage and consumer credit in Europe. It then illustrates the way in which the financial crisis altered that idea by leading to the introduction of new regulatory responses which appear to be aimed at ensuring the stability of the economic system as well as possibly preventing social exclusion in the long term.

In order to highlight the private law dimension in particular, this chapter will also consider a number of topics and their legal regulation that recur throughout the book as a whole, such as the causes of (over-)indebtedness,[6] the concepts of responsible lending and responsible borrowing,[7] the role of credit reference agencies,[8] and the mechanisms for dealing *ex-post facto* with over-indebtedness.[9]

From the United States to Europe

Since the outburst of the financial crisis in 2007–2008 it has become clear that an overextended inclusion of vulnerable consumers in the financial market might be eventually detrimental both to consumers and the financial market itself. For several decades the idea that social inclusion would naturally follow from financial inclusion had been advocated on both sides of the Atlantic. In political terms it was initially in the United States that the consumer became the main focus of an ideology which strived for an egalitarian class-less society in which citizens could purchase more products and services.[10] It is observed in sociological literature that debt has a tendency to disrupt conventional understandings of social class.[11] In economic terms, a mature economic system cannot focus exclusively on supply if this is not supported by constant and growing demand. Especially

hit, how countries dealt with or were forced to deal with the economic downturn'.

5 Chapter 9, this volume.

6 *See* Chapter 9, this volume.

7 *See* Chapter 10, this volume.

8 *See* Chapter 11, this volume.

9 *See* Chapter 12, this volume.

10 Whitman, 2007.

11 Sullivan, 2013, 37.

in the United States the economic system started immediately developing new ways to expand the market in order to foster demand, encouraging internal consumption through consumer credit.[12]

According to broadly Keynesian views this effect could be achieved by means of a more proactive role for the state through government spending. However, the task of enabling consumers to consume more, and by implication to become pivotal economic actors, fell mostly on the private sector. This model started developing in the United States in the 1920s when (industry-financed) research showed that 'consumptive credit', far from being morally irresponsible as it had been generally considered up until that time, instead had a potentially productive function inasmuch as it fostered the purchase of goods and services.[13] Even the consumer who purchases goods and services is a 'productive' economic actor as a result of the fact that they expand the market for the supplier with their demand for new products and services. Providing consumers with the means to purchase everyday products slowly became an industry in the 1930s.[14] By the same token, the policy goals which normally lie behind public policy, and which can include social considerations, shifted to the private sector. Consumer credit was not just a matter of business but it could also offer citizens resources to improve their own welfare. However, in the 1980s such policies achieved their full potential as a result of a wave of deregulation and diminished state control which led to a kind of 'privatized Keynesianism'[15] in which the private sector played the role of the public sector. In this era the role of the state as a 'competitor' to the private sector in providing for services decreased and, at the same time, deregulation facilitated financial innovation. In this context, a possible coincidence of purposes between social and financial inclusion emerged.

It was only later that this view was exported to Europe.[16] Traditionally, European states instead developed welfare systems which fostered internal demand through providing benefits to the citizens. In simple terms: in Europe public indebtedness ideally prevailed over private indebtedness. The spread of consumer credit in Europe can therefore also be historically seen as correlating with waves of deregulation which favoured private instead of public indebtedness. Taking the European Union as a whole, however, the ideology of easy access to credit which emerged in the United States was not completely faithfully replicated on this side of the Atlantic. Rather, the regulation of consumer credit became associated with internal-market goals as laid down in the European treaties. When the EU started drafting rules on the issue, its main objective was to create an internal market of credit within which different actors in different Member States could contract and compete. The expansion of household debt was therefore facilitated by the creation of a common credit market as well as by the later introduction of the common currency, which also led to a convergence and therefore an initial (in some cases significant) lowering of interest rates in some countries.[17]

While the interventions of the EU in relation to consumer credit were therefore expressly mostly aimed at establishing an internal market, considerations related to the possible social function of credit lay in the background of those measures. As the state began to retreat from the provision of certain services to its citizens, reflecting a shift from a welfare state to a new 'market state' model,[18] private debt also began to assume such functions. This development is not limited to consumer credit but also applies to financial services more generally as they began to be more

12 Marron, 2009.

13 Seligman, 1927.

14 Clark, 1931.

15 Crouch, 2008, 476–487; Crouch, 2011.

16 In this context, with a focus on the inclusion/exclusion dimension, *see* Micklitz, 2013, 47–75.

17 For instance for Greece, *see* Pasiouras, 2012, 101; and Chapter 3, this volume.

18 Micklitz and Patterson, 2012.

prominently advertised and promoted to citizens. This development is evident in different sectors traditionally left to the welfare state. For instance private home ownership started to become a form of private insurance as governmental social spending declined.[19] Home ownership was encouraged both for economic reasons and also because it was considered to convey a sense of participation[20] which promotes social inclusion. Mortgages became of fundamental importance in this regard as they enabled (especially low-income) consumers to purchase residential property without having the capital needed for its immediate acquisition. This might have been even more important for countries in which private home ownership was most common and the rental market less developed.[21] In contrast, however, the shrinking role of the state led to the exclusion of the most vulnerable citizens from the housing market, bringing about significant changes in a wide range of areas including the configuration of cities as a result of gentrification.[22]

The increase in financial services and household debt can therefore be linked to the decline of public spending on welfare, incidentally made more compelling by the new macroeconomic objectives as set out in the Maastricht Treaty which required Member States to adopt less wide-ranging spending policies. As the possibility of creating new public debt was reduced and as private credit became increasingly available, especially after the introduction of the common currency, this latter option became a convenient alternative for financing social policies by various Member States. In particular the expansion of mortgage credit, made possible by the deregulation of the mortgage market and the decrease in real interest rates for various countries in the Euro area, contributed to the increase in household debt, while at the same time making those countries more vulnerable.[23] Even several non-Euro Member States encouraged the purchase of a first house through promoting mortgage contracts mostly in convenient foreign currency (the euro or the Swiss franc), often buoyed by overly optimistic (and in hindsight plain wrong) projections about future economic events.[24] At the same time the aforementioned lowered interest rates led to increased liquidity in other Member States which, in turn, boosted the housing market in countries like Spain and Ireland. These developments brought about the conditions for over-reliance on credit and negatively affected European social policies.

Such developments, according to which private credit replaced the role of public spending and in which the inclusion of the consumer in the market appears to be a win-win situation, led to a merger of the concepts of social inclusion and financial inclusion within a more general category commonly referred to as 'democratization of credit',[25] in other words, the easy availability of credit to an ever growing number of people. It is clear that in an advanced capitalist society, the impossibility of having access to even basic financial services – imagine the importance of having a bank account in order to receive salaries and make payments – might determine serious social problems and be associated with forms of poverty.[26] As such, promoting financial inclusion at non-discriminatory conditions can become a social policy. More broadly, advocates of financial inclusion have demonstrated that granting 'productive' credit, even to individuals who do not offer any security over the loan they are granted, in disadvantaged countries might have such positive

19 *See* Conley and Gifford, 2006.

20 For the developments in the United States, *see* Shiller, 2008.

21 Rates of private homeownership are high in the countries considered in the reports in this volume (see chapters in Part II, this volume).

22 Edgar et al., 2002.

23 Ahearne and Wolff, 2012, 11.

24 Chapter 8, this volume.

25 For an overview on the development of 'democratization of credit', *see* Burton, 2008, 92.

26 Bennet, 2010, 223.

economic as well as social effects that access to credit should even be qualified as a fundamental right.[27] Nonetheless, the goals of social and financial inclusion might be separated from each other. It appears that promoting financial inclusion is not sufficient in itself to realise social inclusion and can even be counterproductive in this respect. Whilst social and financial inclusion can perhaps be achieved through the same means in times of economic prosperity, they clearly diverge in periods of economic difficulty. It should be one of the goals of regulation to make sure that this bifurcation is limited.

Limiting the focus to the topic of credit, it can be seen that such bifurcation has been facilitated in recent years by a paradigm shift in lending strategies, characterised by a shift from a 'originate to hold' to an 'originate to distribute' business model. This was particularly clear, again, in the US context. Since low-income consumers being included in the expanding credit market might encounter difficulties in paying off their debts, it became a widespread practice to reduce the credit risk faced by the lender through securitisation,[28] credit default swaps and financial products that eventually practically separated the traditionally interconnected aspects of credit and risk. If the lender can make a profit simply transferring a credit, the solvency of the debtor becomes an almost irrelevant consideration, especially in an institutional framework characterised by insufficient supervision.[29] Indeed, 'a key aspect of securitization is that the creditworthiness of the notes is de-linked from the credit risk of the originator'.[30] A lack of incentive can be seen as the root cause of irresponsible lending practices.[31] This raises a complex question, namely 'can banks simultaneously shed credit risk while retaining the incentive to screen and monitor borrowers?'.[32] Although that question could be answered in the affirmative in theory given a particular set of regulatory and contractual arrangements, in practice a combination of incorrect projections, poorly-designed contracts, possible conflicts of interests within credit rating agencies,[33] and a lack of supervision suggests a less optimistic answer. This laid the foundations for the aggressive subprime mortgage lending and predatory lending practices (associated with opaque securitisation mechanisms) which, in turn, constituted the trigger for the 2007–2008 financial crisis and the subsequent collapse of the housing market in the United States. At the same time, these developments had significant impact on the usual conception of credit which is still mostly enshrined in private law, which, based on the conflicting traditional idea that the solvency of the debtor is in the creditor's own interest, has not represented an adequate limit to the degeneration of those practices. Concepts that could have limited these developments, often opposed by sectors of industry, remain deficient or purely ineffective. On a more general level, 'the process of securitization connected global capital markets to homebuyers and homeowners',[34] which necessarily made those subjects more exposed and vulnerable to the ebb and flow of the global financial market.

At this point, one can critically detect the paradoxical consequence of financial inclusion through the expansion of private indebtedness. Whilst this may initially produce social inclusion, in the long run it may create a cycle of indebtedness leading to over-indebtedness, leading to

27 *See* Yunus, 2001, 280. For a discussion as to the theoretical foundations of a human right to credit, Hudon, 2009.

28 Ashcraft and Schuermann, 2006.

29 Sufi, 2013.

30 de Vries Robbé, 2008, 3.

31 Atamer, 2011, 183.

32 Sufi, 2013, 87, with references and discussion of the literature on the problems of information and incentives in financial intermediation.

33 Immergluck, 2009, 111.

34 Immergluck, 2009, 110.

default, evictions and even homelessness, in other terms: social exclusion. An example from the American subprime market serves to highlight this point. It is calculated that between 1998 and 2006 1.4 million people were able to purchase a home thanks to the subprime credit market which was praised as an efficient mechanism for including individuals who would otherwise have been left out. However, the Centre for Responsible Lending estimated in 2007 that 2.4 million would lose their home due to their inability to meet loan payments,[35] and the figures deteriorated with the subprime crisis.[36] In this context, the original promise of democratisation of credit appeared illusory and more voices called for increased regulation of the sector and outlawing toxic mortgage loans.[37]

This is not to say that, on balance, consumer credit necessarily leads to over-indebtedness and that financial inclusion is a mere chimera, but rather that if the broader governance model is deficient, such results have to be expected.

Between the EU and its Member States

Even though Europe adopted the easy access to credit ideology later than the United States, it does not seem to have yet developed a coherent legal framework to cope with this significant development in order to offer adequate protection to EU citizens active in the financial market. In particular, whilst financial inclusion more clearly became a policy goal in Europe as well, its associated dimension of social inclusion has been neglected, most often being considered a mere positive side-effect of 'democratization of credit' and not an objective requiring a particular set of rules to be achieved together with financial inclusion.

Some Member States with a longer tradition in the regulation of financial services started addressing the topic of financial inclusion quite early. For instance, the report that inspired the UK Consumer Credit Act of 1974 recommended that credit, which was identified as a vital component of capitalist economies, ought to be combined with protective measures to reduce the number of defaulting debtors.[38] That dynamic would later become particularly clear in the case of the housing market, when the supposed boom of the mortgage market was accompanied by a high number of mortgage repossessions, around 90 a day in 1999 in the UK.[39] In other Member States, the development of consumer credit was truncated by more stringent regulations on the banking sector, while social inclusion was mostly pursued through actions by the welfare state.

At the European level, if one considers policy documents and more concrete measures, it took until the second half of the 2000s before social exclusion was explicitly addressed as an issue connected with financial services. Until then, although social exclusion was identified as a problem to be combated it was generally considered to relate to 'employment, housing, training, education, culture and social and medical assistance', as in the Social Charter of the Council of Europe of 1996, without being associated with the financial markets. When financialisation increased, social exclusion also started being addressed in connection with financial exclusion. The issue was approached by the EU institutions mainly through the internal-market rationale: a citizen was considered socially excluded when, lacking basic financial services, they could not actively participate in the internal market, for instance by purchasing goods on the Internet.[40]

---

35 Centre for Responsible Lending, 2007.

36 Immergluck, 2009, 135–140.

37 White, 2008.

38 Report of the Committee on Consumer Credit, Cmnd. 4596/1971, in Ramsay, 1989, 315.

39 Edgar et al., 2002, 46.

40 See for instance COM(2005) 629 final, 4.4.2.

In areas such as mortgage credit, EU interventions remained less developed, despite the fact that the Commission recognised in its 2005 Green Paper on mortgage credit, that 'there is a huge social and human dimension attached to housing and credit, including aspects such as over-indebtedness'.[41] In this context, the main concern appeared to be the inclusion of the citizen in the financial market. The emphasis was therefore most strongly put on the right to have a bank account, 'so that no one in the EU is denied access to a basic bank account',[42] as the Commission declared. This emphasis is striking if contrasted with the primary concern of advocates of financial and social inclusion as a means of promoting decent living conditions and the economic growth of developing countries, who on the contrary had always emphasised the availability of (micro-)credit, an aspect which was considered by the EU to a significantly lesser extent. The lack of appropriate consideration for the dimension of social inclusion at least until the wake of the financial crisis, determined that in practice the measures of the Community first and the Union later tended to understand financial inclusion as market inclusion rather than social inclusion.

This particular approach can (at least partially) be explained not only on the basis of a purely historical argument – namely the delay in the arrival of the US idea of consumer society in Europe – but rather, and most fundamentally, it is consistent with the architecture of the European legal order. The legal design of the internal market on consumer credit in Europe was and still is predominantly governed by the idea of a linear distribution of competences: to put it simply, the market to the EU, welfare to the Member States. At a general level, this is evident in different acts: when in 1997 the Social Policy Agreement of 1991 was incorporated in the Treaty of Amsterdam and the task of combating social exclusion appeared in European primary legislation, the Union was given the task of 'encourag[ing] cooperation between Member States through initiatives aimed at improving knowledge, developing exchanges of information and best practices, promoting innovative approaches and evaluating experiences in order to combat social exclusion' (Art 137.2). With the Treaty of Nice, the goal of 'combat[ing] social exclusion' became an autonomous field in which the Union has to 'support and complement the activities of the Member States' according to the same article.[43] However at the same time the Treaty restricted the powers of the Union in adding to the article a limitation: 'excluding any harmonisation of the laws and regulations of the Member States'. Market and social policies therefore appear not only as different goals, but they even require different methods, whereby the latter appears to be achievable only by non-binding instruments such as the open method of coordination.

This distinction is mitigated only by the new so-called horizontal social clause in Article 9 TFEU, pursuant to which 'in defining and implementing its policies and activities, the Union shall take into account requirements linked to the promotion of a high level of employment, the guarantee of adequate social protection, the fight against social exclusion'. This provision has a strong importance in representing a bridge between market and social rationales, and therefore makes it necessary among other things that the social dimension of financial inclusion is expressly taken into account in all European legislation, including contract law.

41 COM(2005) 327 final, 19.7.2005, 3–4.

42 COM(2008) 412 final, 4.5.

43 On the interpretation of the new wording, Kountouros, 2003.

EU Private Law and the Post-Crisis Reaction

Despite the potentially important role of the horizontal clause of Article 9 TFEU, however, the aforementioned distinction in competences also remains evident in EU contract law and has a direct impact on the way legislation in Europe has addressed mortgage and consumer credit. If EU law understands financial inclusion mostly in the sense of 'inclusion in the market', the possible negative consequences of that inclusion have to be addressed by the Member States. This particular design emerges clearly from the different directives and recommendations in that area.

The field of consumer credit has been regulated in the EU by two directives,[44] which, albeit different in many respects, fundamentally share the same basic preconception of the consumer as an economic actor that should benefit from the credit market and be empowered with a set of pre-contractual and contractual information.[45] Similarly, making such information clearer and transparent was not just a tool to empower the consumer but importantly also allowed for easier comparability of the different credit offers from various financial services providers in Europe with a view to promoting competition. The creation of standardised information to be given to the consumer as required by the 2008 directive is a good example of such an approach. It remained nonetheless questionable whether such a mild regulatory approach was in itself sufficient to ensure financial inclusion.[46]

While European legislation aimed at empowering consumers, paving the way to easy credit which could be employed to promote their social inclusion, it overlooked the social problems that occurred when those consumers did not fulfil their role as efficient economic actors. Those possible problems were to be addressed by the Member States. This division of functions emerges when looking at EU policy with regard to over-indebtedness, which is arguably the most evident drawback of financial inclusion. Despite having shown an interest and having set up several working groups on the issue,[47] the EU merely issued a recommendation to Member States in 2007[48] presenting a rather generic set of options on how to tackle such problems. The recommendation reveals again that even if over-indebtedness is a worrying cause of social exclusion, its consequences are to be alleviated by the Member States, possibly through a series of instruments mainly consisting of access to financial advice and counselling as well as even making 'financial literacy on the rights of consumers in general, and budget management in particular, as part of the national education system'.[49] The recommendation also made a reference to regulation of credit: 'providing the necessary measures and regulations to ensure responsible practices during all phases of the credit relationship including marketing of credit as well as the collection and use of credit data and other financial information'.[50] As to *ex post* actions to be taken by the Member States, the recommendation lists 'mechanisms necessary to facilitate rehabilitation of over-indebted individuals and families and their reintegration into society',[51] ranging from the protection of the essential assets of the debtor to the introduction of measures 'allowing partial or total discharge of the debts of individuals and, where applicable, families in cases of over-indebtedness where other

44 Directive 87/102/EEC; Directive 2008/48/EC
45 Weatherill, 2013, 98.
46 Reifner, 2009, 108.
47 Huls et al., 1994.
48 Recommendation CM/Rec(2007)8.
49 Recommendation CM/Rec(2007)8, 2.b.
50 Recommendation CM/Rec(2007)8, 2.d.
51 Recommendation CM/Rec(2007)8, 4.

measures have proved to be ineffective, with a view to providing them with a new opportunity for engaging in economic and social activities'.[52]

It is common knowledge that the EU can be qualified as multi-level governance and it is perfectly normal that certain competences are attributed to the national instead of the supranational level. Nonetheless, in the area of consumer credit, the linear design of 'market to the EU, welfare to the Member States' was revealed to be overly optimistic. In the first place, it can be said that the ideal division between market and welfare is in reality hardly attainable in practice given the interdependency of the two. More fundamentally, none of those two levels seems to have taken apposite measures within the scope of their competences. On the one hand, EU legislation, despite its apparent shift to full harmonisation in consumer credit law, remained meagre and did not contain sufficiently protective and preventive rules, at least initially turning a blind eye to the most important and potentially dangerous aspects of credit, so that it hesitated to regulate mortgage credit. On the other hand, many Member States did not seem ready to design legal instruments to cope with the social problems arising from over-indebtedness, often failing to perform their task of taking care of the social aspects linked to the market, in the years in which lowered interest rates made credit more available and those legislative measures more needed.

As a result, in the aftermath of the financial crisis, the issue of financial inclusion has been put at the centre of the policy discussion once again, but is now being understood in more critical terms than it was initially. The welfarist justification of financial inclusion has shifted from creating social inclusion to preventing social exclusion. Even more significantly, financial inclusion has been reinterpreted in light of the requirements of financial stability. In particular, to stick with two relevant and telling examples, it was under the proposal of the G20 that the principle of responsible lending was more prominently emphasised in European contract law and it was under the influence of the International Monetary Fund that personal insolvency mechanisms were introduced in indebted Member States. As the G20 principles state, the main reason why 'financial consumer protection should be reinforced and integrated with other financial inclusion and financial education policies' is that '[t]his contributes to strengthening financial stability'.[53] Incidentally, one could certainly question the suggestion that it would be sufficient to improve consumer protection in order to achieve financial stability. At any rate, this view seems to depart from traditional justifications of consumer protection[54] and emphasises again its market functionalisation, as possible evidence of the fact that the new consumer rules represent continuity with, rather than departure from, the neoliberal model.[55]

In particular in the European context, where the financial crisis is associated with a strong political and legitimacy crisis in the EU, the new emphasis on consumer protection is interlinked with a particular moral narrative about the economic and institutional crisis, which emphasises the debtor's responsibilities, de facto associating debt with moral fault, echoing what happened before the development of consumer society. While this view is now widespread when referring to levels of public indebtedness, it also has ramifications for the discussion on household debt and the legal instruments designed to cope with it, as discussed in the following sections.

52 Recommendation CM/Rec(2007)8, 4.h.

53 G20 High-Level Principles on Financial Consumer Protection, October 2011, 4.

54 Williams, 2013, 25.

55 Williams, 2013, 15–45.

Causes of Over-Indebtedness

In the moral narrative, the debtor can be qualified as an individual at fault with a propensity to assume more debt than they can repay, and possibly the propensity to deceive their contractual counterpart with erroneous information, which in the end leads to excessive indebtedness. As it cannot be denied that excessive levels of indebtedness have played a major role in the crisis and that private autonomy cannot be dissociated from individual responsibility, this view, rather than erroneous, is one-sided. To elaborate, it is suggested that this view predominantly focuses on one party to the contract and overlooks on the one hand the interest of the other party in the conclusion of the contract and, on the other hand, the fact that some of the causes of over-indebtedness are independent of the behaviour of the borrower and often hardly foreseeable by the lender. This latter aspect highlights a fundamental piece of the picture that has to be considered, namely the causes of over-indebtedness.

The Bank of France in particular usually draws a distinction between so-called active and passive over-indebtedness, whereby the former situation is determined by the irresponsible behaviour of the debtor, who becomes unable or unwilling to repay debts either through deliberate opportunistic behaviour or financial recklessness. Passive over-indebtedness, on the contrary, is determined by external events such as unemployment, divorce, illness, or any other '*accident de la vie*' which change the debtor's financial situation for the worse. These latter situations amount to a form of 'social *force majeure*',[56] according to the terminology of the European Nordic countries, which legitimise mechanisms of debt relief for blameless debtors. While, on closer inspection, it is clear that the distinction between active and passive over-indebtedness is in practice much more complicated than it is in theory,[57] recent events linked to the financial crisis in Europe have shown how often macroeconomic events can have a significant impact on the solvency of the debtor. Whilst it has been known since at least the 1970s that over-indebtedness often arises as a result of external factors,[58] the recent process of linking the global financial markets and homebuyers[59] made financial crises an even more important determining factor of over-indebtedness.[60] At present, passive over-indebtedness is a much more often recurring circumstance than active over-indebtedness.[61] The levels of over-indebtedness are therefore also dependent on the economic context and policies and are subject to different dynamics in Europe.[62] Such consideration makes it more complicated to perform an accurate creditworthiness assessment as required by the principle of responsible lending and can lead to reconsideration of the traditional responses to debtor insolvency.

Responsible Lending

The most discussed instrument envisaged to prevent over-indebtedness is the concept of responsible lending.[63] The idea of responsible lending was not seen as a particularly attractive one by the

---

56 Wilhelmsson, 1992, 180.

57 Ramsay, 2011, 12.

58 Caplovitz, 1974, 57.

59 Immergluck, 2009, 110.

60 See also the country reports in Part II of this volume.

61 Three cases of over-indebtedness out of four are considered to be 'passive' rather than 'active' over-indebtedness in France: Banque de France, 2008, 4.

62 *See* Chapter 9, this volume.

63 *See* Chapter 10, this volume.

industry in the years of easy access to credit, and the history and *travaux préparatoires* of the 2008 Consumer Credit Directive offer abundant evidence of those debates.[64] While that directive, the main objective of which was to 'facilitate the emergence of a well-functioning internal market in consumer credit',[65] remained mostly loyal to the informative paradigm and had a relatively lax approach to responsible lending, leaving it to the Member States, that concept was back on the European agenda when the Commission included it in its proposal for a Mortgage Credit Directive. The international background of this development is known, since in the aftermath of the crisis the necessity to protect consumers through promoting responsible practices and ensuring that the financial services providers act in the interest of the investor was promoted in Point 6 of the G20 High-Level Principles on Financial Consumer Protection of 2011.[66] This triggered a wave of new regulations on responsible lending in many countries around the world, with the double function of preventing over-indebtedness and promoting a sounder financial system.[67] In the European context too, after initial reluctance to regulate this essential area at the EU level, the directive on credit agreements for consumers relating to residential immovable property was eventually adopted,[68] roughly a decade after the aforementioned Commission Green Paper on mortgage credit.

This instrument is significant owing to its subject matter, since it deals with a topic that, despite its economic and social importance, was not previously an object of EU action and was even explicitly excluded from the scope of application of the Consumer Credit Directive, incidentally giving rise to complicated and controversial judicial after-effects.[69] Notably, in contrast to the Consumer Credit Directive, the Mortgage Directive pays more attention to the idea of responsible lending, which is now formulated in a more accurate provision. The salient point is that the directive prohibits granting credit in cases in which the mandatory creditworthiness assessment has been negative, while the Consumer Credit Directive remained purposely silent on this pivotal aspect[70] leaving Member States the freedom to determine the consequences of a lack of assessment regardless of its professed full harmonisation character.[71] Nevertheless, whilst the new provision of the Mortgage Directive is vigorous in its wording, it is potentially limited in practice since it does not designate remedies in case of violation of the obligation. Much will depend on its implementation by the Member States who can integrate the principle in a supervisory regime – as the directive suggests[72] – or in contract law (or both), possibly strengthening the link between supervision and contract law.[73] As to this particularly important aspect, the different provisions of the two directives derive from the dissimilar economic considerations, and historical moments, which characterised their drafting. Whilst one had the clear function of expanding the credit market, the other aims to establish more rigorous requirements.

---

64 Reifner, 2009, 114; Łobocka-Poguntke, 2012.

65 Directive 2008/48/EC, recital 7.

66 'Financial services providers and authorised agents should have as an objective, to work in the best interest of their customers and be responsible for upholding financial consumer protection.'

67 Wilson, 2013.

68 Directive 2014/17/EU of the European Parliament and of the Council of 4 February 2014.

69 CJEU, C-481/99, *Heininger/Hypo- und Vereinsbank AG*, 13 December 2001.

70 Grundmann and Hofmann, 2010, 481.

71 Cherednychenko, 2011.

72 Directive 2014/17/EU, recital 83: 'Member States may decide to transpose certain aspects covered by this Directive in national law by prudential law, for example the creditworthiness assessment of the consumer, while others are transposed by civil or criminal law, for example the obligations relating to responsible borrowers.'

73 *See* Cherednychenko, 2014, 45.

The shift to a slightly stronger regulatory approach can be justified by the empirical consideration that in many European countries creditworthiness assessments were not performed in an accurate manner, if at all.[74] The reasons why these assessments were not performed in practice, despite the claim that lenders already typically perform such assessment (at least in some countries) because this is in their own best interest,[75] can be easily explained. If the lender has an interest in providing the credit and is at the same time the one initiating and performing the credit assessment, a conflict of interests in broad terms arises. In the field of investment services, proposed solutions to solve the problem consist of distinguishing more clearly between the subject giving advice and the financial services provider, mostly regulating remuneration mechanisms. Following the earlier guidelines of the Commission on remuneration policies in the financial services sector,[76] the Mortgage Credit Directive also touches upon this issue, prescribing that the remuneration policy of the staff responsible for the assessment of creditworthiness and for giving advice does not prejudice their capacity to act in the consumer's interest,[77] though the practical significance of these broad provisions will depend again on the implementation and the supervision by the Member States.

Credit Reference Agencies

Renewed attention is also paid to the topic of credit reference agencies,[78] as an instrument allowing the lender to better evaluate credit risk. The model of assessing creditworthiness based on a simple conversation between the consumer and the bank employee is being replaced by another model in which it is not only the consumer who provides information to the lender, but rather a third party whose job is to gather and provide information on individuals. The idea is that market failures are determined by a lack of information, while building a more efficient infrastructure will help bridge the gap, thereby improving the information paradigm. EU contract law does not impose any specific obligation to consult such databases and rather aims to ensure 'that creditors have access to private or public databases concerning consumers in a Member State where they are not established under non-discriminatory conditions compared with creditors in that Member State',[79] in order '[t]o prevent any distortion of competition among creditors'.[80] According to this legislation, consumers only have to be informed by the lender that a database is to be consulted.[81]

This accommodating regulatory approach is also rooted in the idea that having more information on the consumer is in the interest of the lender. This view, as stated above, is nonetheless incomplete as it overlooks relevant aspects which might lead even lenders to avoid relying on databases, de facto restraining the likely valuable role of credit reference agencies. Indeed, under certain conditions collecting information about the consumer is not necessarily in the interest of the lender, especially when this process is costly. Consequently remuneration mechanisms might play a role; for instance, in cases in which credit reference agencies finance themselves through imposing a

74 National reports in Part II of volume.

75 Kösters et al., 2004, 95.

76 Recommendation 2009/384/EC.

77 Directive 2014/17/EU, Art. 7.

78 *See* Chapter 11, this volume.

79 Directive 2008/48/EC, recital 28. Coherently, the Mortgage Credit Directive states that 'non-discriminatory access for creditors to relevant credit databases should be ensured in order to achieve a level playing field with the provisions laid down in Directive 2008/48/EC', Directive 2014/17/EU, recital 20.

80 Directive 2014/17/EU, recital 60.

81 Directive 2014/17/EU, Art.5(b).

consultation fee. Empirical data confirms that in many cases the consultation of credit reference agencies was not extensive in the European countries affected by the debt crisis.

In this context, while credit reference agencies can be an important player in the credit market contributing to its transparency provided that regulation or even self-regulation guarantees adequate consideration of individual rights,[82] the consultation of databases alone cannot be considered in itself a sufficient replacement for an accurate individual assessment[83] and has to be combined with specific responsible lending obligations. This is all the more important if one considers the aforementioned difference between passive and active over-indebtedness, which would require the lender, in addition, to take into careful consideration macroeconomic indicators besides the good or bad credit history of the potential borrower.

Ex-Post Management of Over-Indebtedness

The complex issue of credit history is related to another aspect which has now emerged as a weakness of the European system and even as a possible cause for its slow economic recovery. Where 'bad credit history' can strongly impact on the inclusion of individuals, the possibility for over-indebted citizens to enjoy a second chance, or a 'fresh start', becomes of systemic importance and is pertinent both from a market and a social perspective. While the United States has insolvency rules which in the end perform the function of a relief valve and can even represent an incentive to renegotiate loans (although subject to recent and contentious reforms meant to limit accessibility and prevent abuses),[84] Europe as a whole does not yet seem to have unequivocal instruments which can perform a similar function.

European law remains generally silent on this issue.[85] Certainly, the aforementioned Recommendation 2007(8) hints at mechanisms of debt renegotiation and even discharge for indebted consumers, but these are mostly left to the autonomous initiative of Member States. This attribution of competence would certainly be unproblematic if Member States had put efficient systems in place. This, however, does not seem to be the case at least for most states. Rather, it was the financial crisis that constituted the trigger for various European states to make changes to legislation, developing different approaches to the issue.[86] In order to alleviate over-indebtedness and the social consequences that this might produce (such as homelessness) a wide range of programmes of debt-renegotiation, moratoria on evictions or procedures of consumer bankruptcy have been introduced among many other options. The solutions adopted not only in Europe but also in the whole world are so disparate and open to meta-legal interpretations that a whole set of comparative research on the issue had arisen even before the financial crisis.[87]

While these procedures diverge strongly between the different states, it also appears that their practical impact to solve over-indebtedness problems might be more limited than one could expect, mostly because of substantive reasons regarding either the conditions for obtaining discharge of

82 For a critical view on credit agencies, data protection and supervision, *see* Ferretti 'A European Perspective on Consumer Loans and the Role of Credit Registries' (2010) 33 *Journal of Consumer Policy* 1–27.

83 Iain Ramsay noted that the quasi-standardised credit scoring model might clash with the requirements of responsible lending, which would on the contrary demand an individual assessment of the client's ability to repay (2005, 59).

84 Bankruptcy Abuse Prevention and Consumer Protection Act, 2005.

85 Niemi, 2012.

86 *See* Chapter 12, this volume.

87 Anderson, 2004.

the debt, or even for procedural reasons which, in some instances, might simply frustrate the original aim of the measure.[88] What is more, these differences, coupled with the provision of the European insolvency regulation[89] enabling the insolvency proceedings to be opened in the Member State where the debtor has the centre of his main interests (i.e. where the debtor conducts the administration of his interests on a regular basis), have already allowed for the emergence of a new phenomenon of personal insolvency tourism;[90] conferring the situation a clear transnational dimension. This occurrence could warrant intervention by the Union, as an occasion for laying down a set of substantive and procedural principles to underpin debt relief schemes in national laws in order to make them more effective.

The Judicial Response

The legislative answers and the legal changes which have been described so far – with a strong view to preventing problems from arising and fixing the financial market – may still appear partially inadequate to cope with all the problems that over-indebted consumers face in times of crisis. However, an important complementary role is played by other societal actors, most importantly by the courts. Courts may employ both private and even constitutional law[91] to deal with some of the important aspects which have been neglected by more specific legislation.

The importance of contract law in addressing the problem of over-indebtedness and subsequent social exclusion becomes evident when looking at a line of cases handed down concerning the resolution of judicial conflicts between borrowers and lenders. A wave of cases linked to over-indebtedness problems are now reaching supranational courts in Europe. The recent but already famous *Aziz*[92] ruling of the Court of Justice of the European Union is paradigmatic. Confronted with the case of an insolvent debtor who lost his home to a bank due to his inability to service his debts following unemployment and the lack of the possibility to invoke potential unfairness of the underlying agreement in the eviction procedure, the Court employed the Unfair Terms Directive[93] in light of a 'hidden' constitutional reading[94] involving the principle of effectiveness and social fundamental rights, with the result of offering Spanish consumers some protection against evictions and leading to the strengthening of remedies in national procedural law. In this scenario, the role of the Unfair Terms Directive is remarkable. Despite its scope of application being limited to business-to-consumer relations, this instrument is now emerging as a form of *lex generalis* which can cut across different fields of sectorial regulations and offer through its unfairness test the strongest weapon offered so far by European law to correct unbalanced contracts.[95] Considering European general principles, the principle of effective remedy could also be of unexpected importance in this context, and offer consumers a legal argument to obtain the strengthening of their national system when this does not appear to offer protection.[96] If a link with EU law could be established that could

88 *See* for example Chapter 3, this volume.

89 Council regulation (EC) No 1346/2000.

90 Hoffmann, 2012.

91 The judicial use of fundamental rights in private law cases relating to financial services is not new, *see* Cherednychenko, 2007.

92 CJEU, Case C-415/11, *Aziz v. Catalunyacaixa*, 14 March 2013.

93 Directive 93/13/EEC.

94 Micklitz and Reich, 2014, 30; Comparato and Micklitz, 2013.

95 Micklitz and Reich, 2014.

96 Reich, 2014, 97.

be an instrument to ameliorate national rules such as those on personal insolvency whenever these appear to be ineffective because of procedural issues for instance. In this context, mention can be made also of a recent judgment of the European Court[97] in which the principle of effectiveness – as laid down in the Consumer Credit Directive[98] and not being drawn from primary EU law – was employed to evaluate and sharpen civil remedies against the non-assessment of creditworthiness as drafted by French legislation in implementation of the Consumer Credit Directive.

This development of course involves domestic courts as well as including those countries not belonging to the European Union but more broadly to the European legal area. In a similar vein, in Iceland judicial scrutiny has affected foreign currency indexation clauses, the main instrument through which the effects of devaluation had been passed on to consumers determining the exponential increase of their debts and that represented a serious social problem in that country.[99] The Icelandic Supreme Court has declared FX-indexation of loans illegal, whereas CPI-indexed loans are currently under consideration with an advisory opinion sought from the EFTA-Court on the issue.

Supranational courts are involved in the solution of these questions especially when the issue cannot be resolved within the domestic legal order. If it is excessive to consider these cases as evidence of a 'political' role of the courts, they nonetheless show the emergence of a new social actor at the European level, which goes beyond the traditional role usually assigned in particular to the CJEU. This new development of a form of judicial activism might therefore be interpreted in different ways, including as evidence of a contrast of economic and social rationales enshrined in internal market legislation, case law and national emergency measures. In the worst-case scenario, this conflict of rationales can be transferred to the institutional level, leading to a radicalisation and the judicial culmination of an inherently political conflict. In this sense, the activism of national and supranational courts is also a warning sign which should be considered carefully, as such activism may eventually come at a price in terms of legitimacy; a particularly dangerous outcome in times of institutional and social crises.

Concluding Remarks

In response to the crisis a plethora of measures of very different nature, with a strong focus on regulation and supervision, are currently being considered at the national and European levels. Those measures have often been previously agreed upon at the global level with a view to correcting the seemingly deficient design of credit,[100] at a time where the need for new legal solutions is clear but in which, at the same time, the reasons behind the crisis are still debated and remain to a certain extent unclear.[101] Even when those interventions pursue the primary goal of mending the financial and economic system and its institutional infrastructure, they will have a strong impact on private relations, possibly affecting financial and social inclusion. The promise of democratisation of credit seems to have remained unfulfilled in the long run, as social exclusion resulted from the sector that was, on the contrary, expected to produce social inclusion.

97 CJEU, C-565/12, *LCL Le Crédit Lyonnais SA*, 27 March 2014.

98 Directive 2008/48/EC, art 8: 'Member States shall lay down the rules on penalties applicable to infringements of the national provisions adopted pursuant to this Directive and shall take all measures necessary to ensure that they are implemented. The penalties provided for must be effective, proportionate and dissuasive.'

99 *See* Chapter 7, this volume.

100 Ferran et al., 2012; Wymeersch et al., 2012.

101 Davies, 2010.

In this context, the combined interaction of regulatory interventions and contract law – regulatory private law[102] – can pursue two main objectives: reconstructing an appropriate regulatory environment and alleviating the negative consequences of previous deficiencies. So far, most initiatives at the European level seem to have been aimed at pursuing that former goal, while the latter is left to a series of diverse emergency interventions in the most strongly affected Member States and, possibly, to the judiciary.

References

Ahearne, Alan and Wolff, Guntram B., *The Debt Challenge in Europe* (2012) Bruegel Working Paper 2012/02, 11.

Anderson, Kent, 'The Explosive Global Growth of Personal Insolvency and the Concomitant Birth of the Study of Comparative Consumer Bankruptcy: Consumer Bankruptcy in Global Perspective, by Johanna Niemi Kiesilainen, Iain Ramsay and William C. Whitford (eds.); Comparative Consumer Insolvency Regimes: A Canadian Perspective, by Jacob S. Ziegel' (2004) 42 *Osgoode Hall Law Journal* 661–680.

Ashcraft, Adam B. and Schuermann, Til, 'Understanding the Securitization of Subprime Mortgage Credit' (2006) 2 *Foundations and Trends in Finance* 191–309.

Atamer, Yeşim M., 'Duty of Responsible Lending: Should the European Union Take Action?', in S. Grundmann and Yeşim M. Atamer (eds) *Financial Services, Financial Crisis and General European Contract Law* (Alphen aan den Rijn: Kluwer, 2011).

Banque de France, *Enquête typologique 2007 sur le surendettement*, September 2008, 4.

Bennet, Paul, 'Geographies of Financial Risk and Exclusion', in Susan J. Smith, Rachel Pain, Sallie A. Marston and John P. Jones (eds) *The SAGE Handbook of Social Geographies* (London: SAGE, 2010) 223.

Burton, Dawn, *Credit and Consumer Society* (London: Routledge, 2008) 92.

Caplovitz, David, *Consumers in Trouble: A Study of Debtors in Default* (New York: Free Press, 1974).

Centre for Responsible Lending, *Subprime Lending: A Net Drain on Homeownership*, Issue Paper 4, 27 March 2007.

Cherednychenko, O., *Fundamental Rights, Contract Law and the Protection of the Weaker Party. A Comparative Analysis of the Constitutionalisation of Contract Law, with Emphasis on Risky Financial Transactions* (Munich: Sellier, 2007).

Cherednychenko, Olha O., 'Full Harmonisation of Retail Financial Services Contract Law in Europe: A Success or a Failure?', in Stefan Grundmann and Yeşim M. Atamer (eds) *Financial Services, Financial Crisis and General European Contract Law* (Alphen aan den Rijn: Kluwer, 2011).

Cherednychenko, Olha O., 'Public Supervision over Private Relationships: Towards European Supervision Private Law?' (2014) 1 *European Review of Private Law* 37–68.

Chmelar, Ales, *Household Debt and the European Crisis*, European Credit Research Institute (2013) 13, 3.

Clark, Evans, *Financing the Consumer* (New York: Harper, 1931).

Comparato, Guido and Micklitz, Hans-W., 'Regulated Autonomy between Market Freedoms and Fundamental Rights in the Case-Law of the CJEU', in U. Bernitz, X. Groussot and F. Schulyok

102 Micklitz, 2009.

(eds) *General Principles of EU Law and European Private Law* (Alphen aan den Rijn: Kluwer, 2013).

Conley, Dalton and Gifford, Brian, 'Home Ownership, Social Insurance, and the Welfare State' (2006) 21 *Sociological Forum* 55–82.

Crouch, Colin, 'What Will Follow the Demise of Privatised Keynesianism?' (2008) 79(4) *Political Quarterly* 476–487.

Crouch, Colin, *The Strange Non-Death of Neo-Liberalism* (Cambridge: Polity Press, 2011).

Davies, Howard, *The Financial Crisis: Who is to Blame?* (Cambridge: Polity Press, 2010).

Edgar, Bill, Doherty, Joe and Meert, Henk, *Access to Housing: Homelessness and Vulnerability in Europe* (Bristol: Policy Press, 2002).

Ferran, Eilís, Moloney, Niamh, Hill, Jennifer G. and Coffee Jr, John C., *The Regulatory Aftermath of the Global Financial Crisis* (Cambridge: Cambridge University Press, 2012).

Ferretti, Federico, 'A European Perspective on Consumer Loans and the Role of Credit Registries: The Need to Reconcile Data Protection, Risk Management, Efficiency, Over-indebtedness and a Better Prudential Supervision of the Financial System' (2010) 33 *Journal of Consumer Policy* 1–27.

Grundmann, Stefan and Hofmann, Christian, 'EC Financial Services and Contract Law – Developments 2007–2010' (2010) 4 *European Review of Contract Law* 467–484.

Hoffmann, Thomas, 'The Phenomenon of "Consumer Insolvency Tourism" and its Challenges to European Legislation' (2012) 35 *Journal of Consumer Policy* 461–475.

Hudon, Marek, 'Should Access to Credit be a Right?' (2009) 84 *Journal of Business Ethics* 17–28.

Huls, Nicolaas J., Reifner, Udo and Bourgoinie, T., *Overindebtedness of Consumers in the EC Member States: Facts and Search for Solutions* (Diegem: Kluwer, 1994).

Immergluck, Dan, *Foreclosed: High-Risk Lending, Deregulation, and the Undermining of America's Mortgage Market* (Ithaca and London: Cornell University Press, 2009) 111.

Köndgen, Johannes, 'Policy Responses to Credit Crises: Does the Law of Contract Provide an Answer?', in Stefan Grundmann and Yeşim M. Atamer (eds) *Financial Services, Financial Crisis and General European Contract Law* (Alphen aan den Rijn: Kluwer, 2011).

Kösters, Wim, Paul, Stephan and Stein, Stefan, 'An Economic Analysis of the EU Commission's Proposal for a New Consumer Credit Directive: Offering Consumers More Protection or Restricting their Options?' (2004) 39 *Intereconomics* 84–96.

Kountouros, Haris, 'The Treaty of Nice and Social Policy: The Amendments to Article 137 EC', in Mads Andenas and John A. Usher, *The Treaty of Nice and Beyond: Enlargement and Constitutional Reform* (Portland: Hart, 2003).

Łobocka-Poguntke, Inga, *The Evolution of EC Consumer Protection in the Field of Consumer Credit* (Frankfurt am Main: Peter Lang, 2012).

Marron, Donncha, *Consumer Credit in the United States: A Sociological Perspective from the 19th Century to the Present* (New York: Palgrave Macmillan, 2009).

Micklitz, Hans-W., 'The Visible Hand of European Regulatory Private Law. The Transformation of European Private Law from Autonomy to Functionalism in Competition and Regulation' (2009) 28 *Yearbook of European Law* 3–60.

Micklitz, Hans-W., 'Access to, and Exclusion of, European Consumers from Financial Markets after the Global Financial Crisis', in Therese Wilson (ed.) *International Responses to Issues of Credit and Over-Indebtedness in the Wake of Crisis* (Farnham: Ashgate, 2013).

Micklitz, Hans-W. and Patterson, Dennis, *From the Nation State to the Market: The Evolution of EU Private Law* (2012) EUI Working Paper LAW 2012/15 ERPL-02.

Micklitz, Hans-W. and Reich, Norbert, 'The Court and Sleeping Beauty: The Revival of the Unfair Contract Terms Directive' (2014) 51 *Common Market Law Review* 1–38.
Niemi, Johanna, 'Consumer Insolvency in the European Legal Context' (2012) 35 *Journal of Consumer Policy* 443–459.
Pasiouras, Fotios, *Greek Banking: From the Pre-Euro Reforms to the Financial Crisis and Beyond* (Basingstoke: Palgrave Macmillan, 2012).
Ramsay, Iain, *Consumer Protection. Text and Materials* (London: Weidenfeld & Nicolson, 1989).
Ramsay, Iain, 'From Truth in Lending to Responsible Lending', in Geraint G. Howells, Andre Janssen and Reiner Schulze (eds) *Information Rights and Obligations: A Challenge for Party Autonomy and Transactional Fairness* (Farnham: Ashgate, 2005) 59.
Ramsay, Iain, 'Between Neo-Liberalism and the Social Market: Approaches to Debt Adjustment and Consumer Insolvency in the EU', in Robert Anderson, Hans Dubois, Anne Koark, Götz Lechner, Iain Ramsay, Thomas Roethe and Hans-W. Micklitz (eds) *Consumer Bankruptcy in Europe: Different Paths for Debtors and Creditors* (2011) EUI Working Paper Law 2011/09.
Reich, Norbert, *General Principles of EU Civil Law* (Cambridge: Intersentia, 2014).
Reifner, Udo, 'A "Call to Arms" – For Regulation of Consumer Lending', in Johanna Niemi, Ian Ramsay and William C. Whitford (eds) *Consumer Credit, Debt & Bankruptcy: Comparative and International Perspectives* (Portland: Hart, 2009).
Seligman, Edwin R.A., *The Economics of Instalment Selling: A Study in Consumers' Credit, with Special Reference to the Automobile* (New York: Harper and Brothers, 1927).
Shiller, Robert J., *The Subprime Solution: How Today's Global Financial Crisis Happened, and What to Do about It* (Princeton: Princeton University Press, 2008).
Sufi, Amir, 'Lender Incentives, Credit Risk, and Securitization: Evidence from the Subprime Mortgage Crisis', in Ralph Brubaker, Robert M. Lawless and Charles J. Tabb (eds) *A Debtor World: Interdisciplinary Perspectives on Debt* (New York and Oxford: Oxford University Press, 2013) 92.
Sullivan, Teresa A., 'Debt and the Simulation of Social Class', in Ralph Brubaker, Robert M. Lawless and Charles J. Tabb (eds), *A Debtor World: Interdisciplinary Perspectives on Debt* (New York and Oxford: Oxford University Press, 2013).
de Vries Robbé, Jan Job, *Securitization Law and Practice: In the Face of the Credit Crunch* (Alphen aan den Rijn: Kluwer, 2008).
Weatherill, Stephen, *EU Consumer Law and Policy* (Cheltenham: Elgar, 2013).
White, Alan M., 'The Case for Banning Subprime Mortgages' (2008) 77 *University of Cincinnati Law Review* 617–644.
Whitman, James Q., 'Consumerism Versus Producerism: A Study in Comparative Law' (2007) *Yale Law Law School Legal Scholarship Series*, Paper 644, 361.
Wilhelmsson, Thomas, *Critical Studies in Private Law* (Dordrecht: Kluwer, 1992).
Williams, Toni, 'Continuity, not Rupture: The Persistence of Neoliberalism in the Internationalization of Consumer Finance Regulation', in Therese Wilson (ed.) *International Responses to Issues of Credit and Over-Indebtedness in the Wake of Crisis* (Farnham: Ashgate, 2013).
Wilson, Therese, 'The Responsible Lending Response', in Therese Wilson (ed.) *International Responses to Issues of Credit and Over-Indebtedness in the Wake of Crisis* (Farnham: Ashgate, 2013).
Wymeersch, Eddy, Hopt, Klaus J. and Ferrarini, Guido, *Financial Regulation and Supervision: A Post-Crisis Analysis* (Oxford: Oxford University Press, 2012).
Yunus, Muhammad, *Banker to the Poor* (Oxford: Oxford University Press, 2001).

PART II
The Country Reports

Chapter 3
Country Report Greece

Georgios Mentis and Katerina Pantazatou*

A. Introduction

Greece was the first victim of the 'Euro-crisis' in the European Union.[1] Many factors led to Greece's dire economic situation, among them its high debt and deficit ratios and the very high rates of tax evasion. Following fears of a Greek default and the 'domino' effect this would bring about in the Eurozone countries, Greece received 'bailout' loans in 2010. The financial aid packages signed between Greece and the Troika governed issues such as fiscal consolidation, significant reduction in pensions and salaries, tax increases and lay-offs both in the public and private sectors. The effect of these packages was a significant increase in the rate of unemployment, an increase in crime, the rise of right-wing parties, social unrest and a governmental crisis. In this political, economic and social environment the number of indebted and over-indebted consumers rose to new heights and the Greek government was forced to adopt new laws to deal with this situation. This chapter will first provide the context within which indebtedness and over-indebtedness arose in Greece, before sketching a picture of indebted and over-indebted consumers, and will critically assess the legal framework that was adopted to tackle the growing problem of indebtedness and over-indebtedness in Greece.

B. The Situation of Indebted Consumers in the Country: Financial and Social Issues

The Problems of Indebted Consumers in the Country

Five years after the outbreak of the financial and economic crisis in Greece, the over-indebtedness of Greek consumers remains one of the main social problems in the country. Levels of both indebtedness and over-indebtedness have been rising continuously in the last five years, exposing especially vulnerable households and creating a significant homelessness problem. Income reduction, high interest rates, the aggressive practices of credit promotion, bad planning, unpredictable 'events' (such as loss of employment), an unforeseeable increase in taxation indirectly imposed by the creditors of the Greek state on even low-income households, and the absence of institutions to support consumers have all contributed to the problem.[2]

The fact that to date household debt amounts to approximately €75 billion for mortgages and €35 billion for consumer credit and credit cards (given a population of 11 million people) is telling of

---

* We would like to thank Mr Viktor Tsiafoutis, Attorney at Law, Athens and Mrs Olga Aloupi, Attorney at Law-LLM Candidate, for their substantial assistance in the preparation of this chapter.

1 The term here is used broadly encompassing the present multiple crises in the EU, financial crisis, economic crisis, political crisis, sovereign debt crisis, legitimacy crisis, crisis of democracy and accountability.

2 See the Explanatory Statement of the Law 3869/2010 which is dedicated to over-indebted households.

how indebted Greece is. More than 12,000 files (which have not yet been digitalised)[3] provided by EKPOIZO, an NGO which undertakes a wide range of activities, but which specialises in assisting consumer claims in various ways, show that on average every household with a mortgage has a debt of €120,000–€150,000. This data, in conjunction with the fact that approximately 1.5 million housing loans have been granted to date, allows us to estimate that the number of consumers who have bank debt is approximately 2 million (estimation according to the 'Bulletin of conjunctural indicators', Bank of Greece, November–December 2013). According to the same source, the total number of loans granted, both private and business, peaked in 2010 and since then has followed a downward trend.

In 2009, a total of 41 per cent of the Greek population was indebted to banks, including mortgage loans, consumer loans and credit cards. Furthermore, 63 per cent of public sector employees and 51 per cent of private sector employees are indebted with loans and credit cards. Meanwhile 77 per cent of indebted consumers have faced difficulties in paying off their debt. In relation to the total population of Greece 32 per cent of Greeks have faced difficulties in paying off their debts.[4]

The term over-indebtedness is only implicitly defined under Article 1 of the new Law 3869/2010,[5] as 'the permanent inability of natural persons[6] to pay their overdue financial debts, as long as this inability is not based on fraudulent behavior'.[7] In other words, over-indebtedness is considered as the surcharge of the consumer with debt that exceeds his financial capacity.[8] Despite the difficulties in defining and measuring over-indebtedness, it can be stated that on average 35 per cent of indebted consumers are, as of March 2014, behind on their repayments (31.2 per cent at the end of 2013 according to the Central Bank of Greece). In terms of absolute numbers approximately 750,000 consumers are behind in their payments with regard to their general consumption loans, approximately 500,000 consumers are behind with their car loans, 150,000 with their motorcycle loans, approximately 750,000 consumers are late with the repayment of their credit card debt and 200,000 with their housing loans.[9] Indicatively, with regard to mortgage payments the percentage of consumers who delay the mortgage loan repayments rose from 3.60 per cent in 2007 to 23 per

3 EKPOIZO, 'The Over-Indebtedness of Greek Households – Registering the Problem and Suggesting Ways to Address it' (Report, Athens, November 2012) (in Greek).

4 Data from the Annual Report of Economic and Social Statistics of VPRC. VPRC is one of the biggest private companies in Greece for statistics and social and political research, a member of ESOMAR (European Society for Opinion and Marketing Research) and WAPOR (World Association for Public Opinion Research).

5 Free translation.

6 And thus not of persons who have the ability to go bankrupt – traders for instance are covered by the 'Insolvency/Bankruptcy Code'.

7 The existence of fraudulent behaviour or 'intention on behalf of the debtor' for the purposes of Law 3869/2010 implies the rejection, by the Court, of the debtor's application to be covered by Law 3869/2010. Intention, in this sense, is understood as the intentional failure to repay the debt, despite the existence of liquidity by the debtor. By way of example, the non-repayment of the debt at issue by the debtor, the transfer of valuable assets to third parties in order to reduce his property and the intentional channelling of his remaining capital to banks outside the country so that it becomes inaccessible to the creditor evidences intentional inability to pay. The burden of proof with regards to intention lies with the creditor.

8 See Georgios Mentis, *Defence and Release of the Over-Indebted Debtor* (Dikaio kai Oikonomia P.N. Sakkoulas 2012) 1 [in Greek: Γεώργιος Μεντής, Άμυνα και Ελευθέρωση του Υπερχρεωμένου Οφειλέτη: Η πορεία προς μια νέα σεισάχθεια στα όρια μεταξύ αστικού δικαίου και νέου πτωχευτικού δικαίου (Δίκαιο και Οικονομία Π. Ν. Σάκκουλας 2012) 1].

9 Data provided by EKPOIZO (n 3).

cent in 2013.[10] The total average amount of outstanding debt is approximately €101,349,000,000 according to the data provided by the Central Bank of Greece. This data allows us to conclude that approximately 700,000 households are now behind with the repayment of their credit obligations and could be considered to be over-indebted. In a similar vein, as of March 2014, at least 100,000 applications have been filed by consumers seeking to benefit from Law 3869/2010 (for over-indebted households), and today the number of applications continues to rise.

Even though it is difficult to clearly understand the vulnerability of certain households to over-indebtedness, it is evident that low-income households and families with children are among the most affected. This conclusion derives from empirical data, although no legislative clear-cut definition of vulnerability exists. The vulnerable *consumer* is not defined in the national legal order (neither in Law 3869/2010), even though Article 8(5) of Law 3869/2010 implies a definition of the term by providing that in exceptional circumstances, like unemployment, health problems and insufficient income to meet basic living needs, the court may determine that the debtor will pay zero instalments (Nullplan) to their creditors, potentially even leading to full discharge of their debts.[11] Consequently, this makes low income one of the factors in determining vulnerability – an indication that is confirmed when looking at the profile of the 'over-indebted' consumers. Thirteen per cent of over-indebted consumers are single, 67 per cent are married, 18 per cent are divorced and 2 per cent are widowed. Approximately 90 per cent of over-indebted consumers have children and 10 per cent do not. From the sample under examination 65 per cent of over-indebted consumers are employed and 35 per cent are not, whereas approximately 17 per cent are pensioners. While it is difficult to establish the percentage of 'low-income' over-indebted consumers due to the absence of such a definition, it is estimated that more than 80 per cent of over-indebted consumers could be considered as 'low-income' consumers.[12]

As a result of the rising over-indebtedness levels, a new social problem in Greek society has arisen in the form of the 'new homeless' people. This can be attributed to the rising number of evictions every year.[13] Approximately 5,000 evictions have taken place every year since 2000, but the figures for the first two months of 2011 alone show the number of evictions reaching approximately 4,000 (whereas evictions for the entire year 2010 were 8,500).[14] The number of

10 Source: Bank of Greece, 'Bulletin of Conjunctural Indicators', Issue 145 July–August 2012 (Τράπεζα της Ελλάδος, 'Στατιστικό Δελτίο Οικονομικής Συγκυρίας', Τεύχος 145 Ιούλιος-Αύγουστος 2012) and Bank of Greece, 'Monetary Policy', 2012–2013.

11 The term 'vulnerable *consumer*' is defined in Article 52 of the Law 4001/2011 where it is provided that the vulnerable consumer benefits from lower tariffs and more favourable regulation in the consumption of electricity. The 'vulnerable costumer' is defined therein as 'persons of low income, families with more than three children, long-term unemployed persons, persons with disabilities, persons living in remote areas and persons that require mechanical/artificial support' (free translation). See also the Decisions of the Ministry of Environment, Energy and Climate Change Δ5-ΗΛ/Β/Φ29/16027/6.8.10 as amended by the Ministerial Decisions Δ5-ΗΛ/Β/Φ29/6713/24.3.11, Δ5-ΗΛ/Β/Φ1.20/οικ.878/17.1.13, Δ5/ΗΛ/Β/Φ29/οικ.21235/20.11.13 and Δ5/ΗΛ/Β/Φ29/οικ.23823/23.12.2013.

12 According to the statistics of the Association of Greek Employed Consumers (October 2013) (http://www.gsee.gr/userfiles/file/2013_BOXES/2013_10_17_%20eeke_statistika.pdf).

13 Approximately 5 per cent of the above total number of evictions take place because of unpaid mortgage instalments. In the last five years the reason for this low percentage is that specific legislation provides the infringement of the enforcement proceedings concerning the main residence of every individual. According to the new legislation (Law 4224/2013) the suspension of the enforcement proceedings is based on stricter conditions which will lead to an increase of the evictions in the near future. Approximately 95 per cent of the above total number of evictions took place because of unpaid monthly rents.

14 http://www.ethnos.gr/article.asp?catid=22768&subid=2&pubid=55606978.

evictions issued by the District Court of Athens increased by 17 per cent between 2010 and 2011.[15] The vast majority of homeless people are men aged 26 to 55 with one out of five having high school or higher education. The main reasons for homelessness are financial difficulties (approximately 30 per cent), unemployment (approximately 17 per cent) and insufficient financial support from the homeless peoples' families (approximately 17 per cent).[16]

Reasons for the (Increased) Levels of Indebtedness and Over-Indebtedness

While the reasons for the high indebtedness of Greek households are numerous, we believe that most probably the biggest macro-economic risk factor in Greece in the years to come is the dramatically high level of unemployment. Since 2008 unemployment levels in Greece have been rising steadily and significantly. In December 2013 unemployment levels reached 27.5 per cent of the total active population,[17] whilst for young persons (those under 25 years old) Greece recorded the highest unemployment rates in the euro area, amounting to 58.3 per cent.[18] A large number of debtors who had a job at the time of the conclusion of the loan contract are now facing the serious problem of no (or less) income while they are obliged to pay the full amount of the instalments of their loans, as otherwise they are charged with default interest for late payment which may be up to 12 or 15 per cent for consumer loans and more than 17 or 18 per cent for credit cards. According to the statistics of the Association of Greek Employed Consumers up until October 2013 approximately 35 per cent of over-indebted consumers were unemployed, as opposed to 65 per cent who were employed.[19] According to the same statistics 26 per cent of the over-indebted consumers were private sector employees, 8 per cent were public sector employees, 17 per cent were pensioners and the rest of them were freelancers or farmers to mention just a few of the many different occupations.

Apart from unemployment, the housing and credit boom in Greece, especially in the years leading up to the crisis, could be considered as the main reasons for the increased levels of over-indebtedness in the country. The demand for real estate in Greece (especially for residential property) was always high due to the tendency of Greek people to prefer to own their own home.[20] Generally speaking, the price of real estate had been going up over an extended period of time. In the decade between 1996 and 2006 the price of real estate increased even more rapidly. This has subsequently, however, been 'corrected' by the crisis. Indicatively, economic studies have shown that during the period between 2009 and 2014 the price of real estate has decreased by almost 40–50 per cent compared to the decade between 1996 and 2006.[21]

15 Data from the First Instance Court of Athens (Protodikeio Athinon), which is geographically competent only for disputes that arise for immovable property in Athens.

16 KLIMAKA NGO's survey on 'Homelessness in Greece-2012'. See http://www.klimaka.org.gr/newsite/KoinApok/Astegoi/Astegoi1.htm.

17 According to Eurostat data. See http://epp.eurostat.ec.europa.eu/statistics_explained/index.php/Unemployment_statistics

18 Ibid.

19 Up until October 2013 (http://www.gsee.gr/userfiles/file/2013_BOXES/2013_10_17_%20eeke_statistika.pdf).

20 The percentage of ownership in Greece amounts to approximately 75 per cent.

21 Sources: Bank of Greece based on data collected by the credit institutions (2006 onwards, apartments only) and weighted index according to the stock of houses in Athens and in other urban areas (up to 2005, all dwellings).

Together with rising demand for private housing we can observe a credit boom in consumer loans from the end of the 1990s. Increased access to consumer credit can be attributed to three factors. First, during the 1980s and early 1990s the Greek financial sector was increasingly liberalised. In this context, the previous ceiling of €25,000 per borrower and bank on consumer loans and any corresponding limits for these loans' subcategories were abolished. Since then, Greek households were able to borrow more easily.[22] Previously, the Greek financial system had been heavily regulated as bank interest rates were set at administered levels and credit was channelled to the economy through investment requirements imposed on banks as regards the financing mainly of the public sector and a complicated reserve or rebate system as regards the financing of the private sector. As a result of the latter, the loan interest rates received by banks were different from the rates charged to borrowers. At the same time, it was more profitable for banks to extend loans to enterprises than to households.[23] In addition, this liberalisation triggered higher demand for loans by firms and households that were previously effectively credit constrained. These factors contributed to the rapid increase in consumer loan growth rates and the corresponding loan-to-GDP ratio.[24]

Secondly, the practice of 'easy lending' on behalf of the Greek banks, coupled with poor control of the candidate borrowers and the sale of risky financial products such as repos, futures, options and swaps contributed to the increased levels of indebtedness and over-indebtedness in Greece. Before Directive 2008/48/EC was transposed into national law by the Common Ministerial Decision (CMD) Z1–699/2010, creditworthiness assessments of the candidate borrower were either imperfect or completely omitted. According to a report by the Association of Employed Consumers (Ενωση εργαζόμενων καταναλωτών Ελλάδας), there are many examples of extreme imbalances between the maximum borrowing capacity of the consumer and the reckless lending behaviour of the banks. Indicatively, there have been cases, in particular in the rural areas of Greece, where banks granted loans of €250,000 to consumers with an annual (declared) income of €9,000.[25] In addition, one can find cases in Greek jurisprudence where credit institutions were giving significant credit to persons with low or no income, such as students.[26] With regard to the 'easy lending' practice, it should also be noted that there are no 'real' credit bureaus in Greece. However, the Credit Consolidation System (CCS or 'white' TIRESIAS), the Default Financial Obligation System (DFOS or 'black' TIRESIAS) and the Mortgages and Prenotations to Mortgages System (MPS) of TIRESIAS Bank Information Systems SA could be characterised as credit bureaus in the broader sense, as they provide credit institutions with data about the financial behaviour of consumers, their indebtedness status, the existence of unpaid debts or of enforcement procedures pending against them in order to facilitate a creditworthiness assessment (see also below). However, since the implementation of Directive 2008/48/EC and the introduction of compulsory creditworthiness assessments the banks have been more careful in their assessments (for details see next section).

Thirdly, the larger conditions in the Eurozone also played a role in the increasing rates of indebtedness. For example, falling interest rates in the Eurozone reflected the process of convergence

22 H. Voridis, E. Angelopoulou and I. Skotida, 'Monetary Policy in Greece 1990–2000 through the Publications of the Bank of Greece' (Bank of Greece Economic Bulletin No. 20/2003) 7–86.

23 Ibid. 11–12.

24 S. Brissimis, E. Garganas and S. Hall, 'Consumer Credit in an Era of Financial Liberalisation: An Overreaction to Repressed Demand?' (Bank of Greece Working Paper 148, October 2012) 11.

25 http://www.gsee.gr/userfiles/file/2013_BOXES/2013_10_17_%20eeke_statistika.pdf.

26 See Case 7241/1999 of First Instance Court of Athens, in which the bank accepted guarantee on a debt of 18,500 euro by a 19-year-old with no income and no property.

towards the levels of EU interest rates and the disinflation process in Greece.[27] Moreover, and as a consequence, banks, consumers and firms expected higher future incomes associated with the benefits from the adoption of the euro in Greece, which led to increased consumption and greater willingness to lend and borrow.[28]

Furthermore, consumers, for their part, made use of the 'easy access to money' framework. As they were generally eager to accept the terms and conditions of the loan agreements, the overwhelming majority did not read their credit agreements before signing.[29] In interviews, more than 90 per cent of the consumers stated that they had not compared offers or asked for explanations before entering into an agreement. In addition, consumers almost never made use of their right to withdrawal within 10 to 15 days from the day the agreement was signed. Moreover, most consumers were not familiar with the legal terms usually used by the creditor (such as payment order). This lack of consumer knowledge and understanding was exacerbated by the indirect pressure of some misleading advertising regarding lending conditions as well as through some aggressive 'distant selling' practices adopted by the banks to promote loans and credit cards, in particular over the phone.[30] In fact, the First Instant Court of Athens has repeatedly ordered the removal of advertisements that have misled consumers, in particular by announcing a low interest rate (for instance 4.97 per cent for one year), while the Annual Percentage of Actual Costs (ΣΕΠΠΕ) appeared on screen as rolling text in very small letters.[31] Moreover, many cases have been reported in which the lender pressed the debtor to sign a refinancing loan in order to repay already existing debts and forced the debtor's relatives to sign as guarantors under the threat that if they did not comply with this, the credit institution would proceed to enforcement procedures on the debtor's assets.[32]

However, since the crisis began, access to credit has become more restricted both legally and in practice. The 'peak' of the credit boom was the year 2009, during which the total amount of loans to private parties reached €119,635 million.[33] In the period from 2009 to 2010, despite the lower ECB interest rates applicable to both business and mortgage loan rates, consumer loan rates did not follow suit. In this loan category, the new importance attached by banks to credit risk and the rising ratio of non-performing loans led to an overall tightening of the credit terms and conditions.[34] Consumer lending in Greece was virtually non-existent in 2013, as gross lending towards consumers (and also businesses) hit an all-time low.[35]

The decline in the granting of loans to individuals can be attributed to the following three factors. First of all, Greek banks faced major liquidity problems, which were compounded even further

27 Brissimis et al. (n 24). Ibid.

28 Ibid.

29 Data provided in this paragraph was collected in interviews with bank employees and consumers with a bank loan. The collected data corresponds also to what is presented by G. Dellios, *Standard Contract Terms* (2nd edn Sakkoulas 2013) 7 *et seq.* [in Greek: Γ. Δέλλιος, Γενικοί Όροι Συναλλαγών (εκδόσεις Σάκκουλα, 2η έκδοση 2013) 7 επ].

30 Information based on interviews with representatives of consumer organisations.

31 See for instance Cases 1212/2007 and 33/2008 of the Court of First Instance of Athens (Πολ.Πρωτ. Αθ).

32 Information based on interviews with consumers and representatives of consumer organisations.

33 ΕΚΡΟΙΖΟ (n 3).

34 Brissimis et al. (n 24) 14.

35 http://www.euromonitor.com/consumer-lending-in-greece/report. According to the same report: 'The only consumer credit category remaining active in 2013 was the so-called green loans, mainly for home energy-saving projects.'

after the events in Cyprus[36] and the banks' involvement in the PSI (private sector involvement, namely the reduction of the public debt through the writing-off of 53.5 per cent of the face value of Greek governmental bonds). Even after strengthening their capital base through re-capitalisation in May 2013, Greek banks have hardly provided any loans.[37] With the rate of non-performing loans (from mortgage loans to credit cards) rapidly increasing, the focus of Greek banks is on refinancing old loans, portfolio rationalisation, keeping non-performing loans from increasing further and making problematic loans serviceable again.[38] Moreover, the ongoing austerity measures and the significant increase in taxation, even for low-income consumers, have diminished consumers' disposable income and have, consequently, undermined demand and made supply more cautious.

C. Legal Framework and the Role of Private Law

Besides the adoption of Law 3869/2010 for over-indebted natural persons (and thus, also consumers) we do not observe an extraordinary change in the legal framework for consumer protection since the beginning of the crisis. Overall, we notice a leniency by the judiciary in the application of the strict terms of credit agreements and a wider use of general Civil Code articles that refer to good faith, fair trading practices and abuse of rights, in favour of the consumer. The *Aziz* case did not have any profound impact on Greek legislation or jurisprudence.

Adjustment with regard to the possibility of raising substantive objections against enforcement was not required in the light of *Aziz*. This case does not give – in our opinion – a clear answer to the problem of high interest rates (ordinary or default interest rates), and it does not provide a solution to the problem pertaining to the Greek banking practice of applying high interest rates without any substantial control by the unfair contract terms Directive 93/13/EEC. Moreover, Greek procedural law already allows substantive objections against enforcement. These objections may relate to the validity of the terms of the loan contract that are important for the specific case, or the validity of the enforceable instrument. For instance, the consumer has the right to file an application for the suspension of the execution procedure until the issuing of the court's final decision concerning the objections (Articles 632 Paragraph 2 and 938 Greek CCP), if the enforcement procedure could cause irreparable damage to the debtor and the main application for suspension (the *anakopi*) is likely to be successful.

Among the objections the consumer may raise, special reference has to be made to the objection of the abuse of the creditor's right based on Article 281 of the Greek Civil Code, according to which the exercise of a right shall not exceed the limits imposed by good faith or fair trading practices or the social or economic purpose of the right. Courts in several cases accept the objection of abuse of the creditor's right to initiate enforcement procedures in order to satisfy their claim. The abuse of right can result from, for example: the initiation of the execution procedure even though the consumer has already commenced the procedure foreseen for over-indebted individuals in Law 3869/2010;[39] the commencement of enforcement procedures by the bank immediately

36 See the Macroeconomic Adjustment Programme for Cyprus and the Eurogroup statement of 25 March with regard to the financial assistance granted. Among the many conditions required by the Troika, the immediate resolution of Laiki Bank – with full contribution of equity shareholders, bond holders and uninsured depositors – had negative repercussions also in the Greek economy.

37 Ibid.

38 Ibid.

39 See of the large number of judgements the cases 8817/2012 of First Instance Court of Athens and 5422/2011 of Magistrate Court of Athens.

after the first delay of the monthly instalment without any notification to the consumer or special reason;[40] or the initiation of enforcement proceedings by the creditor when the amount of the debt is disproportionally low compared to the value of the property under attachment.[41]

It could be said that Greek law aims more at the prevention of over-indebtedness than European law, as it contains tighter rules on the creditworthiness assessment of consumers. First, Article 8 (3) CMD Z1–699/2010[42] on the obligation to assess the creditworthiness of the consumer introduces the legal obligation for a creditworthiness assessment by providing that[43] if the credit institution breaches through its own fault its obligation to assess the creditworthiness of the consumer, the consumer is discharged from the total cost of the credit, including interest, and he has the obligation to pay only the amount of the capital according to the instalments agreed in the contract. The rationale of the provision, the prevention of over-indebtedness, relates strongly to the mandatory character of the creditworthiness assessment. It is the first time that the national law has provided for the discharge (if only partial) of debt because of the inability of the debtor to pay the debt. The main requirement for the application of Article 8(3) is the fault of the creditor, including fraud and negligence. Furthermore, even though not expressly mentioned, the consumer has to be unable to repay his debts.[44] As a consequence, the loan becomes interest-free and the creditor cannot claim his fee for providing the credit, an indication of the punitive character of the provision.

Article 27(3) of the Greek Banking Law (Law 3601/2007) provides further requirements for the creditworthiness assessment by stating that:

> in case of an application for a loan or other credit by a credit or financial institution, the applicant shall provide complete and accurate information for the assessment of his solvency and creditworthiness. Credit and financial institutions have the obligation to take into account in the rating of the risk under this Article, any partial or total refusal of the applicant to provide such information. The information does not include sensitive personal data, as these are defined under the relevant legislation.

The credit institution, when conducting the creditworthiness assessment, checks the total debt burden of a candidate borrower in relation to his income. This percentage must not exceed 30–40 per cent. Another criterion is the existing relationship between the bank and the consumer. The existence of a payroll account or deposits is now at the top of the list of positive criteria in the final assessment process.[45] The bank also takes into account the data provided by TEIRESIAS, a bank information systems company, with regard to the existence of loan agreements between the consumer and other credit institutions and the amount of them ('white' TEIRESIAS); the existence of bounced cheques, insolvency petitions and their evaluation, delays in other loan repayments, payment orders, seizures and auctions, mortgages and their possible removal, terminations

40 See indicatively the case 13/2003 of First Instance Court of Nafplio.

41 See case 60/2004 of the First Instance Court of Mesologgi, in which judged there was an abuse of right if the attachment of an immovable property of value 102,700 euro is exercised for the satisfaction of a debt of 450 euro.

42 Common Ministerial Decision (CMD) Z1–699/2010 almost literally implemented the Directive 2008/48/EC (CCD) into the national legal order, Official Government Gazette (ΦΕΚ) B917 20100623.

43 Free translation.

44 Inability means that the debtor cannot respond to the irresponsibly given credit, keeping at the same time for himself and the persons he is obliged to care of, a minimum standard of living. See Mentis (n 8) 35.

45 Information provided by banking employees and clients of credit institutions.

of loan and credit card contracts and the administrative penalties against violators of tax laws ('black' TEIRESIAS).

Despite these elaborate rules, in the aftermath of the financial crisis, consumer (credit) law has proven to be less important than general contract law. Most of the cases that have reached Greek courts are mainly challenged under Greek contract law and concern issues pertaining to default as well general contract terms and abusive and unfair contract terms. Law 2251/1994 transposed Directive 93/13/EEC into Greek law and constitutes the main legal framework for consumer protection. Article 2(6) of Law 2251/1994 contains the general prohibition of unfair terms (similar to Article 3 of the Directive 93/13/EEC), whereas Article 2(7) provides a non-exhaustive list of 31 specific contract terms that are deemed *ex lege (per se)* unfair, and as such, void and forbidden. The rules regarding the unfairness of contract terms specify the more general rule that exists in the Greek Civil Code, Article 281, according to which any abusive exercise of a right or freedom (in this case, contractual freedom) should be forbidden.

These provisions have been very important in litigation and significant changes in jurisprudence derive from the application of private law principles such as abuse of rights or good faith as contained in the Greek Civil Code (GCC). In general, the creditor has the right to terminate the loan agreement in case of the debtor's default on two or more instalments. If the debtor does not respond to this obligation, the lender can, thus, terminate the loan agreement through an extrajudicial notification. Upon termination of the loan agreement the lender has the right to demand the total amount of the loan (including interest and costs) which is further charged with default interest. Moreover, the lender has the right to notify the TEIRESIAS database of the termination and to initiate enforcement procedures, charging the borrower with the judicial costs, in accordance with Articles 904 *et seq.* of the Greek Code of Civil Procedure.

However, the post-crisis case law now provides that the lender has the obligation to tolerate a reasonable default on monthly instalments (*moratorium, obligation de non petendo*), especially when the default is caused by a temporary financial inability of the debtor and the pursuit of the lender's claim would destroy the former financially.[46] This obligation stems from the principles of good faith and fair trading practices,[47] which govern the enduring contractual relationship of trust between the credit institution and the consumer. Similarly, because of the economic crisis and the rough conditions it has imposed on households, many judgments find the creditor's right to terminate the loan agreement by the first default of the monthly instalments abusive when this action provokes significant damage to the debtor compared to the benefit of the bank.[48] Moreover, Article 288 GCC provides that 'the debtor has to fulfill his obligation in accordance with the principles of good faith and after taking into account the fair commercial practices'.[49] Relying on that provision several court decisions have recognised that in a period of economic crisis the bank has the obligation, in accordance with the principle of good faith, to refrain from the relentless prosecution of the debtor (enforcement procedures), to tolerate the delay and to offer repayment facilities (grace period or extension of the repayment time).[50]

46 See the 15607/2012 case of First Instance Court of Thessaloniki which concerned credit agreement with an open account.

47 See Articles 281 and 288 of the Greek Civil Code.

48 See case 208/2013 of Magistrate Court of Athens.

49 Free translation.

50 The violation of such obligations may lead to the bank's liability to compensation to the debtor. See Decision of the Court of Appeal of Athens 5025/1990 and First Instance Court of Thessaloniki 13035/2013 and 15607/2012.

In contrast to the activism the Greek judiciary has shown in relation to concepts such as the abuse of rights, the Greek judge has been reluctant to adjust contractual terms in cases where the debtor's personal circumstances have changed as a result of the financial crisis. Article 388 GCC provides that:

> if having regard to the requirements of good faith and fair practices the circumstances on which the parties had based the conclusion of a bilateral agreement have subsequently changed on exceptional grounds that could not have been foreseen; and the performance due by the debtor taking also into consideration the counter-performance results in an excessively onerous change, the Court may at the request of the debtor and according to its margin of appreciation reduce the debtor's performance to the appropriate extent or decide the dissolution of the contract in whole or with regard to its non-performed part.[51]

As such, Article 388 of the GCC allows for the heteronomous modification and adjustment of the contract under exceptional circumstances and strict conditions in exception to the rule *pacta sunt servanda*. When applying Article 388 GCC, the judge is called upon to restore the imbalance of rights and obligations of the contract by reducing or increasing the debtor's performance to the appropriate extent, which is determined by the circumstances and good faith. In exceptional cases the court may decide on the total or partial dissolution of the contract. Although Greek law does not provide for the obligation of the parties to renegotiate the terms of the contract before the *ultimum refugium* of the judicial adjustment of their agreement, Greek theory supports such an obligation according to the general principle of good faith.[52]

The application of Article 388 GCC in credit agreements has not been generally accepted by the courts yet, although the majority of the literature is in favour of this.[53] The application of this provision in credit agreements could lead to their reconsideration and adjustment in a period of economic crisis and of over-indebtedness of consumers, by the form of the reduction of the interest rate, the extension of the schedule of monthly instalments, or the obligation of tolerance of the delay (*moratorium*) for instance.

Notwithstanding changes in the application of general contract law in favour of the consumer, consumer protection in the field of consumer credit and mortgages is inhibited in Greece due to procedural congestion. The crisis has also had an impact on the volume of both judicial and non-judicial proceedings. During the period from September 2010 to December 2012, according to data presented by EKPOIZO, 64,772 applications for out-of-court settlement were filed by consumer

51 Translation of the Greek Civil Code by Constantin Taliadoros, Ant. N. Sakkoulas Publishers 2000.

52 Antonios Karampatzos, *Unforeseen Change of Circumstances in the Bilateral Contract* (Ant. N. Sakkoulas 2006) 493 [in Greek: Αντώνιος Καραμπατζός, Απρόβλεπτη Μεταβολή των Συνθηκών στην Αμφοτεροβαρή Σύμβαση (Αντ. Ν. Σάκκουλας, 2006) 493].

53 With the exception of some few but important cases, such as 5025/1990 Court of Appeal of Athens. See Filipps Doris, 'The Judicial Conformation of the Content of Contracts in Periods of Economic Crisis' [in Greek: Φίλιππος Δωρής, 'Η δικαστική διάπλαση του περιεχομένου εκκρεμών συμβάσεων σε περιόδους οικονομικής Κρίσης' ΧρΙΔ 2012], 241 *et seq.*, Georgios Dellios, 'Still On-Going Banking Credit Contracts in Periods of Economic Crisis' [in Greek: Γεώργιος Δέλλιος, 'Εκκρεμείς τραπεζικές πιστωτικές συμβάσεις σε περιόδους οικονομικής κρίσης' ΧρΙΔ 2012], 246 *et seq.*, Mentis (n 8) 1. The majority of the judgments which apply the provision of Article 388 concern contracts for the hire of immovable property (especially commercial lease) and based on that Article they conclude with the reduction of the amount of the rent.

protection organisations to banks.[54] Out of these applications only five were successful.[55] POMEK's (ΠΟΜΕΚ)[56] data show that there are approximately 100,000 phone calls to the organisation's services (representing consumers) requesting out-of-court settlement per year, whereas the cases that address mortgage agreements are approximately 70 per cent of the total number of cases.

Between September 2010 and December 2012, members of POMEK alone filed 44,551 applications. According to EKPOIZO, more than 34,000 applications for court settlement have been filed to the Magistrates' Courts of the country from 2011 to 2012. Out of these applications, 9,335 applications were filed to the Magistrates' Court of Athens, out of which one court settlement was successful, two court settlements were ratified by the Court, 85 decisions were issued by the Court, 469 cases were considered admissible and were processed, and 382 were dismissed as inadmissible. As of March 2014 the number of applications pending in courts all over Greece had reached 100,000 (the number of applications has doubled in almost one year).[57] The increasing number of applications has caused delays in the adjudication of cases. Indicatively, data from other district courts show that the hearing of some cases is likely to take place even later than 2024. This is very problematic, in particular with regard to cases that aim at obtaining (an imminent) debt relief through the newly introduced bankruptcy procedure for consumers (see below).

D. Policy Responses to Over-Indebtedness

Apart from consumers having recourse to judicial and non-judicial settlement procedures, the Greek government has also attempted to alleviate debt burdens, mainly through an innovative bankruptcy legal framework for 'households', and, less importantly, through a temporary debt mitigation programme. In addition, it has suspended eviction procedures while, at the same time, it has provided the possibility to property owners to evict tenants swiftly in case of default on rent payments.

The dire economic situation of many debtors, due to unemployment, huge pay cuts, and over-indebtedness, led the Greek state to introduce for the first time the regulation of the 'insolvency' of over-indebted consumers (non-traders). The relevant Law 3869/2010 has only been in force since 2010 but has already triggered numerous judicial decisions. This led to the amendment of Law 3869/2010 in 2013 by Law 4161/2013, in order to facilitate the procedure and to accelerate the regulation (even temporary) of the debtor's loans. According to Law 3869/2010, as amended by subsequent laws, provided the conditions laid out in Law 3869/2010 are met,[58] the consumer

54 Data from Geniki Grammateia Katanaloti (General Secretariat of Consumers).

55 'Successful' means that the credit institutions agreed to the plan of the settlement proposed by the debtor, including reduction of the monthly instalments, grace period, etc.

56 Πανελλήνια Ομοσπονδία Ενώσεως Καταναλωτών 'Η Παρέμβαση' (National Association of Consumer Protection Organizations 'Paremvasi').

57 Unofficial data provided by EKPOIZO. The data, does not unfortunately, distinguish between mortgage agreements and consumer credit.

58 The material scope of Law 3869/2010 comprises debts of individuals who do not have the legal capacity to go bankrupt (according to traders bankruptcy law) and who have, by no fraudulent intention, permanent inability to pay back their debts. According to Article 1 of Law 3869/2010, debts that have been undertaken during the last year before the submission of the discharging application, as well as debts stemming from illegal acts committed by fraudulent intention, administrative fines/sanctions, fines, tax/debts due towards the state and organisations of local authorities, public law corporate bodies charges and contributions towards social security funds, are excluded from the scope of the provision.

can use mediation and out-of-court settlement (Articles 2 and 7 of Law 3869/2010),[59] court compromise or settlement, and judicial debt settlement (re-organisation), which may entail discharge of debt.

The debtor must be legally unable to file for insolvency and permanently unable to pay his debts and must not have committed fraud in relation to the imputation of financial inability (such as transfer of assets). Fraud does not concern the time of the conclusion of the loan agreement (unless the consumer hid financial evidence in order to misguide the creditor with regard to his creditworthiness assessment), but the time of the imputation of financial inability.[60] However, debts that have been concluded during the last year from the filing of the relevant application to the competent Magistrates' Court (that could be premised on strategic default), debts that have arisen out of a tort committed by fraud, as well as administrative fines, penalties, public taxes, fees to the government and to local authorities, fees to public entities and contributions to social security organisations are exempted from the scope of application of Law 3869/2010.

The debtor seeking settlement and relief from their debts must submit a petition to the Magistrates' Court of the debtor's residence (Article 3 Law 3869/2010).[61] The court can proceed to judicial debt settlement, which sometimes can even result in a complete discharge of debt.[62] Law 3869/2010 provides that the court may, after it has taken into account the debtor's income (personal and family) as well as his family's needs, request the debtor to pay monthly instalments of a specific amount for three to five years,[63] which will be distributed to the creditors equally (Article 8(2) of Law 3869/2010).[64] The amount to be paid by the debtor to the creditors, as ordered by the court, varies between very small and sometimes, even 'zero' sums ('*Nullplan*') if the debtor faces serious unemployment problems (not attributed to the debtor's liability), health or other serious problems, such as serious financial distress that does not allow him to have any income (Article 8(5) Law 3869/2010).

If the debtor complies with the repayment schedule ordered by the court, he will be discharged from all the remaining debt against all creditors (Article 7 and 11(1) Law 3869/2010). The discharge of debt can be attained either through an agreement between the creditors and the debtor on the debt adjustment or settlement ('quasi re-organisation of debt') or through a court decision (Article 7 of Law 3869/2010). Article 11 of Law 3869/2010 provides explicitly for the full relief of the

59 According to Law 4161/2013, the Out of Court Settlement is not any more a prerequisite in order to proceed with the petition. Out of Court Settlement was replaced by a discretionary mediation procedure.

60 See case 193/2012 of Magistrate Court of Lavrio and case 10/2011 of Magistrate Court of Athens. There is also a different opinion of part of judgments concerning the Law 3869/2010 according to which the decision of concluding a loan agreement burdens the consumer who has to be diligent and choose the proper credit contract (see case 1/2012 of Magistrate's Court of Florina). This latter opinion apparently ignores the obligation of the credit institutions to assess the creditworthiness of the consumer.

61 The delivery of the petition does not interrupt the accrual of interest on secured claims (contractual interest rather than default interest applies), unlike for unsecured claims, where interest accrual is interrupted. Creditors have one month from service to provide their comments on the plan. The law provides for a presumption of consent to the plan for creditors that fail to comment.

62 The Greek law does not distinguish between debt relief and debt discharge.

63 Article 8 par. 2 of the Law 3869/2010 was amended by Article 16 of Law 4161/2013 (before the amendment the period of monthly instalments was obligatorily four years).

64 See for instance cases 2/2011 and 4/2011 of Magistrate Court of Patra and case 15/2011 of Magistrate Court of Athens.

debtor and does not leave any space for accepting the remaining of the debt as a non-enforceable legal right, as is sometimes argued by commentators.[65]

According to Law 3869/2010, the debtor is considered debt-free after complying with the three-to-five-year payment schedule. In practice, this is, however, problematic. Although the Law in Article 4 stipulates that the hearing for determining compliance with the given conditions shall be set within six months from the submission of the application, in practice, because of the congestion on litigation procedures, the date of the hearing is usually set many years later, currently even the year 2024. The only solution to this is for the debtor to request temporary injunction according to Article 781 of the Greek Civil Procedure Code.

Unofficial information provided by the Greek courts indicate that since 2011 approximately 5,000 individuals have had debts re-organised through a reduction of the monthly instalments and the interest rates, and have further, made use of the exclusion of the main residence from the liquidation of the assets. However, this a very low number compared with the total number of petitions for debt re-organising (100,000 petitions are pending).[66] Due to the very recent adoption of Law 3869/2010 and the fact that debt relief requires the payment of monthly instalments determined by the court's decision for a period of three to five years, there has not been a completed debt relief yet.

A temporary legal instrument of debt facilitation was introduced with Law 4161/2013,[67] which provides a legal framework for the 'Facilitation of performing debtors'. This law provides for a new path for borrowers who want to settle their loan instalments. It is an extrajudicial procedure, a form of an *ex lege* settlement of the loan. The debtors whose obligations arise from housing, credit or 'reparation' loans that have a mortgage lien to the primary residence of the debtor have the right to request from the credit institution to be included in a programme of 'favourable treatment of their debt'.

This procedure only applied to debtors who filed an application before 14 April 2014 and to mortgage loans which were concluded before 30 June 2010 with a tangible security on the main residence of the debtor (practically, it concerns mainly housing loans). In addition, the objective (taxable) value of the debtor's main residence must not exceed the limit of €180,000, while the value of his total real estate must not exceed the limit of €250,000. Moreover, the total value of the debtor's deposits and other transferable securities (such as shares) must not exceed the limit of €10,000 and the unpaid amount of the remaining capital of the loan (the settlement of which is demanded by the debtor) must not exceed the amount of €150,000.[68] Finally, the debtor must further be either unemployed, an employee in the public or private sector, a pensioner, or a person who provides salaried services – self-employed – and his annual income must have decreased by at least 20 per cent in comparison to the income in 2009. Still the yearly income must not exceed the amount of €15,000 for one person or the amount of €25,000 for persons who provide a joint tax

---

65 See A. Kritikos, *Regulation of Over-Indebted Physical Persons' Debts* [in Greek: Κρητικός, Ρύθμιση οφειλών υπερχρεωμένων φυσικών προσώπων] (2nd edn 2012) 247; M. Stathopoulos, 'Regulation of Over-Indebted Physical Persons' Debts' [in Greek: Σταθόπουλος, Ρύθμιση οφειλών υπερχρεωμένων φυσικών προσώπων] (ΧρηΔικ 2011) 181, I. Spiridakis and E. Georgiakaki, *Regulation of Over-Indebted Physical Persons' Debts* [in Greek: Σπυριδάκης/Γεωργιακάκη, Ρύθμιση οφειλών υπερχρεωμένων φυσικών προσώπων] (2nd edn 2012) 101. For a discussion on this see Mentis (n 8) 1.

66 Indicative of the lately growing rate of applications is that until June 2013 44.262 applications had been filed in all the local Magistrate Courts of Greece.

67 ΦΕΚ 143[A] / 14.6.2013.

68 These limits both with regard to the taxable value of the real estate and the deposits and securities increase if the debtor has three or more children.

return (spouses). The programme of facilitation gives the debtor a grace period of up to 48 months, during which the debtor pays the monthly instalments, which are reduced to an amount equal to 30 per cent of the debtor's monthly family income, without, however, the effect of a reduction of the total loan or a debt discharge.[69] For as long as the facilitation programme runs, any proceedings of the creditor against the debtor and the guarantors are suspended.[70] The debtor can make use of this programme only once.

The effect of this facilitation programme has been rather limited. Until September 2013 only 1,000 applications for inclusion in the programme had been filed to banks. According to EKPOIZO the various and strict conditions have deterred debtors from applying since, in most cases, they do not satisfy *all* the criteria. Moreover, banks have been reluctant to examine the applications and the majority of debtors choose the path of insolvency, which offers the possibility of debt discharge. Law 4161/2013 was also criticised for excluding (not expressly) personal debts (such as housing loans) of traders from its scope of application, leaving them without any possibility to obtain debt relief or discharge (the only exemption is the suspension of auctions of the main residence, a measure initially provided until 31 December 2013 and recently extended until 31 December 2014 under specific conditions, see below).

The legislator has also taken into account the increasing rates of evictions and the danger of homelessness for many people. Article 14(11) of Law 2251/1994 (on consumer protection) provides that a debtor who has no mortgage agreement with the bank can apply for a stay on the seizure of the immovable property that constitutes his sole residence. This provision concerns debts of less than €10,000 arising from consumer credit and credit cards, if the debtor is unintentionally unable to pay. Furthermore, in order to face the large number of auctions held particularly by the banks and with a view to protecting the main residence of the debtor as an asset, the legislator introduced in 2010, in the framework of the new law dedicated to over-indebted households, the suspension of auctions of the main residence of the debtor.[71] Article 9(2) of Law 3869/2010 allows the debtor to submit to the court a petition asking his property to be exempted from execution. In case the only property of the debtor is his primary residence, the debt will be discharged if the amount of the debt to the banks exceeds 80 per cent of the objective value of the property. This case should be distinguished from the debt discharge as provided upon the fulfilment of the conditions of Article 11(1) of Law 3869/2010.

Consequently, by virtue of the Legislative Act of 16 December 2011 and the subsequent Legislative Act of 18 December 2012 the auctions of the primary residence of the debtor were, under conditions,[72] suspended until 31 December 2013. Despite pressures from the Troika to put

69 Only the unemployed debtors have the right to demand to pay zero instalments for six months and to be discharged of the interest for this period of the programme (six months).

70 The credit institution has the right to terminate the programme if the debtor does not comply with his obligations or if the latter is not sincere in relation to the amount of his income or the value of his assets (e.g. if they hide data). In addition to this, the programme is terminated automatically if the debtor files an application of insolvency to the Court according to the Law 3869/2010.

71 The main residence of the debtor as an asset is further protected by the Constitution itself (Article 17 for the protection of the property and Article 21 for the protection of the family). The initial provision stipulated that until 31 December 2013 by virtue of Article 19 of Law 3869/2010 (as it was amended by the Legislative Act of 4–1-2011, by the Article 46 of Law 3986/2011, by the Legislative Act of 16–12–2011 and by the Legislative Act of 18–12–2012) the auction of the main residence of the debtor is suspended.

72 According to these conditions, the objective value of the property should not exceed the minimum taxable limit of the primary residence, increased by 50 per cent, for debts which did not exceed the amount of €200,000.

a halt to the suspension of auctions and allow revenues from the sale of property, Law 4224/2013 extended the suspension of the auctions of the main residence, until 31 December 2014, albeit under strict conditions which excluded many debtors from the protective scope of the measure.

Among the extended strict conditions figure the value of the main residence (which must not exceed the limit of €200,000), the annual income of the debtor (which must not exceed the limit of €35,000), the value of the debtor's assets (which must not exceed the limit of €270,000 including the value of the main residence) and the amount of the debtor's deposits (which must not exceed the amount of €15,000). The suspension of the auction is not automatic. The debtor has to file an application to the credit institution (until 28 February 2014 or two months after the announcement of the formal notice which starts the enforcement procedures) and, upon confirmation that he fulfils the conditions, the auction procedures of the main residence are suspended.

In contrast, the legislature has introduced a new legal framework for the satisfaction of property owners, who can swiftly evict their tenants in case of non-payment of the rent. Law 4055/2012 on a 'Fair Trial' introduced the 'express' procedure for evictions of tenants who have not met their financial obligations. According to the law the tenant has 15 days to pay the lease that has fallen due, upon receipt of the lessor's out-of-court notification. If the lessee does not comply, then the lessor can file an application for an eviction order. If the application is successful then the tenant has 15 days to file a request for the suspension of the eviction. Twenty days after the court's decision has been delivered to the tenant (and provided that the tenant's defence has not been successful), the tenant can be forced to expulsion.

E. Conclusions

The excessive borrowing of Greek consumers in the decade between 2000 and 2010 changed dramatically the financial picture of the average Greek household, which in the past – before the introduction of the euro – did not face any serious over-indebtedness problems. The economic crisis, the excessive Greek deficit and the measures (including high taxation of low-income households) imposed by the country's creditors led to a decrease in incomes, both salaries and pensions, by approximately 50 per cent during the years 2010–2014. Austerity has further contributed to the increase of unemployment to over 27 per cent for the total active population and over 57 per cent for young people, and the fall of real estate prices by an average of 50 per cent. The number of the so-called 'red loans' (non-performing loans) reached approximately 35 per cent of the total amount of consumer loans. The decrease in the values of immovable properties used as a security (mortgage) of the loans deteriorated the situation further with regard to these loans.

While there is a legal framework that aims at helping consumers to alleviate their over-indebtedness and the problems that arise therefrom, by providing even the possibility of a debt discharge, we identify two main problems in the post-crisis consumer legal framework; one in the law's substance and one in its implementation. In many cases a number of very strict conditions are imposed on consumers in order to benefit from the 'facilitative' legal framework, a fact that renders the law eventually ineffective, or applicable to few consumers. We also observe a major problem in the speed of the administration of justice. Judicial procedures are congested because of limited resources and a high number of applications. These bottlenecks may result in the delivery by the courts of a 'debt discharge' decision 12 years after the debtor's application. Such facts reduce the legal framework's effectiveness and create substantial legal uncertainty for both debtors and creditors with subsequent social repercussions. Because of these issues, the protective legal framework for over-indebted persons risks to be rendered ineffective.

References

Books

Dellios, G., *Standard Contract Terms* (2nd edn Sakkoulas 2013) [in Greek: Γ. Δέλλιος, Γενικοί Όροι Συναλλαγών (εκδόσεις Σάκκουλα, 2η έκδοση 2013)].
Karampatzos, A., *Unforeseen Change of Circumstances in the Bilateral Contract* (Ant. N. Sakkoulas 2006) [in Greek: Αντώνιος Καραμπατζός, Απρόβλεπτη Μεταβολή των Συνθηκών στην Αμφοτεροβαρή Σύμβαση (Αντ. Ν. Σάκκουλας, 2006)].
Kritikos, A., *Regulation of Over-Indebted Physical Persons' Debts* (2nd edn 2012) [in Greek: Κρητικός Α., Ρύθμιση οφειλών υπερχρεωμένων φυσικών προσώπων (2η έκδοση, 2012)].
Mentis, G., *Defence and Release of the Over-Indebted Debtor* (Dikaio kai Oikonomia P.N. Sakkoulas 2012) [in Greek: Γεώργιος Μεντής, Άμυνα και Ελευθέρωση του Υπερχρεωμένου Οφειλέτη: Η πορεία προς μια νέα σεισάχθεια στα όρια μεταξύ αστικού δικαίου και νέου πτωχευτικού δικαίου (Δίκαιο και Οικονομία Π. Ν. Σάκκουλας 2012)].
Spiridakis, I. and Georgiakaki, E., *Regulation of Over-Indebted Physical Persons' Debts* (2nd edn Ant. N. Sakkoulas 2012) [in Greek: Σπυριδάκης/Γεωργιακάκη, Ρύθμιση οφειλών υπερχρεωμένων φυσικών προσώπων (Αντ. Ν. Σάκκουλας, 2η έκδοση 2012)].

Articles

Dellios, G., 'Still On-Going Banking Credit Contracts in Periods of Economic Crisis' [in Greek: Γεώργιος Δέλλιος, 'Εκκρεμείς τραπεζικές πιστωτικές συμβάσεις σε περιόδους οικονομικής κρίσης'] *Chronicles of Private Law* [in Greek Χρονικά Ιδιωτικού Δικαίου (ΧρΙΔ)] 2012, 246 et seq.
Doris, F., 'The Judicial Conformation of the Content of Contracts in Periods of Economic Crisis' [in Greek: Φίλιππος Δωρής, 'Η δικαστική διάπλαση του περιεχομένου εκκρεμών συμβάσεων σε περιόδους οικονομικής Κρίσης'] *Chronicles of Private Law* [in Greek Χρονικά Ιδιωτικού Δικαίου (ΧρΙΔ)] 2012, 241 et seq.
Stathopoulos, M., 'Regulation of Over-Indebted Physical Persons' Debts' [in Greek: Μ. Σταθόπουλος, Ρύθμιση οφειλών υπερχρεωμένων φυσικών προσώπων] *Financial Law* [in Greek: Χρηματοπιστωτικό Δίκαιο (ΧρηΔικ)] 2011, p. 181.

Working Papers

Brissimis, S., Garganas, E. and Hall, S., 'Consumer Credit in an Era of Financial Liberalisation: An Overreaction to Repressed Demand?'(Bank of Greece Working Paper 148, October 2012).

Reports

EKPOIZO, 'The Over-Indebtedness of Greek Households – Registering the Problem and Suggesting Ways to Address it' (Report, Athens, November 2012) (in Greek).
Guidelines on International Human Rights Fact-Finding Visits and Reports (The Lund-London Guidelines).
NGO KLIMAKA survey on 'Homelessness in Greece-2012'.
Voridis, H., Angelopoulou, E. and Skotida, I., 'Monetary Policy in Greece 1990–2000 through the Publications of the Bank of Greece' (Bank of Greece Economic Bulletin No. 20/2003).

Cases (in Chronological Order)

Case 5025/1990, Court of Appeal of Athens.
Case 7241/1999, First Instance Court of Athens.
Case 13/2003, First Instance Court of Nafplio.
Case 60/2004, First Instance Court of Mesologgi.
Case 1212/2007, First Instance Court of Athens.
Case 33/2008, First Instance Court of Athens.
Cases 2/2011, Magistrate Court of Patra.
Case 4/2011, Magistrate Court of Patra.
Case 10/2011, Magistrate Court of Athens.
Case 15/2011, Magistrate Court of Athens.
Case 1/2012, Magistrate Court of Florina.
Case 193/2012, Magistrate Court of Lavrio.
Case 15607/2012, First Instance Court of Thessaloniki.
Case 208/2013, Magistrate Court of Athens.
Case 13035/2013, First Instance Court of Thessaloniki.

Chapter 4
Country Report Portugal

Catarina Frade and Mariana Pinheiro Almeida

A. Introduction

Portugal is one of the European countries that has suffered the worst effects of the current economic crisis. Subject to the international trusteeship of the Troika (European Central Bank, European Commission and International Monetary Fund), Portugal has been living under a heavy regime of austerity which has burdened both families and companies. The public finances consolidation plan, agreed with the Troika in May 2011, entailed increasing taxes and cutting salaries and social benefits.

As a result, the economy shrank, public and private investment dropped sharply, credit supply became almost non-existent and unemployment rose sharply to 15.3 per cent in the fourth quarter of 2013, affecting 35 per cent of young people. In 2012, it was estimated that every day 26 houses were turned over to the banks by households and real estate companies, even though this number decreased by 55 per cent in 2013 to seven houses per day. According to the Association of Real Estate Agency (APEMIP, 2013), this decrease was due to an increase in the banks' ability to renegotiate mortgages with their clients in difficulties.[1] The general deterioration of household finances was accompanied by an increase in the number of insolvency cases involving private individuals. Looking at the statistical data of the Ministry of Justice, there was an increase of 1276 per cent in household bankruptcies between 2007 and 2012.[2]

The profile of the people requesting assistance or filing for bankruptcy has also changed since the beginning of the crisis, particularly after 2010. Not only families with low incomes, unemployed people or those with unstable jobs are affected, but also individuals with higher academic and professional qualifications. For the first time, institutions and courts seem to be more conscious of the difficulties faced by families of social and professional standing, with average incomes, even with higher education, who are not able to 'stretch' their money until the end of the month. In courtrooms, social security offices, charity organisations and debt advisory services, families of all social and economic strata are the faces of a severe crisis that stubbornly persists.

The impoverishment of the middle class is the most significant social impact of the crisis and is the focus of the 'mitigation' measures put in place by the government under the tutelage of international financial markets and organisations. The risk of poverty (defined as a monthly income of less than €409) affected, in 2012, 18.7 per cent of the Portuguese population (almost two million people), whereas in 2011 this value was 17.9 per cent.[3] This is the highest rate since 2005, when it reached 19 per cent. Without the social transfers from the state, that rate would have probably risen

1 The legislation adopted by the end of 2012 aiming at promoting extrajudicial renegotiation of debts when debtors enter into arrears may have also contributed to this 'willingness'.

2 Figures obtained from calculations based on quarterly statistical information issued by Direcção-Geral da Política de Justiça do Ministério da Justiça. See http://www.dgpj.mj.pt/sections/estatisticas-da-justica.

3 'Income and Living Conditions' (EU-SILC), National Statistics Office (INE) relating to 2012 and published 24 March 2014.

to 46.9 per cent in 2012.[4] Teenagers under the age of 18 years, couples with dependent children and unemployed individuals are the most vulnerable. In 2012, one in 10 individuals was considered in severe material deprivation (10.9 per cent of the population – rising from 8.6 per cent in 2011).

The worsening of households' labour and financial conditions has not been reflected in an expansion of litigation, apart from insolvency and enforcement proceedings that have greatly increased. Further, the judicial discussion of credit contracts' terms and fairness did not show any relevant results. The legal principle of *pacta sunt servanda* (agreements must be honoured) and the rules of contractual compliance dominate jurisprudence and have not been challenged, despite well-known decisions from foreign courts and the CJEU, such as the *Aziz* case. Due to the nature of the claims in judicial proceedings in Portugal (contract arrears and insolvencies), Portuguese courts have acted as debt collection agencies, without taking a more creative stance that could, somehow, mitigate the contractual imbalances brought about by the crisis.

In the following sections we will try to provide a detailed picture of the financial situation for Portuguese families. While describing the impact of the economic crisis in the deterioration of the living conditions of households, we also highlight the path to mortgage and consumer debt before the crisis. We will examine how access to credit, especially for house purchases, served in the 1990s to improve comfort and quality of life for families, enhancing their social and economic inclusion. And how, by virtue of the changing economic and financial conditions of the country, induced by the financial crisis, the repayment of loans has become an unbearable burden for many households, putting them at risk of social exclusion.

Subsequently, we will discuss the role that law and jurisprudence have played in resolving families' financial difficulties. We will analyse how the legislator was led to create legal solutions designed to facilitate extrajudicial debt arrangements and to safeguard housing, and also how these solutions have had a modest impact on the country's current economic situation. We will also explore the ambiguous role of justice and its resistance to exploring more audacious solutions within the promotion of consumer rights and protection of economic and social rights that are enshrined in the Portuguese Constitution.

One of the biggest challenges when writing this chapter was the lack of detailed statistical data on indebtedness and over-indebtedness issues. We sought to overcome these limitations by contacting several institutions such as the Bank of Portugal (BdP), the Ministry of Justice, the Association of Specialized Credit Company (ASFAC), some financial institutions and various public agencies related to the issues under analysis. We also conducted semi-structured interviews with 29 consumers, four judges (two from first instance courts and two from courts of appeal) and two lawyers. Finally, we received some information from the biggest Portuguese consumer protection association – the Portuguese Consumer Defence Association (DECO).

The availability of consumers, DECO, judges and lawyers for data collection contrasted with that shown by the other institutions contacted. Public bodies always directed us to the data available on their websites and did not provide more disaggregated information. Regarding the financial market entities contacted, we were only able to conduct a brief interview with an employee from one bank. In all other cases, we were refused the information. The reasons for the refusal were that the information is either not available or confidential, and that the data should be provided by the Bank of Portugal regarding the whole market. Despite these limitations, we hope to have gathered some useful qualitative insights that help to understand more deeply the issues under discussion.

4 Ibid.

B. The Situation of Indebted Consumers in the Country: Financial and Social Issues

Prominent Problems of Indebted Consumers in the Country

The terms 'indebtedness', 'over-indebtedness' and 'vulnerability' in the national legal framework
Before analysing the profiles of indebtedness and over-indebtedness of Portuguese consumers and their impact on social and financial inclusion and exclusion, it is useful to clarify some of the fundamental operational concepts and to understand to what extent they are enshrined in the national legal framework or not. In this way, it is possible to facilitate comparability between countries and also to perceive the level of sensitivity shown by national authorities on this issue.

Neither the concept of indebtedness nor that of over-indebtedness is defined by Portuguese law. Despite being commonly used in political and economic discourse, as well as in public opinion, they were defined only by socio-legal scholars. According to Marques et al. (2000), indebtedness means the financial balance of a household, in which a family has at least one credit commitment. If it has more than one credit, the household is said to be multi-indebted. Over-indebtedness represents the situation where a household is unable to meet its payments on time, particularly its credit instalments.

Closely related to the term over-indebtedness and defined by national legal order are the concepts of 'harsh economic situation' and insolvency. The term 'harsh economic situation' was introduced in 2012, when new legal regimes were adopted to help households in financial difficulties in 2008 and the severe austerity measures implemented since 2011 (Law 58/2012, of 9 November 2012). Even though the concept of the consumer in a harsh economic situation may be related to the term over-indebtedness, the former is narrower than the latter. Law 58/2012 defines the parameters for being in harsh economic situation and they are a combination of percentages and proportions of a household's income, effort rate, wealth, and tax value of the property with home ownership and unemployment.[5]

The definition of insolvency in the 2004 Bankruptcy Code ('Insolvency and Corporate Recovery Code') is a more similar (yet distinct) concept to that of over-indebtedness. Following Article 3 of the Bankruptcy Code, the debtor is insolvent when he or she is unable to fulfil their due obligations. For legal scholars, the terms are not coincident: usually, insolvency or bankruptcy refers to a judicial procedure and the condition of the individual that files for it, while over-indebtedness is a broader term and may exist even when consumers do not file for bankruptcy or when this procedure is unavailable to individuals. For instance, a household may be over-indebted because it lacks its own financial means, but is still able to repay its debts thanks to financial support from relatives or friends (Frade et al., 2006).

Similarly, the term vulnerability regarding consumers of financial services is not defined in the national law. The vulnerable consumer as a legal concept was recently introduced into the law but only regarding the provision of utilities. According to Decree-Law 101/2011, of 30 September

5 In 2012, a chapter was also introduced to the 2004 Bankruptcy Code on the recovery of the insolvent individuals, particularly of businessmen. The so-called Special Revitalization Process (PER) has been designed as an alternative to liquidation, for cases where, although the company is in a harsh economic situation or facing imminent insolvency, it is still believed to be recoverable and capable of continuing to operate. In this case, the Bankruptcy Code defines the debtor in a harsh economic situation as an individual who is in serious difficulties fulfilling his/her obligations in a timely manner, either for lack of liquidity or lack of access to credit (Article 17b). In very few cases, the PER process has been used by indebted natural persons individuals, but it is almost always entrepreneurs who want to continue doing business and not infrequently only delay the inevitable – bankruptcy.

2011, and Decree-Law 138-A/2012, of 28 December 2012, a vulnerable consumer has economic and social needs that require protection, including special, more protective measures to guarantee his/her access to gas, electricity and water supply.

The numbers on indebtedness and over-indebtedness

In Portugal, the development of consumer credit started relatively late in comparison with most EU Member States, especially the North European countries. There were converging changes on the side of credit supply – deregulation of the credit market – and demand – low unemployment rates, salary increases, and increased commercial provision – in the favourable social and economic climate of the 1990s, which explains the expansion of credit for consumption and housing purposes.

In a country with 10,562,178 residents and 4,048,559 households, according to the 2011 national census, around 22.5 per cent of residents have a mortgage, while 34 per cent have at least one credit for consumption purposes. This means that 37.7 per cent of households are involved in the credit market – 19.4 per cent with mortgage credit, 11 per cent with credit for consumption and 7.3 per cent with both mortgage and consumption credit (Bank of Portugal, 2012). Mortgages represent approximately 80 per cent of the total credit granted to individuals and are more relevant among medium–high and high income strata. Personal loans are second, followed by loans for cars, household appliances and fittings. The number of individuals using credit showed a decreasing trend since the crisis has settled, reflecting the drop in credit offer and demand as a consequence of the worsening conditions of the country.[6] The same happened to the amounts loaned to individuals and the number of contracts signed. For instance, in 2004, housing loans reached €18.26 million and, in 2007, they achieved the highest value of the decade between 2003 and 2013 with €19.63 million borrowed. Thereafter, housing loans decreased abruptly to about €13.38 million in 2008 and to about €1.94 million in 2012. Since 2013 there seems to have been a slight improvement in the credit market.[7] The Bank of Portugal, in its May 2013 Financial Stability Report, stated that:

> in the first quarter of 2013 there were signs of a less noticeable contraction in the demand, especially in the case of consumer credit and other lending. The decline in consumer confidence and the negative prospects for the housing market continued to fuel the reduction in households' demand for loans.[8]

The decrease in lending was accompanied by an increase of debtors in default. In December 2013, the number of borrowers in the household sector with overdue loans for consumption purposes was 601,749 – 16.6 per cent of the 3,624,996 borrowers with this type of credit in the same period – and for housing it was 145,766 – 6.2 per cent of the 2,351,064 borrowers with this type of credit in the same period.[9] This can be compared with the figures of December 2009, when the number of borrowers in the households sector with overdue loans for consumption purposes was 551,511 – 14.6 per cent of the 3,777,473 borrowers with this type of credit in the same period – and for housing was 125,377 – 5.2 per cent of the 2,411,093 borrowers with this type of credit.[10] In December 2013, the percentage of borrowers in the household sector with overdue loans (housing

6 Bank of Portugal, 2014a.

7 APEMIP, 2013.

8 Bank of Portugal, 2013a.

9 Bank of Portugal, 2014a.

10 The Portuguese Central Bank has provided statistics on the indebtedness of private individuals on a regular basis since 2009, when BdP released the data from the central credit register concerning this type of client. Because of this, we choose to deliver the data from 2009 onwards.

and consumption purposes) affected 14.9 per cent of the 4,440,899 borrowers, that is, 661,694 individuals, while in December 2009, that percentage was 13.3 per cent of a total of 4,571,159 borrowers (607,964 individuals).

Looking at the debtors' profile, families with higher income and wealth are the most involved in the credit market and have the highest amount of debt. Families with children tend to participate more in the housing market, while families with lower incomes, with younger members tend to contract consumer credit instead.[11] The analysis of debt ratios, according to the families' characteristics, suggests that situations of greater vulnerability occur in families who are in lower income and age brackets and in cases where there are mortgage loans, especially if there are simultaneously other debts. The households with low incomes are also those who present a greater financial vulnerability. However, their limited participation in the credit market partly mitigates the overall risk.

Previous studies show that mortgages are the last loan that individuals fail to pay back.[12] When difficulties arise, families first fail to pay small claims and services (telecommunications, property conservation and maintenance costs, and credit card bills). This is followed by the car loan and, in the end, by the mortgage. Along the way, individuals manage to 'creatively' fulfil their debts by alternating their monthly payments between various creditors. After a while, however, they end up failing with all obligations and enter into over-indebtedness and insolvency.

Quantitative data regarding over-indebtedness is scarce and official numbers suffer from underestimation. The available data belongs to the main consumer protection association called DECO.[13] In 2000, DECO established the Over-Indebted Supporting Offices (GAS) in seven branches around the country. In 2000, they opened 152 files in the whole country, but this number increased slowly in the following years, until 2007 when there was an extraordinary growth in numbers from 905 cases opened in 2006 to 1,976 in 2007. Even if we considered these numbers insignificant in the context of around 1,500 million households with credit, they are relevant to mirror the aggravation of Portuguese households' financial well-being at the outbreak of the crisis. In 2013, the number of files decreased (from 5,407 in 2012 to 4,034 in 2013) but, according to the national coordinator of GAS, this is not due to the amelioration of households' financial situations. GAS technicians noticed in 2013 an increase of households in a desperate financial situation that falls beyond DECO's sphere of intervention. When households face enforcement or insolvency proceedings, or when they have tax debts, DECO refuses to intervene. Additionally, according to the same source, even when there are no judicial proceedings going on, many cases are regarded as unrecoverable by means of any sort of debt repayment plan and out-of-court settlement. For those, DECO decides not to open a file. Eventually, the insolvency procedure is recommended.

Following DECO's experience, the majority of over-indebted consumers are married, with children (one or two) and employed. They belong to the middle class (medium income level, meaning up to €1,500 per month and per household) and their severe financial situation results from a current or previous unemployment situation or the downgrading of salaries and social benefits. Since 2013, DECO's professionals noticed an increase in the number of retired people and single parents as well as of civil servants, which is in line with the significant social benefits cuts implemented by the government since 2011 and 2012. It is worth mentioning that civil servants were perceived, for a long time, by financial market as low-risk debtors regarding their working

11 Costa and Farinha, 2012.

12 Frade et al., 2008; 2006.

13 Other institutions from civil society or the market provide debt advice to consumers but they have less impact than DECO. As the biggest consumer association, DECO has the most well-known and well-established network of debt advice services.

status. This perception allowed them to have easier access to loans. However when they suffered several wage cuts due to the austerity programme provisions, they became vulnerable to credit default and insolvency.

The deterioration of the households' financial conditions is plainly confirmed by the continuous rise in the number of insolvencies. According to the statistics from the Ministry of Justice, the number of cases of insolvencies of consumers/households has grown exponentially since the beginning of the economic crisis. In 2011, they even exceeded company bankruptcies (see Table 4.1).

Table 4.1 Number of bankruptcy files, by year

	2007	2008	2009	2010	2011	2012	2013	2014*
Total bankruptcies	2,824	3,856	5,467	6,795	11,228	16,433	17,330	8,152
Total individual bankruptcies	529	759	1,440	2,454	6,214	10,018	11,409	5,615

Note: * – until the first semester of 2014.
Source: DGPJ – Ministry of Justice.

The data on evictions, while not sufficiently updated, seems to be in contradiction with the country's difficult economic and financial situation. According to the Tenants' Association of Lisbon, in 2011 there were 700,000 tenancy contracts in Portugal. Of those contracts, only 0.2 per cent were subject to an eviction procedure.[14] The number of eviction files based on rent arrears provided by the Ministry of Justice has decreased since 2003, from 6,873 to 1,778 in 2007 and 1,399 in 2011. Part of the explanation for this countercyclical path may lie in the complexity and the slowness of the eviction judicial procedure. In 2012, a new Rent Law (Law no. 31/2012, of 14 August 2012) simplified the eviction procedure, creating an administrative office to deal with evictions outside courts – the Balcão Nacional do Arrendamento (BNA), operating since January 2013. Until the end of June 2013, BNA received 1,867 eviction files. From those requests, 193 were granted, 939 were rejected and the remainder were pending. The causes of rejection were not made available.

Statistical data on the profile of people suffering from eviction are missing, forcing us to provide our own perception on the matter and the perception of an interviewed lawyer who is also a member of a consumer association. Unemployed people may be one of the dominant groups. It is worth highlighting that there is a legal provision in the Labour Code that forbids eviction when the tenant does not pay the rent due to wage arrears (but not unemployment). As such we can infer that households affected by unemployment are more likely to be evicted. Also young people with precarious jobs (and with less access to housing credit) are considered a risk group, as well as the elderly. In the past, tenants older than 65 years could not realistically be evicted, even when they

14 Unfortunately there is no available data on evictions from own property. Some indicators show that between 2011 and 2013 many households and homebuilders surrendered their houses/buildings to the banks because they were unable to repay their loans. According to APEMIP, in 2011, an average of 19 houses were surrendered every day by both families and homebuilders, while in 2012 this rose to 26 a day. In 2013 the number dropped sharply to seven houses a day (APEMIP, 2013). Due to this strategy we figured out that evictions due to mortgage default were not very relevant.

did not pay the rent. However, this situation has changed with the new tenancy act which entered into force in 2013.

Explanations for Current Levels of Indebtedness and Over-Indebtedness

Since the 1990s, the indebtedness of Portuguese families coincided with the consolidation of an active and competitive financial market in Portugal. This resulted, to a large extent, from the country's participation in the Economic and Monetary Union. At that time, the expansion of consumer goods supply and the investment in the construction sector, combined with a reduction in unemployment and an increase in confidence regarding the country's economic performance, led many consumers to risk and diversify their consumption patterns. Consequently, consumers increased both their well-being and their vulnerability to financially disruptive situations. If, until the mid-2000s, cases of over-indebtedness were considered negligible by both the market and the state, since the end of the decade they have been recognised as a serious and unavoidable problem.

Access to credit and housing before the crisis and consumers' behaviour

Until the beginning of 2000s, the credit supply and demand in Portugal grew quickly, especially for housing. The household indebtedness ratio stood at 129 per cent of the annual disposable income in 2012, when in the beginning of the 1990s, it barely reached 18 per cent. In spite of the high indebtedness ratio, credit default always remained at very low levels and rose at a moderate pace in the past years (from 1.9 per cent in 2009 to 2.9 per cent in 2013 for mortgage credit, and from 7.3 per cent to 13.1 per cent for consumer credit in 2013).[15]

Several reports argue that Portugal, contrary to other countries, did not experience a housing bubble. Accordingly, house prices fell less markedly throughout the crisis. In its 2010 Annual Activity Report, the Bank of Portugal stated that 'house prices in the period 1997 to 2006 increased at a high rate in Ireland, Spain, France, Greece and the Netherlands (between 6.0 per cent and 10.9 per cent) and more moderately in Italy (2.8 per cent) and Portugal (0.7 per cent). On the contrary, real prices in Germany decreased by an average of around 1.5 per cent'.[16] Similarly, the Portuguese Central Bank refers to the International Monetary Fund (IMF), which claims that:

> the house price gap in 2007 was between 20 and 30 % in Ireland and the United Kingdom, between 10 and 20 % in France, Spain, Italy and the Netherlands and around 7 % in the United States. The deviation in Portugal was close to zero, and in Germany around -5 %.[17]

Finally, in the same vein, the Global Property Guide observes that:

> the house price boom that swept through most of Europe and the developed world from the mid-1990s to 2006 missed Portugal. Except in 2003, house price growth in Portugal has been generally lacklustre. [In] 2003 – 2004, house prices rose by an average of 6.2 % y-o-y (3.3 % in real terms); [in] 2010 – 2012, house prices fell by an average of 3.1 % (-5.5 % in real terms).[18]

15 Bank of Portugal, 2014a.
16 Bank of Portugal, 2011.
17 Bank of Portugal, 2011.
18 See http://www.globalpropertyguide.com/Europe/Portugal/Price-History.

Irrespective of the lack of a housing bubble, Portugal has high rates of home ownership. According to the European Mortgage Federation, Portugal had an owner occupation rate of 74.6 per cent in 2009, more than the EU average of 68.9 per cent. However, only 30 per cent of the population had a mortgage, while 44.6 per cent had no burden of housing, 11 per cent had rented housing and 14.4 per cent paid social rent.[19]

Nevertheless, a drop in house prices was brought about by the financial crisis, due to a decrease in demand, an initial increase in interest rates and more restrictive criteria on the credit supply side. However, in general housing prices have remained relatively stable over time. Stable housing prices and the modest number of credit defaults (at least in housing loans) suggest an efficient creditworthiness assessment of borrowers by banks. For that purpose, the country has two credit bureaus. One is public – Central Credit Register (Central de Responsabilidades de Crédito) – managed and funded by the Bank of Portugal. The other is private – Credinformações – and belongs to Equifax. Since they both have positive and negative record files, they collect the data related to credit contracts between financial institutions and their clients. This includes contract amount, duration and regular payment (positive information), as well as payment incidents (negative information). Decree-Law 139/2009 made consumer creditworthiness assessment mandatory for consumer credit loans only. However, this does not mean that creditors are compelled to consult a credit bureau. They can simply rely on the information provided by the consumer. In any case, if the client is a usual client, the creditor has immediate access to their credit situation because the database of the Bank of Portugal provides regular information to credit institutions on their clients. If it is a new client, the creditor needs his/her permission to access the Bank of Portugal's database. There is no available data about the level of compliance of this obligation, but indirect elements suggest that, at least in mortgage credit, this is a frequent practice. According to the bank employee interviewed, the financial institution's policy regarding households' credit demand (both mortgage and consumer) is to always make a creditworthiness evaluation. This evaluation is based on stricter criteria as regards mortgage credit, as not only the information provided by the debtor is relevant, but also their past history with the institution and his/her record in the credit bureau managed by the Portuguese central bank.

In order to understand the reasons for over-indebtedness, we also have to look at the behaviour of the debtors and their understanding of credit decisions. Following the 2010 Financial Literacy Survey of the Bank of Portugal, 74 per cent of the respondents were said to read in a lot of, or some, detail the information provided by the financial institution when they are about to contract a loan or make an investment decision, while 15 per cent declared not to read the information.[20] This data must be interpreted with caution because the question refers to all information (including brochures and booklets) and not just the contract. Moreover, the effect of the 'politically correct answer' may have distorted the results. Further, even if the results reflect the reality, this does not necessarily mean an understanding of the information provided, as confirmed by other indicators on the survey. The 2010 Financial Literacy Survey shows that, concerning the investment of savings, 56 per cent of the respondents declared not to make comparisons, while, regarding loans, the percentage decreases to 40 per cent.

Analysing the responses from the interviewed consumers, most of them said that they read the contracts before signing. However they also admitted that they were not always able to understand the content. Of 29 interviewees, eight stated that the bank provided the opportunity for them to read the contract and to ask questions before signing the agreement. Ten revealed that the bank

19 CGD, 2011.

20 Bank of Portugal, 2010.

had not given them such an opportunity, even though they had asked for it, while five reported that the bank only allowed such time and just gave clarifications in mortgage loan contracts. Finally, five interviewees said they did not ask for any clarifications and one consumer did not recall the situation. Moreover, eight consumers revealed that they took two or three days before signing the contract. The other 21 consumers said that they signed the contact immediately. They did not experience a refusal on the credit application. One reason may be due to the fact that almost all contracted their loans (especially housing) with their regular bank. Even though, in recent years, banks have tightened lending criteria, it is not possible to know how the rate of denied applications evolved. Available information, concerning 2010, reported an average rejection rate of about 20 per cent of applications.[21] Recent trends in consumer credit – notably for housing – suggest that this rate has risen significantly.

The impact of the crisis on the levels of indebtedness and over-indebtedness

As already mentioned, one of the immediate effects of the crisis on the financial markets was a decrease in credit granted to businesses and families. In the case of households, housing loans became almost impossible to obtain and the applied spreads increased significantly. In 2003, €12,944 million was granted in housing loans. In 2004, credit reached €18,260 million and in 2007 it achieved the highest value of the 2003–2013 decade, with €19,630 million. But after that year, the fall was abrupt, decreasing to €13,375 million in 2008 and to €1,935 million in 2012. From 2013 onwards, there is an improvement in mortgage offer and demand: €1,469 million was granted in housing loans, a slightly greater figure than that of the same period in 2012. This reality is also reflected in the spreads charged by major banks. In 2011 and 2012 the spreads were maintained at the highest values of the last two decades, with the minimum spreads at 4.5 per cent. After 2013, some banks lowered these spreads to around 3 per cent.[22] However, according to the Bank Lending Survey of January 2014, the five largest banks operating in the national market continue to state that they intend to continue using the same restrictive criteria for granting housing and consumer loans that they have been applying in the last two to three years.[23]

The Retail Banking Markets Monitoring Report, published for the first time in 2013 by the Bank of Portugal, states that:

> in 2012, the consumer credit market shrank sharply, even more so than in 2011. The reduction in the number of contracts concluded and the amount of credit provided was very significant and was accompanied by a fall in the average amount provided. The contraction affected all credit types and was accompanied by a rise in the average APRC, which inverted its trend from the fourth quarter of the year. Personal credit, despite the reduction in the number of contracts concluded and the amount provided, continued to be the segment with the greatest share of total credit provided. Car loans lost relative importance since 2010. For revolving credit, where credit cards prevail, the reduction in the number of contracts concluded and the credit provided was not so important. In 2012, the amount for revolving credit exceeded that for car loans.[24] (Bank of Portugal, 2013b)

There has also been a change in the reasons for which credit is sought. According to DECO, until 2008, access to basic assets was the main reason for applying for consumer credit (including

21 Costa and Farinha, 2012.

22 Bank of Portugal, 2014a; 2013b.

23 Bank of Portugal, 2014c.

24 Bank of Portugal, 2013b.

mortgage). Since then, the top two reasons for applying for credit deal with current financial difficulties and the repayment of other loans. This shift is in line with the increasing importance of personal loans and credit cards observed in the last five years.

It was not just the amount of credit and the price that worsened in recent years. The percentages of financing and warranties have also become more demanding since the beginning of the crisis. For example, it is no longer possible to obtain financing for 100 per cent of the property value. Banks now only finance the full value of the property if the immovable property is purchased directly from the banks following judicial collection proceedings, insolvencies or transfers in lieu of payment. With regard to guarantees, there has been an increase in requests for guarantors and insurance from the banking sector, according to the bank employee interviewed.

This trend is also consistent with the deterioration in labour market conditions. The crisis led to a rise in unemployment (from 6.3 per cent in 2003 to 7.6 per cent in 2008 and to 16.3 per cent in 2013),[25] job losses and cuts in overtime. The average salary was reduced while the number of workers earning the minimum wage (of €485 per month) increased, especially since 2011, when the country's bailout programme came into effect. According to the Ministry of Economy and Employment, about 10.9 per cent of full-time employees earned the minimum wage in April 2011 (about 391,000 people) (Ministry of Economy and Employment, 2013). In late 2012, the percentage of employees earning the minimum wage had risen to 12.9 per cent (around 418,000 people). In 2013, this figure decreased to 11.7 per cent of the total workforce (15.1 per cent for women and 9.2 per cent for men), but this data refers only to the first quarter of the year. In 2006, the percentage of employees earning the national minimum wage remained at 4.5 per cent. Since the beginning of the bailout programme in May 2011, it is estimated that there are more than 29,000 employees earning the minimum wage.

In line with the unfavourable developments in the labour market, levels of over-indebtedness and bankruptcies rose. As stated above, the number of individuals seeking debt advice from the association DECO grew dramatically in 2007, with an emphasis on out-of-court disputes and debt rescheduling. With the worsening macroeconomic conditions in the country since 2010, bankruptcy procedures have grown significantly, with a growing number of families facing severe financial difficulties.

This dynamic highlights a social problem, the proportions of which are still being neglected. The Portuguese welfare state has always been less protective than in Northern and Central Europe but its weakness used to be attenuated by informal networks in civil society based in relations of kinship and affection (the welfare society).[26] Parents, other relatives and friends used to help households in financial hardship by providing them with assets, mostly food, clothes, childcare and money. This solidarity helped many families in the past (as it still does today) to remain socially and financially included in society. Many parents depended on their savings and on their retirement benefits to provide support for their children and grandchildren. In the last two or three years, given the growing number of unemployed individuals and the cuts in retirement benefits, the welfare society is reaching its limit with regards to accommodating society's financial needs. Most probably this will mean that the number of individuals defaulting on their commitments and over-indebted individuals will continue to rise in the near future. The social impact will be severe in a time where public expenditure is being significantly cut (for instance, civil servants' salaries, and social benefits) while taxes are being increased.

---

25 See http://www.pordata.pt. In 2003, there were 5,118,000 workers; in 2008, 5,198,000 and in 2013, 4,513,000. It is estimated that, since the beginning of the crisis in 2008, more than 600,000 jobs were lost.

26 Santos, 1991.

C. Legal Framework and the Role of Private Law

The context in which many families face increasing difficulties to fulfil their credit agreements puts pressure on the legal system to respond adequately to this growing social problem. Periods of crisis always challenge the established legal order, forcing it to imagine new ways to promote material justice and fairness.

However, in the case of Portugal, changes have been modest. In 2012, when the crisis was already fully underway, the legislator approved a package of laws designed to help families in difficult financial conditions who possessed loans. The main goals of this package were to promote the settlement of default situations by way of an extrajudicial renegotiation between the creditor and the borrower, and to help preserve the family home or, where this was not possible, to prevent its sale at a bargain price as had been happening. The undisputed merit of these goals collided with the complexity of the procedures that were created and with the tightening of the access to some procedures, particularly those addressing housing protection. Preliminary data on the impact of these measures shows their ineffectiveness.[27]

Similarly, and contrary to what one would expect, courts have not played an especially relevant role in the configuration of social and consumer rights and the interpretation and application of contract law. Judges are overwhelmed by an increasing volume of enforcement and insolvency procedures, in which it is not common to discuss more substantive issues, while remaining reluctant to adopt more daring and creative interpretations of contract law, as has occurred in other legal systems.

Despite these legal and jurisprudential limitations, it is worth describing and discussing the changes in the Portuguese legal system.

Most Relevant Legal Changes in Consumer Credit Legislation Induced by the Crisis

The global economic and financial crisis had some impact on Portuguese legislation on consumer credit. Faced with the worsening of the financial conditions of many households, the legislator sought to find some legal solutions to deal with the increase in credit default. These solutions came in the form of a legislative package adopted in late 2012 and were mostly oriented towards the establishment of special protection for the family home of households suffering from severe financial hardship and the promotion of out-of-court agreements to avoid or mitigate credit arrears. Two laws resulted from this package: Law 58/2012, of 9 November 2012, prescribing an 'extraordinary procedure for households in a harsh economic situation that have a mortgage', while Decree-Law 227/2012, of 25 October 2012, establishes the principles and rules to be complied with by credit institutions to 'prevent and settle cases of default in loan agreements' (consumer credit and mortgage credit excluded from the regime of Law 58/2012) before they can resort to judicial debt collection.

In case of request of a defaulting debtor in a 'harsh economic situation' with a housing loan, the credit institution is obligated to present a plan for restructuring that loan (such as, for example, the extension of the amortisation period of the loan). If the plan is not viable, or if the debtor refuses it, the debtor is entitled to substitutive measures that prevent foreclosure, namely the transfer of the property to the bank in lieu of payment or the exchange for a less expensive house. When a

27 Statistics show that PERSI procedure extinction in 2013 was mostly due to the lack of an agreement between the debtor and the bank (59.8 per cent of the total procedures related to consumer credit and 46.7 per cent of those concerning mortgage credit (Bank of Portugal, 2014b; 2013c).

debtor fails to fulfil the plan or the substitutive measures, he ceases to be covered by this regime and the property can be immediately seized by the creditor. The regime for households in a harsh economic situation is far from being a success. Between November 2012 and June 2013, the entire financial market (20 institutions) received 1,318 cases in total (Bank of Portugal, 2013c). Out of these, 944 (79.3 per cent) were rejected because the debtors did not fulfil the legal requirements for being considered as being in a harsh economic situation in the light of Law 58/2012. Of the files approved (247), only 108 were completed and 84 were successfully concluded either by the payment of the amount in arrears or by a new agreement between creditor and debtor. In March 2014, the Portuguese government indicated its intention to amend the criteria to ensure greater access to the regime.

Under Decree-Law 227/2012, the credit institution is forced to initiate an extrajudicial settlement with the debtor (called Processo Especial de Regularização de Situações de Incumprimento, or PERSI)[28] between the 31st and the 60th day of arrears. During the PERSI procedure, the credit institutions cannot terminate the credit agreement based on default, initiate any legal proceedings in order to satisfy their credit, or transfer their claim or their contractual positions to a third party. Furthermore, credit institutions are forbidden to charge fees when they renegotiate the contract conditions. The data on PERSI shows that 573,732 files were received by financial institutions between January and June 2013 – 446,471 related to consumer credit and 127,261 to mortgage credit (Bank of Portugal, 2013c). Only 32.3 per cent of the total files resulted in the repayment of the amount in arrears or in a new agreement between creditor and debtor. The success rate was higher with regards to mortgage credit (41 per cent of the 127,261 files received by all the financial institutions) than consumer credit (29.9 per cent of the 446,471 files received). In 2013, two reasons for the extinction of PERSI procedure stood out: the lack of agreement between the parties (60.5 per cent) and the payment of the amount in arrears (25.7 per cent).

In addition to these changes in consumer credit regulation, a number of other legal and judicial aspects are worth highlighting, mainly because they concern legal 'opportunities' that are not properly exploited for the benefit of financially stressed families.

Other Legal Impacts of the Crisis

Portugal was diligent in the transposition of Directives CCD 2008/48 and UCT 93/13. While in the first case, Portugal ventured slightly beyond the Directive, in the second Portugal maintained the wide range that already existed in national legal order since 1985. The Directive on Consumer Credit 2008/48/EC was transposed into the national law by the Decree-Law 133/2009 of 2 June 2009, through the mechanism of full harmonisation. This national law excludes mortgages amounting to over €75,000 (Article 2), which means that this legislation is not applicable to the majority of housing loans. For the most part, national law is in line with the CCD 2008/48.

Decree-Law 446/85, of 25 October 1985, establishing the system of standard contractual terms, changed to fit the Directive UCT 93/13 in 1995 and 1999.[29] Portuguese law has always been broader than the Directive 93/13. While the Directive only applies to legal consumer relations, Portuguese law does not contain any restriction of subjective nature, applying to the generality of civil contracts. Moreover, the Directive confines itself to the issue of unfair terms, not truly regulating,

28 PERSI is the Special Regularization Procedure for Default Situations.

29 Amendments were made by the Decree-Law 220/95, of 31 August 1995 and Decree-Law 249/99, of 7 July 1999.

as Portuguese law does, issues concerning communication and clarification of contractual clauses in standard contracts.

As stated above, the Portuguese courts have not been very proactive in the application and interpretation of the law in a way that could suit the needs of over-indebted consumers. For example, according to the Portuguese Civil Code, if the grounds of a contract suffer a fundamental unexpected change of circumstances, it is possible to adjust or terminate the contract (Article 437 of the 1966 Civil Code). Article 437/1 states that 'if the circumstances in which the parties based their decision to contract change unexpectedly, the injured party has the right to terminate the contract, or to alter it according to "fair judgement", as long as the requirement of the obligations which it assumed seriously affects the principles of good faith and is not covered by the actual risks inherent in the contract'. The right of one of the parties to terminate or modify the contract 'according to fair judgment' only exists 'as long as the requirement of the obligations which it assumed seriously affects the principles of good faith and is not covered by the actual risks inherent in the contract'. Some authors, like Ascensão (2005), state that 'the possibility of asking for a modification of the contract, under Article 437, is not restricted to cases where one or both of the contractual partners suffer losses as a result of supervening events. It may also occur whenever the economic balance of the contract is seriously compromised by unforeseeable circumstances' (Ascensão, 2005). Furthermore, jurisprudence understands that the unexpected alteration of circumstances must cause an imbalance in fulfilment, making the performance of the contract excessively onerous or difficult for one of the parties.[30] This has been seen as a 'distant cousin' of the *rebus sic stantibus* ('things thus standing') principle and the theory of unforeseeability.[31]

However, this approach has not been applied to default on credit contracts as such (not even when default is caused by unemployment or illness), in either Portuguese legal thought or in jurisprudence. According to the Ministry of Justice, between 1995 and 2012, there were only 230 judgments of invalidity of unfair contract terms across the three court levels (first and second instance courts and Supreme Court), the majority of them involving banking and insurance, where standard contracts are common. Further, the Supreme Court, in its judgment of 10 October 2013, held that 'the resolution or contract modification for changed circumstances depends on the fulfilment of the following requirements: (i) there is a material change, i.e. abnormal circumstances in which the parties have established a decision to contract and (ii) a requirement to fulfil the obligation to the injured party seriously affects the principles of contractual good faith and are *not covered by business risk*' (which is understood as not being the case for credit contracts).

This is in line with the doctrine that has difficulty recognising the modification of contract terms through change of circumstances, the unforeseeability doctrine, or *force majeure*. According to Monteiro and Gomes (2006), 'the problem of establishing the legal relevance of supervening alteration in circumstances is an old preoccupation in Portuguese Law'. The discussion regarding the *rebus sic stantibus* principle includes several different issues, such as the 'delimitation between the error in the basis of the transaction ("erro sobre a base do negócio") and the regulation for the alteration of circumstances' (Monteiro and Gomes, 2006), the concept of unforeseeability, the abnormality of the change, and the protection of legitimate expectations (Fernandes, 2001).

30 See the Judgment of the Supreme Court of Justice of 30 September 2004.

31 Ordinarily, unforeseeable events may be due to fortuity or to *force majeure*. *Fortuity* is the development of natural forces that remain outside someone's control (flood, fire, etc.). *Force majeure* is an external factor, for which the debtor cannot be liable (war, imprisonment, theft, etc.). The concept of *force majeure* is underlined by the idea of inevitability. Some authors consider 'fortuitous event' and '*force majeure*' to be synonymous, indicating that both concepts report to an event which creates an inability to comply not attributable to the will of the debtor or the creditor.

Impact of the crisis on litigation and out-of-court procedures

The economic downturn and the lengthening of the crisis have had a positive impact on litigation, in terms of an increase in the number of enforcement actions due to contract default and bankruptcies concerning undertakings and individuals. Even though the cases which have been brought reflect the severe economic situation of the country and its impact on the people, it is worth noting that most cases were decided on terms of general civil law rather than consumer law.

The general view of four judges and two lawyers, who we interviewed on this topic, is that, regarding consumer credit, there has been an increase in the number of cases after the crisis, while litigation relating to mortgage loans has not increased and remains scarce. The cases concerning consumer credit crucially did not relate to the validity of contract terms. Here, the judges point out as a fundamental reason the unpreparedness and lack of knowledge of lawyers about consumer law. The lawyers interviewed, while recognising that consumer law is still not widely known or used and that many lawyers continue to use the general rules of civil law that are less protective of consumers, claim that there have been improvements in the dissemination and application of consumer law. However, even judges are still unfamiliar with consumer law and prefer to apply contract law instead. Besides the use of the general scheme of standard contractual terms (Decree-Law 446/85 of 25 October 1985) it is also common to refer to general civil law concepts, such as the abuse of law (Article 334 of the Civil Code) and the expiration of benefits due to default (Article 781 of the Civil Code). Thus, proceedings where the debtor seeks the annulment of the consumer credit contract are based on purely formal issues, such as failure to deliver a copy of the contract breach of the duty of disclosure, the excess of the indemnity clauses, or the right to automatic termination of the contract based on a single default with immediate payment of subsequent instalments.[32]

Notwithstanding the current economic crisis in the country and the importance of mortgage loans in the context of over-indebtedness, litigation concerning mortgage lending remains, as has been said, scarce, especially regarding the discussion of contractual conditions and their equity. One exception is a decision of the first instance court of Portalegre of January 2012. In this case the judge decided that the creditor, by claiming the difference between the value received when repossessing the house through the transfer in lieu of payment and the amount paid in the judicial selling, demanded more than they entitled to, as the transfer of the house to the bank led to the extinction of the credit. This decision, influenced by a decision of the Spanish Court of Navarra in 2010, occurred in a very specific context that is unlikely to be repeated – an inventory process following a divorce that allowed for the discussion of more substantive issues. The argumentation of the decision of Portalegre was weak from a legal perspective but the underlying intention was innovative and caught the attention of legal scholars and courts that, in general, declared their disagreement with the young judge's stand. The Court of Appeal of Lisbon, in a similar case of October 2012, disagreed with the decision of Portalegre, stating that there was no abuse of rights from the bank by claiming the remaining amount and rejecting the perspective adopted by the Court of Portalegre, as well as the Spanish Courts of Navarra (2010) and Barcelona (2012).

All of the judges interviewed recognised little or no influence of the *Aziz* case or other decisions of Spanish on Portuguese jurisprudence. Two reasons were pointed out for this. First, housing credit is only discussed in the context of judicial collection or insolvency procedures, and not in declaratory procedures, and as such there is no place for any in-depth analysis of the validity of the contract terms. The bank resorts to the judicial collection or insolvency in order to avoid discussion

32 Besides the interviews we also collected information through the analysis of 44 Appeal Court decisions.

as to the value of the property or the possibility of transfer in lieu of payment. Second, due to the economic crisis in Portugal, there is an almost total absence of housing credit being granted. Since there is no third party interested in the property offered at auction, the property is awarded to the bank for a lot less than the actual value. As a result, the borrower loses the house and still owes the bank a substantial part of the debt.

According to some of the judges and one of the lawyers interviewed, both jurisprudence and scholarship agree that the Civil Code provisions on fulfilling obligations enable this rather conservative course of action, due to the fact that: (a) the fulfilment of the obligation accounts for all the debtor's assets (Article 601 of the Civil Code); (b) when the property is sold and part of the debt remains, the creditor can attach other assets of the debtor. However, jurisprudence is starting to show some signs of 'sensitivity' to current economic conditions and their effect on the performance of the contracts. At least in the case of companies there are already a small number of judicial decisions on interest rate swaps in which contracts could be terminated or modified based on the abnormal change of the circumstances in which they were signed.[33] The courts have held that the large and prolonged decline in interest rates caused by the financial crisis has created a serious imbalance in the contractual obligations, compared to what the parties had represented as possible and wanted to ensure through those swap contracts. It is argued that this understanding could and should be extended to consumers and households. This would help to create a new balance between the dominant principle of *pacta sunt servanda* and the principle of *rebus sic stantibus*, and would provide new possibilities for balancing the risk of credit default.

Apart from court proceedings, consumers have also had the possibility to benefit from out-of-court procedures to settle problems arising from over-indebtedness. For example, there are the aforementioned legal regimes applied since 2012: the PERSI and the extraordinary procedure for households in a harsh economic situation. The over-indebted supporting offices of DECO and other profit and non-profit debt advice services are the most relevant initiatives seeking to find alternate solutions to insolvency and enforcement proceedings.[34] Through these formal and informal mechanisms, many Portuguese consumers have managed, in recent years, to reschedule their debts without losing their home and other assets. However, with the prolonging of the crisis and the worsening of the labour market conditions, more and more families have become unable to repay their debts, even if they were renegotiated. As DECO data for 2013 shows, there were fewer cases in comparison to 2012, which, according to the association staff, seems to be due to a significant deterioration of household income that pointed to bankruptcy as the last resort. It should be noted that between 2008 and 2010 credit consolidation was a very popular renegotiation measure. Since then, banks have reconsidered the application of this measure given the worsening financial status of the country and the individuals.

D. Policy Responses to Over-Indebtedness

In 2012, the regulator approved several bills aimed at the protection of households in financial distress. The main focus is on mortgage credit default but the limited criteria to access the regime precludes the efficiency of the initiatives.

Apart from the aforementioned Law 58/2012 of 9 November 2012 (providing an extraordinary procedure for households in a harsh economic situation owning a mortgage) and Decree-Law

33 See the Judgment of the Appeal Court of Porto of 14 July 2012.

34 More developments in EUROFOUND, 2012.

227/2012 of 25 October 2012 (PERSI regime) other bills were adopted dedicated to the prevention and resolution of credit default of households. Law 57/2012 allows consumers to mobilise education and retirement saving plans to repay mortgages, in what is a clear political trade-off between the satisfaction of current financial obligations and future educational and retirement opportunities. Law 59/2012 protects the mortgage debtor by forbidding the creditor to terminate the contract before three missed instalments or to increase the credit cost in some cases. Law 60/2012 amends the Code of Civil Procedure by modifying the rules governing the seizures and the determination of the base value for the sale of properties in the foreclosure process. The sale value must be at least 85 per cent of the base value of the property to be sold. The seizure of the house can only occur after the seizure of other assets.

The adoption of this set of rules was an important breakthrough in the fight against over-indebtedness. Its importance derives not so much from the novelty of its provisions, since lenders were already applying some of the measures established as an extrajudicial renegotiation of the debts, but from its compulsory nature, allowing debtors not to depend entirely on the goodwill of creditors to renegotiate. Moreover, the concern with protecting the main residence is worth mentioning especially given the weight of housing loans in household indebtedness (80 per cent of the amount lent to them). Nevertheless, an analysis of the new provisions and of the debates surrounding their adoption reveals certain weaknesses. First, it is clear that the regulator sought to establish very tight rules to prevent any abuse by debtors (any easy 'way out'). As a consequence, the conditions for a 'harsh economic situation' are very hard to fulfil. Second, one must keep in mind that the Bank of Portugal had a decisive role in shaping these schemes and it is more concerned with the prevention of systemic risk and in the promotion of competition than the protection of the interests of bank customers. Furthermore, the banks generally opposed excessive formalities and short deadlines for extrajudicial renegotiation, both within the PERSI and the extraordinary regime. Recently, it was reported that the association representing the banking sector hopes to challenge the new laws based on a cost–benefit analysis.

The 2004 Bankruptcy Code (CIRE) was modified in 2012 but only regarding companies. The debt discharge prescribed by the CIRE to individuals – *exoneração do passivo restante* – allows the discharge of the claims that are not fully paid during the insolvency proceedings, that is, through asset selling (made by the trustee appointed by the court) or in the five-year assignment period that follows asset liquidation (Article 235 of CIRE). When filing for bankruptcy, the debtor must provide a request for discharge (initial requirement of discharge) which must be approved by a judge. If the judge approves this initial request, the bankruptcy procedure continues its regular path of liquidation followed by five years of probation (the assignment period). At the end of the assignment period, the judge evaluates the debtor's behaviour during the assignment period and the creditor's opinion before deciding with the possible discharge of the remaining debts. If the initial request is denied, the procedure will end with the asset being sold and creditors can seize the debtor's remaining debts until their prescription (in some cases, prescription lasts for 20 years). In general, judges have been very strict, leading to a significant number of refusals. The CIRE rules for the acceptance of the initial request did not ameliorate the chances of individuals and the bankruptcy procedure remains highly uncertain for most households. The fresh-start principle announced in the preamble of CIRE appears to be much more of an earned start than a 'fresh' one (Frade and Conceição, 2013).

Regarding evictions, the 2012 Rent Law (Law 31/2012, of 14 August 2012) simplified the eviction procedure by taking it out of the courts. And the newly established administrative office – *Balcão Nacional do Arrendamento* (BNA) – operating since January 2013, is also part of an attempt to overcome the courts' incapacity to solve these actions in due time. As previously shown, the first data concerning the operation of this new regime is not promising.

The general impression arising from the policy responses to over-indebtedness in the wake of the crisis is a prevailing sense of distrust towards consumers and the possibility of them obtaining an 'easy way out' of their obligations. Consequently, the benefit of these measures in dealing with over-indebtedness falls well short of the current needs of Portuguese households.

E. Conclusions

Given the significantly high level of indebtedness of households, banks and the state, being significantly dependent on foreign countries, Portugal was particularly vulnerable to the 2008 global financial crisis. Since the mid-1990s and up to the mid-2000s, Portuguese families enjoyed a burgeoning national financial market, real income growth and the reduction of unemployment, and access to credit (mostly for purchasing a home). In spite of successive record high levels of indebtedness of families, default remained rare. However, since 2007 or 2008 default has become more prominent, both in consumer credit (where the percentage is more relevant), and in housing loans (where the amount owed is higher).

The financial vulnerability of households grew with the crisis, not only because of the global macroeconomic context, but also due to the deterioration of the national labour market, where unemployment levels have more than doubled in the last five years. This proliferation of financial and labour risks for families has created an unusual pressure on informal support networks that have long made Portuguese society a strong welfare society, able to make up for a traditionally weak welfare state.

The rescue programme negotiated by national authorities with the ECB, the European Commission and the IMF, implemented from May 2011 up to May 2014, imposed a wide-ranging austerity programme that negatively impacted on households in precarious economic conditions with lower incomes, while creating a new class of 'new disadvantaged people' from a rapidly shrinking middle class. The dramatic fall in wages, the reduction of social support, namely in pensions, unemployment benefits and social insertion income, along with the increase in taxes and prices of several goods and services has deeply changed the financial equilibrium for an increasing number of households. This 'crisis dynamic' resulted in a rising number of individuals requesting help for renegotiating their debts out of court and, more recently, of requests for insolvency, which have grown at an overwhelming pace since 2010.

The decline of the national and household economy had some effects on the legal framework, although these changes have been generally modest, conservative and disappointing. The same applies to the jurisprudence, which, by inability or unwillingness, has maintained a rigid understanding of the principles of contractual liability. A necessary revision of the 2004 Bankruptcy Code, namely the terms for granting debt relief, did not take place. Instead, in 2012, a legislative package entered into force, with special concerns regarding the prevention and treatment of credit default by extrajudicial means on the one hand, and protection of the family's dwelling on the other. The first results of these measures fell short of the national authorities' expectations and the needs of households. This fact is not in itself surprising if one considers the context of the solutions adopted. With a view to appeasing financial markets, the aim lay more in empowering individuals and families, and in minimising the possibility of relief from their contractual obligations. Accordingly, households have been almost 'pushed' to resort to bankruptcy, notwithstanding the uncertainty and dissatisfaction surrounding its outcome. If preventing over-indebtedness was never seriously addressed, its solution continues to be ineffective.

The economic downturn has especially hit households with low and average incomes, leading to a significant worsening of their well-being and future prospects. Recent data on poverty and social exclusion risk are significant and disturbing. Many young people, especially the most qualified, emigrate in order to find appropriate employment. At the same time, Portugal's population is rapidly aging: in 2013, the birth rate was 8.5 per thousand inhabitants, the second lowest of all EU countries. This crisis has therefore a far longer lasting and profound impact than that immediately resulting from the economic recession. Its effects will be felt for generations.

References

APEMIP (2013), Catálogo de Estudos de Mercado, 23, 4th quarter of 2013.

Ascensão, José de Oliveira (2005), Onerosidade Excessiva por Alteração das Circunstâncias, Revista da Ordem dos Advogados (ROA), 65.

Bank of Portugal (2010), Financial Literacy Survey. URL: http://clientebancario.bportugal.pt/PT/PUBLICACOES/INQUERITOLITERACIAFINANCEIRA/Paginas/InqueritoLiteraciaFinanceira.aspx.

Bank of Portugal (2011), 2010 Annual Activity Report. URL: www.bportugal.pt/en-US/EstudosEconomicos/Publicacoes/RelatorioAnual/RelAnuaisAnteriores/Documents/ra_10_e.pdf.

Bank of Portugal (2012), Household Finance and Consumption Survey 2010 (ISFF). URL: www.bportugal.pt/pt-PT/EstudosEconomicos/Publicacoes/ISFFamilias/Publicacoes/isff_2010_p.pdf.

Bank of Portugal (2013a), Financial Stability Report of May 2013. URL: www.bportugal.pt/en-US/EstudosEconomicos/Publicacoes/RelatorioEstabilidadeFinanceira/REFAnteriores/Documents/REF_may_2013.pdf.

Bank of Portugal (2013b), Retail Banking Markets Monitoring Report 2012. URL: http://clientebancario.bportugal.pt/pt-PT/Publicacoes/RAM/Biblioteca%20de%20Tumbnails/Retail%20Banking%20Markets%20Monitoring%20Report%20(2012)%20-%20Introductory%20Note.pdf.

Bank of Portugal (2013c), Síntese Intercalar de Atividades de Supervisão Comportamental 2013. URL: http://clientebancario.bportugal.pt/pt-PT/Publicacoes/RSC/Biblioteca%20de%20Tumbnails/S%C3%ADntese%20Intercalar%20de%20Atividades%20de%20Supervis%C3%A3o%20Comportamental%20(2013).pdf.

Bank of Portugal (2014a), Statistical Bulletin, March. URL: www.bportugal.pt/en-US/Estatisticas/PublicacoesEstatisticas/BolEstatistico/BEAnteriores/Lists/LinksLitsItemFolder/Attachments/162/BEMar14.pdf.

Bank of Portugal (2014b), The Banking Conduct Supervision Report of 2013. URL: http://clientebancario.bportugal.pt/pt-PT/Publicacoes/RSC/Biblioteca%20de%20Tumbnails/Relat%C3%B3rio%20de%20Supervis%C3%A3o%20Comportamental%20(2013).pdf.

Bank of Portugal (2014c), Bank Lending Survey, January 2014. URL: http://www.bportugal.pt/pt-PT/EstudosEconomicos/Publicacoes/IBMC/Publicacoes/Results_jan14_p.pdf.

Caixa Geral de Depósitos (CGD) (2011), A actualidade do sector imobiliário residencial: ajustamentos e desafios, Nota temática trimestral, November 2011.

Costa, Sónia and Farinha, Luísa (2012), O endividamento das famílias: uma análise microeconómica com base nos resultados do Inquérito à Situação Financeira das Famílias, in Bank of Portugal, Financial Stability Report, May 2012. URL: http://www.bportugal.pt/pt-PT/BdP%20 Publicaes%20de%20Investigao/AR201201_p.pdf.

EUROFOUND (2012), Household Debt Advisory Services in the European Union, Dublin: Eurofound. URL: http://www.eurofound.europa.eu/publications/htmlfiles/ef1189.htm.

Fernandes, Luís Carvalho (2001), A Teoria da Imprevisão no Direito Civil Português – Reimpressão com nota de actualização, Coimbra: Quid Iuris.

Frade, Catarina and Conceição, Ana Filipa (2013), A reprodução do estigma na insolvência das famílias [The Reproduction of the Stigma of Household Insolvency], Revista Crítica de Ciências Sociais, 101, September 2013, 135–152. URL: http://rccs.revues.org/5396.

Frade, Catarina, Lopes, Cláudia, Nogueira, Cláudia, Magalhães, Sara and Brinca, Pedro (2006), Desemprego e sobreendividamento: contornos de uma 'ligação perigosa', Coimbra: CES.

Frade, Catarina, Lopes, Cláudia, Jesus, Fernanda and Ferreira, Teresa (2008), Um perfil dos sobreendividados em Portugal, Coimbra: CES.

Marques, Maria Manuel, Neves, Vitor, Frade, Catarina, Lobo, Flora, Pinto, Paula and Cruz, Cristina (2000), O endividamento dos consumidores, Coimbra: Almedina.

Ministry of Economy and Employment (2013), Inquérito aos Ganhos e à Duração do Trabalho / Earnings and Hours of Work Survey, Lisboa: MEE. URL: http://www.gee.min-economia.pt.

Monteiro, António Pinto and Gomes, Júlio (2006), Hard Core Cases on Unexpected Circumstances. URL: http://www.unexpected-circumstances.org/.

Santos, Boaventura de Sousa (1991), State, Wage Relations and Social Welfare in the Semiperiphery: the Case of Portugal, Oficina do CES, 23. URL: http://www.ces.uc.pt/publicacoes/oficina/ index.php?autor=32;

Chapter 5
Country Report Spain

Pablo Gutiérrez de Cabiedes and Marta Cantero Gamito

Introduction[1]

Spain is one of the countries more seriously hit by the global crisis. The financial crisis was followed by a profound economic and institutional crisis as a result of the negative effects of the housing bubble that had occurred in Spain. Dramatic levels of indebtedness and unemployment, a lack of credit and debt relief policy for households, combined with an underdeveloped legal framework for the protection of over-indebted or bankrupted consumers has led to the radiation of the financial and economic crisis to the social sphere.

The Socialist government, in office since 2004, was accused of denying the existence of the crisis and not making the necessary reforms. General elections held in 2011 saw the People's Party come to power, which worked together with the European institutions and the IMF to improve the country's financial and economic situation. Rajoy's Government introduced highly unpopular austerity budget policies, which included measures such as spending cuts, tax increases and pension reform, in an attempt to reduce the public deficit. In this context, many Spanish households have been struggling with serious financial difficulties to service their housing debt, giving rise to the problems of eviction, social exclusion and public protest.

A. The Situation of Over-Indebtedness in Spain: Economic and Social Issues

In the years during the 'economic boom' in Spain, the national legal framework did not properly address the problem of over indebtedness and the possibility of a financial and socio-economic crisis that would affect individuals and families in Spain.[2] Financial and economic risks increased

---

1 A report with full data on the issues covered in this contribution can be found in I. Domurath, G. Comparato and H-W. Micklitz, 'The Over-Indebtedness of European Consumers – a View from Six Countries', EUI Working Paper LAW 2014/10.

2 It was pointed out in Gutiérrez de Cabiedes, *Comentarios a la Ley Concursal* (ed. Cordón Moreno), 1st edn, Thomson-Reuters-Aranzadi, Navarra, 2004, p. 1247 [*Comments to the Bankruptcy Law*] that '[i]t might be thought that it is not so relevant (in severity or statistical existence). But it should be noted that this approach may be proven increasingly wrong or insufficient' since 'the growing phenomenon of over-indebtedness of individuals (consumers, households, families) could make such a relevance (though still not alarming because fortunately has not turn into defaults and insolvencies) fairly higher, if a change of socio-economic framework (and of certain risk variables therein contained) would take place; and therefore it is absolutely convenient the implementation of a comprehensive policy for prevention and resolution of that over-indebtedness (via bankruptcy and pre-bankruptcy proceedings), approach and response that has been totally omitted by the law'. These issues were developed in the study commissioned by the Government of Spain, Gutiérrez de Cabiedes, *El sobreendeudamiento de los consumidores y la Ley Concursal*, Ministerio de Sanidad y Consumo [*Overindebtedness of Consumers and Bankruptcy Law*, Ministry of Health and Consumer

due to the pervasive effects of unfair financial practices and the high level of debt of companies, credit institutions and households, what made debtors vulnerable to bankruptcy after potential fluctuations in the socio-economic situation.[3] For that reason, the design of a comprehensive legal policy to deal with over-indebtedness based on the guiding principle of responsible lending, a policy establishing a set of preventative measures and a solution to over-indebtedness and consumer insolvency was – by then – suggested.[4] However, at that time, the analysis of that issue was virtually neglected and any attempt to draw attention to this matter, even in specialised *fora*, was considered 'out of focus', if not inappropriate.

In the end, excesses in financial and credit practices occurred in recent years led to the worst economic crisis suffered since the depression of the 1930s. As a result of neglecting what should have been the public and social responsibility, the 'credit boom' gave way to the 'credit crunch'; that is, to a financial crash and a deep economic recession which Spanish consumers are still experiencing, with particularly severe consequences for the country.

1. Concepts and Measurements of Over-Indebtedness and Vulnerability

The term over-indebtedness is not defined in Spanish law. In the literature, over-indebtedness has been defined as 'a situation of financial hardship caused by excessive debt assumption in relation to income and current disposable assets; this is, to be in a situation of such an amount of payment commitments that endangers/impairs the ability to effectively and systematically meet financial commitments'.[5] It is necessary to clarify that the situation of over-indebtedness is different (conceptually and temporally prior) from the ones of arrears and default, which refer to an actual situation of non-compliance with a concrete obligation; and from insolvency (as the effective impossibility of regular performance of the payment obligations) although it may end up constituting the cause of the latter.[6] In addition to the objective understanding of over-indebtedness, at the point where a household is spending more than 30–40 per cent of its income to pay debts,[7] the

---

Affairs], 2004. See also subsequently A. Bercovitz Rodríguez-Cano, 'El presupuesto subjetivo del concurso: en particular, el problema de sobreendeudamiento de los consumidores', *Las claves de la ley concursal*, Thomson-Aranzadi, 2005, pp. 23–24; I. Quintana Carlo, 'El sobreendeudamiento de los consumidores y la Ley Concursal', *Estudios sobre la Ley Concursal. Libro homenaje a Manuel Olivencia*, t. II, Marcial Pons-Unicaja-Caja Sur, Madrid-Barcelona, 2005, p. 2269; L. Muñoz, 'El concurso abreviado', *Anuario de Derecho Concursal*, no. 9, 2006, pp. 107–115 and 142; E. Beltrán Sánchez, 'Insolvencia de las familias en la Ley Concursal Española', *El futuro de la protección jurídica de los consumidores* (ed. J. Tomillo Urbina), Thomson-Civitas, 2008, pp. 199 et seq.; J. Pulgar Ezquerra, 'Concurso y consumidores en el marco del Estado social del bienestar', *Revista de Derecho Concursal y Paraconcursal*, no. 9, 2008, p. 57.

3 Gutiérrez de Cabiedes, *Comentarios* (2004) p. 1255: 'a change in the socio-economic framework triggered by certain risk variables (predictable and visible) could well make change that situation. The fact that it does not exist alarm about this situation (and that it should not be generated) does not preclude the necessity of establishment of standards (and a comprehensive legal policy) that make possible the prevention and solution of that over-indebtedness and, with it, of the non-professional insolvency.'

4 Gutiérrez de Cabiedes, *Comentarios* (2004) pp. 1247, 1255.

5 Gutiérrez de Cabiedes, *El Sobreendeudamiento doméstico: prevención y solución. Crédito, crisis económica, familias y concurso*, Thomson-Reuters-Aranzadi, Navarra, 2009, pp. 24–32 [*Household Overindebtedness: Prevention and Solution. Credit, Economic Crisis, Families and Insolvency*].

6 Gutiérrez de Cabiedes (2009) pp. 30–32.

7 According to the Spanish National Statistical Office, 30 per cent of the salary is the rate from which problems to meet the payment of the mortgage loan may arise. About this distinction and that between active and passive over-indebtedness, see Gutiérrez de Cabiedes (2009) pp. 28–30.

perception of the difficulty of 'making ends meet' gives an indication of the subjective situation of over-indebtedness. However, the term over-indebtedness has been recently taken into consideration in connection with measures to solve the prominent problem of householders' financial difficulties and evictions.[8]

In a similar vein, there is no definition of 'vulnerability' in the Spanish legal framework. An implicit understanding could, however, be inferred from the Royal Decree-Law 6/2012, of 9 March, concerning urgent measures for the protection of mortgage holders who might be in a 'vulnerable' situation, namely that no family member receives any income or holds any other property to satisfy the household's debt, with the mortgage (granted for acquisition of the debtor's only house) payment amounting to more than 60 per cent of the family's net income. In addition, the Royal Decree-Law 27/2012 establishes a moratorium on evictions for those families in a 'situation of special vulnerability', or at 'special risk of exclusion', based on two criteria. The first criterion is subjective and concerns certain social groups (such as large families, single parents, family members with disabilities, etc.) while the second is objective and relates to economic circumstances (such as low income, severe change of economic circumstances, mortgage payment exceeding 50 per cent of the net family income for example). Law 1/2013 mentions the 'special risk of social exclusion' practically in identical terms to those mentioned above.

2. Data on (Over-)Indebted Consumers in Spain

Over-indebtedness in Spain is largely related to the inability to service mortgage loans. Ninety per cent of household indebtedness comes from the financing of investments with real estate assets, mainly loans and mortgages.[9] In 2012, on average 39.4 per cent of the earnings of Spanish people went on paying loans to complete home purchases.[10] The Bank of Spain highlighted that 85 per cent of mortgage secured loans that could not be paid in 2012 were concluded in 2007 or earlier, i.e. during the housing bubble.[11] The situation for young people is even more difficult. In early 2012, a young person paid 52.7 per cent of their net salary to meet the payment of the first instalment of a mortgage for a home.[12]

In addition, Spanish consumers are over-indebted also in terms of the quantity of their credit obligations. When the crisis began 16,921,800 households had some form of debt in Spain.[13]

8 This term is used by the recent Law 1/2013, of 14 May, on measures to reinforce the protection to mortgage debtors, debt restructuring and social rent, whose First Final Provision exceptionally allows the possibility to request the payment of pension plans in order to prevent auction of the dwelling. Similarly, 'over-indebtedness' is mentioned in the Explanatory Memorandum of the Royal Decree-Law 27/2012, of 15 November, on Urgent Measures to Reinforce the Protection of Mortgagors that says this regulation sets an immediate government intervention to ease some of the most desperate social effects of foreclosures 'without prejudice to the need to address a more profound reform of the legal framework of treatment for individuals in situation of over-indebtedness'. However, no definition of this concept is provided.

9 Report by the Spanish Ombudsman, Defensor del Pueblo, *Crisis Económica y Deudores Hipotecarios: Actuaciones y propuestas del Defensor del Pueblo*, 2013.

10 Deloitte, *Report on Real Estate*, May 2012. See also http://www.elmundo.es/elmundo/2012/05/24/suvivienda/1337861452.html.

11 Bank of Spain, *Nota informativa sobre la presentación de una nueva estadística de procesos de ejecución hipotecaria sobre viviendas*, 2013.

12 Consejo de la Juventud de España, *OBJOVI. Observatorio Joven de Vivienda en España*. Spain, 1st quarter 2012, 1/10.

13 Spanish Statistical Office, *Living Conditions Survey*, Special issue on 'Overindebtedness and Financial Exclusion', 2008. This is the last comprehensive study carried out by the Statistical Office, which

According to the Bank of Spain's 'Survey of Household Finances', of the total households surveyed 51.1 per cent reported having some form of loan or credit. With an average net annual income per household of €26,775[14] and an average household expenditure of €28,152,[15] 20.4 per cent of the population resident in Spain was below the at-risk-of-poverty threshold in 2013.[16]

The difficulty of 'making ends meet' also gives an indication of the increasingly common situation of over-indebtedness in Spain. Between 2002 and 2008, the percentage of those with difficulties in dealing with payments relating to their debts doubled.[17] In 2013, 38.7 per cent of Spanish households reported 'difficulties or serious difficulties' (18.5 per cent of them serious difficulties) in meeting their commitments.

The households particularly affected were those whose heads were young people, the elderly and retirees.[18] Households with the lowest levels of income and under 35 years were those suffering significant over-indebtedness. In addition, indebted households with low incomes or those in which no member of the household is working are those with the highest median debt burden ratios and, therefore, with highest levels of financial pressure.[19]

3. The Problem of Increasing Evictions in Spain

The most obvious consequence of this situation has been the rise in evictions that Spain has experienced in recent years. A clear increase in the number of foreclosures since the beginning of the crisis[20] shows the extent of the social problem triggered by the over-indebtedness and unemployment situation in the aftermath of the financial crisis. According to the available data provided by the Spanish General Council of the Judiciary, there have been a total of 485,828 evictions since 2007, albeit without a distinction being drawn between evictions of residential properties and non-residential properties.[21] As a result of the crisis in 2008, in just one year the number of foreclosures culminating in evictions doubled and since then continued to rise until 2013.

According to the data, there were 91,622 foreclosure orders in 2012 (517 per day in the first trimester).[22] More specifically, the Bank of Spain and the filtered data from financial institutions that managed more than 85 per cent of mortgage lending reported that, in 2012, there were 32,490 foreclosures of home residences from which 14,110 were given as *datio in solutum* (43 per cent of total) and the other 4,215 were voluntary surrenders.

---

dates back from 2008.

14 Spanish Statistical Office, *Living Conditions Survey*, 2013 (last publication May 2014).

15 Spanish Statistical Office, *Household Budget Survey*, 2012 (last publication July 2013).

16 Spanish Statistical Office (2013).

17 Economic and Social Council, *Memoria CES 2012. Life Quality and Social Protection*, 2013.

18 A. Valiño Castro, 'Efectos de la crisis en la accesibilidad a la vivienda de las familias en función de su composición y residencia', *Información Comercial Española, ICE: Revista de economía*, Nº 867. Economía de la vivienda en España, 2012.

19 Banco de España, *Encuesta Financiera de las Familias* [Survey on Household Finances], 2010.

20 Consejo Económico y Social, *Memoria CES 2012. Calidad de vida y protección social*. 14 March 2013.

21 General Council of the Judiciary, *Data on the Effect of the Crisis in the Judiciary*. Last data from third quarter 2013.

22 Ibid.

4. Causes of Over-Indebtedness in Spain

Even though the causes of over-indebtedness are numerous in Spain, the consequences of the connection between the financial and economic crisis in Spain have been exponentially amplified due to the structural focus of the economy on the housing sector.[23] Economic policies in Spain have long considered the real estate and the property sector as the main economic driver of the country.[24] As a result, when the housing bubble burst the credit system was strongly affected, which in turn had a huge impact on the real estate market. Many companies in the building and other economic sectors that revolved around the sale of property were forced to declare bankruptcy.[25] That situation led to a rise in unemployment and to the economic recession (turning what were situations of householders' over-indebtedness into bankruptcies) and to a severe credit crunch (as a consequence of the financial crisis in the banking system itself and its reluctance to continue giving credit).

a. Macro-economic risks factors: the housing bubble

There is a direct link between the increase in house prices and over-indebtedness. Spain's *credit boom* (from the mid to late 1990s to mid-2000s)[26] was mainly a consequence of the ease of access to the mortgage market. The situation of extraordinary liquidity forced up house prices, giving rise to a real estate market based on expectations of obtaining benefits, based on the general belief that prices *could never go down* and, in turn, leading to an excessive increase in the price of real estate acquired on credit. In many cases this involved consumers, often speculatively, turning their main dwelling into an investment. These factors resulted in a so-called state of 'hypertrophy of credit'.[27] At the same time, the price of housing increased exponentially, resulting in a huge overvaluation of real estate.[28]

Due to the rise in housing prices, the value of mortgage loans increased as well, and loans were granted at a 100 per cent loan-to-value ratio. Hence, during this period the grounds were laid for most of the mortgage problems that Spanish households are currently facing.

---

23 La Caixa Foundation, Report 'Crisis and Social Fracture in Europe: Causes and Effects in Spain', *Social Studies Collection*, 35, 2012.

24 See R. Vergés Escuín, 'El mercado residencial español, 1987–2006. Expectativas de vivienda y suelo', *Revista de Economía y Financias de Castilla y León*, 5, pp. 73–85; and J.M. Naredo, 'El modelo inmobiliario español y sus consecuencias', *Boletín CF.+S*, 44, 2010, pp. 13–27; also Deutsche Bank, Press Release, 'Spanish Construction: All Good Things Come to an End', 9 June 2008.

25 In 2008, the closure of around half of the real estate agencies in Spain. See http://elpais.com/diario/2008/01/17/economia/1200524403_850215.html.

26 See the description of the genesis of this situation in Gutiérrez de Cabiedes (2009) pp. 18–24. Among the economic causes of this phenomenon, there are mentioned the reduction in interest rates (low-cost credit – rates at historic lows in the Eurozone – resulting in economic attractiveness and ease to resort to it) coupled with the creation of jobs and increased disposable income and therefore more confidence and consumer optimism in the economic situation, with better expectations and welfare derived from that situation.

27 See Gutiérrez de Cabiedes (2009) pp. 20–21 and 117–124 (situation against which an actual setting of the responsible lending principle is proposed).

28 See *The Economist*, 'Global House Price. Ratio Rentals', 30 December 2009.

b. Micro-economic risk factors: irresponsible lending and borrowing

The behaviour of consumers and credit entities in the credit market was also a risk factor for the increase of over-indebtedness. In the years prior to the housing bubble, some creditworthiness assessments by the lender were performed and those with a negative outcome usually resulted in the credit being denied.[29] However, in the years of the housing bubble, loans were often granted even though banks were aware of the risks involved.[30] Today, it is known and recognised that mortgage lenders granted loans to borrowers in many cases without carefully examining their actual ability to service their debts. This was the reason why atypical or imbalanced guarantees were requested from third parties, usually borrowers' relatives.

Consumers also ignored warning signs and risks. The fact that many consumers have several loan obligations shows that some might have engaged in irresponsible borrowing practices. Furthermore, in mortgage agreements, for instance, despite the role of the notary and intervention in property deals,[31] it was not uncommon that consumers did not fully understand all the financial and legal consequences of the loan agreement. In this regard, empirical data shows that most consumers (58 per cent of the population surveyed) who contracted a financial product or service usually did not receive information concerning the service or product.[32] As a matter of fact, it was usually the bank officer who performed marketing strategies. In addition, even where prior information was provided, 48 per cent of the surveyed consumers have reported that the information was not appropriate and that it did not provide a proper understanding of the specific characteristics of the product or service. Only 24 per cent said that they received proper and sufficient information.[33] Likewise, 39 per cent of the surveyed consumers claimed that they were not allowed to take any document containing information out of the financial institution's premises. Only a third of the surveyed consumers declared to have carefully read the contract.[34]

However, as a result of the financial crisis, the situation has been now completely reversed.[35] Currently, there is an absolute restriction of access to credit for consumers, in contrast to the ease that existed in previous years, both in terms of quantity and conditions of availability, which have both tightened. The uncertainty in which financial credit institutions have operated since the financial crisis, increased default rates and the current aversion of the banks to any risk is exacerbating the lack of credit (and there are low expectations that the situation will get better in the short term). It has been a constant public demand that public money that has been used for private banks' recovery flow to taxpayers. Yet, despite the policy announcement from the government of

29 This assessment involved income tax statements (offering insight into the financial capacity of the borrower) and the last pay cheque (to verify income) as well as a check of defaults and credit records, managed by credit bureaus.

30 S. Nasarre Aznar, 'Malas prácticas bancarias en la actividad hipotecaria', *Revista Crítica de Derecho Inmobiliario*, no. 727, pp. 2665–2737.

31 Mortgage loans are always signed in front of the notary. The role of the notary is to guarantee the legality of the deal and, among other things, to ensure that property buyers or sellers are aware of what they are signing, which includes reading the contract to the parties.

32 Adicae, *Los hábitos y experiencias de los consumidores ante la publicidad, la transparencia al contratar y las reclamaciones en consumo financiero*, 2014 (survey among 3,960 consumers).

33 Adicae (2014). Sixty-nine per cent of surveyed consumers were not provided with written information and 14 per cent claim that they did not receive any kind of information (either written or oral).

34 Adicae (2014).

35 In the legal field, Article 14 of the Spanish Law 16/2011, of 24 June, on Consumer Credit Agreements (Ley de Contratos de Crédito al Consumo) currently provides that before the consumer credit contract is signed, the lender shall evaluate the creditworthiness of the consumer.

a boost in the activity of the Official Credit Institute (*Instituto de Crédito Oficial*, ICO) with new policies to facilitate access to credit, the flow of credit to families and SMEs has not actually been facilitated in reality.

B. Legal Framework and the Role of EU Law

1. The Impact of EU Law on the Spanish Legal System

EU law has had a fundamental impact on the Spanish legal order, contributing to the re-design of the Spanish consumer protection law. In particular, the issue of foreclosure proceedings in Spain has been the subject of an extensive debate drawing attention to the deficiencies of such procedure in a situation of crisis like the one Spanish households are experiencing. Further, the role of the Court of Justice of the European Union (CJEU) has been crucially important in 'fine-tuning' the national legal provisions in light of the European legal instruments.

Directive 93/13 on Unfair Contract Terms (UCT Directive) was transposed into the Spanish legal system by the Standard Contract Terms Act (Law 7/1998). In some aspects the Spanish legislation, now mainly reflected in the Consolidated Text of the General Act for the Protection of Consumers and Users of 2007 (hereinafter, TR-LGDCU) has even gone beyond the provisions of the Directive: for instance, in relation to the black list of unfair terms. However, the CJEU ruled that Spain had failed in fulfilling its obligations of transposing into the national legal system Articles 5 and 6(2) of the Directive.[36]

Furthermore, the potential that might be drawn from the interpretation of Directive 93/13 in the case of *Caja Madrid v Ausbanc* should not be disregarded,[37] in combination with the cases *Banco Español de Crédito*[38] and *Aziz*,[39] according to which judges are entitled to declare the invalidity of terms related to remunerative interests in mortgage loans and, because of lack of price, to declare the nullity of the whole contract, with the reimbursement of the loan without interest. Once the nullity of the loan is declared, as the Supreme Court has recently ruled in some judgements, the annulment of the mortgage is also possible given that it is an accessory to the principal contract.[40]

Moreover, the aforementioned Spanish Law on Consumer Credit Agreements transposed Directive 2008/48, although excluding mortgage-secured loans, which remain regulated by Law 2/2009, by the general mortgage regulation and by specific banking regulations. Nonetheless, Spanish law goes beyond the Directive in other aspects, given that the Spanish Law on Consumer Credit maintains provisions from the former legislation that provide a higher protection to credit consumers –although they were not required by EU legislation. Finally, most of the legal amendments that may be derived from the Mortgage Credit Directive were already implemented in Spain (by the Law 1/2013 and other previous banking regulations).

36 Case C–70/03 *Commission of the European Communities v Kingdom of Spain* [2004] ECR I-07999.

37 Case C-484/08 *Caja de Ahorros y Monte de Piedad de Madrid v Asociación de Usuarios de Servicios Bancarios (Ausbanc)* [2010] ECR I-04785.

38 Case C-618/10. *Banco Español de Crédito SA v Joaquín Calderón Camino*; not reported yet.

39 Case C-415/11 *Mohamed Aziz v Caixa d'Estalvis de Catalunya, Tarragona i Manresa* (Catalunyacaixa); not reported yet.

40 S. Cámara, 'El control de cláusulas abusivas sobre el precio: de la STJUE 3 junio 2010 (Caja Madrid) a la STS 9 mayo 2013 sobre cláusulas suelo', *Revista CESCO de Derecho del Consumo*, no. 6/2013, pp. 98–115.

Lastly, the recent enactment of Law 3/2014 of 27 March is aimed at the transposition of Directive 2011/83/EU on Consumer Rights. Thereby the Spanish legislature enacts a (minor) reform of the TR-LGDCU, in an attempt to comply with the CJEU Judgment in *Banco Español de Crédito* by modifying the wording of Article 83 TR-LGDCU 2007 in the interest of a proper transposition of Article 6(1) of UCT Directive. Accordingly, the integration of the contract by the judge once the term has been found unfair is banned, and the contract will remain being binding on the parties, provided that it can be upheld without the unfair term(s).

2. Mortgage Enforcement Proceedings

The legal framework for the procedure of mortgage enforcement has traditionally been considered burdensome for the debtor in Spain. Until the *Aziz* ruling and Law 1/2013, the debtor could not stop the mortgage enforcement procedure, even if the contract contained unfair terms. The potential unfairness could only be claimed in a separate declaratory proceeding. As a consequence, in some cases it happened that the foreclosure procedure had come to an end when unfairness was declared and the debtor had already been evicted.

Moreover, the minimum awarding price of the dwelling has always been very low in these proceedings (50 per cent of the appraised value in judicial auction and no minimum limit at the out-of-court enforcement, before the notary, in case it is forfeited, which occurred in many cases).[41] This resulted in a practice of the public auction of the mortgaged properties at bargain prices, usually awarded to the real estate agencies from the creditor entity attending the auction.

Additionally, Spanish law does not provide the borrower with the possibility to get a discharge of the remaining debt after the mortgaged property is awarded to a third party by public auction or to the mortgage holder (in case of lack of bidders).[42]

This means that the eviction does not put an end to the obligations secured by the mortgage. It is important to note that as a result of the *unlimited personal liability* principle enshrined in Spanish law,[43] after the mortgage foreclosure proceedings the creditor may continue collecting the outstanding debt (considered not satisfied) in an ordinary enforcement proceeding from the debtor's remaining and even future assets (which are able to be seized and sold at public auction or awarded); and even after the bank has sold the house for a higher value of the awarding price.

a. Possibilities for consumers to raise substantive objections against enforcement

In Spanish mortgage enforcement proceedings, there have been traditionally quite restricted possibilities of opposition for the defendant because of the alleged 'special nature' of this procedure.

---

41 Article 129 of the Spanish Mortgage Law (before the amendments introduced by the aforementioned Royal Decree-Law 6/2012, analysed below).

Now this practice has been confirmed by the CJEU in the *Barclays case* (Case C-280/13, Judgement of the Court of 30 April 2014, *Barclays Bank SA v Sara Sánchez García and Alejandro Chacón Barrera*). The Court has held that it does not fall under the scope of the Dir. 93/13, since it is related to a national statutory legal provision (Article 1(2) UCT Directive) that has already struck a balance between the rights and obligations of the parties (para. 41).

42 If there are no bidders or they do not meet the minimum awarding amount required by law, the creditor may request the Court to award the mortgaged property to him.

43 This is what Article 1911 of Civil Code establishes as an absolute principle, in a categorical and solemn way: 'The debtor is liable for the performance of his obligations with all his assets, present and future.' And according to Article 105 of Mortgage Law, enacted in 1946, 'The mortgage (…) will not alter the unlimited personal liability of the debtor provided in Article 1911 of the Civil Code'.

At the procedural level, Spanish legislation lists the reasons by which a debtor may contest the procedure of foreclosure (Article 695 of the Spanish CPA). These reasons were very limited before *Aziz* and potential unfairness of a contractual term could only be invoked in a separate declaratory procedure that does not suspend the foreclosure proceedings.[44] Thus, in the Spanish eviction procedure, the final awarding of a mortgaged property is, in principle, irreversible. As a result, if the decision of the judge hearing the declaratory proceedings concerning the possible unfairness of a clause in the loan agreement at stake –entailing the annulment of foreclosure proceedings– is pronounced after the eviction has taken place, that decision can only ensure compensatory *ex post* consumer protection, given that the evicted consumer will not be able to recover its property at that point in time.[45]

However, until the *Aziz* case, Spanish courts had not challenged these procedural rules. In 2011, the Spanish Constitutional Court refused to admit the exceptions of unconstitutionality of Articles 579, 695 and 698 of the Spanish CPA.[46] The Constitutional Court held that the foreclosure proceeding does not infringe the principles of effective judicial protection and procedural fairness between the parties, and that the absence of procedural contradiction within the mortgage enforcement procedure does not cause inability to defend given the possibility of initiating a subsequent assessment procedure (declaratory proceedings).[47] Furthermore, the Spanish Supreme Court ruled that the creditor's performance cannot be considered abusive when claiming the enforcement of her rights according to the powers granted by the law, as expressed in the claim of the difference between the total of the credit by which it was executed and the amount for which it was awarded.[48]

Against this background, the CJEU in the *Aziz* case considered that the Spanish judicial system undermines the effectiveness of the protection provided by Directive 93/13 on unfair terms in consumer contracts. This lack of effectiveness would apply in all cases where the execution of the eviction of immovable property takes place before the court hearing within the declaratory process to declare the unfairness of a contract term on which the mortgage is based and, consequently, the nullity of the enforcement procedure.[49] Indeed, given that the court competent for the declaratory process is not able to suspend the enforcement proceedings, the declaration of nullity only ensures mere subsequent consumer protection granting damages.[50] Such compensation results are incomplete and insufficient to prevent the continued use of such (unfair) clauses. Thus, the initiation of foreclosure proceedings is enough to deprive consumers of the protection ensured by

44 Article 698(1) of the Spanish CPA: 'Any application made by a debtor, third-party debtor or other interested party, which is not covered by the preceding articles, including applications concerning nullity of title, maturity, certainty, extinguishment or the amount of the debt, shall be settled by an appropriate judgment, without ever having the effect of staying or terminating the judicial enforcement proceedings provided for in the present chapter.'

45 This procedure has cast on doubt the effectiveness of the Directive 93/13 on unfair terms in consumer contracts (see *Aziz* case).

46 Order of the Constitutional Court 113/2011, of 19 July 19.

47 Ibid. In the same vein, the Constitutional Court in Judgments of the Constitutional Court 41/1981, 18 December; 64/1985, 17 May; 41/1986, 2 April; 8/1991, 17 January; 6/1992, 16 January; 296/1993, 18 October; 69/1995, 9 May.

48 Judgment of the Supreme Court, of 16 February 2006 and of 25 September 2008. In this regard, there is case law both in favour and against this doctrine by the different Spanish Courts of Appeal.

49 Case C-415/11 *Mohamed Aziz v Caixa d'Estalvis de Catalunya, Tarragona i Manresa* (Catalunyacaixa); not reported yet. Para. 60.

50 Ibid.

the Directive on unfair contract terms. Accordingly, the Court found that the Spanish legislation does not comply with the principle of effectiveness, to the extent that makes it impossible or excessively difficult, in foreclosure proceedings, applying the protection that the Directive confers on consumers.[51]

The *Aziz* judgement has brought about a long-awaited legal reform on the Spanish mortgage foreclosure system in the Law 1/2013. Through the introduction of a more effective protection of consumers in these foreclosure proceedings, this case has altered this essential feature of the mortgage foreclosure procedure and the possibility for defendant mortgagors to raise substantive objections against enforcement in those proceedings.[52]

Yet, these legal amendments following *Aziz* have given rise to a new (or subsequent) problem:[53] the Spanish legislation continued to limit the possibility of filing an appeal against the decision solely on the ground that the court of first instance has declared the unfairness of a contractual term that constitutes the basis for the enforcement, establishing a difference in treatment between the professional and the consumer. Thus, the consumer can only appeal the decision solely if the opposition has been considered justified, whereas the businesses are entitled to appeal against a decision that is contrary to their interests.[54] This imbalance of procedural means accentuates the inequality between the contracting parties.[55] The CJEU holds that the design of the procedure for opposition to foreclosure provided for in Article 695 CPA is 'contrary to the principle of equality of arms or procedural equality'.[56] Therefore, in a second 'call for attention' to the Spanish legislator, the Court has stated in 2014 that the 'new' procedural measures are incomplete and insufficient to secure the cessation of application of an unfair clause in the mortgage secured loan contract that serves as a basis for the seizure of the property.[57]

b. Adjustment of contractual terms in case of 'unforeseen/unforeseeable events'

Generally adjustments of contractual terms can only be made with the agreement of the two parties.[58] However at the same time, the Spanish Civil Code takes into account in many articles the institutions of 'caso fortuito' ('*fortuitous event*') and 'fuerza mayor' ('*force majeure*'), generally and implicitly defined by Article 1105 Civil Code: '[o]utside the cases expressly mentioned in the law, and those in which the obligation should require it, no one shall be liable for events which cannot be foreseen or which, being foreseen, should be *inevitable*'.[59] The wording of Article 1575 Civil Code makes reference to '*unforeseen* fortuitous events', describing them shortly after as '*extraordinary* and *unaccustomed* events which the contracting parties should have been *unable* to foresee *reasonably*'.[60] Consequently, they must be understood as supervening exceptional circumstances that are outside the control of the parties, which makes impossible performance of

51 Ibid. Para. 63.

52 The specific legal amendments are analysed in section C of this chapter.

53 Addressed by the CJEU Judgment of 17 July 2014, Case C169/14 *Sánchez Morcillo Abril García v Banco Bilbao Vizcaya Argentaria, S.A.* (not reported yet) issued just when the edition of this book is being closed.

54 Para. 30.

55 Para. 46.

56 Para. 48.

57 Para. 49. Emphasis added.

58 The Civil Code sets as a general rule in Article 1256 that 'compliance of obligations cannot be left to the will of only one of the parties'.

59 Emphasis added.

60 This is a special provision for leases of rural properties. Emphasis added.

the contract. Thus, predictability leads to terms of no reasonable probability that, not constituting an inherent element of the contract or will of the parties, relieves the debtor of her responsibility. Likewise, 'force majeure' provides a ground for exclusion of liability of a party for non-performance of the contract; i.e. usually relieves one or both parties to a contract of their contractual obligations.[61]

Furthermore, the Spanish Civil Code, which enshrines the principle of *pacta sunt servanda,* does not consider the possibility of reviewing or cancelling a contract on the basis of the alteration of circumstances. However, the Spanish Supreme Court started to apply the *rebus sic stantibus* doctrine after the Spanish Civil War, which is similar in nature to the frustration of contract or of purpose. In the current situation, the possibility of application of the *rebus sic stantibus* principle to mortgage loans has been raised and discussed again,[62] in order to be able to request the modification of the contract terms or the termination of contracts, according to each particular case. Thus, that formula would be applied in the event of severe alteration of the circumstances in which mortgage loans were signed compared to a subsequent situation, for instance, due to the current economic crisis. Nonetheless, the case law of the Spanish Supreme Court and many decisions from appealing courts had declared that the economic performance of a country and the global or particular situation of economic crisis cannot imply a general justification for the breach of the contractual obligations.[63]

More recently, the Spanish Supreme Court has dealt with this issue in its Decision of 17 January 2013 where it defined the criteria for the application of the *rebus sic stantibus* principle and analysed the predictability of the current economic crisis for its consideration as a factor that could lead to a change in the circumstances. The Court has followed this approach by reviewing to a certain extent the prior doctrine, facilitating the application of the principle. Nonetheless, despite its exceptional nature, the decision admits that a situation of economic crisis might imply an extraordinary alteration of the circumstances.[64] The Court also refers to the circumstances that may lead to the application of the principle. *Ad exemplum*, it takes into account 'the economic situation of the buyer at the time of execution of the contract and the time of having to pay the outstanding part of the price that she was expected to finance; the actual degree of impossibility of funding and specific causes added to the general economic crisis'.[65]

Finally, it can be said that this substantial and supervening alteration of the circumstances, which is closely related to ('passive') over-indebtedness, has been indirectly addressed, in the most recent regulatory provisions passed by the Spanish government: the aforementioned Royal Decree-Law 27/2012 and the Law 1/2013.

---

61 Article 1105 Civil Code.

62 See Judgment of Provincial High Court of Madrid, Sección 11ª, 27/2013, 10 January.

63 See the Supreme Court's decision of 27 April 2012. A vast number of decisions from Provincial High Courts had also rejected in the last years the application of this principle concerning the current economic crisis in property purchases.

64 And so, the Decision states: 'A situation of economic recession as the current one may be regarded if the contract had been concluded before the external manifestation of that crisis, as an extraordinary manifestation of the circumstances, capable of originating … an exorbitant disproportion and out of all calculation of the performance of the parties.'

65 The Decision considers other nearby criteria: the destination of the house, purchased as a principal or a second residence; the contractual allocation of risk of not having funding and the level of promised cooperation by the seller for purchase, distinguishing between contractors who are professionals of real estate and those who are not; or the conditions imposed by the banks to provide financing.

3. Bankruptcy Proceedings

Besides the inadequacy of the mortgage enforcement proceedings explained above, Spanish law does not provide for consumer bankruptcy rules in its Insolvency Law. Unlike many other countries in Europe and all over the world, in Spain, bankruptcy is not an adequate solution for obtaining some form of debt relief since mortgage debt (the main part of credit in every household in Spain) is specifically excluded from the non-professional bankruptcy scope and solutions (composition settlement with the creditors or liquidation).

There is no automatic stay for mortgage debts: foreclosure of immovable property can be stopped for any kind of debtor (companies and entrepreneurs or self-employed persons) but not for consumers. And there is no possibility of discharge. Hence, there is no reason for the debtor (or incentive for the creditor) to file for bankruptcy, widely used in other countries. In fact, in 2013, personal bankruptcies were less than 7 per cent of the total.

4. Changes in Litigation since the Crisis

The economic crisis has led to a clear increase in litigation in Spain.[66] In actual fact, the litigation rate presented a moderate growing trend from the last years of the 1990s to 2007, but it rose sharply from 2007 to 2009, declining in 2010 and 2011, and stabilising in 2012 and 2013. Currently, these figures are dropping as a result of the reintroduction by Law 10/2012 of court fees (now applicable also to individual persons).[67]

The issues that have been challenged (particularly since the entry into force of the recently passed Law 1/2013) are related to, besides foreclosure proceedings, default interest rates (or penalty interest) applied by banks on mortgage loans and aforementioned floor clauses. As for foreclosure proceedings, many of them have been dismissed after the amendments introduced by the Law 1/2013, both through the presentation of opposition by the debtor, as *ex officio* by the judge which requires the claimant to make a new settlement debt. Other 'minor' challenged issues, thereby unfair terms and abusive practices, also affecting the mortgage payment, are: very high spreads (to compensate the EURIBOR's fall) or benchmarks, abusive increasing fees, abusive repayment systems, and monthly financial obligations imposed by the bank (taking another 'product' shape), and marketing of swaps, clearly linked to the mortgage (for the same amount and signed at the same time).

C. Policy Responses to Over-Indebtedness

1. Social Response and Judicial Activism

There has been a strong *social response* against the Mortgage Enforcement Legislation (and protests against the eviction of thousands of families from their homes while still being obliged to honour outstanding debts) especially after a number of suicides of people who were to be evicted from their homes. What needs to be stressed is not so much the impressive demonstrations that

66 General Council of the Judiciary, *The Spanish Judiciary in Figures: 2012.*

67 It has fallen by 15 per cent, as observed by the Statistical Service of the Spanish General Council of the Judiciary, at CGPJ, *Boletín Información Estadística*, no. 34, 2013.

were held all over Spain in 2012 and 2013,[68] but the 'Citizens' Legislative Initiative' that was submitted to the Spanish Parliament with the support of 1,402,854 signatures seeking reform of the legislation that set up the *datio in solutum* (the so-called 'giving-in-payment') of the house. The government and opposition parties were forced to submit their respective draft law on this matter in the parliamentary proceedings of this Initiative. The outcome of these proceedings was the abovementioned Law 1/2013.

Another remarkable phenomenon is that of the unprecedented *judicial activism* of lower courts attempting to curb the banking sector practice in foreclosure proceedings and evictions by considering it as an 'abuse of rights', an 'anti-social exercise' or an 'abuse of authority' – banned by Spanish Civil Code[69] – regarding the rights derived from the mortgage;[70] and, on this basis, some courts denied the right of the bank to pursue the collection of the outstanding amount of the mortgage on the remaining assets of the mortgage holder. In particular, several decisions of the Provincial Court of Navarra, mainly the one of 17 December 2010, in which the bank was obliged to accept the solution of '*datio in solutum*' to extinguish and cancel the debt. Those decisions were followed by other courts, which remarked that judgments should reflect the current economic and social reality, one of the main criteria of legal interpretation established by Article 3(1) of the Civil Code,[71] which is quite different from the one that existed when the contract was signed. Some of the decisions even add certain systemic or socio-political considerations to their reasoning.[72]

However, the Court of Appeal of Navarra soon issued conflicting decisions (mainly on 4 February 2011). And finally, the Supreme Court rejected the approach of the lower courts and ruled that the creditor's performance does not constitute an abuse of rights when claiming the enforcement of their rights according to the powers granted by the law and if the foreclosure proceeding has been followed according to the legal procedure. In addition, the Court holds that preventing the lender from exercising those rights would undermine the general confidence in the performance of contractual obligations.[73] In the same vein, the Constitutional Court, in its Decision 113/2011 of 17 August, curbed such judicial practice, stating that those judges, decisive in the application of the law, exceed their interpretative role and force the existing legal framework, which, in a system of law such as that of Spain, can only be modified by the legislature. That is the reason why the legislature itself decided to intervene in order to remedy or, at least, to relieve the severity of the social-economic situation.

---

68 Promoted principally by the 'Platform for Mortgage Victims' (*Plataforma de Afectados por la Hipoteca*: PAH).

69 Article 7(2).

70 The Court of First Instance of Lleida, 29 December 2011, considers that the '*venire contra factum proprium*' doctrine, analogue to the estoppel doctrine, applies here. If the bank, the dominant party in the contract of adhesion with the borrower, appraised the property at a certain amount, it cannot then incorporate as its own the property without giving it the value that itself set, which allows its *unjust enrichment*.

71 'The law will be interpreted … according to the social reality at the time they should be applied'.

72 For example, the aforementioned Order of Court of First Instance of Lleida No. 5, 29 December 2011, stating: '[T]he 2011 economic outlook has nothing to do with the economic outlook of 2006, 2007 and 2008 … Nowadays, the Spanish economy, as well as the world economy, suffers a deep economic crisis and for this reason, surely, the property adjudicated to the bank … now has a market value below the price agreed in the mortgage loan, but is it fair that the debtor suffers all the consequences of this fall? Would it not be fairer that the financial institutions also bear part of this decline? Economists are unanimous in considering that the real estate value losses have been caused by the financial institutions themselves with their mismanagement of the financial system.'

73 The judgments of Supreme Court, of 16 February 2006 and 25 September 2008, hold that to exercise the legal rights in order to obtain 'admissible economic benefits' in those transactions is not *per se* abusive.

Subsequently, first instance judges began questioning the compliance of this legislation with the protection afforded by European Consumer Law, giving rise to the well-known *Aziz* case. Shortly after, the Spanish Supreme Court did take another major step in correcting another of the Spanish system failures: it declared the 'floor clauses' abusive in the way they have been used and, therefore, null and void, ordering the banks to remove them from their agreements.

The political response, initially reluctant, was pushed by the social and judicial initiative. Even into the crisis and increasing evictions scenario, the Spanish law surprisingly remained motionless in providing a solution to the problem of household over-indebtedness. In this context, several parliamentary groups from the opposition started pushing for amendments of foreclosure proceedings, including the possibility for allowing '*datio in solutum*' (that is, to relieve the mortgage defaulters from debts with the bank by recovering the property). However, the government (first, the Socialist Cabinet of José Luis Rodríguez Zapatero, and later on, the People's of Mariano Rajoy) has opposed such a major change in mortgage credit laws, claiming that the Spanish system of personal guarantees prevented its banks from the turmoil experienced in the United States.

2. Legal Amendments

As a result, the Spanish government decided to adopt certain extraordinary and urgent measures aimed at reinforcing the protection of the most vulnerable mortgage holders from eviction, with the purpose of reducing the number of evictions that affect the most vulnerable mortgage debtors. The government first approved the Royal Decree-Law 8/2011 of 1 July, concerning measures in support of mortgage holders, only touching upon some procedural aspects,[74] reforming the Civil Procedure Act (CPA). Awarding price rules intended to ensure that, in foreclosure proceedings, the debtor receives a more adequate price for the immovable property that allows him to minimise the remaining debt. The creditor shall not be awarded the debtor's assets for an amount below 60 per cent of their appraisal value (modified in 2013, for 70 per cent if the property is the main dwelling, and 50 per cent in other cases). The legislation also exempted personal property from seizure: the legal limit of that which is 'exempt' is increased by 50 per cent, and an additional 30 per cent of the minimum wage for each household member who does not receive regular income.

Afterwards, the aforementioned Royal Decree-Law 6/2012, seeking to address the social evictions problem (and protests) establishes a voluntary system of mortgage debt renegotiation by means of a 'Code of Good Practice' that applies only to those financial institutions who voluntarily adhere to it (soft law) and only to 'particularly vulnerable' mortgage holders, who experience extraordinary difficulty to meet the payment of their mortgage obligations. Mortgage holders in such situation have different possibilities. First, they may request from the lending bank the restructuring of the mortgage debt that makes its performance viable by the debtor in the medium and long term. The restructuring plan must include a four-year grace period on the repayment of the capital, an extension of the loan repayment term of up to 40 years, and a reduction in the rate of interest applicable, which, during the grace period, will be determined according to the EURIBOR index plus 0.25 per cent. If restructuring is not feasible, the consumer may ask the lending institution for a debt write-down over the capital to be repaid. If neither of the two measures is able to reduce the debtor's mortgage stress to attainable limits for his financial viability, he may

74 For further reference P. Gutiérrez de Cabiedes, 'El Real Decreto 27/2012, de 15 de noviembre, de medidas urgentes para reforzar la protección a los deudores hipotecarios', *Revista de Derecho Concursal y Paraconcursal*, vol. 18, 2013, pp. 479–483, considering this reform 'a partial and insufficient measure'; and J. Marco Molina, 'Spanish Law in 2010–2012: The Influence of European Union Law and the Impact of the Economic Crisis', *Journal of Civil Law Studies*, vol. 6, 2013, pp. 426–434.

seek the '*datio in solutum*', whereby the bank accepts the transfer of the mortgaged property in payment of the outstanding debt, which will definitely extinguish the obligation. An additional and interesting protective measure is that the debtor (upon request) may stay as a tenant for a period of two years, paying an annual rent equivalent to 3 per cent of the total debt outstanding at the time of the delivery of property.

Subsequently, when social concerns and demonstrations against housing evictions arose, the government passed the Royal Decree-Law 27/2012 on urgent measures to reinforce the protection of mortgage holders, whose purpose is to reduce the number of evictions. Its main goal consists of 'the immediate suspension, during two years, of evictions on the families that are in a situation of *special risk of exclusion*'. It applies to foreclosure proceedings in which the primary home was awarded and to persons who are in a 'situation of special vulnerability'.

Lastly, the amendment of the Spanish mortgage legislation performed by Law 1/2013, on measures to reinforce protection of mortgagors, debt restructuring and social rent, tries to complete and strengthen the rules providing protection to mortgagors. This law develops four types of measures.

First, it provides for a *moratorium* on evictions of mortgagors at special risk of social exclusion, as an exceptional and interim measure where the law, without altering the foreclosure procedure, prevents the eviction of people belonging to particular social groups exposed to social exclusion. It also foresees, as a consequence of the *Aziz* ruling, the *suspension* of the eviction order in case of unfair contract terms, what is the main innovation of the reform together with the former.[75] The reform also sets a new minimum quantity of defaults according to which the entity may seek enforcement of a mortgage. This minimum has shifted from one to three unpaid instalments.

Second, the Law 1/2013 introduces some amendments to Mortgage Law: (1) limitation of *late-payment or default* interest on mortgages on principal residence;[76] and (2) the rules on out-of-court mortgage foreclosure *proceeding* (before a notary), set out in Article 129 of the Mortgage Law, have been amended. The *value* set by the parties as the starting price of the property at auction cannot differ from the value, if any, set for the direct judicial foreclosure proceeding, and cannot, under any circumstances, be lower than 75 per cent of the value set in the appraisal used to grant the mortgage. The notary is authorised to warn the parties that some of the mortgage clauses on which the sale is based may be *unfair terms*. Last, but not least, the notary will place a suspension on the sale if a party evidences that he has submitted to the courts that unfairness (new grounds for opposition).

Third, this major reform carried out by Law 1/2013 introduces some changes to the judicial foreclosure procedure: (1) control of unfair terms: the judge, at his own motion or at the request of the interested party, is able to assess the existence of unfair clauses;[77] (2) new grounds for

75 The new law provides the judge with the ability to temporarily stop an eviction where the concerned consumer claims the unfairness of the contract term(s). In cases where the eviction is motivated for one unfair clause, the judge may definitely paralyse the process, whereas if there is an unfair term although it is not enough to trigger the eviction, the procedure will continue without the application of such contract term. The law also gives similar powers to the notary, who may suspend, in similar terms, a foreclosure on extrajudicial procedures.

76 Default interest currently stands at rates that may range from 18 per cent to 30 per cent. The reform narrows the charges that the bank can impose on the debtor up to three times the legal interest rate.

77 Article 552(1) CPA. If clauses are found to be unfair, the court will rule that the foreclosure is unjustified, or it will carry out the foreclosure, but without applying those unfair clauses, when appropriate (Article 561(1) CPA).

opposition to enforcement proceedings;[78] (3) other amendments affect the costs of main dwelling's foreclosure proceedings, which cannot exceed 5 per cent of the sum claimed. Finally, the Law contains in its Annex a Code of Good Practices for financial entities on the feasible restructuring of debts with a mortgage guarantee over the main residence.

A particular initiative to highlight, in addition to those mentioned, is that of the Regional Government of Andalucía which enacted a – quite controversial – Decree[79] which authorised the temporary *expropriation* within three years of the use of houses 'in imminent' eviction and if there is the 'risk of social exclusion or threat to the physical or mental health of the people'. The Constitutional Court of Spain has decided the interim suspension of the application of this Decree, by accepting the constitutional proceedings brought against it by the Central Government. It considers the Andalusian rule 'affects the essential content of the right to private ownership, which is a reserved rule to Parliament, establishes a punitive liability regardless of fault principle that is required by the Constitution and establishes a regulation contrary to the equality principle'.

Recently, a discharge regulation has made its first (and limited) appearance in the Spanish law. Law 14/2013 of 27 September, on support for entrepreneurs and their internationalisation, known as the 'Entrepreneur's Act' (*Ley de Emprendedores*), introduces changes to the Spanish Bankruptcy Act (Law 22/2003). In that framework, the Law foresees a kind of '*fresh start*' regime, by which an individual debtor is able to cancel the debts that could not be satisfied with his present property and assets, within a bankruptcy process. Nonetheless its scope is quite restrictive, because it will only apply to certain type of debtors and it will not apply to public law claims, also requiring the debtor to satisfy certain classes of claims in full (preferred claims especially, which include those secured by a mortgage or pledge).

One of the last reforms introduced by the Spanish Government by the time this contribution was written is the so-called 'second chance' mechanism.[80] This measure allows, through a bankruptcy process, discharge from all debts to companies and individuals upon the liquidation of the debtor's assets, even in those situations in which the value of the assets does not cover the entire amount of the commitments. In other words, the mechanism introduces the possibility of negotiation a potential '*datio in solutum*'. The aim is to reconcile the interests of creditors and debtors by guaranteed procedures aimed at facing payment of debts in an orderly manner, through settlement agreements via mediation performed by notaries or by the Chambers of Commerce. During this negotiation procedure, evictions are suspended. In addition, among other additional measures, the Government has increased the protection of the most vulnerable groups by extending until 2017 the moratorium on evictions expiring as of May 2015 and excluding the application of floor clauses in mortgage contracts to the beneficiaries of the Code of Good Practices.

---

78 Article 557(1) CPA now list contractual unfairness as ground for opposition. If that ground is upheld, either the foreclosure will be dismissed (if it was based on the contractual clause in question) or it will proceed, without application of the unfair clause (following the ruling of the CJEU in *Aziz*).

79 Decree-Law 6/2013, of 9 April, on measures to ensure the fulfillment of the social function of housing. The (financial or real estate) entities affected by the expropriation would receive 2 per cent as fair value in exchange.

80 Introduced by the Decree-Law 1/2015, of February 27, on second chance mechanism, reducing financial burden and other measures of social order.

D. Conclusions

The Spanish legal framework turned out to be inadequate in dealing with the solution to the problem of over-indebtedness in the aftermath of the crisis bringing about evictions and social exclusion. Spanish consumers experienced how the legal system remained silent before a growing phenomenon of 'homes without people and people without homes'.

The latest reforms carried out – some of them correcting clear shortcomings of Spanish legal order, such as those related to the mortgage foreclosure proceedings for instance – are certainly steps in the right direction. However, some shortcomings remain. Despite some emergency laws adopted to mitigate the most serious consequences (and protests) triggered by the crisis for extremely vulnerable groups, the measures taken are still insufficient and the underlying problems substantially persist.

There is still a lack of a comprehensive approach to household over-indebtedness resolution, and an absence of an insolvency culture and praxis. A major problem is that the Spanish law does not properly provide consumers with the possibility of release from their remaining debt even if the mortgage property is awarded to the mortgage holder.[81] Filing for bankruptcy is not an adequate solution for obtaining debt relief either, given that mortgage debt (which is the most common household debt in Spain) is excluded from its scope. In addition to this, both out-of-court and formal insolvency schemes remain inefficient and are not widely used.

Accordingly, the Spanish foreclosure and insolvency frameworks require further reform, providing for an effective system of debt restructuring, as well as a clear 'fresh start' for non-fraudulent debtors as the key issue.. This necessity is grounded not only in human and social reasons (to avoid poverty and exclusion) but also in economic ones.[82]

Furthermore, the credit crunch caused by the financial crisis has exacerbated the economic problems and social exclusion of thousands of consumers. Therefore, another key policy that must be implemented is that related to the access to credit, which should be encouraged, making it available to consumers on the basis of the principles of responsible credit lending and borrowing.

Spain's recovery started already in 2013, in a difficult deleveraging process reflecting the 'collective efforts of Spanish society' (austerity policies on spending, taxes and pensions), but people are still suffering from the legacy of the economic crisis, and some risks still remain.[83]

To conclude, it is necessary to point out that the crisis we are living through may and *must* be the occasion for a real catharsis, to set up a new financial and insolvency culture in Spain and a system able to achieve a fairer and more effective management and resolution of the serious situation that the country has reached. There is much at stake: not only the necessary, fair and equitable, reasonable and proportionate distribution of burdens of the crisis (with all concerned –institutions, financial entities and consumers – taking responsible action) but also the very regeneration and even legitimacy and social recognition of the institutions and the potential for the economic recovery of the country.

---

81 Recent amendments provide actually rather limited and partial discharge possibilities. In mortgage foreclosure, only 20–35 per cent debt can be discharged after the repossession of the main dwelling, within quite a long period of time (5 or 10 years). Insolvency proceedings reform excludes pre-insolvency mediation for consumers and provides for a practically useless discharge solution for them.

82 An argument for the implementation of a fresh start in Spain on economic and insolvency systemic grounds, also refuting the moral hazard and potential abuse concerns, in Gutiérrez de Cabiedes (2009) pp. 201–223. Backing these grounds IMF, *IMF Country Report No. 13/245. Spain: Selected Issues*, August 2013.

83 IMF, *Spain: 2014 Article IV Consultation*, 27 May 2014.

Chapter 6
Country Report Hungary

Mónika Józon

A. The Situation of Indebted Consumers in the Country

Despite the economic and social impact of the large number of badly performing loans in Hungary there is no legal definition of or doctrinal debate about the concepts of indebtedness and over-indebtedness. Banking practice and central statistics operate with the concept of payment delay (more than 90 days' delay is considered as payment difficulty) with different scales of severity when recording the actual status of the debtors on the 'market of loan reimbursement'.

According to the assessment of the Hungarian National Bank the outstanding debt of the Hungarians amounted to 6893.6 billion HUF in November 2013.[1] The same assessment reports that in December 2013 18.8 per cent of the households' debts were in payment delay over 90 days. Out of this the restructured debts under the different debtor rescue schemes amounted to 50.3 per cent.[2] According to the 2012 official statistics of the National Bank of Hungary households' debts made up 32.56 per cent of GDP of which the foreign currency denominated loans represent 18.54 per cent of GDP. In March 2013, the NPL-rate of foreign exchange loans was 20.2 per cent.[3]

In Hungary the most affected debtors are those who contracted mortgage loans denominated in foreign currency and, consequently, policy and judicial discourse in Hungary is strongly focused on the payment difficulties of such loans and on mortgage loans for housing purposes. However, these are not the only problems relating to over-indebtedness in Hungary.[4] The ratio of non-housing loans in Hungary is higher than in most European countries (excluding Bulgaria and Romania) and Hungarian interest rates on non-housing loans are the highest within the entire European Union.[5] At end of 2013, there were 287,407 mortgage contracts for non-housing purposes against 213,683 housing mortgages and only a slight fall can be noticed in the demand for current account debts (3,083,147 at the end of 2010 and 2,873,920 at the end of 2013) and credit card debts after the crisis (1,007,038 at the end of 2010 and 942,404 at the end of 2013).

In the aftermath of the financial crisis, the indebtedness of Hungarian consumers turned into over-indebtedness. In 2010 a Hungarian household with a mortgage loan spent on average 19 per cent of the total income of the household on mortgage payments. However, in the case of 12 per cent of the debtors this amount is above 30 per cent, whereas 25 per cent of the debtors were using 20–30 per cent of their full income for mortgage payments. Just one year later, those numbers had risen significantly. In 2011 almost 60 per cent (59.9 per cent) of the expenditure of the Hungarians (spending per person) was related to household costs (25 per cent for housing maintenance and energy and 22.8 per cent for food).[6]

1 The exchange rate of HUF/EUR on 25 June 2014 was 305.7 HUF for 1 EUR.
2 Report of the Hungarian Financial Supervisory Authority on Financial Stability (November 2013).
3 Risk Report of the Hungarian Financial Supervisory Authority (June 2013).
4 For more information see: Józon (2014).
5 Szigel and Fáykiss (2012: 27ff.).
6 'Level and Structure of Household Consumptions 2011' (2012).

Comparing the expenditure for household costs (60 per cent) with that spent on mortgage payments (19 per cent) reveals that families with mortgage loans can hardly make any savings. Most families which contracted mortgage loans for housing purposes are families with a higher number of family members than average. Although these households might have higher income levels than average, because of the higher number of family members these families belong to the lower income per capita category.[7] A study conducted by the National Bank of Hungary shows the ratio of non-performing debtors increased from 1.5 per cent at the end of 2008 to over 11 per cent at the end of 2011 and that from 2001 to September 2011 the household credit-to-GDP ratio increased from 10.7 per cent to 40.6 per cent.[8] According to this study, the bank credit interest burden of Hungarian households is among the highest in Europe; the interest payments-to-GDP ratio in Hungary is also higher in comparison with the Central Eastern European region; and the nominal interest rate on housing loans is the second highest in Europe behind Bulgaria.

B. The Causes of Over-Indebtedness in Hungary

The causes for the over-indebtedness of Hungarian consumers are various. They range from the widespread use of unfair and unclear contractual terms, the marketing of risky financial products for consumers with regards to the reimbursement scheme (such as loans denominated in foreign currency) and exploding demand for housing and easy access to credit. Banking practices that distorted the informed choice and consent of the Hungarian customers were employed on a young credit market with underdeveloped regulation (and missing codes of conduct). The Hungarian mortgage market has existed only since 2001, only a few years after the enactment of Law XXX of 1997. A housing and mortgage boom in the young and unregulated market led to risky contracting behaviour. The banking code of conduct was only launched by banks in 2009.

One of the major causes for over-indebtedness derives from unilateral adjustment of interest rates and other costs of mortgage credit through the bank. Contractual clauses were widespread, that put on the shoulders of the consumers the full risks of consumer crediting, allowing the bank unilaterally to amend the interest rate, other costs and charges in case it would increase the interbank interest rate or the consumer price index, the basic interest rate of the Hungarian National Bank, the costs of financing sources of the creditors, the costs of credit account administration, or in case of any other changes in the risk factors of consumer crediting.[9] In addition, the typical contract contained a clause stating that during the existence of the contract (almost 20 years) the 'actually applicable and future general terms and conditions as well as the actually applicable and future announcements of the credit institutions, without any additional legal act being necessary for this purpose' will be binding on the debtor.[10] Thus one could say that the consumers contracted mostly open-ended obligations for long terms.

Such types of contract clauses were largely employed in Hungary although the implementing norms of the UCT Directive 93/13 were in place and in 2006 the Hungarian Competition Authority had warned the stakeholders well in advance, before the global financial crisis, that the tools available under competition law do not suffice to effectively protect the consumers against unfair

7 Report of the Hungarian Statistical Office on Housing (2010).

8 Szigel and Fáykiss (2012: 27ff.).

9 Pécsi Ítélőtábla, Pf. VI. 20. 238/2013/9 (decision of the Pécs Court of Appeal on loan denominated in foreign currency, contract concluded in 2007).

10 Decision of 6 December 2013 of the Court of Appeal of Budapest.

contracting practices.[11] Such warnings had no impact on the legislature before 2010 due to the far-reaching regulatory liberalism that prevailed in Hungary and the absent consumer law approach in the field of consumer credit. As a consequence, Article 210(3) of Law CXII of 1996, which allowed for unilateral amendment by the banks of the interest rate, charges and other contract conditions under the 'conditions and circumstances established by the financial institutions' if the contract makes this explicitly possible in a separate clause, remained in force until 8 August 2009. Only in September 2011 the banks could make actual use of the clause on the unilateral amendment of the contract defined by the Highest Court (the predecessor of the Kúria).[12] The Court had ruled that the actual change in the circumstances must exceed the normally affordable level of the business risk and that the amendment of the contract must be proportional with the effects of the changes in circumstances, and the occurrence of the change and its actual effect on the interest rate, charges and costs should not be foreseen even by a professional market player.

Contractual liberalism in the field of consumer credit also made possible the introduction of new products, such as the loans denominated in foreign currency, with which the banks transferred the risk of exchange rate fluctuations onto the consumers. Under this scheme the credit institutions record and relate the value of the loans and the payable monthly instalments to a foreign currency. It was common practice for many banks to apply at the moment of the loan transfer the selling exchange rate of the National Bank of Hungary, whereas the reimbursement exchange rate was established by the credit institution *ex post* following market movements. Furthermore, the banks applied a large variety of different costs and charges that were not defined clearly which made it very difficult for the consumers to compare different offers. Cost and charges were neither governed by laws nor controlled by banking regulations before 2008. The Hungarian Competition Authority suggested in 2006 to the authorities with regulatory competences in the financial sector to limit the variety of costs and charges in order to make the comparison of different offers easier for the consumer, but the competition arguments of the HFSA prevailed over those on consumer protection.

Within such a poor regulatory framework on consumer credit marketing and contracting, the credit institutions were engaging in risk competition. A lack of rules on creditworthiness assessments led to banks securing the credit risk of low-quality loans through risk clauses, under which the credit institutions could unilaterally amend the payment obligations of the debtors, even though most banks have risk insurance. At the first manifestations of the global financial crisis, banks significantly lowered their lending conditions in Hungary. For instance, the average value of the LTV[13] was between 50–60 per cent in 2008, whereas for certain mortgage loan categories the banks applied a 100 per cent LTV.[14] Such financial products were promoted by aggressive, misleading or manipulative advertisement practices, mostly through intermediaries. Around 50–60 per cent of the new mortgage loans contracted before 2008 were marketed by intermediaries, under a poor legal framework on the activity on licensing, and supervision of such intermediaries. Only in 2010 were stricter rules introduced on eligibility and professional training of banking intermediaries.

The public policy of access to housing and credit also played a significant role in the exacerbation of indebtedness levels in Hungary. There was no social housing system, the housing construction

11 Report of the Hungarian Competition Authority on market assessment conducted in the field of mortgate loans 2006 (http://www.gvh.hu/dontesek/agazati_vizsgalatok/2366_hu_jelentes_a_jelzaloghitelezes_targyaban_lefolytatott_agazati_vizsgalatrol.html)._

12 Decision no. 211 of the Highest Court (Gfv. IX. 30. 211/2011 határozat).

13 The loan to value (LTV) ratio is a financial term used by lenders to express the ratio of a loan to the value of an asset purchased.

14 Király and Nagy (2008).

industry was stagnating and the consumer mortgage schemes were subsidised from 2002 to 2006 when the Hungarian economy was performing well. The demand for housing rapidly increased in Hungary due to the collapse of the social housing system after the changes in 1988, when large public housing assets created by the nationalisation of privately owned houses after the Second World War were either reclaimed by the previous owners or sold to the current tenants at affordable (social) prices. Thus, the public housing asset of the state and of the local communities suddenly disappeared and with 90 per cent ownership of the total housing Hungary became the leader in Europe in the number of privately owned residences. Moreover, the supply side on the housing market could not satisfy the demand generated by the increase in salaries around the year 2000. All these factors contributed to a significant increase in housing prices. Between 1998 and 2000 real estate prices increased by 132 per cent and the income of private persons increased by 46 per cent, whereas housing construction stagnated. Only 20,000 to 30,000 new homes were built annually. In addition, the loan subsidy programme was introduced in a period of low growth (between 2001 and 2003), when unfavourable developments in the domestic monetary and fiscal markets caused high level of interest rates for loans in HUF. At the beginning of 2002 the interest rates for loans in HUF ranged from 12.74 to 20 per cent.[15] After the introduction of the housing subsidy programme interest rates fell behind the interest rates of the market, with the consequence that the market of new houses started rising by 50 per cent annually. In the period between 2002 and 2004 subsidised mortgages amounted to 90 per cent.[16]

Even though the housing subsidies programme came to an end in 2004 and the construction market started declining, credit continued being supplied and demand for housing continued to remain high. Consumers continued seeking ‘easily’ affordable loan schemes, and foreign currency denominated loans provided the solutions. Between 2004 and 2008, the share of foreign currency denominated loans rose to 90 per cent.[17] This development was caused by mainly two factors.[18] First, interest rates for HUF loans were unfavourable compared to the interest rates for loans denominated in foreign currency. Second, foreign currency loan agreements often offered more attractive reimbursement characteristics, such as delayed reimbursement schemes. This was especially appealing to young people with families, who believed in an improvement of their reimbursement capacity over time. Moreover, the possible prospect of joining the Eurozone area generated the belief that the currency risks may be short term.

In general, little research can be found in Hungary on irresponsible borrowing or customer behaviour during the credit boom. However, assessments of debtor behaviour identified overconfidence, misplaced optimism concerning the labour market and income levels, and confirmation bias on loan risks as factors contributing to consumer over-indebtedness.[19] The optimism at the time of the credit boom (2005–2007) was based on the increase of the gross wages of full-time employees by 8–9 per cent and in the real value of the earnings by 40 per cent.[20]

15 Report of the Hungarian Competition Authority on market assessment conducted in the field of mortgage loan, made public in 2006.

16 Report of the Hungarian Competition Authority on market assessment conducted in the field of mortgage loan, made public in 2006.

17 Hegedűs (2013).

18 Kovács (2013).

19 Schepp and Pitz (2012: 18).

20 Government Ordinance no. 12/2001. (I. 31.) on housing state aids (21/2001, (I.31.) Korm. rendelet a lakáscélú támogatásokról) and Government Ordinance no. 4/2005 (I.12.) on state security on housing loan granted to young people (4/2005. Korm. rendelet a fiatalok lakáskölcsönéhez kapcsolódó állami kezesség vállalásának és érvényesítésének részletes szabályairól).

According to the statistics of the Hungarian National Bank 87 per cent of the housing mortgage loans, 89 per cent of the foreign currency loans, and 86 per cent of HUF loans were contracted by families in which at least one person was employed.

Another important factor for over-indebtedness is the market entry of people with poor financial education and skills to assess the medium- and long-term consequences of the complex long-term financial contracts, during the credit boom. Taking into account the use of unfair contractual terms on behalf of the banks, irresponsible borrowing could be defined as irresponsible contracting rather than irresponsible self-assessment of own reimbursement capacity in the medium and long run. The reimbursement obligations have so much increased upon the activation of the risk clauses by the credit institutions that even regardless of the effects of the financial crisis on employment and on real income, it would have been heavy burden for the debtor to repay the loans under the changed reimbursement conditions.

In conclusion, the consequences of market failures on the consumer credit market escalated with the global financial crisis. A lack of acknowledgement of the need for regulatory intervention in order to correct market failures and of the need for a consumer approach on private borrowing (more specifically the lack of effective judicial enforcement of the UCT Directive to stop the widespread use of unfair terms) created favourable grounds for the introduction and widespread use of risky loan schemes for consumers on the Hungarian consumer credit market, such as the loans denominated in foreign currency.

C. Legal Framework and the Role of Private Law

Regulatory measures limiting the far-reaching contractual freedom of the credit institutions and rules preventing irresponsible borrowing were introduced only at the beginning of 2010. In the absence of a more interventionist regulatory framework on consumer credit, general contract law is given increased importance. Since irresponsible lending practices were perceived as legally correct market behaviour at the time, many contracts reflecting such practices could not be challenged successfully under the general principles of contract law. At the same time, the consumer perspective based on European unfair contract terms law was missing from the judicial discourse of the courts during the first years after 2008.

Civil law courts played a fundamental role in the attempt to solve over-indebtedness problems, as they were the first ones, upon the initiative of the debtors, to react to the consequences of the risky loan agreements. The most common cases concerned the validity of the contract in order to stop enforcement, mostly challenging the clauses on unilateral amendment of the contract by the banks – or concerning the exchange rate mechanism in case of loans denominated in foreign currency. A significant number of cases are built on the private law concepts such as usury, sham, immorality, error, good faith and good morals, amongst others.[21] However, most of these cases failed, since the validity of the clauses transferring the full risk of the loan onto the debtor could not be successfully challenged under the general rules on contract validity of the Civil Code, which is based on the equality of the parties.

In contrast, no significant case law on the specific problems of mortgage law can be reported. Even though Hungary extended the material field of application of Directive 2008/48 through Law no. CLXII of 2009 to mortgage loan agreements, the Directive has so far not had any impact on

21 More details on the first-generation case law on consumer loan and the case law assessment of the Kúria in Józon (2014).

litigation. The few judgments issued before 2013 which employed the Hungarian implementing norms (Article 209 of the Civil Code) of the UCT Directive as legal basis show that the case law of the CJEU did not have significant impact on the Hungarian courts. According to the case law assessment of 2012 commissioned by the Kúria there was only one case in which the court conducted by its own motion an analysis of unfairness, despite the settled case law of the CJEU on the matter of *ex officio* assessments. This mirrors a lack of recognition of the Hungarian implementing rules as a mandatory law, which must necessarily apply in the specific case of consumer contracts. Both the legal literature and the Kúria remained mostly silent on the new problems of interpretation of domestic consumer credit law, while a wave of regulatory interventions into the loan agreements under the debtor rescue schemes implemented by the government started in 2010.

At the same time, the Hungarian courts did not make full use of the tools available under the Civil Code either in order to restore the contractual equilibrium between the parties affected by the global financial crisis. For example, lawyers and the courts were reluctant to make use of the *rebus sic stantibus* principle, ignoring that in long-term agreements the obligations of the parties may be imbalanced by unforeseen circumstances at contract conclusion. In its law unification decision no. 6/2013 issued in December 2013,[22] the Kúria emphasises that the courts may intervene into individual contracts concluded in the past only exceptionally under Article 241 of the Civil Code,[23] because it is impossible to solve in a satisfactory manner the social consequences of contracts for large groups through individual litigations. It considered the judicial problem solving to be time-consuming and costly compared to the possibilities of legislative intervention. One can perceive in this statement a larger concern for social issues than for prompt individual justice. Even though the Kúria rejected the potential of the principle *rebus sic stantibus* to remedy contracts with large social and economic impact, the Constitutional Court in its decision of 17 March 2014 reinforced the legitimacy of legislative intervention into contracts concluded in the past, with the reasoning that the change in circumstances affects large masses and can re-establish contractual balance under the same principles as those established by the *rebus sic stantibus*.[24] However, none of these highest courts acknowledged the specific regulatory needs and judicial needs of the debtors, as consumers. This is a paradox of the highest judicial level in search for ways out from the legal crisis generated by consumer over-indebtedness in Hungary

Perhaps the most unusual, paradigmatic feature of the judicial culture is that invalidity is perceived not as a way to terminate the contractual relation between the credit institution and the customer, but as a tool to stop or to delay contract enforcement and eviction. Thus, Article 249A of the Civil Code allowed the defendant to ask the court for a declaratory judgment when challenging contract validity, without an actual ruling on the legal consequences of the invalidity between the parties. Therefore, in many cases the parties had to deal with the consequences of invalidity by themselves either through an out-of-court settlement, including a deal with the bank, or within a subsequent litigation. This phenomenon cannot be considered an effective tool of contractual justice. Often, as a result of the legal uncertainty surrounding invalidity and its legal consequences, the debtors stop paying monthly instalments, without cooperating with the credit institutions, in order to render the contractual relationship in the hope of new rescue measures from the government. At the same time, the banks did not insist on evictions either. The eviction quota introduced in 2011was never fully used.

22 Decision no. 6 of 2013 of the Kúria.

23 Article 241 Civil Code: the court may amend long-term contracts when circumstances subsequent to contract conclusion substantially affect the interest of one of the contracting parties.

24 Decision no. 8 of 2014 of the Constitutional Court.

The *Kásler*[25] reference marked the beginning of a new development stage, where the courts started using the case law of the CJEU. By the end of 2013, the first final judgments were delivered, which were based on the UCT Directive 93/13 and the case law of the CJEU, most prominently the *Banco Español* case.[26] Even though the *Kásler* ruling raises further questions, the case should be qualified as a major step on the road to more effective enforcement of unfair contract terms law in Hungary. It was now confirmed by the CJEU that where the contract could not be kept in force without the unfair term, courts can substitute the term with provisions of national law. Besides the answers of the CJEU on the specific questions referred to it by the Hungarian Kúria, the *Kásler* ruling provides impetus to the Hungarian courts as regards the value and role of individual justice in the field of consumer over-indebtedness.[27]

However, the CJEU ruling, which put end to the standby attitude of the Kúria for unfair contract terms law, it did not fully overturn the Kúria's stance concerning the role and share of individual justice and case-law in remedying contractual injustice for over-indebted consumers. Although the law unification decision of 16 June 2014[28] issued upon the *Kásler* ruling of the CJEU, presents the idea that mandatory rules will in the future substitute unfair contract terms when unfairness would endanger the existence of the loan agreement, it narrowed down the room of the courts to the dispositive rules (*lex generalis*) of the old Civil Code (Article 234, Paragraph 2) in place at the moment of contract conclusion until special mandatory rules will be adopted in the future. The Kúria was bound both in the *Kásler* judgement issued on 3 June 2014 in the case that gave rise to the preliminary ruling and in the law unification decision issued on 16 June 2014 to its own wording of the question referred to the CJEU, which limited the judicial intervention to dispositive rules of the private law. Although the CJEU in its ruling answered the question in general terms, meaning that the national courts can substitute the unfair terms with the provisions of the private law, the Hungarian version of the ruling of the CJEU uses the initial wording of the reference in light of the policy of the referring court (the Kúria), as confirmed by its subsequent judgment and the law unification decision. This means that upon the ruling of the CJEU the Hungarian highest court is (even if temporarily) again back in the safe harbour of general contract law. It also shifts the policy decision to the legislature with regard to the consequences for the parties of finding unfairness of a contract term. Thus, the Hungarian courts do not have the instruments required to provide individual justice to over-indebted consumers under the *Kásler* judgment and law unification decision of the Kúria. Instead, the Kúria has again invited the government to take legislative measures. In fact the Kúria was seeking the green light from Luxembourg for further retroactive legislative intervention into contracts concluded in the past.

In this context is worth mentioning that at the end of 2013, in an attempt to persuade the judiciary in the direction of a more proactive attitude on handling the private law consequences of consumer over-indebtedness, the government requested constitutional judicial review of the laws under which the loan agreements were concluded in the past, of the civil court decisions, and of the loan agreements. The government proceeded this way, although in Hungary the probability to persuade the courts by constitutional tools in the direction of more effective consumer protection is low, because in the new Hungarian Constitution enacted in 2011 consumer protection is an ancillary obligation of the state rather than an independent right of consumers.[29] Although in its

25 Case C-26/13 *Kásler and Hajnalka Káslerné Rébai v. OTP Jelzálogbank Zrt.*

26 C-618/10 *Banco Espaniol de Credito SA v. Joaquin Calderon Camino.*

27 On the policy impact and judicial reaction on the Kásler ruling of the CJEU see Józon (2014).

28 Decision no. 2 of 2014 of the Kúria.

29 Article M (2) of the Constitution stipulates that 'Hungary shall ensure the conditions of fair economic competition and act against any abuse of a dominant position and shall defend the rights of consumers'.

decision issued on 17 March 2014 the Constitutional Court declined to deal with this issue, the request for constitutional review was a useful exercise for opening in Hungary the policy and academic debate on the borderlines of fundamental rights and consumer law.

We can conclude that in recent years there has been a lot of confusion about the function and role of private law and regulatory law with regard to consumer over-indebtedness. The post-*Kásler* judicial developments seem to confirm this. However, the government has always given the floor to the judiciary first before advancing legislative intervention into private law in the form of mandatory rules.

D. Policy Responses to Over-Indebtedness

In 2010, a new government took over, committed to mitigate the social and economic consequences of over-indebtedness. It limited the extent of market liberalism and unfair marketing practices in order to stop the accumulation of new badly performing debts. It also had to cure the social and macro-economic impacts of over-indebtedness taking into account distributive justice and social solidarity, instead of considering over-indebtedness as a private matter. Hungary does not yet have in place a law on bankruptcy of private persons.

Among the new regulatory measures governing consumer credit, the most important ones are those on compulsory creditworthiness, the establishment of a central credit information system, compulsory pre-contractual information, conditioning of foreign currency denominated loans on earnings in foreign currency, the introduction of new loan-to-value criteria in granting loans, limitations on unilateral amendments of the contracts, mandatory requirements on the description of the financial burden of the debtors, and stricter rules on the professional training and activity of the financial intermediaries.

As regards loans denominated in foreign currency, Law no. XCVI of 2010 prescribes that the conversion of HUF both at the time of the availability of the loan for the client and at the time of reimbursement should be either at the exchange average rate established by the bank or at the official exchange rate of the National Bank of Hungary. In addition, Article 209(1)(g) obliges financial institutions to determine in the general conditions and terms, the calculation method employed and the point in time in which the amount in HUF will be established for the reimbursement of the loan. Moreover, the total loan indicator may not contain the prolongation costs, default payments and other charges related to non-performance, insurance fees and security charges, and the cost of banking transfer. Law CXXI of 2011 also establishes in Article 200(5a) that in case of loans denominated in foreign currency the credit institution can charge the debtor in that currency only those costs which are directly related to the acquisition of the foreign currency necessary for the implementation of the loan agreement, including the interest rate. This excludes the costs related to contract conclusion, correspondence, statistics, certificates, loan monitoring, termination of the contract, assessment of the security or replacement of the security, amendment of the contract, insurance, as well as costs and charges related to the loan agreement management or the loan account. Financial institutions are allowed to conclude mortgage loan agreements in foreign currency only with persons who have at the moment of the submission of the loan request a monthly net income in the currency of the loan that is equal to 15 times the value of the basic income of a full-time employee, as established by the National Bank of Hungary. This restriction does not apply to financial leasing.

Creditworthiness assessment became compulsory with the implementing rules of Directive 2008/48 (Law CLXII and Government Ordinance no. 361/2009). According to Article 3(1) it is forbidden to grant loans only on the basis of the loan risk ratio. The credit institution must assess the creditworthiness and solvency of the person in every single case based on the assessment of the incomes of the applicant and on the credit limit based on income. This law obliges the financial institutions to hand over to the potential debtor the information published on the website of the Hungarian National Bank and HFSA on the risks of indebtedness.[30] Furthermore, specific loan limits are established for different loan types. Accordingly, the monthly reimbursement limit at the moment of approval of the loan request cannot be higher than 80 per cent of the loan limit for euro-based loans. The threshold is 60 per cent for loans denominated in other foreign currencies. The limitations do not apply when the debtor has regular income in the currency of the loan and this income is at least equal to all his monthly reimbursement obligations. When establishing the loan limit, the financial institution must take into account all loans the applicant may have with the same or other financial institutions. The credit institution is also obliged to act with 'due care' and make use of all information available in the credit information systems. The rules on loans granted for the purchase of automobiles establish a risk exposure of 75 per cent of the market value of the automobile of 75 per cent for financial leasing in HUF, and of 60 per cent for euro loans. For other currencies the rate is 45 per cent for mortgage and 50 per cent for financial leasing. Special rules apply for mortgage loans. For example, for HUF loans the risk exposure cannot exceed 75 per cent of the commercial value of the immovable, whereas for mortgage loans in euro this is 60 per cent.

The Central Credit Information System (CCIS) based on mandatory information sharing by banks was set up in 2011 by Law CXXII of 2011. The CCIS is administered by BISZ Zrt. (a profit-oriented limited liability company).[31] The CCIS records both positive and negative data on consumer credit, including information on credit agreements, default or bank card fraud.

New rules in force since 2010 limit the possibility of unilateral amendment of loan agreements and financial leasing agreements as regards the interest rate, charges and costs of credit (see Law no. LXXXVI of 2009). However, the creditors can only exercise their right to unilaterally amend the contract if the contract explicitly contains the objective circumstances of such amendment. Furthermore, Law XCVI of 2010 introduces a new provision prohibiting – under the sanction of nullity – the unilateral amendment of loan and leasing agreements for housing purposes to the detriment of the debtor.

Finally, the framework law on the functioning of the financial institutions was replaced at the end of 2013 by Law CCXXXVII of 2013, which includes strict provisions on debtor protection, such as rules on mandatory pre-contractual information, the calculation of costs and charges, the unilateral amendment of the contract, as well as notification obligations of the credit institutions during contract implementation. Moreover, according to Article 266 a loan agreement which is secured by the immovable, which the debtor actually uses as home, is void. It is forbidden to apply a THM (*teljes hiteldíj mutató*, or total loan indicator) which exceeds by more than 24 points the basis interest rate of the National Bank of Hungary. Consumers are protected against arbitrary amendments of the loan agreement by the banks by the rule that interest rates, charges, costs and fees can be amended only on the basis of the actual influence of reasons that justify the amendment and that if circumstances justify the reduction of costs and charges, the reduction should take place. The Law also provides that the reasons of amendment should be assessed in their interplay and their actual effects on the costs, charges and fees. Fees and charges can be amended once a year on the basis of the consumer price index of the Central Statistical Office.

---

30 The information is available at http://felugyelet.mnb.hu/data/cms2152112/tajek_tulzott_eladosodas.pdf.

31 More information on the CCIS at www.bisz.hu/english.

In order to mitigate the social and economic effects of loans contracts denominated in foreign currency, several provisions establish rules concerning the final payment of the debt, an interest rate cap and prolonged reimbursement of the loan, reconversion of the loan from foreign currency into national currency, purchase of the debt by the state with the possibility of use and subsequent repurchase of the immovable by the debtor. The debtor rescue schemes targeted different categories of debtors in payment difficulty and were not introduced at the same time as alternatives, but as part of a process, one measure following the other. The government adopted a progressive, step-by-step strategy testing the reaction of the market and of the judiciary.

Final mortgage repayment was the first rescue measure for debtors with foreign currency mortgage loans. Under Law CXXI of 2011, debtors having loans in foreign currency have the possibility to reimburse the loan at once at a fixed exchange rate set by law (1 CHF = 180 HUF and 1 EUR = 280 HUF). During 2011–2012 169,256 persons indebted with loans in foreign currency made use of final mortgage payment and 23 per cent of the performing foreign exchange loans were repaid.[32] Moreover, Law XVI of 2012 set a deadline of 31 August 2012 for the credit institutions to convert existing loans denominated in foreign currency into HUF at the average exchange rate of the National Bank of Hungary during the period of 15 May 2012 to 15 June 2012. Under this scheme, debtors could choose to convert foreign currency loans in default for at least 90 days into HUF facilities, with a simultaneous write-off of 25 per cent of their entire debt, provided that the value of the mortgaged immovable was less than 20 million HUF and not yet under eviction. The credit institutions were not allowed to charge the debtors with extra costs and fees for the reconversion of the loan into HUF.

An exchange rate ban was introduced by Law LXXV of 2011. It involves the possibility for debtors to repay the loan during a five-year period (between May 2012 and May 2017) at a fixed exchange rate (1 CHF = 180 HUF, 1 EUR = 250 HUF and 1 Japan JPY = 2.5 HUF). In turn, debtors are relieved of the interest rate for the amount above the fixed exchange rate, which is being paid by the state and the bank. The difference between the actual exchange rate and the fixed exchange rate accumulates on a pool account, which constitutes a HUF-based loan. After five years the debtor will start paying the initial loan at the actual exchange rate and, in addition, he will reimburse the debt accumulated on the pool account. The amount to be reimbursed cannot be higher than 15 per cent of the last instalment paid by the debtor before the termination of the interest rate ban, including the interest rate and other costs of the loan and the period of reimbursement of the amount accumulated on the pool account cannot exceed the length of the initial loan with more than 30 years. This scheme was available to those with payment delays of not more than 90 days, a loan expiring before 31 December 2014 and a mortgaged immovable property with a commercial value of not more than 30 million HUF, not yet under eviction. Until August 2012, when the programme on the conversion of foreign currency denominated loans into HUF ended, HUF 23 billion worth of defaulted foreign currency loans were converted, amounting to a 4 per cent participation rate. Thus this programme did not have any measurable impact on the NPL rate.[33] Until 30 April 2013 more than 158,000 contracts were signed for the repayment of the loans at a fixed exchange rate. For nearly 150,000 of these cases a pool account was also opened. Loan agreements protected by an exchange rate barrier represent more than half of the restructured mortgages, 35 per cent of the eligible consumers joined the programme on exchange rate ban.[34]

32 Risk Report of the Hungarian Financial Supervisory Authority (June 2013).

33 Risk Report of the Hungarian Financial Supervisory Authority (June 2013).

34 Risk Report of the Hungarian Financial Supervisory Authority (June 2013).

For both HUF and foreign currency debtors in default for over one year, Law CLXX of 2011 provides an ultimate solution to have the debts and immovables purchased by the state. The National Asset Management Company (NAMC) purchases the mortgaged immovable property at a discount price from the credit institutions and will then use it for renting purposes. The immovable properties are bought by the state at a price of 55 per cent (in Budapest and cities) and 35 per cent (in rural areas and villages) of their commercial value as established in the mortgage agreement. This scheme was introduced to assist households in social difficulty, who resided in the mortgaged immovable property before 28 September 2011, with a commercial value of the mortgaged immovable at contract conclusion of not more than 20 million HUF in Budapest and other cities, and no more than 15 million HUF in other areas. At the end of 2013, 13,000 properties were available for purchase by the NAMC. The budget of the NAMC allows the acquisition of another 25,000 properties until the end of the programme.

At the same time, an eviction quota system was established in 2011 and periodical eviction bans were adopted to stop and mitigate the rising number of evictions.[35] Since the number of evictions was low even before the introduction of the quota, the quota was never exhausted by the banks.[36] This means that the debtors are not threatened by the credit institutions to terminate the contracts and enforce the mortgages.

E. Conclusions

A major finding of the research carried out for the purposes of this chapter is the role of paradigms within the development of financial products and marketing techniques of the credit institutions, the reaction of the Hungarians to these products, the reaction of the state institutions and of the society to over-indebtedness. Paradigms are more powerful than policies and politics and therefore strongly frame the search for the ways out from the crisis. Considering the paradigms of the past and present in designing regulatory solutions and judicial policies may act as an engine of the reforms since different interest groups share 'commons' rooted in paradigms that may promote the dialogue of stakeholders in the search for affordable economic, social, political and legal solutions.

The main lesson from the crisis of Hungarian private law is that despite painful legislative interventions into private law, crisis management is strongly influenced by judicial paradigms and less by the positive law, being that European or domestic. The post-*Kásler* developments in the Kúria's policy reinforced that judicial culture continues to be a strong driving force of developments in consumer contract law in Hungary.

The debtor rescue measures prevented large-scale evictions in Hungary and thus social exclusion of over-indebted citizens. However, the assessment of the consumer credit case law revealed that *consumer justice*[37] did not develop under the new judicial needs generated by consumer over-indebtedness into a fully functioning tool. The reaction of the Hungarian judiciary to consumer over-indebtedness brought to the surface how weak was the manner in which consumer policy is entrenched in Hungarian private law thinking and judicial culture. Indebted consumers protected by the debtor rescue measures continue to remain highly vulnerable, lacking a firm consumer-oriented private justice that views the debtors as the weaker party in need of special protection.

35 Law LXXV of 2011.

36 More information on the use of the eviction quota is available at https://felugyelet.mnb.hu/data/cms2409345/fv_kockazati_jelentes_2013_II.pdf.

37 With the term 'consumer justice' the author refers to individual justice provided to consumers under consumer legislation.

A change seems to have occurred in 2013 at the level of first instance courts and appeal courts in Hungary and upon the Kásler ruling of the CJEU at the Kúria in mid-2014. However, it is too early to evaluate the impact of the recently issued law unification decision no. 2/2014 of the Kúria on this positive development.

The regulatory measures adopted during the period of 2010 to 2013 aim at preventing the accumulation of new badly performing debts, protecting private persons from irresponsible lending through restrictions imposed on credit institutions and through opening the possibility to either terminate the contract by performing under different conditions than initially agreed with the bank, or to continue contract implementation under a more affordable reimbursement scheme (interest rate caps and extension of the period and lower monthly instalments). However, consumer over-indebtedness is still prevalent in Hungary and tools are still needed to address the *process* in its full dimension, not only the phenomenon, including the consequences of the *contractual dynamism* resulting from regulatory interventions and that of finding unfairness.

At the beginning of 2014, there were more than 2,000 pending civil law litigations in Hungary, and several thousand indebted consumers under contracts concluded under the legal framework of the past waiting for the *Kásler* ruling of the CJEU to proceed in court. The main question was what kind of restoration is possible in these cases, after the past years were spent on gaining time by delaying evictions and keeping in effect the loan agreements under restructured burdens or delayed enforcement. Most of the legislative interventions in contracts did not tackle the very heart of the private law dimension of long-term, sophisticated financial contracts.

Hungarian private law and the judiciary were unprepared to handle the judicial needs arising from global financial services. One could even say that consumer over-indebtedness resulted in a crisis of private law and civil justice in Hungary. Consumer over-indebtedness has challenged the unity and pureness of Hungarian civil law more than the European private law did over the past 15 years. The lack of systemic approach and the delayed and defective reaction of civil judiciary resulted in the past in the misuse of other instruments, such as the attempt to achieve constitutional review of the private law rules, civil court decisions and private contracts, in search for remedies or the outsourcing of the crisis of Hungarian private law to the CJEU in Luxembourg.

Regulatory law cannot and should not substitute the role and function of private law and individual justice. Otherwise the system of private law would be threatened by the monopolising character of regulatory law, and the effectiveness of regulatory law would be at stake, since general contract law deals with many aspects of consumer credit that are outside the domain of regulatory law.

The legal consequences of consumer over-indebtedness are as important as the economic and social ones. The assessment of national policies, regulatory measures and judicial responses to the crisis necessarily touches upon broader, theoretical issues. Countries struggling with consumer over-indebtedness are 'exporting' judicial problems to the EU level, seeking solutions within the EU law. In this way, the CJEU assumes an increasing role in the judicial unification of the unfair contract law in Europe. This process raises further regulatory questions for Europe, such as: whether traditional contract law or even the European unfair contract terms law effectively handle the enforcement problems of long-term financial contracts; what would be the new division of tasks between private law and regulatory law, codified and court-made law in response to the specific regulatory and judicial needs of consumer credit; can national or European policies on financial services effectively control the cross-border externalities of the financial markets that are led by global policies; is the 'information and choice based' consumer law sufficient, given national or European to cure financial market failures; what room should be left to the Member

States for market intervention along domestic conditionality under the EU policy on consumer credit and financial services?

The factors resulting in consumer over-indebtedness question the suitability of the information and choice-based approach of the European consumer policy with regard to its ability to prevent and remedy the information asymmetry of private persons in the financial services market. The information asymmetry of the private persons on highly technical markets such as banking and finance renders them incapable of being active market players able to correct market failures. More state intervention into the market and more paternalism is thus justified, in the form of collective protection, including procedural rules.

The potential of the European unfair contract terms law should be further explored by the Member States and the CJEU in the search for legal solutions, especially on the consequences of finding unfairness in the case of standard contracts being employed by the banks on a large scale, bearing in mind the requirements of efficient administration of justice when large categories are affected by the same legal problems. Upon the recently issued *Kásler* ruling, it seems that the CJEU had actually assumed this task, as it acknowledged that in case of long-term contracts, where the circumstance may change in time, instruments should be in place that are able to handle the effects of unforeseen circumstances. Solutions that focus on the moment of contract conclusion may not suffice for this purpose. The problems of interpretation related to unfair contract terms law demonstrate that a fully functional unfair contract terms law demands the modernisation of the principles of general contract law and also of the civil procedural law having in mind the specific enforcement problems of long-term consumer contracts.

The questions of how private law can handle irresponsible lending and borrowing and what future there is for self-responsibility in consumer contract law in an interplay of self-governance and regulatory law on the consumer credit market remain unanswered.

References

Case Law Assessment on Unilateral Amendment of Consumer Credit Contracts, commissioned by the Kúria. A fogyasztói kölcsönszerződésben pénzügyi intézmény által alkalmazott általános szerződési feltételekben szereplő egyoldalú szerződésmódosítás tisztességtelensége megítélése tárgykörben felállított joggyakorlat-elemző csoport összefoglaló véleménye. Available at: http://www.lb.hu/sites/default/files/joggyak/joggyakorlat_osszefoglalo_velemeny.pd.

Hegedűs, J. 2013. '"Unorthodox" Housing Policy in Hungary: Is there a Way Back to Public Housing?' in J. Chen, M. Stephens and J.Y. Man (eds) *The Future of Public Housing: Trends in the East and the West*, Springer, pp. 279–302.

Józon, M. 2014. 'Hungary' in I. Domurath, G. Comparato and H-W. Micklitz (eds) *The Over Indebtedness of European Consumers – a View from Six Countries*, EUI Working Paper LAW no.2014/10.

Király, J. and Nagy, M. 2008. 'Jelzálogpiacok válságban: Kockázatalapú verseny és tanulságok' ['Mortgage Markets in Crisis: Risk Competition and Lessons'], *Hitelintézeti Szemle*, 7(5), pp. 451–480.

Kovács, L. 2013. 'A devizahitelek háttere' ['The Background of Loans Denominated in Foreign Currency'], *Hitelintézeti Szemle*, 12(3), p. 184.

'Level and Structure of Household Consumptions 2011'. 2012. *Statisztikai Tükör*, VI(106) (A háztartások havi fogyasztásának színvonala és szerkezete, 2011, *Statisztikai Tükör*,

VI. évfolyam, 106. szám, 2012. December 20). Available at: http://www.ksh.hu/docs/hun/xftp/stattukor/haztfogy_haztfogy11.pdf.

Report of the Hungarian Competition Authority on market assessment conducted in the field of mortgage loan, made public in 2006. Jelentés a jelzáloghitelezés tárgyában lefolytatott ágazati vizsgálatról. Available at: http://www.gvh.hu/dontesek/agazati_vizsgalatok/2366_hu_jelentes_a_jelzaloghitelezes_targyaban_lefolytatott_agazati_vizsgalatrol.html.

Report of the Hungarian Financial Supervisory Authority on Financial Stability, November 2013. Jelentés a pénzügyi stabilitásról, 2013 November. Available at: http://www.mnb.hu/Root/Dokumentumtar/MNB/Statisztika/mnbhu_statisztikai_idosorok/penzugyi-stabilitasi-statisztikak/H34_Tajekoztato_2013_q4_hu.pdf.

Report of the Hungarian Statistical Office on Housing, 2010. *KSH Társadalmi Helyzetkép* 2010, Lakáshelyzet, pp. 18–19.

Risk Report of the Hungarian Financial Supervisory Authority. June 2013. *PSZÁF Kockázati Jelentés*, 2013 június. Available at: https://felugyelet.mnb.hu/data/cms2401408/kockazati_jelentes_2013_I.pdf.

Schepp, Z. and Pitz, M. 2012. 'Lakossági devizahitelezés Magyarországon: problémafelmérés és a frankhitelek banki árazásának empirikus vizsgálata' ['Consumer Loans Denominated in Foreign Currency in Hungary, Problem Setting and Empirical Study on Pricing of Loans Denominated in Foreign Currency'], Műhelytanulmányok [Working Paper] 2012/3, p. 18.

Szigel, G. and Fáykiss, P. 2012. *The Effect of Indebtedness on the Financial and Income Position of Hungarian Households*, MNB Bulletin, February.

Hungarian Cases

Decision no. 8 of 2014 of the Constitutional Court (8/2014 (II.2) AB határozat http://public.mkab.hu/dev/dontesek.nsf/0/EE3A84E45401B26EC1257C32006000E6?Open Document).

Decision no. 6 of 2013 of the Kúria (6/2013 sz. PJE határozat http://www.lb.hu/hu/joghat/62013-szamu-pje-hatarozat).

Decision no. 2 of 2014 of the Kúria (2/2014. számú PJE Határozat http://www.lb.hu/print/joghat/22014-szamu-pje-hatarozat).

Judgement no. GfV. IX. 30. 211/2011 of the Kúria (Gfv. IX. 30. 211/2011 no. 6 adopted on September 27, 2011).

Press release of the Kúria on case GFv. VII. 30.078/2013 (Sajtóközlemény a Gfv.VII.30.078/2013 számú ügyről, http://www.lb.hu/hu/sajto/sajtokozlemeny-gfvvii30078 2013-szamu-ugyrol).

Judgement of December 6, 2013 of the Appeal Court of Budapest (http://fovarosiitelotabla.birosag.hu/sajtokozlemeny/20131210/fovarosi-itelotabla-5-pf-tanacsa-2013-december-6-devizahitel-ugyben-).

Judgement no. 9 of 2013 of the Court of Appeal of Pécs.

CJEU Cases

Case C-26/13 *Kásler and Hajnalka Káslerné Rébai v. OTP Jelzálogbank Zrt.*

Case C-618/10 *Banco Espaniol de Credito SA v. Joaquin Calderon Camino.*

Chapter 7
Country Report Iceland

M. Elvira Méndez Pinedo and Irina Domurath[1]

A. Introduction[2]

Iceland was the first European country that was hit by the global financial crisis. Within a few weeks in October 2008, all three main commercial Icelandic banks faced bankruptcy. An emergency law[3] was adopted that gave the Financial Supervision Authority the powers to initiate the winding-up and resolution of the old banks and the creation of new banks, to which all resident deposits in Iceland were transferred. With the procedure still ongoing, two banks (Arion, Íslandsbanki) were privatized again, while the other (Landsbanki) is still in public hands – its resolution complicated by the 'Icesave-case' concerning guarantees towards depositors from the UK and the Netherlands.

The financial crisis was followed by a deep economic and political crisis. Public protests in late 2008 and early 2009 forced the social-democrat and conservative government to resign. New elections led to a social-democratic-left Green coalition, which worked together with the IMF to stabilise the country's financial, monetary and economic policies. Even though Iceland has recovered remarkably well in macro-economic terms, many Icelandic households are still struggling with high levels of indebtedness. In the boom years between 2000 and 2007, indebtedness had been growing significantly,[4] until it turned into over-indebtedness in the aftermath of the financial crisis. In the context of falling housing prices, the rise of unemployment, the indexation of credit to foreign currencies and/or inflation, and a dramatic devaluation of the local currency, indebted households were no longer able to service their debts. Many had to take recourse to different procedures to alleviate their monthly debt burdens and/or rearrange their financial commitments to serve outstanding debts. Despite important efforts of the government to address over-indebtedness and alleviate debt burdens in the last years, debt relief for households was an important issue in the general elections held in 2013, in which the liberal party, which had promised debt relief for households,secured 24.4 per cent of votes and entered a coalition with conservative party that had won 26.7 per cent of votes. The coalition was led by a Prime Minister that put debt-relief top of the agenda.

1 The authors would like to thank Gudmundur Àsgeirsson and Sigurdur Sigurdsson for their valuable assistance in the data collection.

2 Data on the issues covered in this contribution can be found in I. Domurath, G. Comparato and H-W. Micklitz (eds) *The Over Indebtedness of European Consumers – a View from Six Countries*, EUI Working Paper LAW no.2014/10.

3 Act No 125/2008 on the Authority for Treasury Disbursements due to Unusual Financial Market Circumstances … adopted 08.10.2008, available (in Icelandic) at www.althingi.is.

4 T.T. Ólafsson and K.A. Vignisdóttir, 'Households' Position in the Financial Crisis in Iceland', Central Bank of Iceland Working Paper No. 59, June 2012, p. 76, available at http://www.cb.is/library/Skrper centC3per centA1arsafn---EN/Working-Papers/Workingper cent20Paperper cent2059.pdf.

B. The Financial and Social Problems of Over-Indebted Consumers in Iceland

While indebtedness levels in Iceland have largely followed international patterns, they have traditionally been higher than elsewhere – as for example in the United States, Norway or the Euro area as a whole. When the crisis struck, Icelandic households were among the most indebted in world.[5] In the year 2012 there were between 120,745[6] and 154,694[7] households with some kind of loan (mortgage, car loan or overdraft). This means that almost 80 per cent of Icelandic households, or 38.59 per cent of the total population (including children) are indebted.

Even though over-indebtedness is difficult to measure due to a lack of a uniform definition of 'over-indebtedness' and the use of different parameters to grasp the difficulties of Icelandic consumers, it is clear that following the crisis and the deterioration of the financial situation of many households, over-indebtedness levels have risen. The Central Bank of Iceland uses the term 'households in distress', which is defined as households with 'a negative financial margin', meaning that 'their disposable income is insufficient to cover both debt service and necessary minimum living expenses'.[8] Even though 'financial distress' alone does not necessarily lead to default on debt payments,[9] it is illustrative to note that the share of households in distress almost doubled from 12.05 per cent to 23.05 per cent between early 2007 and autumn 2008, with 'acute distress' rates nearly quadrupling over the same period. The share of households in distress then peaked at 27.05 per cent in autumn 2009, before falling to about 20 per cent at the end of 2010, in the context of governmental forbearance efforts aimed at providing temporary breathing space.[10]

Total numbers on over-indebtedness in Iceland provided by the Central Bank and the Statistic Office (Statistics Iceland) are relative and must be set in context.[11] According to information from the Tax Authority based on the fiscal year 2013, Icelandic households had a total debt of 1,785,000 million ISK (around 11.61 million EUR).[12] Divided by 145,137 families the average debt is about 12.3 million ISK per family. According to Statistics Iceland, the average debt per family in Iceland is 10.2 million ISK (around 66,346 EUR) and average mortgage per family is 6.5 million ISK taking into account all population. If we take into account only indebted families, the average debt is 12.4 million ISK (around 80,650 EUR). Average debt is as follows. 76,464 individuals owe on average 6.5 million ISK, 14,748 single parents owe on average 11.6 million ISK, 32,000 couples without children owe on average 14.3 million ISK and 31,482 couples with children owe on average 25.4 million ISK.[13]

5 Ólafsson and Vignisdóttir (2012), pp. 8 and 9.

6 Ólafsson and Vignisdóttir (2012) p. 15.

7 In 2014 there was a total of 126,581 housing units in Iceland. Data from Statistics Iceland available at www.statice.is.

8 Ólafsson and Vignisdóttir (2012) p. 4.

9 Ólafsson and Vignisdóttir (2012) p. 30.

10 Ólafsson and Vignisdóttir (2012) p. 5.

11 The Icelandic Central Bank uses primary data from tax authorities combined with primary data provided by financial institutions. Statistics Iceland uses tax return data in combination with independent analysis based on household survey which is estimated and represented as such. The different methodologies rely on a similar definition of 'household', with a tendency to overestimate the number of singles and underestimate the number of nuclear families. For example, individuals older than 16 are considered to be independent households although they may still live with their parent(s).

12 Exchange rate 153.74 ISK = 1 EUR, as of 9 June 2014.

13 Data from Statistics Iceland available at www.statice.is.

Most Icelandic consumers have more than one kind of credit obligation. The vast majority of the debt consists of mortgages (84,600 households), motor vehicle loans (46,900 households) or a combination of the two (34,900 households).[14] Credit card and overdraft facility credit agreements are also widespread. Motor vehicle debt contracted during the boom years 2004–2008 proved to be a particularly difficult source of debt as the vast majority was denominated in foreign currency (FX-nomination). This led to one of the major problems of over-indebtedness in Iceland (see below).

Housing loans play an important role in the indebtedness and over-indebtedness of Icelandic consumers. Home ownership in Iceland is one of the world's highest.[15] In 2009 the total of privately owned property was 99,965 or 77 per cent of all residential property. Just over 85 per cent of all Icelandic people lived in their own property in that year.[16] The number of new mortgages rose continuously in the last decades until 2007, from 5,809 in 1990 and 10,100 in 2000 to 15,252 in 2007.[17] This changed in the aftermath of the financial crisis. In 2012, this figure had decreased to 7,623. Simultaneously, the financial situation of households deteriorated very quickly. For almost 30 per cent of households housing cost was considered a heavy burden and around 10 per cent are in 'arrears' on mortgage or rent payments.[18]

The incidence of negative housing equity (amount owed is higher than the registered/market value of the property) increased 'dramatically' from around 6 per cent in 2007 to 37 per cent of indebted homeowners in 2010.[19] In the last years, the Ministry of Labour has observed a slightly favourable trend. While the number of families with negative housing equity remained stable until 2007 (around 5,000–7,000 households), and went up to 25,000 at end of 2010, in 2011 this figure went down to 21,000 households, and further down in 2012 to 17,780.[20] Since 2013 a rapid diminution of the incidence of negative housing equity has been expected, following the re-calculation of FX-indexed loans, and debt-mitigation and fiscal public policies implemented in 2011 and 2012 (see below).

It is difficult to provide a coherent picture on the households that are most affected by over-indebtedness. There is no definition of 'vulnerability' in the Icelandic legal framework or in European consumer credit law. However, the Icelandic Central Bank equates simultaneous 'financial distress and negative housing equity' with 'exceptional' or 'high' vulnerability.[21] This vulnerability seems to be common among low-income singles and middle-income families with children, many of which had foreign-denominated loans.[22] Young parents, who entered the housing market late in the housing upswing between 2004 and 2008 are in an 'exceptionally vulnerable position' as regards housing equity.[23] This can probably be explained by the participation of younger people in the

14 Ólafsson and Vignisdóttir (2012) p. 16.

15 For further reference see J.R. Sveinsson, 'The Formation of Urban Homeownership in Iceland', Cambridge Conference Paper, available at https://borg.hi.is/Theper cent20Formationper cent20ofper cent20Urbanper cent20Housingper cent20Policyper cent20inper cent20Iceland.pdf.

16 Ministry of Welfare, 'Skýrsla samráðshóps um húsnæðisstefnu' ('Report of Specialist Group on a Housing Policy') 2011, pp. 21 and 22, available at http://www.velferdarraduneyti.is/media/frettir2011/19042011_Skyrsla_samradshops_um_husnaedisstefnu.pdf.

17 National Registry, Chart 2012 available at http://www.skra.is/library/Samnyttar-skrar-/Markadsfrettir/tafla2.1_2012.xls.

18 Data from Statistics Iceland available at www.statice.is.

19 Ólafsson and Vignisdóttir (2012) p. 5.

20 Data from Statistics Iceland available at http://www.statice.is/pages/2980.

21 Ólafsson and Vignisdóttir (2012) p. 6.

22 Ólafsson and Vignisdóttir (2012) p. 6.

23 Ólafsson and Vignisdóttir (2012) p. 55.

housing boom, while older people may have inherited their property or have been further along in the repayment of their mortgages when the crisis hit. Moreover, by entering the market in the years of the housing boom, young people entered the housing market also at a time when FX-nomination was a widespread practice.

If we look at the parameters of financial distress and negative housing equity separately, the following picture emerges. Financial distress affects young individuals,[24] low-income consumers, families with children, and those with foreign-denominated debt.[25] In October 2010, these were around 47 per cent in the lowest income quintile group, 20 per cent in the middle-income quintile, and only 2 per cent in the highest income quintile group.[26] As regards negative housing equity, the picture is inverted. Negative housing equity is more widespread among high-income households.[27] This can be explained by the phenomenon that this group purchased more expensive property, while having higher purchasing power, which enabled them to make larger down payments. Many high-income households – especially young households that had experienced rapid income increases in the years before the crisis – made use of their debt service capacity to take on large mortgage debt. So they purchased real estate with high loan-to-value ratios and combined foreign- and ISK-denominated mortgages, thereby exposing themselves to both exchange rate and inflation risk.[28] Furthermore, it is likely that financial institutions were more reluctant to grant loans with high loan-to-value ratios to low-income families.[29]

In general, over-indebtedness, negative equity and financial distress in a context of an economic crisis tend to increase the number of evictions and forced sales of property. This has not been the case in Iceland, since the regulator implemented several (also temporal) measures to prevent the turning of non-performing housing loans into evictions (ie. moratoria).

C. Causes of Over-Indebtedness in Iceland

The causes of the over-indebtedness of Icelandic households are manifold and reflect the interplay of many different factors, as they range from economic and structural problems to behavioural issues.

Macro-Economic Causes

First of all, when we focus on over-indebtedness and mortgage credit, we have to take into account that Iceland – with limited exceptions in some remote areas – has experienced a housing bubble in the years before the crisis, the bursting of which has left many households with negative housing equity. Real house prices (albeit deflated by the consumer price index, CPI) had been rising steeply (about 120 per cent) between 1997 and 2007, with the largest increase in 2005 (by one-fourth).[30] After October 2008, the property market fell approximately 34 per cent (figure adjusted after inflation) and at one point more than 27 per cent of households were left in negative equity. The

24 This is also confirmed by data provided in Statistics Iceland, Statistical Series 2013:3 'Wages, Income and Labour Market – Household Finances', April 2013, Table 5, p. 16.

25 Ólafsson and Vignisdóttir (2012) p. 5.

26 Ministry of Welfare, press release from 9 April 2013 on the basis of information published by Statistics Iceland in 2012 at http://www.velferdarraduneyti.is/frettir-vel/nr/33814.

27 Ólafsson and Vignisdóttir (2012) p. 5.

28 Ólafsson and Vignisdóttir (2012) p. 5.

29 Ólafsson and Vignisdóttir (2012) p. 74.

30 Central Bank of Iceland, Monetary Bulletin 2001–2 available at www.sedlabanki.is.

situation has improved lately, mainly because of debt-relief measures and policy instruments that temporarily reduced the burden of mortgage debt, as well as a series of Supreme Court rulings that led to the re-calculation of illegal FX-indexed loans (see below).

Second, Icelandic households were also affected by an unprecedented rise in unemployment. Evidence suggests that unemployment and levels of over-indebtedness correlate directly, as the capacity to withstand a rise in debt service after the financial crisis was compromised by declining wages and the loss of employment.[31] Even though the unemployment rate is relatively low (7 per cent) compared to other European countries, the extent of the sudden increase in unemployment after the financial crisis should not be underestimated.

Third, and probably most importantly, the indexation of loans, both to foreign currencies (FX-indexation) and inflation (CPI-indexation) contributed to over-indebtedness. In order to avoid the traditionally high interest rates and inflation associated with a volatile micro-currency (Icelandic Króna ISK), a law adopted in 1979 allowed the indexation of savings and financial obligations to the consumer price index (CPI-indexation). For decades, the public Housing Financing Fund (HFF) only provided CPI-indexed type of credit. When the credit market was liberalised, the new privatised banks and the private pension funds also promoted indexed loans, in order to circumvent the less favourable interest rates of the Icelandic Central Bank. At the end of 2009, a total of 74,000 households had a CPI-indexed mortgage on their residential property.[32] In addition, from 2004, indexation to foreign currency indexes (FX-indexation) became widespread practice. Close to 84 per cent of total outstanding motor vehicle and 15 per cent of mortgage debt was foreign-denominated in 2008.[33]

Due to the substantial devaluation of the Icelandic Króna in the aftermath of the financial crisis, consumers with FX-indexed loans became more indebted than consumers with ISK-denominated loans. Twenty-three per cent of households with FX-indexed debt had monthly debt payments exceeding 40 per cent of their disposable income, rising to 66 per cent in 2009 and decreasing to almost 33 per cent in 2010. In contrast, the number of households with ISK-denominated loans rose from just above 7 per cent in 2007 with a heavy debt burden to 14 per cent in 2009, while falling to 9 per cent in 2010.[34] The nominal outstanding amounts for FX-indexed loans nearly doubled in the autumn of 2008. Even though this situation improved when those loans were deemed illegal by the Supreme Court from June 2010 and were re-calculated (see below), the share of FX-borrowers in distress was roughly twice as high as that of ISK borrowers.[35] Since high-income households were more likely to have FX- denominated debt,[36] the second-highest quintile benefited most from the re-calculation of foreign-denominated loans, as the share of those households in distress declined by 4.3 percentage points following re-calculation compared to 1.2 percentage points in the lowest and 2.3 percentage points in the second-lowest quintile.

In a nutshell, these macro-economic issues combined had a dramatic impact on Icelandic households: a currency depreciation of circa 60 per cent, the consumer price index rising 37.5 per cent, real wages declining by 13.5 per cent, unemployment rising by 8.5 percentage points, and the fall in real house prices by 34 per cent over a four-year period led to a significant increase in the

31 Ólafsson and Vignisdóttir (2012) p. 72.

32 Data from Prime Minister's Office, Government Action Plan for Household Debt Relief, available at http://eng.forsaetisraduneyti.is/news-and-articles/nr/7808.

33 Ólafsson and Vignisdóttir (2012) p. 18.

34 Ólafsson and Vignisdóttir (2012) pp. 41–42.

35 Ólafsson and Vignisdóttir (2012) p. 76.

36 Ólafsson and Vignisdóttir (2012) p. 34, Figure 4.1c.

households' debt service burden, debt levels and living costs, while housing wealth and disposable income declined deeply.[37]

A Culture of Easy Access to Credit

When looking at the causes of over-indebtedness one must also take into consideration that in the years before the financial crisis, there was a 'culture' of easy credit and overspending in Iceland. Home ownership was promoted, for example through tax subsidies to cover the high interest rates. There was no organised rental market and many were pushed into the mortgage market.[38] However, people did not only buy residential property, but also SUVs, designer furniture, expensive clothes, flatscreen TVs, etc. Consumers were encouraged to invest savings into financial products (bank shares, investment funds, other shares). Equity was drawn from residential property to finance consumption.

In order to enable Icelanders to consume, creditors were easily granting credit. Advertising of mortgage credit and consumer credit was paramount in the years before the crisis. In 2004, when the HFF started competing with the commercial banks, 90 per cent Loan to Value Ratio loans – which required only savings of only 10 per cent or less – and even 100 per cent loans were offered. FX- and CPI-indexed loans offered beneficial interest rates. The Home Association SH confirmed in an interview with the rapporteurs a general practice of the banks to merely ask: 'How much do you want?'. The association of financial institutions, SFF, reported, on their side, cases of consumers asking: 'How much can I get?'.

There was a common overestimation of the sustainability of the credit system: benevolent circumstances of rising housing prices, low inflation, stable exchange rates and low interest rates.[39] Consumer interviews with the rapporteurs confirm that that loan agreements – even without direct pressure from the lender – were often done in much haste and without too much hesitation. Comparison of offers was not broadly practised. Explanations were only rarely sought from the lender. Consumers who asked relevant questions signed the contracts without getting satisfying answers and were sometimes even given wrong or misleading information.

The extension of credit permeated all segments of the Icelandic society. Banks expanded their lending activities to low-income and previously credit-constrained groups, distributing risk across the financial system through securitisation.[40] At that time, creditworthiness assessment was only obligatory for loans in cases in which a third party – mostly family members – issued a personal guarantee against the debt. It is impossible to know to what extent that obligation was observed in practice, as credit could have been granted despite a negative outcome of the test. What is known for sure is that loans were also given to households already in distress, especially low-income households. In 2007–2008, up to 34 per cent of households were granted loans even though they were already financially distressed.[41]

This situation has changed. The new standards of banking regulation adopted in Europe and the new Basel III rules will now tighten access to credit (i.e. international rules on expansion of banks' balance sheets in relation to own capital and new liquidity ratios depending on risks for different

37 Ólafsson and Vignisdóttir (2012) p. 72.
38 Ólafsson and Vignisdóttir (2012) p. 10.
39 Ólafsson and Vignisdóttir (2012) p. 7.
40 Ólafsson and Vignisdóttir (2012) p. 7.
41 Ólafsson and Vignisdóttir (2012) Abstract.

assets).[42] Moreover, the new Act no. 33/2013 on consumer loans puts in place tighter requirements concerning the checking of information provided to the bank by the potential debtor and testing credit history and real capacity of payment. The criteria for creditworthiness assessment are for the first time defined and take into account of the debtor's assets, debts, expenses and income (Article 5 lit. d) of new Act no. 33/2013 also makes mandatory the use of the Icelandic credit bureau that collects information on the past financial history of payment compliance and on present financial commitments.

D. Legal Framework and the Role of Private Law

The Icelandic legal framework applicable for consumer credit and mortgages has changed since the financial crisis. However, despite important reforms, protection through consumer law can be regarded insufficient for Icelandic consumers. It was litigation before the Icelandic courts on the basis of domestic contract law that led to the most significant improvement of consumer rights in the area of credit and mortgages. Thus, the legal framework is still being shaped by national jurisprudence, especially concerning FX- and CPI-indexation, while EU/EEA consumer (credit) law is only reluctantly and recently been taken account of.

The Icelandic Legal Framework Applicable to Over-Indebted Consumers

All new EU consumer law is incorporated into Annex XIX to the EEA Agreement by decisions of the EEA Joint Committee. In Iceland, Directive 93/13/EEC on unfair terms in consumer contracts has been transposed by Act no. 14/1995 amending Act no. 7/1936 on contracts, agency and void legal instruments. Directive 2005/29 on unfair commercial practices has been incorporated to Iceland through Act no. 57/2005 on supervision on commercial and marketing practices.[43] In November 2013 Act no. 33/2013[44] implemented Directive 2008/48/EC on consumer credit agreements extending its scope to mortgages. This decision was not new. The Act no. 121/1994 transposed Directive 87/102/EEC into Icelandic setting forth information disclosure requirements regarding consumer credits and was amended in 2000 as to apply also to mortgage credit. *De lege ferenda*, adjustment of the national law will be necessary after the incorporation of the Mortgage Credit Directive 2014/17 into the EEA and Icelandic legal order.[45]

One important reform in favour of over-indebted individuals was introduced with Act no. 23/2009 on bankruptcy. A new rule of reimbursement of claims following a forced sale and eviction has been adopted in order to secure a fair price resulting from the public auction. Moreover, claims now prescribe two years after the termination of the bankruptcy proceedings, which in the end

42 For a summary of the content of the Act no 33/2013 in English and its potential impact on the Icelandic credit system see Central Bank of Iceland, Financial Stability Report 2014–1, pp. 71–72, available at http://www.cb.is/library/Skrper centC3per centA1arsafn---EN/Financial-Stability-Report/2014–1/Financialper cent20Stabilityper cent202014_heildarskjal.pdf.

43 On the status of EU/EEA law consumer acquis in Iceland see Ministry of Presidency, 'Neytendavernd á fjármálamarkaði' ('Report on Consumer Protection in Financial Markets') 2013, p. 47.

44 The EFTA Court declared that Iceland violated the EEA Agreement for the late incorporation of EEA legislation EFTA Court in the judgment of 15 May 2013, case E-12/12 *EFTA Surveillance Authority v Iceland*, not yet reported.

45 A full list of the recommendations is provided by the Ministry of Presidency (2013) pp. 83–88. The Report refers to a similar conclusion reached by the Financial Supervisory Authority FME in 2011.

amounts to a discharge of the remaining outstanding debt (but this provision may be re-evaluated by the parliament again as there is a sunset clause). However, the number of bankruptcies has been relatively small, probably due to lack of information, legal uncertainty regarding indexed loans, a public policy of debt-relief, cost of the proceedings, and promises of future further action for those indebted.

In general, the standard of consumer protection in Iceland under European law in the area of consumer/mortgage credit needs to be ameliorated.[46] This applies, first and foremost, to the incorporation, application and enforcement of European provisions through the national legal order. Just to name a few issues:[47] until October 2013, Article 7 of the Directive 93/13 had not been properly implemented (lack of competent authority to enforce the provisions of the UCT Directive and/or domestic provisions on interest and indexation (Act 38/2001)); the Directive 2008/48 was incorporated by Act 33/2013 on consumer credit only after a respective ruling of the EFTA Court; there was a general reluctance of national judges, including the Supreme Court, to adjudicate private law cases on the basis of European consumer (credit) law; and, last but not least, the case-law from the CJEU (i.e. the *Aziz* case in Spain[48]) on seminal cases has had no impact on the interpretation of the national provisions. For example, the Icelandic consumer cannot raise substantive objections against the enforcement of a mortgage contract. Thus, similarly to the situation leading to the *Aziz* case, a substantive assessment of abusive clauses cannot be requested. According to Article 22(2) Act no. 90/1991 on Forced Sale, objections shall not stop an auction, unless they are of a formal nature – which the Commissioner is obliged to examine *ex officio*[49] – or if the Commissioner considers it otherwise uncertain that the lender has the right to demand an auction. Basically, the borrower can only stop the auction if he/she can provide substantial evidence that the claim has been fully paid. This is just one example of the reluctance to take into account developments on the European level.

FX- and CPI-Indexation of Loans Before the Courts

Litigation in private law matters has been the most important tool for Icelandic consumers to address problems of over-indebtedness, both with regard to guarantees given by third parties and FX- and CPI-indexation. The extensive use of FX-indexation has given rise to several cases, the adjudication of which has ameliorated the financial situation of consumers and small companies. It remains to be seen whether ongoing litigation relating to also widespread CPI-indexation will have similar effects.

The Icelandic Supreme Court has used the general Article 36 of Act no. 7/1936 to declare some contracts void, partly or as a whole, and to adjust them if they are considered unfair or against good business practice to uphold them. According to Article 36c a contract is unfair if it is not in compliance with good business practices and if it disturbs substantially the status of obligations and rights of the contracting parties to the detriment of the consumer. However, until October 2013, the provisions of European law (Directive 93/13 incorporated by a modification of Act no.

46 Ministry of Presidency (2013) p. 61.

47 Ministry of Presidency (2013).

48 CJEU, Case C-415/11 *Mohamed Aziz v Caixa d'Estalvis de Catalunya, Tarragona i Manresa (Catalunyacaixa)* [2013].

49 Those objections concern formal conditions such as the obligation of the Commissioner to send a registered letter to the borrower about the sale, the advertisement of the sale with all required information and within time limits, Articles 16, 19 and 20 and also if the auction request was sent to a Commissioner in another district than the one where the jurisdiction belongs to, Article 13, paragraph 2.

7/1936 in a new addition to Art. 36 (letters a–d)) have not been applied by the Icelandic courts to adjust contractual terms in consumer mortgage agreements and/or to declare null and void unfair contract terms. For example, as regards third-party guarantees, the Supreme Court decided in cases 4/2013 and 127/2013 to declare null and void the guarantee given by a third party on a loan taking into account defects in the contracting stage (lack of information and due consent of the individual providing guarantee).[50] This was decided under general Art. 36 of Act no. 7/1936 of contract law. In other relevant cases 213/2012 and 343/2013 the Supreme Court decided, nevertheless, that the breach of information duties did not comply with all requirements set by national legislation and did not cancel the guarantee given.[51] The Supreme Court has been reluctant to adjust contractual terms in the case of unforeseen or unforeseeable events (this has been tried in one case invoking the occurrence of the financial crisis as such an unforeseen/unforeseeable event), given the difficulty of imposing the burden of the change of circumstances on one of the parties.

However, in two seminal cases in 2010,[52] the Supreme Court ruled that the Icelandic Act no. 2001/38 on interest and indexation – a public law statute that allows private parties to decide contractually on interests and indexation for financial obligations – did not allow FX-indexation and declared the challenged car loan agreements partially null. On the basis of general (Icelandic) contract law, FX-indexed loans were to be re-calculated in ISK without the indexation clause. This illegality was later extended to other kinds of loans (i.e. house loans) and declared applicable both to companies and consumers, while loans in foreign currency remain possible as long as their nature and form does not reflect an indexation practice.[53]

The re-calculation of the principal of many illegal FX-indexed loans proved difficult and led to subsequent litigation.[54] More than a thousand consumers complained to the EFTA Surveillance Authority, the European Commission and the Committee of Petitions of the European Parliament about the detrimental retroactive effects of Act no. 151/2010, which stipulated that FX-linked loans were to be re-calculated *ex-tunc*, replacing the (usually lower) interest rates that the parties had agreed on by the (higher) ones of the Icelandic Central Bank, with the effect that consumers ended up owing and paying higher interests for credit instalments already paid in the past. In 2012, the Supreme Court declared Act no. 151/2010 partially unconstitutional and allowed the re-calculation on the basis of the Central Bank interests *ex-nunc*, as they would only apply after the time of the ruling.[55] The Supreme Court took into account the good faith of the consumers as well as the protection of property rights guaranteed by the Icelandic Constitution (Article 72) and the European Convention of Human Rights.[56] This jurisprudence has since then been confirmed[57] and further clarified[58] in a way that additional payments cannot be demanded from the debtor in

50 Ministry of Presidency (2013) p. 54.

51 Ministry of Presidency (2013) p. 59.

52 Supreme Court of Iceland. Cases no. 92/2010 and 153/2010.

53 Supreme Court of Iceland. Case no. 524/2011.

54 Supreme Court of Iceland Case no. 471/2010.

55 Supreme Court of Iceland. Case no. 600/2011 (in connexion with previous case 604/2010) on a mortgage loan where one of the authors (M. Elvira Méndez Pinedo) was a claimant.

56 On case no. 155/2011, the Supreme Court took a similar approach for companies (Motormax case). In that decision, an FX loan agreement between a legal entity and a financial institution was declared illegal for the first time, extending the scope of the doctrine on partial illegality of illegal FX-car loans to loans falling under company law.

57 Supreme Court of Iceland. Case no. 464/2012.

58 Supreme Court of Iceland, Case no. 600/2011 and Supreme Court of Iceland. Case no. 50/2013.

relation to already paid contractual credit claims. Further litigation concerning difficult cases of FX-indexation is ongoing.

Litigation on CPI-indexation has tried to follow the successful path taken by debtors with FX-indexed loans. In 2013 a CPI-indexation clause in a car loan was declared null and void.[59] It was the first time that the Supreme Court applied consumer credit law (Act no. 21/1994 on consumer loans incorporating European law) dealing with the consequences of a lack of contractual transparency and clarity.[60] Further cases are being dealt with by district courts, for example concerning the lack of due disclosure of financial obligations under Act no. 121/1994. Moreover, cases concerning indexation of mortgage loans are still open, both before the Icelandic Supreme Court and district courts. One case, brought by the Consumer Association *Samtök heimilana* SF against the HFF is built on Act no. 121/1994 on consumer loans and EEA consumer law (Directive 93/13/EC unfair terms in consumer contracts and requirements of transparency and disclosure of financial obligations).[61] In two more cases, one tried by private parties supported by a trade-union against *Landsbanki*,[62] and another brought by a private party against Íslandsbanki,[63] advisory opinions from EFTA Court were requested by the Reykjavík District Court. The opinions were delivered in 2014 and the Court found that, although indexation of credit per se is not directly forbidden by European consumer law, the creditors cannot calculate and disclose the cost of credit with a 0 per cent inflation rate ignoring real final cost.[64] At the same time, the Icelandic legislator as well as the Committee on Consumer Protection on Financial Markets[65] have expressed their concerns about the potential illegality of CPI-indexation under EU law, while leaving the competence to clarify the legality of the question to the courts.

E. Policy Responses to Over-Indebtedness

Besides the re-calculation of illegal FX-indexed loans, there has been a range of temporary and permanent measures adopted since 2009 to alleviate debt burdens and decrease over-indebtedness. The different policy measures adopted in the aftermath of the crisis were summarised by the IMF in 2010.[66] The Central Bank of Iceland has also assessed the effectiveness and economic impact of later measures in 2012.[67]

---

59 Supreme Court of Iceland. Case 672/2012.

60 Neither the contract nor the payment plan contemplated indexation of the car loan nominated in ISK and the variable interest rates applicable. In these circumstances, the Court finds that the creditor cannot claim respective payment afterwards. The creditor had argued that the debtor – by not protesting at the beginning – accepted the methodology of calculation. The creditor lost the case and had to refund what the individual had paid in excess.

61 It was dismissed in 2015 by the district court but will be appealed to the Supreme Court.

62 Case E-338/2013 (District court). See also Ministry of Presidency (2013) p. 61.

63 Supreme Court of Iceland. Case 489/2013.

64 EFTA Court, cases E-25/13 (Íslandsbanki) and E-27/13 (*Landsbanki*) decided on 28 August 2014 and on 24 November 2014 respectively.

65 Prime Minister's Office, 'Report of the Committee on Consumer Protection in the Financial Markets', April 2013.

66 IMF, Country Report (Iceland) 10/95, Staff Report for Second Review Under Stand-By Arrangement 4 (2010) 43 available at imf.org/external/pubs/ft/scr/2010/cr1095.pdf.

67 Ólafsson and Vignisdóttir (2012) pp. 26–28.

Initially, Iceland preferred a hybrid way of debt reorganisation and debt-relief over a flat reduction of debt (2009–2013). It encouraged direct collaboration between creditors and debtors to reorganise and restructure debt (voluntary additional measures of debt-relief). Later on, a framework was set up with supporting measures for debt-mitigation and the creation of a new Debtor's Ombudsman as well for possible debt write-off (the so-called 110 per cent way – a tool to readjust eligible mortgage debt to market value) and special tax subsidies. The new prime minister promised further legislative action. In May 2014, the parliament approved a new plan to provide financial relief to indebted households with CPI-indexed loans. The plan has been executed successfully.

Debt Mitigation, Debt-Relief and Debt Restructuring Policy 2009–2013

In 2009 the Icelandic authorities started attempts to provide solutions to over-indebted households. The policy consisted of both centralised and de-centralised measures.[68] In the first place, the authorities promoted voluntary measures between banks and their debtors in light distress through the payment rescheduling (payment smoothing) of credit, introduced changes to several benefit schemes and allowed private pension fund pay-outs. Other de-centralised measures were directed towards households in more complex/serious difficulties which would otherwise end in bankruptcy: bank-administered out-of-court voluntary debt restructuring, voluntary mediation of a new Debtor's Ombudsman in the process of debt restructuring,[69] and banks' own initiatives under guidelines applicable to financial institutions. Some banks decided to offer a variety of voluntary work-out measures beyond the minimum requirements in the agreed guidelines, including payment smoothing to specific groups of debtors, loan conversion with some reduction, interest rate reimbursements, reduction of interest rates, maturity extension, and the possibility of debt write-offs. This led to different treatment of debtors of different banks, which gave rise to social discontent.

Together with the promotion of voluntary measures, some legislative acts were put in place for the temporary mitigation of debt,[70] allowing debtors to pay in accordance with their financial situation for a limited period of 1–3 years under administrative/judicial supervision. It can imply revision of terms of payment, reduction or cancellation of individual claims under the supervision of a representative appointed to that effect. For real state credit, the procedure falls under judicial scrutiny and it may lower the debtors' financial burden for the duration of up to five years. Temporary debt mitigation was an important instrument used to help households in financial distress and/or with negative housing equity through the widespread freezing and/or payment smoothing of instalments and interest payments.[71] However, these debt-smoothing or mitigation measures were only temporary solutions to give the private sector (households and small business)

68 In general see Ólafsson and Vignisdóttir (2012) and in particular see T.T. Ólafsson, 'Crisis Responses to a Housing Bust and Households' Debt Problems: The Icelandic Saga', lecture at the conference 'The Nordic Housing Markets: Main Lessons and Remaining Challenges', Stockholm, 15 November 2013, available at http://www.sedlabanki.is/library/Skrper centC3per centA1arsafn/Rper centC3per centA6per centC3per centB0ur--erindi-og-greinar/Theper cent20Nordicper cent20housingper cent20marketsper cent2015per cent2011per cent202013.pdf.

69 Act no. 100/2010 on the Ombudsman for Debtors in relation with Act no. 101/2010 on debt mitigation for individuals, both available (in Icelandic) at www.althingi.is. The Office of the Debtor's Ombudsman is to oversee and provide advisory and mediation services related to debt mitigation procedures.

70 Act no. 24/2009 and Act no. 50/2009.

71 Ólafsson (2013).

time to reassess their financial position.[72] Popular discontent continued, reaching a peak in October 2010 when more than 5,000 people protested before the parliament.

Additional special measures were put in place in 2010. Apart from Act no. 151/2010 intended to deal with the re-calculation of illegal FX-indexed loans,[73] two further measures were introduced at the end of 2010 for debt-restructuring and debt-mitigation: the so-called 110 per cent option and special interest rebates. The first option allowed households with mortgages exceeding 110 per cent of their underlying property value to apply for write-offs. The second instrument was a general measure, interest subsidies dependent on mortgage indebtedness and independent on income for 2011 and 2012, and financed by a tax levied on financial institutions.

Moratoria on Evictions and Reform of Bankruptcy Law

In addition, a moratorium on evictions was adopted and renovated periodically. This was a measure which aimed to avoid or delay evictions from residential property under certain circumstances and which has been extended several times for different reasons. The latest moratorium – leading to the interruption of eviction proceedings – is related to the legal uncertainty surrounding certain mortgages (i.e. re-calculation of illegal FX-indexed loans).[74] In a parallel way, a reform of bankruptcy law and several other measures relating to the enforcement of mortgage contracts and forced sales (property auctions) were adopted to attenuate the social repercussions of over-indebtedness (see above).

Moreover, the new Article 87 of Act on Bankruptcy no. 21/1991 allows individuals going through bankruptcy proceedings to remain in housing or have certain items (for example cars) at their disposal for up to 12 months. Rent has to be paid for the use and the trustee in bankruptcy may require the posting of security for any damage to the possession. A similar change was made to Act on Distress Sale no. 90/1991, Article 28, which gives the individual the right to live in the property for up to 12 months from the time at which the auction's commissioner received a payment of the auction prize. Rent has to be paid, the monthly fee corresponding to the amount which the Commissioner finds appropriate. Specific debt-restructuring and debt-mitigation procedures, under the supervision of the Debtor's Ombudsman, both provide for the affected persons to stay in their homes while proceedings are ongoing.

A New Debt Relief Package for 2014 to 2017

In 2013, the Icelandic government announced a new four-year debt-relief plan for the write-off of a substantial part of CPI-indexed household mortgage debt starting in 2014.[75] The aim is to correct households' inflated balance sheets through debt relief amounting to a total of ISK 150 billion (around 8 per cent of Iceland's estimated GDP in 2014). It was approved by the parliament in May 2014 and it will be funded by an increase in the levy on financial institutions. The plan consists of two parts: first, a direct write-down of inflation-indexed mortgage principal of up to

72 Ólafsson (2013).

73 Act 151/2010 was declared partly unconstitutional, see *supra*.

74 Act no 9/2014 on financial aid for the payment of bankruptcy procedure fees/guarantee.

75 Prime Minister's Office, Government Action Plan for Household Debt Relief (2013) available (in English) at http://eng.forsaetisraduneyti.is/debt-relief/. For a comment in English see Omar Valdimarsson, Iceland Defies Creditor Backlash With Debt Relief: Nordic Credit, Bloomberg, 28 November 2013 available at http://www.bloomberg.com/news/2013–11–28/iceland-defies-creditor-backlash-with-debt-relief-nordic-credit.html.

13 per cent, amounting to a total of ISK 80 billion over a four-year period; and second, a 6 per cent tax exemption that will cost the Treasure 20 additional billion over a three-year period. The tax exemption relates to payments that households (and their employers) would otherwise have been able to make towards their private pension funds. According to the government, the plan will lower the outstanding mortgage principal by up to 20 per cent until 2017 and will be available to 80 per cent of Icelandic households. Earlier mortgage relief transactions will be taken into account as the maximum debt relief under the first option is ISK 4 million per household, while the second option is limited to a total of ISK 1.5 million over the three-year period. Most households have mortgages of ISK 25 million or less.[76] Latest data from the media at the end of 2014 reflects that more than 95,000 individuals have requested relief under this new plan. Public financed debt-relief has therefore had a wide impact for up to 75.000 households.

Even though this governmental initiative is to be welcomed, the plan does not solve the main root of the problem that lies in a credit system anchored in the indexation of credit to inflation. Political plans to abandon indexation are not yet realistic.[77] It is therefore vital that the Supreme Court decides on the legality and fairness of CPI-indexation in the light of European consumer law.

F. Assessment of Debt Relief Possibilities

The IMF has cited Iceland as an example of good practice due to its policy of household debt-restructuring with a view towards economic recovery.[78] In the words of the IMF: 'government policies can help prevent prolonged contractions in economic activity by addressing the problem of excessive household debt. In particular, bold household debt restructuring programs such as those implemented in the United States in the 1930s and in Iceland today can significantly reduce debt repayment burdens and the number of household defaults and foreclosures'. This stance does, however, not reflect the main causes of the success of the debt-relief provided and the important role of private litigation in the re-calculation of FX-indexed loans (in the period 2010–2012).

According to the Association of Financial Institutions SFF, all in all, 83,677 households had obtained some form of debt-relief as of 12 March 2012. Icelandic households had a total of 196.3 billion ISK (about 1 billion pounds) written off their debts.[79] The most updated data from the Central Bank calculates debt write-offs amounting to 244 billion ISK (14 per cent of the GDP at the end of 2013).[80] The Central Bank of Iceland reports in 2012 that household deleveraging has progressed more rapidly in Iceland than in many previous crises and that debt-relief measures and the re-calculation of illegal exchange rate-linked loans have allowed thousands of households to alleviate distress.[81]

76 Prime Minister's Office, Debt Correction Action Plan (*Leiðrétting*) (2013–2014).

77 Central Bank of Iceland (2014) pp. 66–70.

78 International Monetary Fund "Dealing with Household Debt", Chapter 3 in *World Economic Outlook*, pp. 89–124, April 2012, Washington: International Monetary Fund, available at: imf.org/external/pubs/ft/weo/2012/01/pdf/c3.pdf.

79 Reply from Minister of Work and Innovation to the question of MP Einars K. Guðfinnssonar at http://www.althingi.is/altext/141/s/pdf/0575.pdf. As it can be seen in this reply referring to data in 2012, the restructuration of the debt has been three times more important for illegal FX-indexed loans than for CPI-indexed loans (estimation of 149 billion ISK versus 53 billion ISK).

80 Most recent data provided by Central Bank of Iceland, see especially Chart 4, 'Post-crisis write-off of household debt', Central Bank of Iceland, Monetary Bulletin (2013) p. 36.

81 Ólafsson and Vignisdóttir (2012) pp. 26–28.

Administrative interventions by the legislator were relatively successful but the most substantial debt-relief came via court rulings that led to the re-calculation of illegal FX-indexed loans. Until 2012, banks have re-calculated a total of 68,348 loans, 14,179 of them FX-denominated mortgages, 45,668 FX-denominated motor vehicle loans, and 8,501 ISK-denominated portions of mixed loans.[82] This resulted in a debt discharge of 108 billion ISK through the re-calculation of illegal FX-indexed mortgage loans and of 38.5 billion ISK deriving from the re-calculation of illegal exchange-rate-linked car loans. In contrast, a relatively small write-off of 6 billion ISK came from the adjustment of residential mortgages based on 110 per cent of the market value and another 6.2 billion ISK from another debt-relief provided for households in 'serious' difficulties. The share of households in distress declined by only 1.5 per cent percentage points through such measures,[83] which are, moreover, viewed critically, as their benefits were not evenly distributed. Households in distress received only 23.5 per cent of the write-offs from the 110 per cent option and 27 per cent of the special interest rebate. All in all, the 110 per cent option resulted in a debt discharge of approximately 3 per cent of GDP and the special interest rebates led to financial assistance for 1 per cent of GDP.[84]

In short, debtors with FX-indexed credit/mortgage loans benefitted from a 246.5 billion ISK write-off financed by the private and public banks (2010–2012) following judicial litigation (private law remedies) while debtors witn CPI-indexed mortgage loans will benefit during 2014–2017 from 100 billion ISK write-off financed by the Treasury (tax payers) (public policy).

This data makes clear that, even after the 2014 plan, the re-calculation of illegal FX-indexed loans has so far been the most important tool for indebted and over-indebted Icelandic consumers to alleviate their debt burden. That the cost of this debt write-off is borne by the financial sector should not be a surprice. It must be borne in mind that the claims that financial institutions had to re-calculate were based on illegal commercial practices or unfair contractual terms respectively. A violation of Act 38/2001 through the practice of FX-indexation led to a situation of widespread use of unfair terms embedded into the private law structure in Iceland. The legislator tried to intervene with the passing of Act no. 151/2010 on the re-calculation of loans, but this attempt come about only after respective jurisprudence and the Act was later also declared partially unconstitutional for expropriating consumer´s property rights (regarding past and completed repayment of claims).

G. Conclusions and Challenges for the Future

The lessons from Iceland after the financial crisis in the area of consumer law are both positive and negative. On the one hand, Iceland has led pragmatic efforts in Europe to provide temporary debt-relief and debt-discharge to over-indebted households. Households' and firms' financial situation and balance sheets have ameliorated slowly since 2012 and 2013.[85] This positive trend is expected to continue because of the new plan implemented in 2014. The total debt burden has continued to fall in 2013 due to restructuring and write-downs, rising asset prices and increased household income.[86] At the end of the day, debt-restructuring, re-calculation and write-downs have helped Iceland, households and small firms. This has also helped economic recovery, as appreciated by the IMF.

82 Ólafsson and Vignisdóttir (2012) p. 27.
83 Ólafsson (2013).
84 Ólafsson (2013).
85 Central Bank of Iceland (2014) pp. 55–61.
86 Central Bank of Iceland (2014) pp. 51 and 55–61.

On the other hand, the success of the Icelandic approach during 2010–2012 rests less on a public policy of debt-relief but more on a series of seminal judgments delivered by the Supreme Court on the basis of private contract law. The re-calculation of illegal FX-loans as the most effective tool of debt-relief and debt write-off was a consequence of private litigation between different parties (consumers, financial institutions, companies). The uncertainty surrounding CPI-indexation is – even if not specifically mentioned – the main reason for still uncertain asset values of the banks and the public HFF.[87] Considerable risk still lies ahead.[88] The assessment of the legality and fairness of indexation of loans to inflation *ex-post* in the light of EEA consumer law is still ongoing as a final judgment must be given by the Supreme Court. The opposite can be said in 2014, where the government executed a new debt-relief plan for CPI-indexed mortgage loans.

Because of its complexity, opacity and general structure of adjusting interest rates after the contract formation, which make the compliance with information disclosure obligations *ex-ante* almost impossible, Icelandic price-indexation of general consumer and mortgage credit seems highly problematic in the light of European consumer law. A legality and fairness test of this practice seems unavoidable. The Icelandic public and media follow the respective cases before the courts very closely. The judicial approach will definitely have an impact on Icelandic financial, banking, housing and pension systems, and will affect the future practice of indexation of credit.

Further governmental action and continuous effort is necessary to help Icelandic households. Over-indebtedness is still an important issue, especially for those with CPI-indexed loans. Indexation of credit embedded into private contracts passes the risks of the financial sector directly to the balance sheets of households and small companies, for which the nominal figures of debt have practically doubled in the five years following the crisis. The success of the new debt-relief will be limited as long as indexation of credit to inflation is still in force. Iceland is at the crossroads of having to solve a major underlying problem of endemic high inflation associated with the use of its small local currency which indexation is supposed to combat since its adoption 35 years ago. In no other country in Europe is indexation of credit an institutional feature of the economy. The Prime Minister's promise of putting an end to indexation of credit will have to be faced before next legislative elections.

A well-intentioned public policy of debt-relief must go hand-in-hand with the protection of consumer individual rights under both European and national public and private law. A combination of different measures could be envisaged for Iceland: from a political and economic perspective, an end could be put to indexation for both old and new loans (maybe more effective than the new 2014 plan of debt-relief) and a policy of sustainable access to housing and pension policies for the next generations has to be designed. From a legal perspective, both European and domestic law need to be applied and effectively enforced. In general, legal theory could contribute to a theory of finance that accommodates different interests of societal groups and makes clear the role of the legislative and judicial powers in providing justice for debtors.[89] But in order to prevent similar problems in the future, a radical reform must take place on the global level if the roots of the financial crisis are to be addressed in a sustainable manner. Law, political economy, political philosophy and the

87 Central Bank of Iceland (2014) p. 3.

88 Central Bank of Iceland (2014), p. 3.

89 A new trend in legal thought is focusing on already existing private law principle in order to provide justice, for example K. Pistor, 'Towards a Legal Theory of Finance', CEPR Discussion Paper no. 9235, London, Centre for Economic Policy Research, 2012, available at http://www.cepr.org/pubs/dps/DP9235.asp; already in 1959: K. Rohde, *Adjustement of Contracts on Account of Changed Conditions*, Stockholm Institute for Scandinavian Law, Stockholm, 1959.

design of a sustainable international monetary system not exclusively based on the creation of money, debt and credit by the financial institutions lie at the heart of the problem.

References

Reports and Public Official Documents

Central Bank of Iceland, Monetary Bulletin (2001–2) available at www.sedlabanki.is.

Central Bank of Iceland, Monetary Bulletin (2013) available at www.sedlabanki.is.

Central Bank of Iceland, Financial Stability Report (2014–1) at http://www.cb.is/library/Skrper centC3per centA1arsafn---EN/Financial-Stability-Report/2014–1/Financialper cent20Stabilityper cent202014_heildarskjal.pdf.

IMF, Country Report (Iceland) 10/95, Staff Report for Second Review Under Stand-By Arrangement 4 (2010) 43 available at imf.org/external/pubs/ft/scr/2010/cr1095.pdf.

IMF, Country Report (Iceland) 13/256, Article IV Consultation and Third Post-Program Monitoring Discussions (2013) available at http://www.imf.org/external/pubs/ft/scr/2013/cr13256.pdf.

IMF, 'World Economic Outlook: Growth Resuming, Dangers Remain', Chapter 3 'Dealing with Household Debt', 4 (2012) pp. 89–124, available at imf.org/external/pubs/ft/weo/2012/01/pdf/c3.pdf.

Ministry of Presidency, 'Neytendavernd á fjármálamarkaði' ('Report on Consumer Protection in Financial Markets') 2013.

Minister of Work and Innovation, Reply to the question of Member of Parliament Einars K. Guðfinnssonar at http://www.althingi.is/altext/141/s/pdf/0575.pdf.

Ministry of Welfare (in collaboration with other ministries), 'Greinargerð um fjárhagsstöðu heimilanna' ('Report and Analysis of the Financial Situation of Households') (2013) available (in Icelandic) at http://www.velferdarraduneyti.is/media/Rit_2013/Greinargerd-um-fjarhagsstodu-heimilanna_april2013.pdf.

Ministry of Welfare, press release from 9 April 2013 on the financial situation of households according to data collected by Statistics Iceland in 2012, available at http://www.velferdarraduneyti.is/frettir-vel/nr/33814.

Ministry of Welfare, 'Skýrsla samráðshóps um húsnæðisstefnu' ('Report of Specialist Group on a Housing Policy') (2011) available (in Icelandic) at http://www.velferdarraduneyti.is/media/frettir2011/19042011_Skyrsla_samradshops_um_husnaedisstefnu.pdf.

Ministry of Work, 'Skýrsla eftirlitsnefndar til efnahags- og viðskiptaráðherra, samkvæmt lögum nr. 107/2009 um aðgerðir í þágu einstaklinga, heimila og fyrirtækja vegna banka- og gjaldeyrishrunsins' ('Report on Actions Adopted for Homes and Companies due to the Financial Crisis according to Act no.107/2009') (2011) available (in Icelandic) at http://www.atvinnuvegaraduneyti.is/media/Acrobat/Eftirlitsnefnd.pdf.

National Registry, Chart 2012 on numbers of registered mortgages, available at http://www.skra.is/library/Samnyttar-skrar-/Markadsfrettir/tafla2.1_2012.xls.

OECD, OECD Economic Surveys: Iceland 2013, available at http://dx.doi.org/10.1787/eco_surveys-isl-2013-en.

Ólafsson, T.T., 'Crisis Responses to a Housing Bust and Households' Debt Problems: The Icelandic Saga', lecture at the conference 'The Nordic Housing Markets: Main Lessons and Remaining Challenges', Stockholm, 15 November 2013 available at http://www.sedlabanki.is/library/Skrper centC3per centA1arsafn/Rper centC3per centA6per centC3per centB0ur--

erindi-og-greinar/Theper cent20Nordicper cent20housingper cent20marketsper cent2015per cent2011per cent202013.pdf.
Ólafsson, T.T. and Vignisdóttir, K.A., 'Households' Position in the Financial Crisis in Iceland', Central Bank of Iceland Working Paper No. 59, June 2012, available at http://www.cb.is/library/Skrper centC3per centA1arsafn---EN/Working-Papers/Workingper cent20Paperper cent2059.pdf.
Prime Minister's Office. Government Action Plan for Household Debt Relief (2013) available at http://eng.forsaetisraduneyti.is/news-and-articles/nr/7808.
Prime Minister's Office, 'Skýrsla um skuldavandi heimilanna' ('Report on the Household's Indebtedness Problems') (2010) available (in Icelandic) at www.forsaetisraduneyti.is/media/Skyrslur/skyrla-skuldavandi-heimila.pdf.
Prime Minister's Office, 'Neytendavernd á fjármálamarkaði' ('Report on Consumer Protection in Financial Markets') April 2013, available (in Icelandic) at http://www.forsaetisraduneyti.is/media/Skyrslur/neytendavernd-a-fjarmalamarkadi.pdf.
Statistics Iceland, general data on households, available at www.statice.is.
Statistics Iceland, Statistical series – National Accounts, 'Liabilities, Assets and Net Worth of Individuals 1997–2011', 2013: 9.
Statistics Iceland, Statistical series – National Accounts, 'Liabilities, Assets and Net Worth of Individuals 2012', 2013: 11.
Statistics Iceland, Statistical series – Prices and Consumption, 'Household Expenditure Survey 2010–2012', 2013: 1.
Statistics Iceland, Statistical Series – Wages, Income and Labour Market, 'Household Finances 2012', 2013: 13.
Sveinsson, J.R., 'The Formation of Urban Homeownership in Iceland', Cambridge Conference Paper, available at https://borg.hi.is/Theper cent20Formationper cent20ofper cent20Urbanper cent20Housingper cent20Policyper cent20inper cent20Iceland.pdf.

Table of Cases before European Courts

CJEU

Case C-415/11 *Mohamed Aziz v Caixa d'Estalvis de Catalunya, Tarragona i Manresa (Catalunyacaixa)* [2013].

EFTA Court

Judgment of 15 May 2013, case E-12/12 *EFTA Surveillance Authority v Iceland*, EFTA Court Reports [2013] n.y.r.

Advisory opinions requested from Reykjavík District Court. Pending cases E-25/13 (*Gunnar V. Engilbertsson v Íslandsbanki hf.*) and E-27/13 (*Sævar Jón Gunnarsson v Landsbankinn hf.*).

*List of Most Relevant Cases before the Icelandic Supreme Court (*Hæstiréttur*)*

Case no. 92/2010 Óskar Sindri Atlason v. SP. fjármögnun hf. Judgment of 16 June 2010.

Case no. 153/2010 *Lýsing hf. v. Jóhanni Rafni Hreiðarssyni og Trausta Snæ Friðrikssyni*. Judgment of 16 June 2010.

Case no. 471/2010 *Lýsing hf. v. Guðlaugi Hafsteini Egilssyni og gagnsök*. Judgment of 16 September 2010.

Case no. 604/2010 *Sigurður Hreinn Sigurðsson og Maria Elvira Mendez Pinedo v. Frjálsa fjárfestingarbankanum hf.* Judgment of 14 February 2011.
Case no. 155/2011 *Landsbankinn hf. v. Motormax ehf.* Judgment of 9 June 2011.
Case no. 600/2011 *Sigurður Hreinn Sigurðsson og Maria Elvira Mendez Pinedo v. Frjálsa fjárfestingarbankanum hf.* Judgment of 15 February 2012.
Case no. 524/2011 *Þorsteinn Hafsteinsson og Marsibil Baldursdóttir v. Íslandsbanka hf.* Judgment of 7 June 2012.
Case no. 464/2012 *Borgarbyggð v. Arion banka hf.* Judgment of 18 October 2012.
Case no.672/2012 *Lýsing hf. v. Bjarnþóri Erlendssyni og gagnsök.* Judgment of 24 April 2013.
Case no. 50/2013 *Plastiðjan ehf. v. Landsbankanum hf.* Judgment of 30 May 2013.
Case no. 489/2013 Íslandsbanki hf. v. Gunnari V. Engilbertssyni. Judgment of 8 October 2013.

Chapter 8
Country Report Romania

Beatrice Andresan-Grigoriu and Madalina Moraru

A. Introduction

Romania's accession to the EU was one of the significant factors that boosted consumer confidence in the domestic economy. The general perception of accession as an opportunity for new jobs and higher income created a positive attitude towards taking credit.[1] As such, by the end of 2008, two years after Romania's accession to the EU, household debt reached a historical peak of almost half of the total private loans. The reasons for the contracted loans were similar to those that existed in the pre-accession period: rising income, optimistic expectations of future income, the significant interest of consumers in acquiring immovable property, and the banks' household-credit oriented strategies.[2] In the following years, the rate of consumers taking on credit started to decrease. This trend can be seen as one of the many effects of the financial crisis. The fluctuations in the level of household indebtedness did not affect consumers negatively on their own. Rather, it was the increased risk in foreign exchanges, the depreciation in value of the assets guaranteeing consumer loans, increased living costs,[3] and other specific characteristics of the Romanian consumer credit market[4] (see sections A and B) which led to increased levels of consumers' over-indebtedness and evictions.

With this contribution we aim to provide information on the under-researched situation of Romanian indebted and over-indebted consumers. In section B part I we will briefly provide empirical data showing the numbers of indebted and over-indebted consumers in Romania detailed by type of credit agreements, currency of the credit and the structure of the income of these consumers. We will then provide in part II of section B an analysis of the potential causes of the high number of indebted and over-indebted consumers, including social-economic reasons, before proceeding in section C to the analysis of the specific legal framework and jurisprudence[5]

---

1 NBR Financial Stability Report, 2007, 19. See also G Morosan, 'Effects of the Romanian Economic Crisis upon the Banking System' (2011) The Annals of the Ştefan cel Mare University of Suceava. Fascicle of the Faculty of Economics and Public Administration 245–255.

2 NBR Financial Stability Report, 2007, 69. For example, according to the NBR calculations, in December 2008 the total level of debt was five times higher than in December 2004.

3 M Stanculescu and M Marin, 'Report on Impacts of the International Economic Crisis in Romania 2009–2010: A Panel Study based on Qualitative Methods', UNICEF study, available at http://www.unicef.org/romania/Impacts_of_the_international_crisis.pdf [last visited on 30 June 2014]. G Zaman, 'Criza economică şi financiară în România. Cauze, provocari si remedii pe termen scurt si lung' ['The Economic and Financial Crisis in Romania: Causes, Challenges and Remedies on Long and Short Term'], paper available online.

4 For instance, in 2008 the majority of the household loans were foreign currency and foreign currency denominated loans, see World Bank, *Diagnostic Review of Consumer Protection and Financial Literacy* Volume I, Key Findings and Recommendations (February 2009), 15.

5 The legislative and jurisprudential framework were assessed according to their status available until 30 June 2014.

on mortgage secured credit agreements contracted by consumers. We will conclude with section D on the legislative and policy changes that have had and could have a positive impact on the difficult situation that Romanian over-indebted consumers continue to face. Our conclusion is that Romanian consumers are slowly overcoming the high level of over-indebtedness and evictions as a result of being increasingly aware of the most risky types of credit agreements, taking advantage of the many consumer-friendly legislative amendments, the favourable reaction of courts to consumer claims, and strict regulatory norms imposed by the National Bank of Romania (NBR). These changes have had such an impact that renowned practitioners and academics have[6] stated that the Romanian consumer market has empowered consumers to such an extent that the traditional power balance between banks and consumers has been called into question, with the latter no longer being in a vulnerable position.

B. The Situation of Indebted Consumers in the Country: Financial and Social Issues

The Evolution of Indebtedness and Over-Indebtedness of Romanian Consumers

Before analysing possible causes for the Romanian consumer indebtedness and over-indebtedness, we would first like to mention the definition of the concepts of 'indebtedness' and 'over-indebtedness' in national legal instruments or jurisprudence. While the concept of 'indebtedness' is defined by Article 13 of Regulation No. 17/2012 of the NBR[7] concerning conditions of indebtedness as the ratio between the total value of obligations arising from loans and other financing agreements and the value of eligible income,[8] the concept of 'over-indebtedness' is not defined as such. The NBR does not use the concept of 'over-indebtedness', instead it refers to the following concepts, which have similar definitions: 'overdue loans', 'overdue payments ratio', 'non-performing credit/loan'[9] and 'defaulter'.[10]

Since 2000, the number of indebted consumers has increased in Romania every year, reaching a peak in 2008, when the total level of household debt was five times higher than in December 2004.[11] Due to the impact of the financial crisis, the number of indebted consumers has been slowly

6 M Avram, 'Clauzele abuzive în contractele de credit – o temă incandescentă în dreptul naţional şi cel european' ['Unfair Terms in Consumer Credit Agreements – a Hot Theme in National and European Legislation'] (2014) Revista Română de Arbitraj, available also at http://www.juridice.ro/326335/clauzele-abuzive-in-contractele-de-credit-o-tema-incandescenta-in-dreptul-national-si-cel-european.html [last visited on 30 June 2014].

7 Official Journal of Romania, Part I, 855, 18.12.2012.

8 Eligible income is the income left after deducting subsistence expenses from the total value of the income.

9 The NBR defines the non-performing loan as 'the share of loans overdue for more than 90 days and/or for which legal proceedings have been opened' (definition provided in relation to loans to companies, but which applies also to the loans to individuals), see NBR Financial Stability Report of 2013, 110, footnote 37 (report available online).

10 NBR Financial Stability Report of 2011, 100; NBR's Monthly Bulletins. In addition, the NBR Financial Stability Report uses also the term 'arrears' which is defined as payments overdue for more than 90 days.

11 According to the data provided by the NBR Financial Stability Report of 2008 and 2004; more details in M Moraru and B Andreşan-Grigoriu, 'The Over-Indebtedness of European Consumers after the Financial Crisis: Country Report Romania', 2014 in I Domurath, G Comparato and H-W Micklitz (eds), 'The Over-Indebtedness of European Consumers – a View from Six Countries', EUI Working Paper LAW 2014/10.

decreasing every year.[12] However, in spite of a decline in the total number registered in June 2012, a high percentage of the active population (43 per cent) remained indebted. The average loan duration has also remained high since 2009. In 2013, it was reported to be 21 years for mortgage-backed exposures and six years for consumer loans other than mortgages.[13] The fact that a high percentage of these mortgage-backed credits were contracted either directly in a foreign currency or forex-denominated (euros, Swiss francs and US dollars) has increased the risk of default for this type of credit.

The main type of loans contracted by households is consumption loans, followed by real estate credit. While 55.5 per cent of the total number of loans were taken for consumer purposes, 35.5 per cent were taken for housing purposes.[14] Around 60 per cent of the total number of loans are secured with a mortgage.[15] A look at the statistics provided by the NBR for the period 2008–2013 shows that the total number of consumption loans, in spite of a slow decrease, was higher than the real estate loans. All real estate loans as well as a large proportion of those taken for consumption purposes were secured with mortgage guarantees. This type of mortgage secured loan has steadily increased every year since 2008. Credit card debt has also contributed to raising the indebtedness level of consumers. The number of consumers with credit cards has increased every year since 2008 until 2013 when a slow decrease was registered. At the same time, the debt accumulated by credit card holders doubled between 2008 and 2012.[16]

It is important to note that in Romania – a country outside the Eurozone – many credit obligations, and the majority of the mortgage secured loans,[17] were contracted directly in foreign currency with the consumer bearing the obligation to buy the foreign currency and pay the monthly instalment in the contracted foreign currency, or forex-denominated loans (2004–2006 mainly in Swiss francs; afterwards in euros), while the income of consumers was and is paid in the national currency (the Romanian leu, RON).[18] In spite of the fact that these two types of loans have been one of the main causes of over-indebtedness and evictions in Romania, and the increasing publicity of

12 Total number of indebted households in December 2009: 4,070,031; in December 2010: 3,929,726; in December 2011: 3,791,204; in December 2012: 3,809,976; in September 2013: 3,662,835 (NBR, reply to questionnaire from 14 November 2013).

13 NBR Financial Stability Report of 2013, 131.

14 NBR Bank Lending Survey, May and August of 2013.

15 In 2006, 62 per cent (NBR Financial Stability Report of 2007); in 2013, 60 per cent (NBR Financial Stability Report of 2013).

16 M Moraru and B Andreşan-Grigoriu (n 11).

17 See NBR Financial Stability Report of 2013.

18 The Romanian banking market includes approximately 40 credit institutions. In December 2012, 89.9 per cent of the total assets of the Romanian banking sector belonged to those with foreign capital, which could be an explanation for the foreign currency denominated loans focused strategy of the Romanian banking sector. As regards the origin of the shareholders function of assets, the banks with Austrian capital hold a market share of 37.7 per cent, followed by the banks with French capital with 13.6 per cent and those with Greek capital with 12.2 per cent (data provided by the Romanian Banking Association, available at http://www.arb.ro/en/sistemul-bancar-din-romania/sistemul-bancar-din-romania [last visited on 30 June 2014]). In addition to the high share of foreign banks in the Romanian banking market which had advantageous interest rates for foreign currency and forex-denominated loans, another cause for the high indebtedness of consumers in foreign currencies was the consumers' high confidence in the stability of the Swiss franc as a foreign currency, and later on in the euro, without predicting the subsequent high depreciation of the national currency in relation to these foreign currencies.

the problems faced by consumers for this type of loan,[19] a high percentage of credit continued to be taken directly in euro, or as forex (mainly euro) denominated loans.[20]

Starting in 2008, the level of over-indebtedness grew rapidly, to the extent that by the end of 2008 the volume of overdue payments had tripled. Similarly, throughout 2009 and 2011, overdue payments and the non-performing loans (NPLs) continued to increase.[21] A study commissioned by the European Commission shows that in 2011 more than three in 10 households were in arrears.[22] While in 2012, on average, every fourth household declared arrears in repaying at least one loan.[23] Loans denominated in a foreign currency accounted for one third of the total overdue payment in February 2008, and this percentage has risen in the following years.[24]

In the first half of 2013, signs showing that households were starting to improve their debt servicing capacity started to appear. For example, the recovery rate of loans overdue for one day to 90 days rose slightly in the first trimester of 2013 (84 per cent compared to 82.5 per cent in 2012). The number of consumers that were registered with payment delays of more than 90 days for the first time during the period between January 2012 and June 2013 diminished by 6.4 per cent compared to the same six-month period in the previous year. Banks' rescheduling strategies[25] played a part in this improvement. However, they failed to reach their full potential in relation to preventing or decreasing the number of NPLs. Although there are several possibilities for debt reorganisation, of which the most common is loan rescheduling and refinancing, they have not proved to be sufficient in helping borrowers to fulfil their payment obligations on time.[26] Rescheduling did not lead to a significant improvement in non-performing loans, as proved by the fact that recovery rates were relatively similar for both rescheduled and not rescheduled credit. At the same time, refinancing was

19 Starting with end of 2009, financial journals, lawyers and the National Authority for Consumers' Protection started to raise the awareness of the public on the different problems faced by consumers with foreign currency denominated loans (increasing rate interests due to depreciation of the RON to euros and the banks' so-called abusive strategies to cover this risk, as well as those stemming from the financial crisis) and the legislative amendments.

20 In June 2012, real-estate loans and mortgage-backed consumer loans were still granted in overwhelming numbers in foreign currency (95.5 per cent of real-estate loans and 91 per cent of mortgage-backed consumer loans, banks and NBFI), amounting to 68 per cent of all household loans being foreign currency denominated loans.

21 Short study published by the Financial Companies Association, 17 November 2011; NBR Annual Report 2011, 38, available at http://www.bnro.ro/Regular-publications-2504.aspx_[last visited on 30 June 2014].

22 Report 'The Over-Indebtedness of European Households: Updated Mapping of the Situation, Nature and Causes, Effects and Initiatives for Alleviating its Impact', study conducted by Civic Consulting of the Consumer Policy Evaluation Consortium in January 2013 for the European Commission available at http://www.bristol.ac.uk/geography/research/pfrc/news/pfrc1301.pdf_[last visited on 30 June 2014].

23 P Anioła and Z Gołaś, 'Differences in the Level and Structure of Household Indebtedness in the EU Countries' (2012) Journal of Contemporary Economics 46.

24 For more data, M Moraru and B Andreşan-Grigoriu (n 11).

25 Romanian legislation does not provide rules for the personal bankruptcy of natural persons. When consumers are in a situation where they can no longer fulfil their payment obligations towards banks or financial institutions, the only solution is reorganisation of debt (loan rescheduling or refinancing). If these measures prove unsuccessful, the creditor will start eviction procedures. For more details, M Moraru and B Andreşan-Grigoriu (n 11).

26 NBR Financial Stability Report 2013.

not possible for a large percentage of the foreign currency denominated loans since the guarantees given, including the immovable ones, could not cover a loan refinancing.[27]

Against this background, the difficulties in meeting the payment requirements were experienced mostly by young families, the unemployed and borrowers with a salary income lower than the average salary,[28] mostly for foreign currency and forex-denominated credits concluded between 2006 and 2010 for housing purposes. The lower the monthly income of consumers was, the lower their capacity to pay the interest on the credit. For instance, the overdue payments ratio for the category of debtors with the lowest income (below 500 RON which is approximately 110 euro) was about five times higher than those receiving the average income. In 2012, the population with an income below the minimum wage of 700 RON (approximately 150 euro) per month had the highest level of underperforming loans.[29]

In sum, the consumers with a monthly net income below the average monthly salary represented and continue to represent more than half of the debtors with NPLs.[30] Borrowers with a net income below the minimum wage thus experienced the highest level of indebtedness, the highest level of over-indebtedness, and the highest risk of facing problems in repaying their financial obligations on time.

In conclusion, the significant over-indebtedness of consumers in general is determined to a large extent by the high non-performing loan ratio of below-average income earners, a category of consumers that, under the negative impact of the financial crisis on monthly salaries and the depreciation of RON to euro and other foreign currencies, widened considerably after 2009.[31]

Causes of Indebtedness and Over-Indebtedness in Romania

The causes of over-indebtedness in Romania are manifold. Among the most significant factors are: the housing and credit bubble; a high unemployment rate;[32] the practice of foreign currencies and forex-denominated loans, making the amount of monthly instalments contingent upon fluctuating exchange rates; the high fluctuations in the interest rate due to the depreciation of the RON to the foreign currency of the contracted loan, and to the bank's policies responding to the legislative amendments implementing the relevant EU consumer protection.[33]

---

27 A large number of indebted consumers saw their interest rates, especially for foreign currency denominated loans, rise considerably from the first year of the contracted loan. See on this topic, surveys indicating the percentage of increase in loan payments for different banks on the financial website of economica.net.

28 The average salary is approximately 2,200 RON (approximately 500 euro). Data collected through interviews with consumers and financial reports of the NBR and National Institute of Statistics.

29 With rates of 25 per cent for consumer credit and 11 per cent in mortgage credit.

30 In 2012 the NPLs of consumers with a monthly net income below the average salary represented approximately 70 per cent of the total number of those with NPLs. According to the NBR Financial Report of 2013, in 2013, it is still this category of consumers that holds a significant share of the banks' portfolio of NPLs. In addition to the NBR Financial Report of 2013, see also http://www.business-adviser.ro/bnr-romanii-sunt-printre-cei-mai-indatorati-dintre- Europeni.html [last visited on 30 June 2014].

31 NBR Financial Stability Report 2013, 130.

32 Compared to 2007, in 2010, the number of unemployed individuals has increased by more than 13 per cent; see L Mărcuța, A Mărcuța and C Angelescu, 'Effects of the Economic Crisis on the Standard of Living in Romania' (2013) Procedia Economics and Finance 6 89–95.

33 NBR Financial Stability Report of 2013, 129. See more details on the banks policies' responding legislative amendments implementing the EU Directives 93/13/EC and 2008/48/EC in section B.

There has long been a cultural desire for home ownership in Romania after its communist past. The percentage of private ownership increased steadily[34] until 2012 when it reached a level where the housing market was approximately 95 per cent owner-occupied.[35] This high growth in home ownership was possible due to the policy of several banks,[36] beginning in the late 1990s, of expanding their mortgage lending practices. Such expansion also led to irresponsible lending practices. At some point, credit was even given based solely on showing the national identity card.[37] In parallel to the cultural characteristic of strong housing ownership, in the period between 2006 and 2008, the economy was flooded with foreign capital and much of the money ended up being real estate investments.[38] In addition, the National Housing Agency (ANL), which acts primarily as a housing development and construction agency, started to provide subsidised loans to eligible borrowers.[39] In order to respond to the Romanian consumers' high demand for houses and to partially alleviate the cumbersome long-term and high interest bank credits for housing purposes, the government developed the 'First House' programme,[40] improving access to mortgage credit. Fifty-three per cent of the housing loans granted in 2011 and the first half of 2012 were contracted under this programme. At first, these loans were almost exclusively (99 per cent) denominated in foreign currency[41] but later shifted to loans predominantly in the national currency.

Increasing demand coupled with easier access to housing credit led to a substantial increase in housing prices. In 2009, when the financial crisis hit several countries, Romania was the country with the highest price for houses per income ratio in the world.[42] In the following years housing prices contracted, however, in 2013 Romania was still among the top 30 countries in the world in this regard. However, the NBR considered the rising housing prices (in 2007 more than 50 per cent

34 From 5.3 in 2007 to 8.4 in 2013. Distribution of population by tenure status, type of household and income group, see ECRI Statistical Package 2013: *Lending to Households 2013*.

35 Housing Europe Review 2012, *The Nuts and Bolts of European Social Housing Systems*, CECODHAS Housing Europe's Observatory (Brussels, October 2011), available at http://www.housing Europe.eu/www.housing Europe.eu/uploads/file_/HER percent202012 per cent%20EN %20web2_1.pdf [last visited on 30 June 2014].

36 Such as BCR, HVB, Alpha Bank, Raiffeisen and Ro-Fin.

37 For more details, M Moraru and B Andreşan-Grigoriu (n 11).

38 Declaration of the NBR President at the NBR colloquium on 25 June 2014, warning of the possible return of the housing bubble experienced by Romania in 2006–2008, available at http://www.bnro.ro/Colocviu-Statistica-sectorului-extern-in-contextul-noilor-standarde-metodologice-11152.aspx [last visited on 30 June 2014].

39 The Urban Institute, *Developing Secondary Mortgage Markets in Southeast Europe: Assessment of the Mortgage Market in Romania*, available at http://www.ceemortgagefinance.org/pdfs/Romania_assessment.pdf [last visited on 30 June 2014].

40 The 'First House Programme' is part of the anti-crisis measures initiated by the government to support the priority economic sectors. The main objective is to unlock lending and support the construction sector, which was aimed to have positive effects on the economic activity and create new jobs. Furthermore, the programme was aimed to improve the population's access to mortgages. For this purpose, the state offered to guarantee 50 per cent of the loans granted by banks, provided they gave cheaper loans to individual consumers. Legislative framework includes OUG no. 60/2009 concerning certain measure on the implementation of the programme 'First House' and Decision no. 717/2009 concerning the adoption of the norms implementing the programme 'First House'.

41 NBR Annual Report 2011.

42 More details on the house prices in Romania and their evolution from 2009 onwards is available at http://www.globalpropertyguide.com/ Europe/Romania [last visited on 30 June 2014].

of the average value per square metre of a standard dwelling) to be normal consequences of the economic growth.

Another specific cause of the Romanian consumer over-indebtedness was the rising foreign exchange rate coupled with the high number of loans contracted directly in a foreign currency or denominated in a foreign currency.[43] The irresponsible lending practices followed by the banks before the start of the financial crisis also contributed towards encouraging consumers to undertake obligations that were not sustainable in the long run and gave them a false impression of what the interest rate would be throughout the course of a long-term credit agreement.[44] At the beginning of the financial crisis, the national currency depreciated against the euro by up to 40 per cent,[45] placing consumers with forex-denominated loans in an extremely difficult position.[46]

In short, an analysis of the evolution of the households' non-performing loans shows the persistence of four main causes. First, the persistently high number of household credit in foreign currency and forex-denominated loans,[47] for which the credit risk is higher than those relating to domestic currency loans. This is due mainly to the increase in the exchange rate, to which the other effects of the financial crisis (such as, *inter alia*, unemployment, rise of taxes and prices) added. Second, in spite of the fact that the NPLs in foreign currency received greater attention from banks with respect to restructuring,[48] this type of loan continued to create outstanding payments and led to evictions. The failure of the loan reorganisation process was due also to the limited methods which banks could employ, as refinancing was often not possible due to the fact that the guarantees that had been given could not cover refinancing. Third, instead of drafting rescheduling plans that would tackle the new problems faced by consumers under the impact of the financial crisis, the banks' loan strategies after the entry into force of OUG 50/2010[49] were more concerned with how to keep their high interest rates for credit and circumvent the safety rules imposed by the new legislative measures aimed to protect the consumer from abusive behaviour in credit contracts. Among their strategies, banks chose to unilaterally increase the variable interest rate or introduced new types of commission. In the following paragraphs, we will examine this issue, along with the

43 World Bank, *Diagnostic Review of Consumer Protection and Financial Literacy in Romania*, July 2009, 1. For example, in early 2007, foreign currency mortgages accounted for 85.5 per cent of total mortgage loans to households. Thus, of the approximately 7.9 billion RON lent by banks to customers who wanted to buy a home, the equivalent of 6 billion was borrowed in euro and 0.7 billion in other foreign currencies, especially Swiss francs and dollars. At the end of 2007, over half of all households' debt was in foreign currency.

44 In 2013, it was reported that the average duration of mortgage-backed exposures was 21 years and six years for non-mortgage consumer loans (NBR Financial Stability Report 2013, 131).

45 E Beckmann and IJ Fidrmuc II Helmut Stix, 'Foreign Currency Loans and Loan Arrears of Households in Central and Eastern Europe', available at http://econpapers.repec.org/paper/onboenbwp/181.htm [last visited on 30 June 2014].

46 In 2012 more than half of the households loans were in euro; loans taken for housing purposes were approximately 90 per cent in euro with the majority of the rest in other foreign currencies, and the remaining smallest percentage in the national currency. Consumer loans and loans for other purposes where given mostly in RON, followed at a small distance by loans in euro, and very few in other foreign currencies. See for more details, M Moraru and B Andreşan-Grigoriu (n 11).

47 Before the start of the financial crisis mortgage loans were in majority contracted in foreign currency or forex-denominated, and, in spite of the decline in recent years, they continue to have a high share in the private loans portfolio.

48 About 80 per cent of the volume of restructured loans targeted non-performing loans in foreign currency, number corresponding to loans outstanding in May 2013.

49 The law transposing Directive 2008/48/EC. See section B below.

overall reaction of the banks to the legislative amendments introduced by the OUG 50/2010 and other legislative acts, as well as the reaction of private and public consumer associations and courts.

C. Legal Framework and the Role of Private Law

In this section we will see that the legal framework applicable for consumer and mortgage credit has improved since the start of the financial crisis, mainly due to choices of the legislator when transposing Directive 2008/48/EC. The relevant provisions set out by the Civil and Civil Procedure Codes also helped by allowing the consumer to raise substantive objections when opposing enforcement (including on the basis of the unfair character of the contractual terms) and by codifying previous jurisprudential developments on adjustment of contracts in cases of hardship. However, despite several attempts, a special law on insolvency of natural persons is still missing from the legal framework. Moreover, a countrywide debate and analysis of the enforcement procedure from the perspective of consumers' protection against unfair terms has not yet taken place.

Implementation of European Instruments in the National Legal Order

The EU instruments relevant for our discussion were integrated in the Romanian legal system by the adoption of two special statutes: Law No. 193/2000 regarding unfair terms in contracts (Law 193/2000)[50] transposing Directive 93/13/EEC (UCT Directive),[51] and Government Emergency Ordinance No. 50/2010 (OUG 50/2010) on credit agreements for consumers, transposing Directive 2008/48/EC (Consumer Credit Directive).[52] Articles 3 and 4 of the UCT Directive were transposed almost literally in Article 4 of Law 193/2000. As we will see below, the terms that could be deemed as relating to the object of the contract have been the subject of ample litigation.

Making use of the margin of discretion in the transposition of the Consumer Credit Directive, Romania decided to extend the required substantive and temporal scope of the EU Directive. First, it modified the temporal scope of the Directive, stating that its provisions were to apply also to credit agreements in place at the time of its entry into force. Both the constitutionality and the compatibility of this provision with Directive 2008/48 and several provisions of TFEU were challenged by a Romanian bank in proceedings for the annulment of sanctions applied by the National Authority of Consumer Protection (NACP) for abusive behaviour.[53] The proceedings included a preliminary reference to the CJEU. Only four months after the entry into force of OUG 50/2010, and before the answer of the CJEU, the legal provision on the temporal application of the OUG was amended to the effect that the act was only applicable to future credit agreements. This gave rise to further problems in practice and increased litigation before the national courts. Second, the transposition act extended the material scope of the Directive, making it also applicable to credit agreements secured by mortgages or by other rights on immovable property (Article 2); this too was challenged by the same credit institution mentioned above. Third, a series of detailed

50 Official Journal of Romania, Part I, No. 506, 10.11.2000. Last amended by Law No. 76/2012 implementing Law 134/2010 on the adoption of the Code of civil procedure, which introduced the so-called collective action from 1 October 2013.

51 Also known as the Unfair Contractual Terms Directive (UCT Directive).

52 Official Journal of Romania, Part I, No. 389, 11.06.2010.

53 NAPC is the public institution with legal personality, functioning under the direction of the Ministry for Economy, Commerce and Environment, which is responsible for the coordination and implementation of governmental policy on the protection of consumers.

conditions on information duties binding the creditor were introduced. They go beyond those required by the Directive and also apply to credit agreements secured by mortgages or by other rights in immovable property.[54]

Possibilities for Consumers to Raise Substantive Objections Against Enforcement in Case of Default

The legal framework regulating credit agreements and the assessment of potentially unfair terms therein is not complete without a description of the enforcement stage. According to the new Code of Civil Procedure (NCCP),[55] the consumer may raise objections against the enforcement order within the special procedure called 'objection to enforcement' (*contestatie la executare*). In cases where a bank enforces the contract directly, the consumer may oppose the enforcement proceedings initiated by the creditor based on the unfairness of the contractual term. Article 712(2) NCCP does not explicitly mention it as a ground, but the language is such that it can be interpreted as including it ('legal or factual grounds regarding the substance of the right').[56]

During the objection to enforcement, the debtor or the creditor may ask the court to stay the enforcement proceedings. According to Article 718(1) NCCP, the court has the power to suspend the enforcement proceedings for 'reasonable grounds'. The general wording of the provision allows the judge to interpret them as including the 'unfair' character of the contractual term among the reasons for suspending the proceedings. It follows that the judge may exercise this power only in the second situation described above, where there were no previous judicial proceedings disputing the legality of the contract. However, while the court enjoys discretion regarding the evaluation of the grounds for ordering a stay of enforcement proceedings, the mandatory condition laid down at paragraph (2) of the same article might raise problems similar to those in *Aziz*.[57] According to this paragraph, the person who asks for a stay of enforcement proceedings must lodge a deposit in an amount that varies according to the value in dispute, which might prove to be difficult or even impossible for an over-indebted person.

Possibility of Objecting to Enforcement Based on Unforeseen Events Such As Unemployment or in Case of Frustration of Contractual Purpose

Article 38 of OUG 50/2010 on the reimbursement of credit provides that, in the case of overdue credits,[58] where the consumer or their spouse is unemployed, deceased or their salary has been drastically reduced,[59] the applicable interest rate cannot be above two percentage points the interest rate applicable when the payment is not overdue. The debtor may benefit from this reduced overdue interest rate until the circumstance ceases, but no longer than 12 months, with a minimum of six

54 M Moraru and B Andreşan-Grigoriu (n 11).

55 The NCCP entered into force on 15 February 2013 and it applies to proceedings initiated after the date of entry into force.

56 When enforcement is based on a court judgment, the objection to enforcement may regard only new issues that appear during the enforcement proceedings, in consideration of the *res judicata* effect of the judgment.

57 *Aziz*, C-415/11, EU:C:2013:164.

58 Art. 38 OUG 50/2010 applies to the limited circumstances of overdue credits, which implies the moment in time after the formation of the credit contract.

59 This latter circumstance is defined as a reduction of at least 15 per cent of the amount of the salary.

months in the case of death.[60] In addition to this special provision there is the general rule of contract law under Article 1271 of the NCC that allows for the adjustment of contractual terms for 'hardship' ('impreviziune'). The rule that the contract has the power of law between the parties is emphasised in paragraph 1 which states that parties to a contract must fulfil the terms of the contract, even if performance of the contract becomes 'more onerous', either because of an increase in the costs of a party's performance or a decrease in the value of the performance a party receives. Article 1271(2) lays down an exception for the situation where the performance of the contract may become '*excessively* onerous due to an *exceptional* change in the circumstances that would render the obligation of the debtor to perform the contract manifestly unjust'.[61] The courts may order a revision of the terms of the contract ('the equitable distribution between the parties of losses and gains which result from the change in circumstances') or termination of the contract.

The concept of 'hardship', which is not new to Romanian contract law, is yet to be tested in court in its present form. While absent from the former Code, it was present in a few special laws such as the law on copyright[62] and the law on concessions.[63] Under the influence of the doctrine, there are judicial decisions, albeit only a few, where it was acknowledged that in the case of contracts with subsequent execution, unforeseen events such as the liberalisation of prices or the considerable drop in the market value of real estate may affect contractual balance to the detriment of the debtor and to such extent that an adaptation of the contract was ordered.[64]

Under the new Article 1271 NCC, it is anticipated that it will be difficult for the courts to distinguish 'excessively onerous' from 'more onerous' in a uniform and predictable manner. One author suggests an interpretation consistent with Article 6.2.2 UNIDROIT, which defines hardship where 'the occurrence of events fundamentally alters the equilibrium of the contract either because the cost of a party's performance has increased or because the value of the performance a party receives has diminished'.[65] The High Court of Cassation and Justice acknowledged hardship in a decision from 2003 where performance of the contract became impossible or the new circumstances make it radically different from the initial obligations.[66] It is expected that the new provision will be

60 Article 38 of OUG 50/2010 should be read jointly with OG 13/2011 regarding the legal compensatory or penalising interest for money obligations and other financial-fiscal measures in the banking sector (Official Journal of Romania, Part I, No. 607, 30.08.2011). This act defines the penalising legal interest as the interest owed by the debtor for overdue payments and sets a value of 4 percentage points above the level of the reference interest rate of the National Bank.

61 Emphasis added. The conditions to be met for the application of this provision are: the change in circumstances must have occurred after the agreement was concluded and was not and could not have been reasonably foreseen by the debtor when the agreement was concluded; the debtor did not accept the risk of the change in circumstances and it could not have been reasonably considered to have accepted it; the debtor tried in a reasonable time limit and in good faith to negotiate the reasonable and equitable adjustment of the agreement.

62 Law 8/1996 (Official Journal of Romania, Part I, No. 60, 26.03.1996).

63 Law 219/1998, currently repealed.

64 G Viorel and LA Viorel, 'Configurația impreviziunii în Codul Civil' ['The Configuration of Hardship in the Civil Code'] (2012) Dreptul 30, 31–32.

65 G Tița-Nicolescu, 'Excepțiile de la principiul obligativității efectelor contractului prevăzute de Noul Cod civil' ['Exceptions from the Binding Effect of the Contract provided by the New Civil Code'] (2012) Pandectele Române 9, 17.

66 Decision No. 1122/2003, cited in G. Viorel and L.A. Viorel (n 64) 35. This type of decision is not binding on lower courts, but it certainly informs their analysis in similar cases.

interpreted in a manner consistent with previous case-law and doctrine, but the range of unforeseen events that qualify for its application remains to be determined.[67]

Changes in Litigation Since the Crisis

The wave of consumer complaints before judicial and non-judicial bodies has grown as a result of a combination of mainly three legal and non-legal factors. The first factor is the financial crisis putting a large number of households in financially difficult situations; the second is Romania's legislative choices for transposing the relevant EU legislation on consumer credit contracts which had considerably raised the standards of consumer protection imposed by the EU legislation (by way of extending protection to a wider category of credit contracts and limiting the types of fees that banks could claim, and recently expanding the category of claimants with *locus standi* before courts that could claim sanctions for abusive contractual clauses[68]); and the third factor is the banks' unfortunate choices for credit contract amendments and arrears management in reaction to the Romanian specific legal framework transposing Directive 2008/48 and the financial crisis.

Regarding the type of claimants initiating court proceedings related to consumer protection in credit agreements, there has been an evolution, starting with individual actions brought by tens and later even hundreds of individual consumers, some of these claims being joined due to their similar subject matter. Subsequently, a second wave was started by the banks and financial institutions challenging the administrative sanctions imposed by the NACP. The latest wave of claims started after 1 October 2013, which are the so-called collective actions initiated by the NACP and other consumer protection associations.[69]

Litigation concerning consumer credit agreements has reached all levels of court jurisdiction, including the supreme court of Romania – the High Court of Cassation and Justice[70] – and has also spread geographically. So far, eight preliminary references[71] on the interpretation of provisions of Directive 93/13 and Directive 2008/48 were sent to the CJEU in proceedings concerning loan agreements from different regions of the country. Moreover, the Constitutional Court rejected, on the merits, several pleas of unconstitutionality of OUG 50/2010, which were raised in proceedings concerning consumer loan agreements.

---

67 For a thorough analysis of hardship, see C Zamşa, *Teoria impreviziunii. Studiu de doctrină şi jurisprudenţă* [*The Theory of Hardship: A Study of Doctrine and Case Law*] (Hamangiu Press 2006). For an argument that there is nothing to prevent its use in the context of credit agreements, E Mihai, 'Principiul echilibrului contractual în noul Cod Civil şi dreptul consumului' ['The Principle of Contractual Balance in the New Civil Code and Consumer Law'] (2013) 1 Pandectele Române 18, 24.

68 M Avram, 'Clauzele abuzive în contractele de împrumut bancar: legislaţie europeană vs. cea naţională. Jurisprudenţa recentă a CJUE' ['Unfair Terms in Consumer Credit Agreements: European v. National Legislation. Recent Case Law of the CJEU'], paper presented at the conference *Probleme actuale de drept european instituţional şi privat* [*Current Issues of Institutional and Private European Law*], 5 June 2014, University of Bucharest.

69 The former president of the NACP declared that the so-called type of collective action was introduced against 11 banks, while the Romanian banking market comprises a total of 40 credit institutions (see, inter alia, files nos: 317/3/2014, 37822/3/2013, 5410/3/2014, 316/3/2014, 36773/3/2013, 36772/3/2013 and 314/3/2014, available at http://portal.just.ro/SitePages/acasa.aspx [last visited on 30 June 2014]).

70 According to procedural rules establishing competence, in private proceedings (not involving the NACP) the amount in dispute is one of the criteria determining which court is competent to hear a case. Thus both local courts and county courts may hear cases in first instance. If a case started before the county court, the second appeal will be heard by the High Court of Cassation and Justice.

71 Since accession to the EU and before 1 June 2014 (out of a total of 73).

Even though there is no official data available on the total number of consumer complaints about the use of unfair contractual terms in credit contracts,[72] it can be stated that the number of cases brought both before the NACP or national courts reaches tens of thousands (one bank alone was involved in over 2,000 cases). Consumers especially make use of the administrative complaint procedure prescribed by Law 193/2000 before the NACP. In 2008, the number of complaints reached 4,000, half of which were registered in October 2008, when banks started to unilaterally increase the interest rates in credit agreements secured with mortgages. An amendment to Law 193/2000 that gave the NACP power to ask for collective remedies contributed to keeping the number of complaints before the NACP high.[73] Articles 12–13 of Law 193/2000 on the protection of consumers regarding unfair terms in contracts introduced a sort of collective remedy for consumers injured by unfair contractual terms. Accordingly, the NACP has the competence to initiate investigations into the practice of financial institutions and, upon a finding that the contracts under inspection include unfair terms, it must file an action before the competent court asking it to order the removal of the unfair terms from the contracts in progress. Furthermore, a similar type of collective action can be submitted also by consumer associations against sellers of goods or suppliers of services who use unfair terms in their consumer contracts.[74]

Under the new provisions,[75] if the court deems that the contract comprises unfair terms for consumers, it can order the supplier to modify all of its ongoing contracts containing unfair terms by removing such unfair terms from the contract, or (where the associations of consumers initiated the proceedings) to remove the unfair terms from all its standard contracts. A fine is also to be applied. While such judgment has wider effects than a judgment *inter partes*, it will produce effects limited to the contractual relationships between that particular supplier and its consumers. This means that other professionals who use the exact same unfair terms in their standard contracts will not be affected by a judicial decision delivered against them directly.[76]

72 There is no comprehensive database of case-law in Romania, but only local databases serving each court (approximately 100 which would have on their docket relevant case-law), which are not interconnected and which can be checked only on local computers. Relevant case-law is not archived under a particular heading and therefore data cannot be extracted by way of a keyword search.

73 The former president of the NACP declared that this type of collective actions were introduced against 11 banks, while the Romanian banking market comprises a total of 40 credit institutions (files nos: 317/3/2014, 37822/3/2013, 5410/3/2014, 316/3/2014, 36773/3/2013, 36772/3/2013 and 314/3/2014, available at http://portal.just.ro/SitePages/acasa.aspx [last visited on 27 June 2014]).

74 According to the revised version of Law no. 193/2000. This procedure became applicable in October 2013.

75 Before this new provision, some consumers who concluded contracts with the same bank organised themselves and used the procedural means provided by the Code of Civil Procedure to achieve a similar result. To this end, they could file civil actions individually and subsequently petition the court to join them based on the similarity of object. Several such disputes were filed before different regional courts (files nos. 6169/337/2010, 2133/216/2010, 11652/306/2011); the Tribunal of Bucharest reviewed cases with 100 or 80 complainants. However, this led to protracted proceedings and limited legal effects (only *inter partes*).

76 A thorough analysis of more issues that raise doubts about the efficacy of the new provisions in L Bercea, 'Acţiunile colective în eliminarea clauzelor abuzive din contractele standard de consum. *Cui prodest*?' ['Collective Actions for the Removal of Unfair Terms in Standard Contracts. *Cui prodest*?'], 20 June 2013, available at www.juridice.ro [last visited on 30 June 2014].

Predominant Issues in Litigation

Before the NACP, the most common type of complaint relates to the illegal increase in interest rates and commission, the introduction of commission that was not initially included in the credit agreement, closure of accounts that are not operated in a timely manner, and misleading promotions such as bonuses on deposits or low initial interest. According to NACP's statements, a considerable part of these complaints were closed after the imposition of fines to credit institutions.

In the past years, Romanian courts became gradually aware of the European origin of the legislation on consumer protection. Law 193/2000 was adopted well before accession to the EU and was used in a variety of proceedings, mostly concerning telecommunications services and insurance contracts. Issues litigated before accession and the financial crisis included the obligation of assessment of the unfair nature of the terms *ex officio*.[77] In contrast, by the time of the adoption of OUG 50/2010, the publicity surrounding its nature as an act implementing an EU Directive greatly contributed to making its compatibility with the Directive a forefront issue, especially in the context of the financial crisis.[78] This prompted two identical preliminary references concerning the extension of the material and temporal scope of Directive 2008/48 by OUG 50/2010, to which we will refer below.

The three most important issues in litigation concerned the potentially unfair character of the unilateral increase of the variable interest rate by the credit institutions in relation to 'significant changes on the financial market',[79] the material and temporal scope of OUG 50/2010 in comparison to its parent Directive 2008/48, and the question whether the notions of 'subject-matter' and 'price' referred to in Article 4(2) of Directive 93/13/EEC cover the annual percentage rate in a credit agreement secured by a mortgage. With respect to the unilateral increase of the variable interest rate, it was challenged whether such a contractual term was unfair and what the legal effects of such a finding would be. The background to the dispute is provided by the Annex to Law 193/2000, which declares unfair a term that allows the unilateral change of the contract without a clearly specified reason, but makes an exception for suppliers of financial services, who are allowed to change the interest rate without notification if they have a 'valid reason' and inform the consumer as soon as possible.

Regarding the unfairness of the unilateral increase of the variable interest rate, two lines of thought emerged in the jurisprudence. The majority of the courts held that 'significant changes on the financial market' was a wide and ambiguous expression, which may include any kind of fluctuations in the market, in the absence of any kind of reference point, and therefore does not qualify as a 'valid reason'. Other courts argued the contrary, on the grounds that all banking institutions take into account the policy of the National Bank, which determines the reference interest rate and the interest rates on the interbank market. Thus, the rate cannot only increase, but also decrease, and therefore qualifies as a 'valid reason'. In addition, it was considered that the elimination of the clause as unfair would lead to a change in the contract from a variable interest

77 *Océano Grupo Editorial*, Joined Cases C-240/98 to C-244/98, EU:C:2000:346.

78 D Efrim, M Moraru and G Zanfir, 'The Hesitating Steps of the Romanian Courts Towards Judicial Dialogue on EU Law Matters', available at http://papers.ssrn.com/sol3/papers.cfm?abstract_id=2261915 [last visited on 30 June 2014].

79 Lending institutions had 90 days from the entry into force of the OUG 50/2010 to amend this type of clause.

rate credit agreement to a fixed interest rate one, which was not intended by either party when the agreement was concluded. The courts that found the term unfair also refuted this latter ground.[80]

For several years, national jurisprudence was also divided on the effects of an assessment of unfairness. According to Law 193/2000, the 'unfair' term does not 'produce effects on' (cannot be opposed to) the consumer, which is an ambiguous and nonsensical choice of words from the perspective of Romanian contract law, probably made by the legislator in a misguided attempt to transpose the Directive literally. The expression was interpreted to imply the nullity of the term, but there was divergence as to the type of nullity, which was a significant issue for the application of the statute of limitations. Based on the general interest of consumer protection, the High Court of Cassation and Justice decided last year that the appropriate sanction is absolute nullity. The High Court based its reasoning entirely on the interpretation of the objective of the Directive in the case law of the CJEU.[81]

The second important issue in the litigation concerned the question whether the extension of the material and temporal scope of Directive 2008/48 by its transposition law was within the margin of discretion of the state. As shown above, OUG 50/2010 included in its material scope credit agreements secured by mortgages and applied initially to contracts in progress. It also provided an exhaustive list of the types of commissions a bank may charge. These issues were dealt with by the CJEU in C-602/10 *Volksbank (I)*.[82] The Court decided that the national legislature was free to extend the scope of application of the Directive to other types of contracts, such as credit agreements secured by mortgages, that were, *in casu*, the object of the main proceedings. It also stated that its maximum harmonisation nature applied only to the contracts within its scope, therefore in the absence of other EU legislation, Romania was free to regulate other matters not covered by the Directive, such as the type of commission a bank may charge in contracts not covered by its material scope, such as credit agreements secured by mortgages.[83] The Court's ruling would have probably led to an outcome favourable to the consumer, but in the particular proceedings the referring court dismissed the case.[84] The reason for the dismissal was the referring court's interpretation of the change in national legislation, which occurred shortly after the preliminary reference was sent to the CJEU and before the delivery of the preliminary ruling. According to Law 288/2010 approving with amendments OUG 50/2010, the obligations imposed on lending institutions would no longer apply to contracts in progress, except in very limited exceptional situations, but only to future credit contracts.[85] This amendment raised further problems connected to the application of

80 A detailed description of both lines of reasoning in N Țăndăreanu, 'Clauze abuzive. Clauza de ajustare a ratei dobânzii în raport de schimbările semnificative de pe piața monetară' ['Unfair Terms: Changing the Interest Rate According to Changes on the Financial Market'] (2012) 6 RRDJ 51.

81 Decision no. 686/2013.

82 *Volksbank*, C-602/10, EU:C:2012:443. The charge in dispute was the so-called 'risk charge' equal to 0.2 per cent of the balance of the loan which had to be paid monthly by the consumer throughout the loan term. In the saga of 'risk charge' which divided the courts, there have been recently (in 2013) a few confusing decisions of the High Court regarding the notion of risks in loan agreements, ranging from the opinion that banking is a business where banks assume no risk (Decision No. 3913/13 November 2013), to the opinion that the security provided by the consumer covers all the risks (Decision No. 1393/2 February 2013) or that risk analysis goes beyond the knowledge of the courts and therefore such assessment should be made by experts (Decision No. 3920/13 November 2013).

83 Except for the newly entered preliminary reference of 2014, most of the references were either withdrawn by the referring courts as parties reached settlements or addressed similar issues.

84 Judgment of the First instance court of Călărași, 26 November 2012.

85 This law was unsuccessfully challenged as unconstitutional, Decision of the Romanian Constitutional Court no. 1656/2010, Official Journal of Romania, 31 January 2011.

the constitutional principle of the more favourable law applicable to administrative and criminal offences, which led some courts to decide on the annulment of NAPC's administrative act imposing sanctions on the bank, without further discussion on the merits.[86]

The third issue in litigation built upon the question whether the concepts of 'subject-matter' and 'price' referred to in Article 4(2) of Directive 93/13/EEC cover, in the context of a credit agreement secured by a mortgage, the annual percentage rate. The stakes of this determination are high: if the annual percentage rate is the 'price' of the financial services provided, its adequacy may not be subjected to judicial control under Article 4(6) of Law 193/2000 which transposes Article 4(2) of Directive 93/13. Some of the courts dealt with this issue as a matter of national law, analysing the nature of this commission as part of the total cost of the credit, and the outcome was divergent on the substance of the matter. Other courts sought the opinion of the CJEU and referred very specific questions on this matter. Four such attempts were removed from the docket of the Court following the withdrawal of the references by the courts pursuant to settlements in the main proceedings, however one is still pending.[87]

A new wave has started to develop initiated by individual and collective actions in relation to forex-denominated loans (Swiss francs and euros) seeking a freeze in the exchange rate at the time of conclusion of the loan agreement.[88]

D. Policy Responses to Over-Indebtedness

The several legislative acts[89] on which consumers successfully relied in their negotiations or judicial litigation against banks for the purpose of alleviating their increasing financial burden, have not necessarily been the result of conscious policy choices of the legislature or government targeting consumer credit reforms and aiming to help consumers to overcome financial difficulties. The adoption of OUG 50/2010, extending the protection offered by the Consumer Credit Directive to both future and ongoing consumer credits secured by movable as well as immovable property, and the entry into force of the amended Law 193/2000 making available collective remedies to consumers did ensure contractual discipline, consumer protection and compliance by credit institutions of both internal and European law in the field of unfair contractual terms. However, the entry into force of the OUG 50/2010 and the discussion preceding the entry into force of the amendment of Law 193/2000 raise questions about the true reasons behind these legislative options. With the financial crisis threatening the banking market, the legislator responded to the pressure of the banks by limiting the initial *ratione temporae* of the consumer protection rules imposed by OUG 50/2010 only to future loans.[90] A similar fate befell the other legislative instrument protecting consumers from abusive behaviour of professionals.[91] After several postponements of the entry into force of an amendment with possible consumer protection effects, it was again close to being excluded or again postponed, before its final entry into force on 1 October 2013.

As a result of the entry into force of the new Code of Civil Procedure, consumer protection was enhanced by measures such as the possibility of raising the issue of unfair terms in all stages of judicial proceedings, including during eviction proceedings, and the prohibition on evictions during

86 E.g. Decision of Tribunal of Vâlcea, 8 September 2011.
87 *Matei and Matei*, C-143/13.
88 M Avram (n 6).
89 Such as OUG 50/2010 and Law 193/2000 with its current amendment permitting collective remedies.
90 Law 288/2010 approving with amendments OUG 50/2010.
91 Law 193/2000.

winter.[92] However the Code also introduced amendments which are not necessarily in the favour of consumers, such as shortening the eviction proceedings and making them less procedurally cumbersome.[93] Furthermore, the NBR has been under pressure to solve the dispute between the consumers and the banks, with consumers on the one side asking for stricter regulatory, supervisory and sanctioning measures, and the banks asking for support of their position in a country severely hit by the financial crisis. The NBR has mostly remained neutral in the dispute between consumers and banks, and when pressed to intervene has referred to its limited power which does not include contracts between banks and consumers.

However, following the irresponsible and opaque credit practice of banks, which was increasingly sanctioned by courts and consumer protection public authorities on grounds of banks' abusive credit behaviour, the NBR did adopt a new regulatory banking behaviour act[94] establishing: detailed obligations on the part of credit institutions to inform the consumers that ask for a loan in foreign currency or forex-denominated of possible deterioration of the exchange rate of the loan's foreign currency to the national currency throughout the consumer's payment obligations schedule; explicit provisions on the loan-to-value ratio based on the borrower's capacity to cover the exchange rate risk through their income, which was differentiated by currency (RON, euro and other foreign currency); a maximum level of indebtedness for consumers; a ceiling in terms of the percentage of consumer income that can be given as guarantee for both RON and foreign currency denominated loans[95] and the percentage of the mortgage guarantee that can be used for real estate investment.[96] In parallel, monetary policy measures were adopted with the aim of balancing market conditions and the general economic backdrop. Its decision to gradually lower the monetary policy rate from 6.5 per cent in March 2010 to 4.25 per cent in September 2013 has contributed to the reduction of the interest rates of the new loans to households, and, consequently, to the improvement of the reimbursement rate of the household debt service.[97]

In addition to the changes in the national legislation and policies, there has also been a change in the conduct of the consumer, especially after their experience with the foreign denominated loans. Since 2011, as a result of consumers being more and more aware of the high risks of over-indebtedness associated with credits in euro, there has been an increase in consumer demand

92 Article 895 of the Code of Civil Procedure; for more details see M Moraru and B Andreșan-Grigoriu (n 11).

93 M Moraru and B Andreșan-Grigoriu (n 11), section V Enforcement of consumer credit contracts.

94 Regulation 17/2012 on regulating conditions on granting loans to households and companies published in the Official Journal 855/2012, which was also meant to bring the national regulatory norms in line with the Recommendation of the European Systemic Risk Board (ESRB) on lending in foreign currencies (ESRB/2011/1).

95 The maximum total indebtedness is limited to 35 per cent and the maximum indebtedness for a credit for consumption denominated in foreign currency or indexed to the exchange rate of a currency other than that of the eligible income of the borrower cannot exceed 10 per cent. See Art. 16(1) of the NBR's Regulation 17/2012.

96 The amount of credit for real estate investments may not exceed 85 per cent of the mortgage collateral for loans in RON; while in the case of loans denominated in a foreign currency or indexed to the exchange rate of foreign currencies, in case the borrower obtains eligible income denominated or indexed in the currency of the credit, the value of a real estate investment loan is limited to 8 per cent of the mortgage (Article 16 and 18(3) of NBR's Regulation 17/2012).

97 See also the NBR Regulation No 5/2013 on prudential requirements for credit institutions, which entered into force on 1 January 2014 (certain provisions will be applicable from 1 January 2015 or 2016); this Regulation also implements Regulation (EU) No. 575/2013 on prudential requirements for credit institutions and investment firms.

for loans in domestic currency. The share of new euro-denominated loans to households shrank considerably in the case of consumer loans.[98]

E. Conclusions

The significant over-indebtedness of Romanian consumers can be ascribed to a number of factors. First, an increasing amount of credit was taken by consumers with high expectations concerning the rise of the domestic economy in the period immediately before and after the accession of the country to the EU. Second, most of the mortgage-backed loans, including those for housing purposes, were contracted in foreign currencies or forex-denominated (euros, Swiss francs and US dollars). Third, following the crisis, the exchange rate of the RON vis-à-vis the euro and other foreign currencies increased considerably and left many Romanians with ever-higher monthly instalment obligations. Last but not least, the banks have not sufficiently employed strategies that were adjusted to the Romanian consumers' over-indebtedness problems. Even though reorganisation of loans was used for the targeted NPLs, it proved to be inefficient, sometimes even putting consumers in a more financially burdensome situation than before.

These problems have been remedied to a certain extent by way of legislative amendment with the adoption of OUG 50/2010 (transposing Directive 2008/48/EC) which provides strict rules aimed at securing correct, clear and complete information of the consumer of their rights, obligations and risks. Nevertheless, the period following its entry into force was one of confusion since banks challenged it by using all available procedural means (pleas of unconstitutionality and preliminary references), and the legislature hurried to modify it without need, which led to serious problems of application in time and judiciary's confusion on the precise extent of the legislator's margin of appreciation in transposing the Consumer Credit Directive.

Finally, the legal framework lacks an important instrument – a law regulating personal bankruptcy. In its absence, the theory of hardship which was developed in the case law and then codified as positive law in 2012 by the New Code of Civil Procedure is the only one that can help consumers unable to fulfil their obligations. The language of the provision on 'hardship' is wide enough to permit a variety of legal interpretations in favour of consumers. Additionally, the New Code gave standing to organisations, institutions or authorities acting for the protection of a group interest or in the public interest, in the conditions laid down by law. However, in the consumer law field, the right of action in favour of associations of consumers introduced in 2013 by an amendment to Law 193/2000 (transposing Directive 93/13/EC) has serious limitations. On one hand, it alleviates the procedural problems that previously burdened the courts seized with hundreds of cases brought by the consumers of the same credit institution. On the other hand, the provisions regulating it are not drafted precisely enough, and are not corroborated with each other and with the other provisions defining the mandate of the judge pursuant a finding of unfairness. The language is ambiguous enough as to leave room for arbitrary results and divided legal interpretation and jurisprudential trends. For instance, some courts have interpreted the provision as requiring a complete elimination of the unfair term, without substituting it with a legal provision, while other courts may have opted for the replacement of the void unfair contractual term with a legal provision of general application. Moreover, a judgment delivered within such actions has effects

98 From 35.7 per cent in 2011 to 10.3 per cent from December 2011 to August 2013, and to a lesser extent when looking at housing loans (from 97.8 per cent in 2011 to 86.4 per cent from December 2011 to August 2013).

only with respect to the standard contracts of the bank party to the case. In addition, there are no indications regarding the criteria to be taken into account for the assessment *in abstracto* required when removal of the unfair terms from the future pre-formulated contracts is sought.

In sum, the legislature has not always been of help in ensuring the required foreseeability and clarity of the national legislation on consumer protection. The opportunity to refine the legal norms was missed. As a consequence, the heaviest burden was placed on the courts. Although there is no uniform jurisprudence on any given issue connected to unfair terms, the courts have been playing a very important role in ensuring the protection of consumers subject to unfair terms in contracts. In certain cases judges are overwhelmed by the complexity of the analysis required and unprepared for the economic assessment of credit risks.

In parallel to the judicial trials, these credit agreements have been the subject of critical assessment resembling a 'trial' also in the media. It soon escalated to such a wide media coverage and mainly consumer-biased critical assessment, that it remains to be seen whether the vast media coverage served to aid the development of a stable and balanced legal and regulatory framework. However, the role of professional websites and other media as main vehicles for the dissemination of information about the latest decisions of the CJEU cannot be denied, despite the fact that they are always presented as being 'in favour of the consumer'.[99]

Finally, the media has functioned as a channel of communication between the legislator and the Romanian consumer explaining in common language the benefits brought by the convoluted and technically drafted legislative and regulatory amendments. It thus helped, to a certain extent, the Romanian consumer in making him aware of the risks stemming from one of the most regularly concluded type of consumer credit and which gave rise to numerous evictions proceedings – loans denominated in foreign currency and secured with mortgages.

99 The following judgments of the CJEU are now present in all conferences, law curricula (including of the National Institute for the Magistracy, the institution responsible for the initial and ongoing training of the judiciary) *Océano Grupo Editorial* and online articles and discussions: Joined Cases C-240/98 to C-244/98, EU:C:2000:346), *Pannon* (C-243/08, EU:C:2009:350), *Schneider* (C-137/08, EU:C:2010:659), *Banco Español de Crédito* (C-618/10, EU:C:2012:349), *Pereničová* (C-453/10, EU:C:2012:144), *Aziz* (C-415/11, EU:C:2013:164), *Caja de Ahorros y Monte de Piedad* (C-484/08, EU:C:2010:309), *Volksbank* (C-602/10, EU:C:2012:443), *Jőrös* (C-397/11, EU:C:2013:340) and most recently *Kásler/OTP* (C-24/13, EU:C:2014:282). The latter will hopefully be of help to settle with authority the issue of the effects produced by the elimination of the unfair term.

PART III
The Different Issues of Over-Indebtedness

Chapter 9
Over-Indebtedness and its Causes Across European Countries

Elaine Kempson

There are very wide variations in both the levels and nature of over-indebtedness across Europe and also in the extent to which households have been affected by the economic crisis in 2007 and the subsequent economic downturn. For some countries, over-indebtedness was already an established problem even before the economic crisis; for others it was largely triggered by the downturn and the subsequent responses to it.

In general, in countries that have faced a long-term over-indebtedness problem, it is primarily caused by poverty and the restructuring of economies that took place in the newer member states in Central and Eastern Europe. And it manifests itself primarily in arrears on household bills such as those for utilities. Romania and Bulgaria are prime examples.

At the other extreme are countries where arrears were barely a problem before 2007, but a housing bubble with concomitant imbalance in the economy and high levels of household borrowing had exposed households to the consequences of the downturn. This was exacerbated by the steps these countries had to take to deal with their economies and as condition of the financial bailouts they received. Iceland and Ireland are the two key examples. Yet others, such as Greece, had structural budget deficits which the downturn laid bare. The steps needed to tackle the Greek budget deficit made an already bad over-indebtedness problem even worse. In all these countries arrears were commonplace across all types of commitment.

In this chapter we begin by providing an overview of the prevalence and nature of over-indebtedness across Europe, before looking at the situation with regard to arrears on different types of household commitments. We conclude by setting out three important influences on over-indebtedness that merit analytical consideration: the nature of a country's economy as the economic downturn hit; the state of household finances at that point in time, as well as the policy measures adopted in the aftermath of the crisis. In doing so we draw on comparative statistics for individual countries as well as information contained in the six detailed case studies reported in Part II.

Overall Levels of Over-Indebtedness

Across the 28 countries of the European Union, 12 per cent of households were in arrears with their mortgage, rent, utility bills or consumer loans in 2013. But this average hides a wide variation across countries: from just 4 per cent in Luxembourg to 10 times that number in Greece (Figure 9.1).

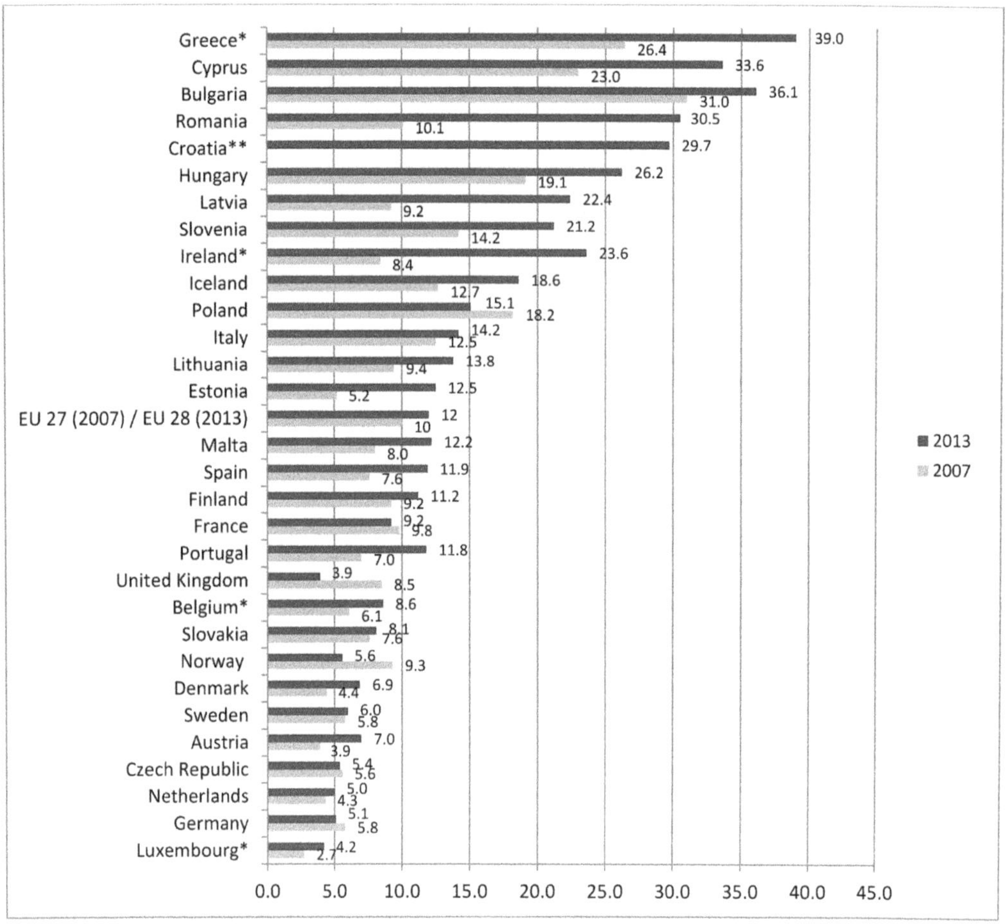

Figure 9.1 Percentage of households with arrears on key commitments (mortgage or rent, utility bills or consumer loans) by country (2007 and 2013)

Notes: * 2013 figures, ** figures not available before 2010.

Source: Eurostat, SILC data [code: ilc_mdes05].

On the whole, newer member states had much higher levels of arrears than the longer-standing members. So that all but four of the 15 countries with above-average levels of arrears were new member states – the exceptions are Greece, Ireland and Iceland.

In contrast, the lowest levels of arrears tended to be found in Northern Europe and only three of the 14 countries with below-average arrears levels were newer member states, with Slovakia and the Czech Republic particularly standing out.

Across the European Union as a whole there was a fairly modest increase in the level of over-indebtedness since the onset of the economic crisis in 2007. Between 2007 and 2013, the proportion of households in arrears with their mortgage, rent, utility bills or consumer credit commitments increased from 10 to 12 per cent, with most of that increase occurring in the period up to 2009. But, again, this average hides some large differences between countries (Figure 9.1).

Most countries saw some increase following the start of the economic crisis, but not all. Arrears levels did not increase in Germany and did so only marginally in Luxembourg, the Netherlands, Sweden, Finland and the UK. All these countries had levels that were below the EU average.

Others, most notably the Czech Republic, Slovakia and Poland, had high but falling levels of arrears up to and including 2008, and although this decline was halted and arrears levels rose slightly in that year they have since remained fairly flat.

Yet others, Bulgaria in particular, and almost certainly Romania too,[1] entered the economic downturn with very high levels of arrears, which increased relatively little in the following years, although there was an upturn in Bulgaria between 2012 and 2013.

But the more general picture is one of rising arrears, albeit from different starting points and at different rates. Countries faring particularly badly include:

- Greece, Cyprus and Hungary, which saw their already high levels of arrears climb steeply.
- Ireland and Iceland, which had near-average levels of arrears until the economic downturn but then experienced a very rapid escalation in over-indebtedness.
- The Baltic countries, Estonia, Latvia and to some extent Lithuania, which saw their long-term trend of falling arrears turn around and increase steeply.

Disaggregating Over-Indebtedness

Although over-indebtedness is commonly associated with arrears on credit commitments, across Europe as a whole it is arrears on utility bills that are most common. Across the 28 countries of the European Union 10 per cent of households were in arrears with utility bills, compared with 4 per cent that had arrears on their rent or mortgage and 3 per cent on consumer loans (Figures 9.2, 9.3 and 9.4). Of course, while almost every household has to pay utility bills and a large proportion pay either rent or mortgages, in most countries only a minority tend to have consumer credit commitments. It is, therefore, important to interpret these figures accordingly.

Just about all countries followed this general pattern, with utility bills being most commonplace, and little difference in the level of arrears between rents and mortgages and consumer loans. The main exceptions were Bulgaria, Romania and Cyprus where levels of arrears on consumer credit were at least three times those for rents and mortgages.

Most of the increase in the level of over-indebtedness in Europe has been driven by an increase in utility bill arrears, which rose from 7 per cent in 2007 to 10 per cent in 2013. Rent and mortgage arrears have risen only slightly over that time period (from 3 to 4 per cent), while consumer loan arrears stayed flat at 3 per cent. This has not, however, been the case across all countries, as we show below.

Arrears on Utility Bills

The highest levels of arrears on utility bills in 2013 were to be found in the low-income countries in South Eastern Europe – Greece, Romania, Bulgaria, Croatia and Hungary (Figure 9.2). All these

1 We do not have figures for Romania from the period before 2007 and the arrears level in that year was implausibly low (10 per cent), suggesting measurement error as it stood at 25 per cent the following year.

countries had high levels of utility bill arrears in 2007 that increased steeply in all except Bulgaria over the following six years to 2013. There has, however, been a sharp increase in Bulgaria between 2012 and 2013. In all likelihood, these high levels of arrears have resulted from a combination of poverty[2] and a rapidly rising cost of living (and of utility bills in particular)[3] following the restructuring of their economies.

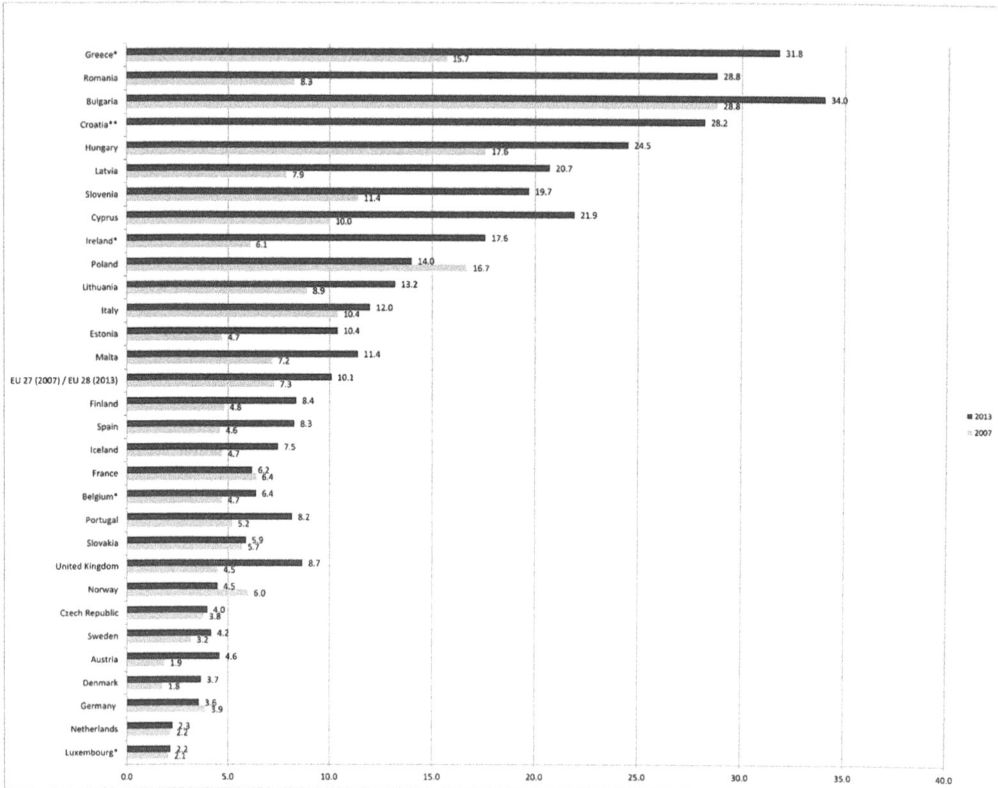

Figure 9.2 Percentage of households with arrears on utility bills by country (2007 and 2013)

Notes: * 2013 figures, ** figures not available before 2010; latest figures 2013.
Source: Eurostat, SILC data [code: ilc_mdes07].

Utility bill arrears were also high in countries that were hit hard by the economic downturn. This was particularly the case in Greece, but also in Latvia, Cyprus Slovenia, Iceland and Ireland. All had experienced very steep rises since 2007, which are almost certainly the result of rising unemployment and falls in real household incomes, in part due to austerity measures leading to

2 Eurostat statistics of real adjusted disposable income of households per capita [tec00113].
3 Eurostat HICP data [prc_hicp_aind].

cuts in wages and social security payments. Previous research has shown that when household budgets are under pressure, utility bills are one of the first commitments to go unpaid.[4]

Arrears on Mortgage or Rent Payments

Three countries stand out as having very high levels of arrears on mortgage or rent payments in 2013: Greece, Ireland and Iceland. And in all three cases the level has increased steeply since 2007 (Figure 9.3).

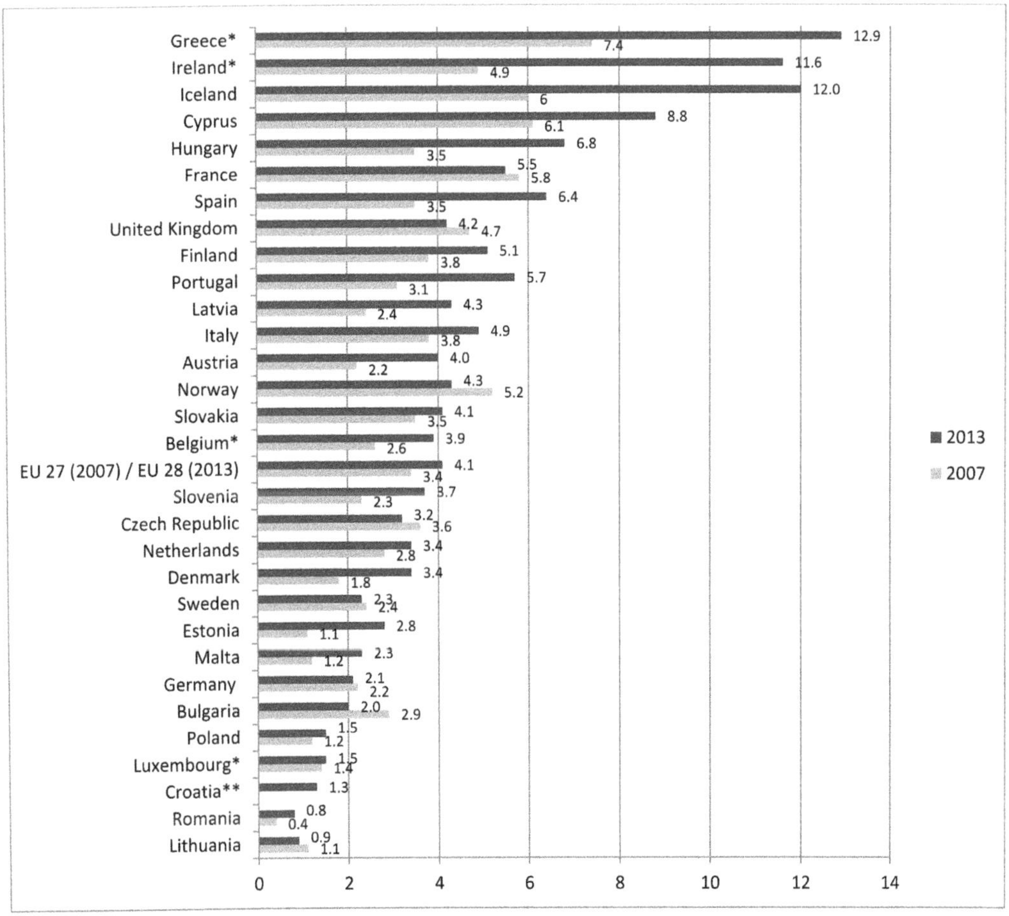

Figure 9.3 Percentage of households with arrears on mortgage or rent payments, by country (2007 and 2013)

Notes: * 2013 figures, ** figures not available before 2010; latest figures 2013.
Source: Eurostat, SILC data [code: ilc_mdes06].

4 For an overview of research into the causes of over-indebtedness see Davydoff et al. 2008, updated by Civic Consulting of the Consumer Policy Evaluation Consortium 2014.

In Greece, this rise is almost certainly associated with falls in real incomes as a result of the austerity measures, putting pressure on household budgets and on paying both mortgages and rents. A high proportion of households own a home without a mortgage, just 15 per cent of households have a mortgage to pay and 30 per cent pay rent. This means that the rate of arrears among those with housing costs to pay will be a great deal higher.

The situation in Iceland and Ireland is somewhat different. Both experienced a housing bubble with large increases in house prices up to 2007 that caused households to over-stretch themselves with mortgages. This was followed by a dramatic fall in house prices that has led to negative equity for many households and stagnation in the housing market. As a result of the economic downturn, they have experienced high and rising levels of unemployment[5] and austerity measures following financial bailouts have led to falls in income.[6] All of these are factors that fuel high levels of mortgage arrears.

In Iceland, the rise in mortgage and rent arrears took place between 2008 and 2010, while in Greece and Ireland the situation continued to deteriorate through to 2012. This is almost certainly attributable to the measures taken by the Icelandic government to deal with the economic crisis, compared with those that the Irish and Greek governments were obliged to take.

Other countries have also experienced house price bubbles (Netherlands, Denmark, the UK and Spain) although only Spain has needed a financial bailout as a result of the economic crisis. But none of them has seen the rapid rise in mortgage arrears experienced in Ireland and Iceland. We cover possible explanations for these anomalies below.

Arrears on Consumer Loans

The highest levels of arrears on consumer loans in 2013 were in Cyprus, Greece and Iceland. All three entered the economic downturn with levels of arrears that were already higher than average and these increased further in subsequent years. In Iceland, however, these peaked at 15 per cent in 2010, since when they have fallen to 10 per cent. Ireland has also a experienced steep rise, from 2 per cent of households in 2007 to 8 per cent in 2012 (Figure 9.4).

Other countries, such as Luxembourg, Estonia, Latvia, Austria and Portugal, have seen arrears on consumer loans double or more but in each case from a very low level in 2007.

Non-Performing Loans

As we note above, countries vary markedly in their levels of borrowing, both as mortgages and as consumer loans. It is, therefore, useful to consider figures published by the World Bank on the percentage of bank loans that are 90 days or more past the due date.

In 2007 none of the 28 European Union countries had levels of non-performing loans that were above 5 per cent and nor did either Iceland or Norway. However, by 2013, 10 countries had rates that were in double digits and all of them had seen the level of non-performing loans rocket (Figure 9.5). These 10 countries were either low-income countries in Eastern Europe that have seen the rapid development of a still immature credit market (Romania, Bulgaria, Slovenia, Lithuania and Croatia), or they were countries that had been hit very hard by the economic downturn (Greece, Cyprus, Ireland, Portugal and Italy). Spain also saw a steep rise from 1 to 8 per cent in this time

5 Eurostat news releases.

6 Eurostat statistics of real adjusted disposable income of households per capita [tec00113].

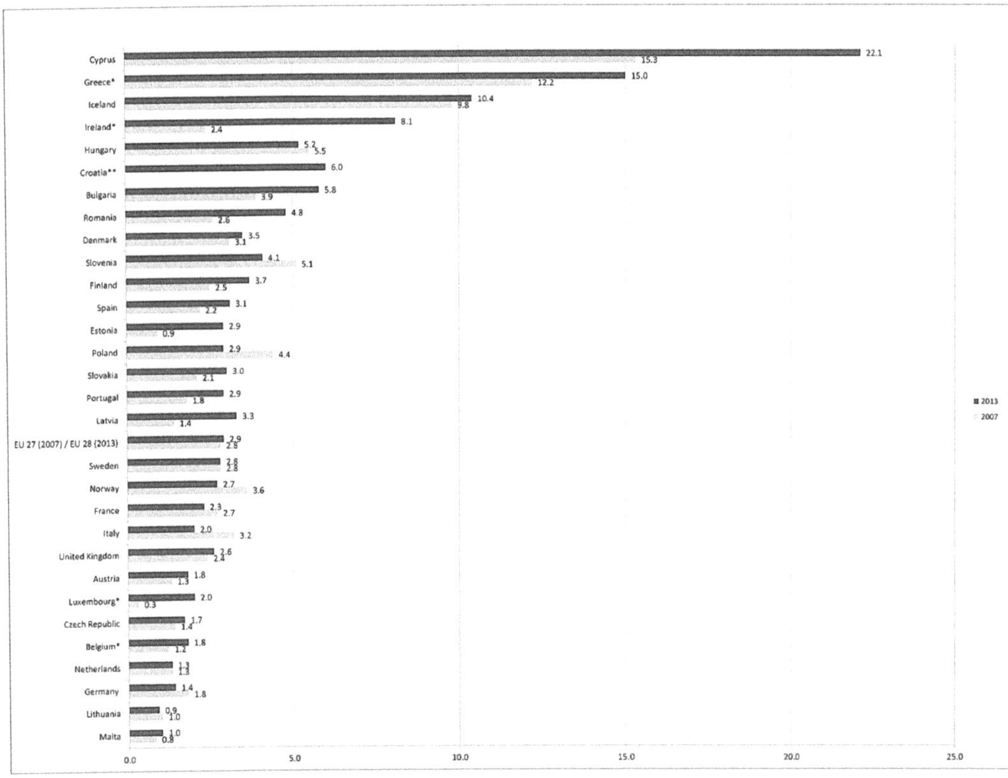

Figure 9.4 Percentage of households with arrears on consumer loans by country (2007 and 2013)

Notes: * 2013 figures, ** figures not available before 2010; latest figures 2013.
Source: Eurostat, SILC data [code: ilc_mdes08].

period. In all these countries there was a steady rise over this seven-year period, with the single exception of Lithuania, where the peak of 23 per cent was reached in 2010, since when rates have been falling steadily.

In addition, Iceland and Latvia had also experienced a very steep increase in the level of non-performing loans to 2010 but they have since fallen back to more moderate levels. In Iceland they rose from 1 per cent in 2006 (2007 figures are not available) to 18 per cent in 2010 but had fallen to 5 per cent by 2013. While in Latvia, they increased from 1 per cent in 2007 to 16 per cent in 2010, reducing to 6 per cent by 2013.

Households in a number of other countries had entered the economic downturn with very high levels of borrowing, notably Denmark, the Netherlands, Luxembourg, Sweden and Norway.[7] But all of these countries, except Denmark, have been relatively unaffected by the economic downturn and levels of non-performing loans in 2013 were very low indeed. In Denmark, although the rise in non-performing loans was fairly steep it was from a very low base: from 1 to 5 per cent between 2007 and 2013.

7 Eurostat: Gross debt-to-income ratio of households [tec00104].

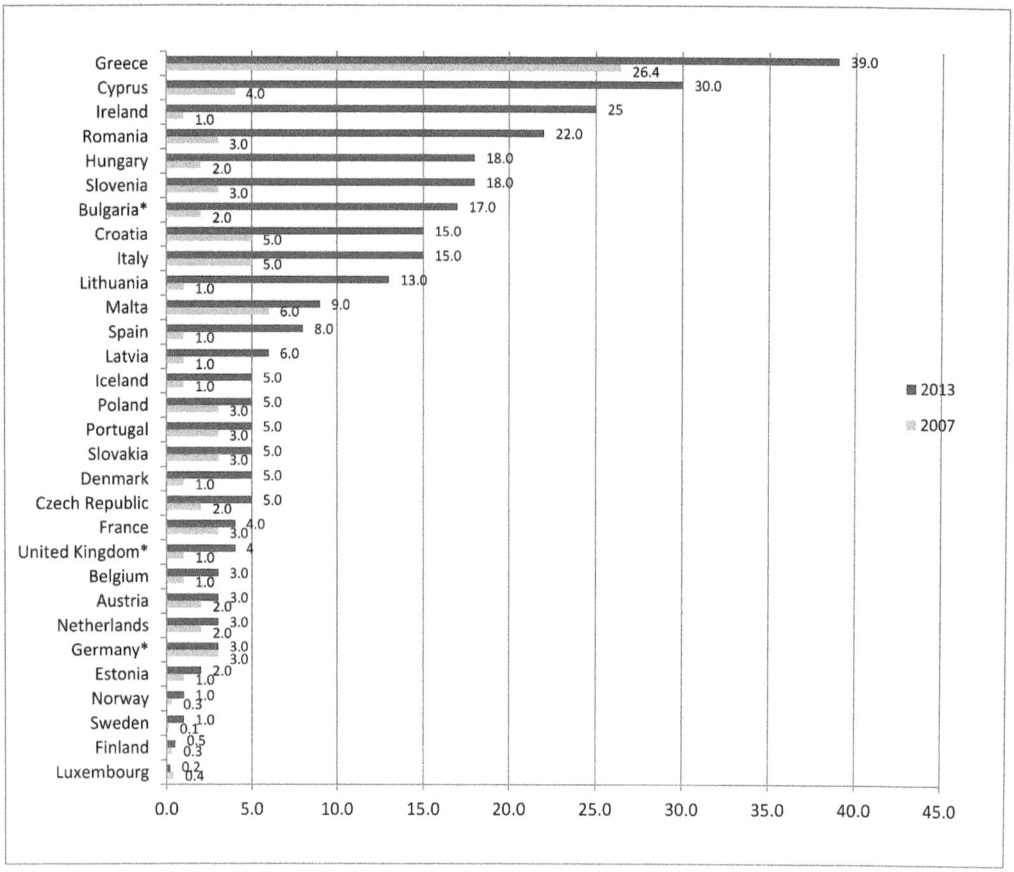

Figure 9.5 Non-performing bank loans by country (2007 and 2013)
Source: World Bank [code:FB.AST.NPER.ZS].

Explaining the Differences Between Countries

As we have seen, both the prevalence and nature of over-indebtedness varies greatly across Europe as does the extent to which the situation has deteriorated since the economic crisis hit in 2007. It is also clear that the causes of the problems in the worst-hit countries vary markedly. Drawing on our six case studies as well as the above analysis we can identify three factors that are important:

- The nature of a country's economy as the economic downturn hit.
- The state of household finances at that time.
- How countries dealt with or were forced to deal with the downturn.

It is the interaction between these three factors that largely explains the impact of the downturn on levels of over-indebtedness across countries.

Nature of the Economy

At the macro-economic level, countries were made vulnerable to the economic downturn in a number of ways: through the management of their economy; the privatisation of essential services and financialisation of social welfare, which was compounded by a failure of regulation of mortgage and consumer credit markets.

Management of the economy

Some countries had been made very vulnerable by the build-up of unsustainable structural budget deficits – most notably in Greece but in also in other countries such as Italy, Spain and Portugal. Other economies (Iceland, Ireland, Spain and the UK in particular) had become over-financialised, with a heavy reliance on the banking sector and on consumer spending fuelled by ready access to credit. This was accompanied by house price bubbles that eventually burst, which left governments with the need either to take banks into public ownership or to let them fail.

In many newer member states, persistent poverty has been the main problem. Three countries stand out in this respect: Latvia, where real adjusted disposable household income per capita was 7,927€ in 2012 compared with the European Union average of 20,059€, Bulgaria (8,499€) and Romania (8,131€ in 2011).[8]

Privatisation of essential services and financialisation of social welfare

Here have been two important trends. In the former communist states in Central and Eastern Europe, there has been a programme of privatisation of utilities and other essential services, which in turn have led to rapid price rises and increases in the cost of living that have outstripped the rise in incomes. This dismantling of state provision of (often subsidised) essential services in Central and Eastern Europe has been most problematic in countries with the lowest incomes.

In addition a number of governments have reduced spending on state welfare provision, transferring responsibility to individuals and households who are required to make their own provision through the financial markets – a process known as financialisation. This has fuelled an increase in households with mortgages, private pensions and insurances. But it has also included a reliance on consumer credit to maintain living standards. In newer member states, such as our case study countries Romania and Hungary, this has arisen as a result of a restructuring of their economies. In others it occurred as a result of a long-term trend of encouraging growth in home ownership, using consumer credit to boost living standards and tackling the pension gap that is occurring as populations age. For countries that received financial bailouts, cuts in public spending were a condition of that finance, as we discuss below. In some cases these cuts came on top of a long-term trend of such financialisation.

Regulation of banks

It is very clear, particularly from the country reports contained in this volume, that there was a regulatory failure in some countries; which included failures in the provisions of the regulatory regime itself and also in its enforcement. This occurred at the prudential level, for example, in Iceland, the UK and Ireland. But it also occurred at the conduct of business level too. Many of the countries that have been hit hard by the recession had an over-reliance on foreign currency loans that left households vulnerable to currency fluctuations. Lending (and borrowing) practices were often irresponsible, leading to households taking on more borrowing than they could sustain. The

8 Eurostat statistics of real adjusted disposable income of households per capita [tec00113].

way that banks have responded to people who fall into arrears with their mortgages or other loans has also proved variable. In some countries, such as the UK, forbearance measures have been widely used by banks; but in others (Ireland, for example) they have been much slower to develop.

State of Household Finances

At the micro-economic level, individuals and households were vulnerable to the economic downturn for a number of reasons. Poverty and restructured labour markets, leading to less secure employment and often no guaranteed working hours, have undoubtedly put households at risk. When unemployment started to rise steeply, more and more people would have been put at risk of falling into arrears with their regular commitments. A large number of research studies have, over the years, shown that the two main causes of over-indebtedness are long-term low incomes that mean people have little financial resilience and sudden drops in income that leave people with unsustainable commitments.[9] So levels of over-indebtedness were high both in countries, such as Romania, where there is persistent poverty and also in countries where high levels of unemployment and large cuts in social welfare spending, pensions and public sector wages have resulted in a fall in real incomes across the population as a whole. Here Greece is the extreme example.

Pressure has been placed on household budgets by rapid rises in the cost of living and these tend to be most problematic for households on low incomes for whom such essential services account for the major part of their spending. Where a high proportion of a country's population lives on a low income this translates into a much wider problem of over-indebtedness. This can be seen clearly in the poorest countries such as Romania, Bulgaria and Latvia.

A further pressure is also placed on household budgets by high levels of borrowing. The exact relationship between levels of household borrowing and over-indebtedness is complex. Only a minority of people in surveys attribute their financial difficulties to over-borrowing, but it is clear from research that high levels of borrowing increase the risk of a household becoming over-indebted and falling into arrears – not only on their credit commitments but also on their other regular bills too. At the same time, borrowing can be a consequence of being in financial difficulty, as households rely on consumer credit to deal with a sudden fall in income. If short-term, it may help them over a difficult period. More often it leads to a downward spiral of financial difficulty.[10]

But there are two factors that can help to protect households from financial difficulty: access to savings and support from family and friends. Unfortunately, though, these have become eroded over time in many countries as societies have become more consumerist and more individualistic. Spain and Portugal stand out in this regard as countries that have avoided this trend.

Actions by Governments and Regulators to Deal with the Economic Crisis

Levels of household over-indebtedness were also affected by the ways that governments and regulators responded to the economic crisis – or were forced to respond if they received financial assistance from third parties such as the International Monetary Fund, the European Central Bank or the European Commission.

9 See Davydoff et al. 2008, updated by Civic Consulting of the Consumer Policy Evaluation Consortium 2014.

10 See Davydoff et al. 2008, updated by Civic Consulting of the Consumer Policy Evaluation Consortium 2014.

The effect of these responses was often to transfer the consequences of the economic downturn to (powerless) individuals. Unemployment levels rose steeply in countries like Greece and Spain as firms were hit by recession and government cutbacks led to job losses. Wage levels fell in real, and often absolute, terms as a result of cuts in public sector wages and pensions. And increases in the cost of living occurred, putting further strain on already stretched budgets. These effects were most extreme in countries that had received a financial bailout, especially if they were in the Eurozone and had less freedom of manoeuvre than Iceland, which was outside it.

Some countries took decisive action to deal with abusive lending and introduced systems to help individuals and households facing serious over-indebtedness. Actions by the Icelandic government and regulators in 2010 to recalculate foreign exchange loans and make them illegal, along with provisions for debt relief and debt write-off will have played an important part in arresting the deterioration in over-indebtedness in that year and turning it round. The introduction of debt relief schemes and fixed exchange rates for foreign exchange loans by the Hungarian government in 2010 have had a similar effect. While in Spain legislation relating to mortgage repossession in 2013 has helped to contain the consequences of the burst housing bubble and high levels of unemployment.

Understanding the Interactions between these Factors

The case studies show that to understand the outcome of the economic crisis in terms of household over-indebtedness across Europe it is necessary to consider how these factors have interacted in individual countries.

Romania

In Romania, it is almost certain that arrears levels on household commitments were already high and rising when the economic crisis hit in 2007[11] and that these were primarily driven by a combination of low incomes and a rapid rise in the cost of living as the government restructured the economy to satisfy the requirements to join the European Union in January 2007 – just before the onset of the economic crisis.

Real adjusted gross disposable incomes of households were one-third of the European Union average in 2007.[12] And although they had been rising quite steeply over the preceding four years, that growth slowed appreciably in the following five years. At the same time, restructuring of the economy and a programme of privatisation led to the most rapid increase in cost of living experienced by any country in the European Union over the 10 years from 2003 to 2013. The cost of living index rose from 81.94 in 2003 to 152.61 in 2013[13] and far outstripped real increases in income. This meant that household finances were already stretched when the economic crisis hit and it manifested itself in very high levels of arrears on utility bills.

As part of the economic restructuring, an emerging consumer credit market grew at a considerable rate. As noted in the country report, consumer lending was just 7€ per capita in 2000 but had grown to 920€ by 2007. Borrowing has been concentrated in a small number of households and has been largely related to consumer spending, fuelled by consumer optimism related to access

11 Figures for household over-indebtedness are not available for the years leading up to the economic crisis and ones for 2007 look implausibly low. It is almost certain that the situation will have been very similar to Bulgaria and levels of over-indebtedness will already have been very high before the economic downturn.

12 Eurostat statistics of real adjusted disposable income of households per capita [tec00113].

13 Eurostat Household Index of Consumer Prices (2005=100) [prc_hicp_aind].

to the European Union. Around half of new loans were in a foreign currency in 2007 and this proportion rose over the early 2000s. Exchange rate changes since the onset of the economic crisis have hit borrowers hard.

Mortgage lending in contrast was low, fewer than 1 per cent of households were buying a home on a mortgage, and mortgage lending was constrained by liquidity restrictions until early 2007. This is reflected in the arrears figures, with very low levels on rents and mortgages but rather higher levels on consumer loans. Indeed, taken together this suggests that a minority of households were building (or maintaining) their standard of living on unsustainable loans. Indeed statistics from the World Bank show that non-performing loans in Romania increased from 3 per cent in 2007 to 22 per cent in 2013.

Lack of debt advice or debt relief provision (there is no personal bankruptcy law for example) means that households in financial difficulty have to rely on their creditors' goodwill in dealing with their problems (see Chapter 8 for more detail).

Iceland

In a detailed review of the position of Icelandic households in the financial crisis, the Icelandic Central Bank acknowledges that, although the economy was strong fiscally, there was an over-reliance on the banking sector and the banks themselves were over-extended.[14] It has similarly acknowledged that Icelandic households were severely hit by the global finanical crisis as a result of over-borrowing. The Central Bank estimated in its review that, on the eve of the banking collapse in 2008, around 90 per cent of Icelandic households owed money they had borrowed. Seven in 10 of these households held mortgages; four in 10 had car loans and almost seven in 10 had overdrafts.

Mortgage lending, both as first mortgages and also as equity withdrawal, escalated creating a house price bubble that, ultimately, burst, leaving large numbers of households with negative equity. Moreover, housing policy led many more lower-income households to enter home ownership with a mortgage. The Central Bank reports that:

> The absence of an organised rental sector, together with clear political aims to encourage widespread home ownership and easy access to credit, pushed many low-income families into the mortgage market.[15]

In other words, this was a classic case of the financialisation of household economies.

The state-owned Housing Finance Fund played its part in starting the mortgage boom by raising both the maximum loan to value ratio and maximum nominal loan amounts to historic rates. The private sector soon followed its lead. During the ensuing house price bubble, house prices rose 120 per cent in the 10 years from 1997 to 2007 and in 2009 around 12 per cent of households were spending over 50 per cent of their disposable income on mortgage repayments.

Running alongside the rapid growth in mortgage lending was a similar boom in consumer credit, with car loans featuring prominently in this. The Central Bank reports that, in 2008, 11 per cent of households spent over 30 per cent of their disposable income on car loan repayments. This meant that, in total, 17 per cent of households were spending over 50 per cent of their disposable income on mortgages, car loans or other forms of borrowing.

---

14 Olafsson and Vignisdottir 2012.

15 Olafsson and Vignisdottir 2012.

Like a number of other countries, Iceland entered the economic downturn with households already showing signs of financial distress. Levels of arrears on mortgages/rents and consumer loans in 2007 were well above the European average (Figures 9.3 and 9.4). A steep increase in the cost of living between 2010 and 2013,[16] and rising unemployment[17] as the government sought to deal with the financial crisis, put further pressure on already stretched budgets.

The other important feature of the Icelandic situation was the heavy reliance on foreign currency-linked loans (to the euro, yen, Swiss francs, or a mix of currencies). And, during the second credit boom that took place in 2007–8, these loans were increasingly granted to low- and middle-income households, many of whom were already in financial difficulty. The large devaluation in the Icelandic krona in 2008 had a major impact on households holding these loans. The Central Bank estimates that roughly a fifth of household borrowing at the time of devaluation was in foreign-currency-linked loans: approximately eight in 10 car loans were linked in this way; mortgagors, on the other hand, were much less exposed and just one in 10 mortgages were foreign-currency linked.

Arrears levels on mortgages and consumer loans that were already high in 2007 increased steeply (Figures 9.3 and 9.4). These peaked (at 11 per cent and 15 per cent respectively) in 2010 and have reduced since then. Similarly the level of non-performing loans (Figure 9.5) rose from 1 per cent in 2006 (2007 figures are not available) to 18 per cent at their peak in 2010. They had, however, fallen back to 5 per cent in 2013.

The crisis was stemmed in Iceland by decisive actions that were taken by the government and financial regulators. Forbearance measures, debt restructuring and court decisions regarding currency-linked loans all played a part. Also important was the fact that Icelandic households, which had high levels of pension savings, were allowed to withdraw considerable amounts of their third pillar pension fund savings (see Chapter 7 for more detail).

Hungary

In many ways, Hungary has experienced similar but less extreme influences to those in both Romania and Iceland.

Household incomes were only a little over a half of the EU average in 2007 and were growing more slowly than those in Romania.[18] And, like Romania, restructuring of the economy had led to one of the highest increases in the cost of living in the last decade: from 90.5 in 2003 to 144.55 in 2013,[19] exceeding the real increases in incomes.[20]

Hungary had a low household debt-to-disposable-income ratio as it went into the recession – 50.55 compared with the European average of 94.09 – but this had grown very steeply from the beginning of that decade (it was 12.65 in 2001).[21] This was a new consumer credit market with inexperienced borrowers.

About 80 per cent of total lending in 2013 was in the form of mortgages. Levels of home ownership in Hungary were high (90 per cent in 2012) but only 22 per cent of households were buying a home on a mortgage in 2013. That proportion had, however, grown rapidly over the preceding decade with no commensurate increase in home ownership. A mortgage loan subsidy scheme that was introduced in 2001 led to a boom in house building and mortgage lending. When

16 Eurostat Household Index of Consumer Prices (2005=100) [prc_hicp_aind].

17 Eurostat news releases.

18 Eurostat statistics of real adjusted disposable income of households per capita [tec00113].

19 Eurostat Household Index of Consumer Prices (2005=100) [prc_hicp_aind].

20 Eurostat statistics of real adjusted disposable income of households per capita [tec00113].

21 Eurostat: Gross debt-to-income ratio of households [tec00104].

the level of subsidy was cut in 2004, foreign exchange loans emerged and were especially common in young families. The subsidy scheme stopped altogether in 2009. The Icelandic Central Bank report[22] notes that Hungary stands out as having a large share of total borrowing held by the lowest income quintiles and a very high share of foreign-currency loans (higher even than in Iceland). Hungary also experienced a house price bubble up to 2007, followed by falling house prices from 2008.

Given the size of its markets for mortgages and consumer lending, the proportion of Hungarian households in arrears with their mortgage/rent and consumer loans is surprisingly high (Figures 9.3 and 9.4). In fact, the level of non-performing loans in 2013 was one of the highest in Europe (Figure 9.5) and had risen steeply from 2 per cent in 2007 to 18 per cent in 2013. This indicates that not only were the borrowers inexperienced but that lenders had clearly failed to assess the real risks of their lending or to see the potential consequences of risky lending for their customers.

Indeed, Hungary has experienced greater over-indebtedness than other countries with similar levels of income who joined the European Union at the same time. However, like Iceland, levels of over-indebtedness have remained relatively flat since 2010, almost certainly helped by the introduction of debt relief schemes by the government in that year. The introduction of fixed exchange rates for foreign exchange loans in 2012 for a five-year period can also be expected to help stem the level of arrears (see Chapter 6 for more detail).

Greece

Without doubt, Greece has fared worse than any other country in Europe – although Cyprus runs a close second. As the economic crisis hit in 2007, both the Greek economy and a large proportion of Greek households were running a structural budget deficit. Bank of Greece statistics show that consumer borrowing in relation to gross incomes grew very rapidly indeed – 600 per cent between 2000 and 2009 (see Chapter 3). Around one-third of the money borrowed by households was consumer credit; two-thirds in mortgages. But unlike other countries there was no house price bubble.

The restructuring of the economy as the government has sought to meet the terms of its financial bailouts has further worsened an already bad situation. Steps taken by the government to cut the budget deficit have led to a significant fall in real household incomes, from 18,623€ in 2008 to 15,177€ in 2012.[23] Cuts in public sector wages and pensions as well as rising unemployment have all played their part in this decrease. Unemployment was already high in 2007 but soared from 8 per cent to 27 per cent in 2013.[24]

At the time that the economic crisis hit, Greek households already had a level of arrears that was one of the highest in Europe (26 per cent of households were in arrears with one or more household commitments in 2007). And the increase since then has outstripped all other countries so that Greece tops the list not only for the overall level of arrears, which in 2012 were standing at 39 per cent (Figure 9.1) but also for arrears on all three main types of commitment (Figures 9.2, 9.3 and 9.4) and non-performing loans, which were fairly steady up until 2008 at around 5 per cent, have since rocketed to 31 per cent in 2013 (Figure 9.5). The breadth of the arrears problem in Greece is in contrast to most other countries with very high overall arrears, where the problems tend to be focused on utility bills.

22 Olafsson and Vignisdottir 2012.

23 Eurostat statistics of real adjusted disposable income of households per capita [tec00113].

24 Eurostat news releases.

Taken together, this suggests that Greece had a problem of household arrears before the economic crisis, but the crisis itself and government responses to it have had a huge effect on households such that arrears levels seem still to be increasing (see Chapter 3 for more detail).

Spain and Portugal

Both Spain and Portugal were running large budget deficits at the time of the economic downturn and have required a bailout from the so-called 'troika' (the European Central Bank, European Commission and International Monetary Fund) following the economic downturn. Spain (but not Portugal) experienced a house price bubble and banking collapse not unlike those experienced in Ireland and Iceland. But as house prices rose, the average term of mortgages also increased significantly from 10–15 years to 30 or even 40 years. This had the effect of reducing payments and might well have helped to protect many households from the risk of mortgage arrears.

Both governments have implemented a set of austerity measures aiming to reduce public debt and budget deficit. These have included public sector wage cuts, tax rises, cuts in social benefits as well as increases in the costs of transport, utilities, health and education. Both countries entered the economic downturn with unemployment rates that were only slightly above the EU (Spain 8.3 per cent and Portugal 8.9 per cent in 2007) but have increased to well above the average rate since (Spain 26.4 per cent in 2013, Portugal 16.5 per cent).[25] But while real household incomes in Spain have fallen from 19,130€ in 2008 to 18,439€ in 2012, those in Portugal have remained more or less flat.[26] And notwithstanding the price rises noted above, neither country has seen an above-average increase in the cost of living.[27]

Despite the problems these two countries have faced, household budgets have remained remarkably resilient. In both cases levels of arrears on household commitments are close to the European average both in terms of the level and the increase since 2007 (Figures 9.1 to 9.4). And, judged by the average statistics, they appear to have fared far better than other countries that have needed a financial bailout and even countries, such as Italy, that have avoided one.

The explanation for this apparent conundrum seems, in large part, to lie in how households have managed their finances in Spain and Portugal. Compared with other European countries, households in neither Spain nor Portugal had particularly high levels of borrowing either as the economic downturn hit or in 2012.[28] In Portugal saving rates were still 8 per cent in 2007 as the crisis hit, despite having fallen, and have since recovered to almost 14 per cent in the third quarter of 2013.[29]

Perhaps significantly both countries are good examples of what sociologists call a weak welfare state combined with a strong welfare society model.[30] The welfare state has always been less protective than those in Northern Europe, while informal networks based on kinship relations continue to play a much larger role. Traditionally, parents, other relatives and even friends help out financially when someone close to them is in financial difficulty. And in contrast to state provision, which has been cut, this informal support has increased in recent years. It is, however, being put under strain with rising unemployment and cuts in retirement benefits and public sector salaries.

25 Eurostat news releases.
26 Eurostat statistics of real adjusted disposable income of households per capita [tec00113].
27 Eurostat Household Index of Consumer Prices (2005=100) [prc_hicp_aind].
28 Eurostat: Gross debt-to-income ratio of households [tec00104].
29 Instituto Nacional de Estatistica 2013.
30 Esping-Andersen 1990 and 1996.

This apparently benign picture is, however, at odds with the protests that have taken place in Spain and Portugal, against financial service providers for their part in causing the financial crisis and the politicians for the way they have handled it. The full effects of the financial downturn, as measured by levels of arrears, are almost certainly being masked by these mitigating factors. But the mitigations can only be temporary as there are finite limits to savings and family support. The consequences of them not being available can already be seen and are described in the case study (see Chapter 4 and Chapter 5 for more detail).

As noted above, Spain experienced a house price bubble which might have been expected to result in a mortgage arrears and possession crisis such as occurred in Ireland. But this has undoubtedly been constrained by a major change in the legislation in 2013 that came about as a result of social unrest, coupled with the European Court of Justice ruling in the *Aziz* case. This legislation introduced a requirement on judges to analyse the fairness of the mortgage contract in determining whether a lender should be allowed to foreclose on a mortgage loan that is in arrears (see Chapter 5).

Concluding Remarks

The effects of the economic crisis on household over-indebtedness have varied widely across Europe. In some countries, the effects have been severe and the situation is still deteriorating; some of these already had high levels of arrears before the economic downturn, others did not. At the other extreme, there are other countries where levels of household over-indebtedness were low when the economic crisis occurred and remained so in the following years. Two key factors seem to explain these differences: first the nature of a country's economy as the crisis struck and, second, the state of household finances at that time. Countries where the economy was being run with a budget deficit or was over-exposed to the banking sector suffered badly and have been forced to make adjustments that have proved painful at the household level. The impact of those adjustments on household budgets, in the form of arrears, also depended on the degree of resilience households had. Countries where households were poor or already overstretched financially and had no reserves either in the firm of savings or kinship financial support have seen steep rises in over-indebtedness. Moreover, the causal picture is more complex in the more advanced economies where financialisation was more extensive exposing many households to risk in the event of the economic downturn. This is seen in the breadth of the problems in the countries badly affected by the crisis. In many of the low-income countries of Central and Eastern Europe, the situation is more focused and primarily linked to poverty.

The length and seriousness of the over-indebtedness problem in individual countries has been determined by the actions that their governments took (or were forced to take) to deal with the problems they faced. In some countries, such as Greece, the actions taken have not stemmed the rise in arrears (indeed they have almost certainly increased them). The governments of other countries, Iceland and Hungary for example, succeeded in turning round the situation so that while levels of arrears are still high, they are falling. Both countries took swift action in 2010 to introduce debt relief schemes and introduced legislation to deal with foreign-currency-linked loans. And both succeeded in reversing the mounting arrears problem. In Spain, legislation introduced as a result of social unrest and the European Court of Justice ruling in the *Aziz* case has undoubtedly avoided the high levels of mortgage repossessions despite the bursting of the housing bubble and very high levels of unemployment.

References

Civic Consulting of the Consumer Policy Evaluation Consortium (2014) *The Over-Indebtedness of European Households: Updated Mapping of the Situation, Nature and Causes, Effects and Initiatives for Alleviating its Impact*, available in two parts at: http://ec.europa.eu/consumers/financial_services/reference_studies_documents/docs/part_1_synthesis_of_findings_en.pdf and http://ec.europa.eu/consumers/financial_services/reference_studies_documents/docs/part_2_synthesis_of_findings_en.pdf.

Davydoff, D., Jentsch, N. and Kemosin, E. (2008) *Towards a Common Operational European Definition of Over-Indebtedness*. European Commission (Directorate-General for Employment, Social Affairs and Equal Opportunities).

Esping-Andersen, G. (1990) *The Three Worlds of Welfare Capitalism*. Polity Press, London.

Esping-Andersen, G. (1996) *Welfare State in Transition: National Adaptions in Global Economies*. Sage Publications, London.

Instituto Nacional de Estatistica (2013) *Quarterly National Sector Accounts*.

Olafsson, T.T. and Vignisdottir, K.A. (2012) *Household's Position in the Financial Crisis in Iceland*. Reykjavik, Central Bank of Iceland.

Chapter 10

A Map of Responsible Lending and Responsible Borrowing in the EU and Suggestions for a Stronger Legal Framework to Prevent Over-Indebtedness of European Consumers

Irina Domurath

Introduction

This chapter deals with the concepts of responsible lending and responsible borrowing and how they are conceptualised in the EU legal order. The claim is made that EU consumer law implements *responsible lending* and *responsible borrowing* only in a narrow way and, as a consequence, misses a chance to contribute to the prevention of over-indebtedness of consumers.

Two assumptions are inherent in the claim. First, it is assumed that EU consumer law (not national consumer law) should prevent over-indebtedness. This is, of course, a much disputed issue rooted in the division of competences between the EU and its Member States.[1] However, in a pragmatic way, this contribution takes into account that the EU competence in this field is already often exercised, albeit shared, deriving from Article 114 TFEU. The field of consumer and mortgage credit is already harmonised to a large extent at the EU level. Thus, the argument could be framed as, now, the 'job should be done properly'.[2] The second – normative – assumption of this contribution is that EU consumer law should have as its goal the prevention of over-indebtedness. This could derive from Article 114 in connection with Article 169 TFEU, according to which the EU should aim at a 'high level of consumer protection', which can include the prevention of over-indebtedness.[3] In parts of the academic literature it is already acknowledged that the prevention of over-indebtedness should be a goal of EU consumer law.[4] Policy seems to slowly follow. Albeit not specifically stated as an 'aim' of its provisions, the Mortgage Credit Directive 2014/17 mentions the need for using appropriate tools to prevent household over-indebtedness, which can be interpreted as an acknowledgement of the need for such a perspective in EU law.

The aim of the chapter is to assemble the scattered and disconnected proposals on *responsible lending* and *borrowing* and put forward suggestions for a broad legal framework for those concepts with a view to effectively addressing the most important causes of over-indebtedness. We will see that the EU will not have to reinvent the wheel. Useful ideas are already being developed. What is still missing is a holistic appraisal and realisation of the most effective solutions. This contribution hopes to provide an impetus to such an encompassing, holistic approach with a view to setting up

1 For example Weatherill (2010, 2011), Loos (2010), Poncibó (2007).

2 The expression is borrowed from Twigg-Flesner (2010), who however uses it the context of arguing for a regulation instead of consumer directives.

3 The author elaborated on this issue also in Domurath (2013).

4 See for example Atamer (2011), 185ff.

a framework of *responsible lending* and *responsible borrowing* that can, in fact, help to prevent over-indebtedness and its adverse socio-economic consequences.

The chapter is broadly divided into four parts. In order to put the contribution into context, first, the political, economic and social role of consumer and mortgage credit will be elicited. It will become clear that law, especially contract law, is of pivotal importance for the understanding and tackling the problems of over-indebtedness. Second, the most prominent causes of over-indebtedness will be described. Here, insights from the country reports in this volume as well as other studies, including from other disciplines, will be used. The causes will be the basis for, third, mapping the concepts of *responsible lending* and *responsible borrowing* in order to analyse to what extent those concepts are conceptualised in the EU legal order and address the causes of over-indebtedness. Together with policy papers, the pertinent EU directives in the field will be analysed. The author will show that the EU understanding of the two concepts and the way in which they are implemented is rather narrow and that further tools could be put into place. These tools will be described in the fourth part with a view to contributing to a debate about the improvement of *responsible lending* and *responsible borrowing* as implemented in the EU legal order so as to prevent over-indebtedness.

The Role of Credit and Housing in Modern Consumer Societies and the Lessons from the Financial Crisis

In the last few decades credit markets have grown rapidly. The availability of 'cheap credit' is considered a central element in the functioning of modern market economies and a driver of economic growth.[5] It is inherent in the need of modern market economies to grow – though not only through credit and monetary systems, but also through increasing commodification, consumerism and the creation of competitive markets through infrastructure.[6] Against this background, the expansion of credit has become an ideology also in the EU policy and is connected to the important political, economic and social functions both consumer and mortgage credit have taken on in the modern economies of the EU.

First and foremost, in the EU, consumer credit is regarded as a part of a more general programme to boost the economy.[7] The consumers are to be encouraged to engage in cross-border shopping for products and services and thus exercise their political and economic role as consumer-citizens in the functioning and fostering of the internal market.[8] In this context, enabling easy access to credit gives consumers and companies the possibility to borrow at affordable rates and use borrowed funds to buy goods and services on the market.[9]

At the same time, consumer and especially mortgage credit also enable the provision of welfare,[10] and thus fulfil an important social role. With regard to the pressure put on the public finances through an ageing population, the states increasingly withdraw from the provision of

5 'Financial Activity Report of the Group of Specialist for Legal Solutions to Debt Problems (CJ-S-DEBT of the Council of Europe' (2007), 19.

6 Beckert (2012), 4.

7 This development started in several countries after the Second World War, for example in France, see Effosse (2012), 188, and in Germany see Belvederesi-Kochs (2012), 46.

8 Concerning consumer citizenship see, for example, Reich (2004).

9 Banks (2009), 54.

10 Korczak (2001), 8; therefore in more developed welfare states, consumers need to rely less on borrowing in order to secure oldage provision, see Prasad (2012), 227ff.

old-age welfare, instead expecting consumers to care themselves for their own private and work-based retirement schemes.[11] Borrowing fulfils two purposes in this regard. It gives households the possibility to supplement current income to manage financial difficulties.[12] But it is also regarded as a social 'equaliser', a tool to improve standards of living and realise consumerist desires.[13] Private home ownership is of pivotal importance here and a prominent measure for the privately produced old-age welfare. In fact, research has shown that in states with a weak public pension system the lack of social welfare is compensated by private home ownership, which reduces the need for income through public pension schemes – a credit-welfare trade-off.[14]

In order to enable widespread private home ownership, in the last few decades, almost all European countries publicly promoted private home ownership as part of larger social policy and facilitated easy access to mortgage credit.[15] Households were encouraged by the financial sector to take consumer loans and mortgages.[16] Targeted marketing and advertising practices coupled with the spreading of the consumer society have led to a broadly accepted practice of over-indebtedness.[17]

However, the financial crisis has revealed substantial shortcomings in this environment of credit-welfare trade-off and the extended access to consumer and mortgage credit. The decline in the US housing market lead to widespread default on home loans granted to borrowers of less desirable financial capacities.[18] Together with a 'toxic blend' of loose monetary policies, rising (and falling) real estate prices, complex risk structures, punitive market-to-market accounting principles, lax regulatory oversight, poor corporate governance, and inadequate risk management practices, the subprime mortgage crisis finally led to a financial disaster.[19] Through a globally connected finance and banking system, this cocktail caused – also in Europe – massive unemployment, turned indebtedness into over-indebtedness, and evoked a wave of evictions leading to further social problems. Countries with high home-ownership rates proved to be more vulnerable to mortgage crises than the jurisdictions with high rental housing shares.[20]

Calls for more and 'better' regulation have become louder with the spreading of the – albeit not unequivocal – opinion that unfettered markets are not self-correcting and that regulation is needed to correct market failures.[21] The problems of over-indebtedness are not automatically – without regulatory pressure – cleared out through a wave of insolvencies, credit crunches and the adoption of more conservative lending policies.[22] Intervention is also desirable if we believe that it is still the function of the state to not only maintain and foster a free market economy, but also to provide for a minimum level of welfare.[23] Even literature arguing against more regulation acknowledges

11 See for example Commission Green Paper on Retail Financial Services in the Single Market, 30.04.2007, COM (2007) 226 final 4.

12 Vandone (2009), 4.

13 Marron in Logemann (2012), 3.

14 Castles (1998), Dalton Conley (2006), 55.

15 See for example the country reports from Hungary, Romania and Iceland. As regards the larger development all over Europe, see Bill (2002).

16 Georgarakos et al. (2010), 6.

17 Korczak (2001), XXII.

18 Banks (2009), 154.

19 Banks (2009), 154.

20 See (Dübel and Rothemund (2011), 26 and country reports in Part II of this volume.

21 For example Atamer (2011), 186 with further reference to *Stiglitz*; Dübel and Rothemund (2011), 28; Financial Services Authority (2010).

22 Dübel and Rothemund (2011), 28.

23 Atamer (2011), 186.

the need for better regulation that is based on sound economics, enriched with insights from other disciplines in order to achieve healthy competition that constraints firms' opportunistic behaviour.[24] There is no reason to not discipline private economic power and 'reclaim' the governance potential of private law to overcome the conceptual divide between politics and markets that has led to supreme economic power in confrontation with public sovereign authority.[25]

This chapter argues that regulation through contract law is needed. This is so because of the 'public dimension' of consumer and mortgage credit contracts that derives from their nature as substitutes for state support and from the individualisation of risk under conditions of uncertainty.[26] State intervention into the substance of those contracts is also pertinent given the widespread use of *standardised* contracts. Not only does widespread standardisation lead to a global law by contract that amplifies risks inherent in those contracts,[27] but standard terms were also often abused before the crisis and subject to the possibility of unilateral alterations by the lender.[28] What is more, the normative power of contractual consent to standard terms is weakened through misconceptions on behalf of the consumer based on cognitive 'defects', as consumers tend to accept standard terms as lawful.[29] Thus, individuals fail to make intentional choices among available options.[30] Counteracting the opinion of those who are against a restriction of autonomy through more regulation, it can be argued that regulation does not necessarily mean a limitation of autonomy, but an increase of individual autonomy, if the latter is interpreted as the residual that is left after desires are eliminated that are formed by irrational preferences.[31]

Against this background, the claim is made that adequate protective provisions in consumer credit and mortgage contracts need to be put in place in order to protect consumers from over-indebtedness and enable them to exercise the political, economic and social role allotted to them in the public dimension of the societies at large. The widespread use of standard terms calls upon legislators to set a default option for such terms that prevents the over-indebtedness of these important consumer-citizens.

The Causes of Over-Indebtedness

The causes of over-indebtedness have been the subject of much debate, especially after the financial crisis. It is clear that over-indebtedness cannot exclusively be ascribed to one cause or risk factor. The country reports included in this volume show that over-indebtedness can derive from multiple causes and is often the result of the interplay of several risk factors, such as lack of information or information overload, the inability to understand information, or over-commitment. These risk factors can lead to so-called active over-indebtedness, acknowledging the role of the consumers in their formation.[32] However, there are also external factors that can lead to passive over-indebtedness – 'external' relating to outside of the contract and the ambit of the contracting parties. Those factors are the extension of credit to segments of society with higher credit risk and

24 For example Inderst (2009), 462–464.

25 Muir-Watt (2011), also MacNeil and O'Brien (2011), 6.

26 As for the 'public dimension' of consumer credit see Ramsay (2004), 16.

27 MacNeil and O'Brien (2011), 6.

28 See Chapter 6 in this volume as well as, more generally, Warren (2007), 12, 19.

29 In this vein see Atamer (2011), 186 and Shiller (2008), 131.

30 Shiller (2008), 130.

31 Ramsay (2004), 16.

32 As for the terms of 'active' and 'passive' over-indebtedness see Comparato, Chapter 2 in this volume.

unexpected adverse events, such as unemployment or the sudden decrease of housing equity. In sum, the causes of over-indebtedness that will be dealt with in the context of responsible lending and responsible borrowing in the EU for this chapter are: the lack of information, the inability to understand information, over-commitment and irresponsible borrowing choices, unexpected adverse events, and increased access to credit.

Information about financial products is of seminal importance. If, for example, information is obfuscated[33] or simply not provided by the lender, the borrower cannot make an informed decision on whether the product fits his needs. Similarly, the borrower can become over-indebted if he does not understand the information that was provided or evaluates it in a non-rational way. Moreover, irresponsible borrowing practices, such as the excessive use of credit and a lack of self-discipline,[34] are often highlighted as causes of over-indebtedness. As the Icelandic contribution for this volume describes, for example, many made use of the easy credit to buy luxury consumption goods such as big TVs and cars.

In addition to the provision and understanding of information concerning the financial product, it is unexpected adverse events that are one of the major causes for over-indebtedness, as many studies, including the ones contained in this volume, have confirmed. Usually, the payment ability of the household is adversely affected by either a reduction of income or an increase of expenses.[35] The reduction in income often follows the loss of employment or reduction of working hours, a change in the composition of the household, or sickness.[36] By changing the ability of the household to meet financial obligations through the current income, an often acceptable and unproblematic situation of indebtedness is turned into a situation of being threatened by and falling into over-indebtedness.[37] Besides the reduction of income, another adverse event played a decisive role in the bringing about of over-indebtedness in the aftermath of the financial crisis: sharply declining housing prices. As mentioned above, the financial crisis commenced with a decline in the housing market, after years of excessive house price levels[38] in almost all countries that were hit by the crisis. Iceland, Spain, Portugal, Romania, Hungary and Greece all have experienced housing bubbles or increasing housing prices in the years before the crisis, followed by a sharp decline of housing prices when the crisis hit. This left many consumers with negative equity on their homes.

Another acknowledged but often neglected factor for over-indebtedness is the excessive expansion[39] and the increased marketing of credit. It is the practice of granting credit in itself that lays the foundation for over-indebtedness in the future[40] and giving credit easily can result in over-indebtedness.[41] The increase in the availability of inexpensive capital across borders in increasingly integrated global and regional capital markets,[42] coupled with increased competition on financial markets, has incentivised lenders to expand lending into more segments of society. As Rona-Tas explains in Chapter 11 of this volume, the expansion of lending does not only mean that

33 Warren (2007), 11.

34 For example Warren (2007), 11, Dübel and Rothemund (2011), 24.

35 Korczak (2001), 60.

36 Heuer et al. (2005), 4; Vandone (2009), 74; see also Korczak (2001), XVII and XVII for Germany (English summary).

37 Korczak (2001), 60.

38 Dübel and Rothemund (2011), 24.

39 Dübel and Rothemund (2011), 24.

40 Korczak (2001), 55.

41 'FINAL ACTIVITY REPORT of the Group of Specialist for Legal Solutions to Debt Problems (CJ-S-DEBT of the Council of Europe' (2007), 2.

42 Dübel and Rothemund (2011), 11.

riskier loans are granted but also that new, riskier borrowers from lower economic groups enter the market. As more borrowers enter the credit market who are more vulnerable to exogenous shocks and the subsequent inability to service debt burdens, credit expansion and the easy availability of credit in itself can be risk factors for over-indebtedness.

Finally, the behaviour and knowledge of consumers, often diverting from the rational-consumer model, influences most of these causes and risk factors of over-indebtedness. Insights from behavioural economics have shown that individuals do not behave in a rational way and are subject to cognitive biases that lead them to under-estimate their own exposure to risk and long-term benefits and costs, and hence to under-estimate their risk of not being able to meet their financial obligations.[43] Oftentimes, unrealistic optimism can lead consumers to misjudge the probability of the occurrence of adverse events.[44] Consequently, such events do not form part of the assessment whether the consumer will be able to repay the loan. Consumers can also adopt excessively optimistic views, because they learn about and judge the information that others have and base their own decisions on actions of others.[45] This thinking can lead to social contagion and 'rational bubbles'.[46]

In what follows, the policy tools that address these causes for over-indebtedness in the EU legal order will be explored. More specifically, it will be examined to what extent the concept of *responsible lending* and *responsible borrowing* are understood and implemented in the pertinent EU directives. We will see that the lack of and inability to understand information as well as irresponsible borrowing choices – concerning 'active' over-indebtedness – are more addressed by those concepts. The author will also elicit the potential of some specific private law tools to address 'passive' over-indebtedness and to broaden the two concepts.

The Concepts of Responsible Lending and Responsible Borrowing in the EU Legal Order

Very often, and more intensely after the financial crisis, there has been talk about responsible lending and responsible borrowing as policy tools to combat and prevent over-indebtedness.[47] The concepts are, however, elusive and difficult to define. In their broadest sense, the concepts refer to credit practices in which the lender shares the responsibility for the repayment ability of the borrower.[48] Considering the many different factors that can impair the repayment ability of the borrower and lead to over-indebtedness (see above), it is difficult to fan out the precise policy tools that determine this shared responsibility of borrower and lender. In the EU legal order, an analysis of the policy tools shows that *responsible lending* is understood as the responsibility of the lender to seek for and provide accurate, transparent, intelligible and comparable information and advice to the borrower, while *responsible borrowing* concerns the responsibility of the borrower to make informed decisions and provide all necessary information from within his ambit. This will become obvious when looking at the conceptualisation of those two concepts in the relevant consumer

43 Vandone (2009), 19–20, Vandone (2012), 73–74, Shiller (2008), 47.

44 Atamer (2011), 184.

45 Shiller (2008), 46–47.

46 Shiller (2008), 46. At the same time, many have refuted that over-consumption is one of the leading causes of over-indebtedness, as it does not match with data available concerning those who are most indebted, see Nogler and Reifner (2014), 14.

47 See for example Weatherill (2005), 91, Dübel et al. (2009), 337ff., Grundmann and Atamer (2011), 185, Reifner in Twigg-Flesner et al. (2007), 420ff.

48 Benedict (2008).

acquis, namely the Consumer Credit Directive 2008/48 (CCD), the Mortgage Credit Directive 2014/17 (MCD), and in the more general Unfair Contract Terms Directive 93/13 (UCT) and Unfair Commercial Practices Directive 2005/29 (UCP).

Responsible Lending in the EU Legal Order: Information Disclosure and Assessment of Creditworthiness

In the EU legal order, *responsible lending* is mainly equated with 'better' information disclosure and creditworthiness assessment. For example, the European Commission connects responsible lending to advertising, marketing and information practices before the lending transaction, business practices related to creditworthiness, as well as suitability assessments and advice.[49] In this context, the responsibility of the creditor lies in ensuring that the consumer receives the relevant information before the formation of the contract,[50] and in the verification of the information submitted by the consumer on the basis of which a creditworthiness assessment is to be carried out.[51] The mandatory obligation to provide transparent and complete information aims at giving individuals the essential information necessary in order to make an informed and responsible borrowing decision.

The two credit-specific directives (CCD and MCD) contain extensive provisions and novelties relating to the transparency and completeness of information, which are complemented by more general provisions in the UCP and UCT. Both directives also contain elaborate provisions concerning the completeness of the information that is to be provided to the consumer at different stages of the contractual process.[52] Even after the contract has been signed, the CCD and MCD oblige the lender to inform the consumer about any changes in the borrowing rate before that change enters into force.[53] In this way, they take a big leap forward – compared to pre-crisis legislation – with regard to the standardisation of information provided. Article 5 CCD and Article 14(3) MCD introduce the requirement of providing pre-contractual information on the Standard European Consumer Credit Information form – in Annex II CCD – and the European Standardised Information Sheet (ESIS) – in Annex II MCD – respectively. This enables consumers to compare different offers more easily and, since specific information has to be included in the standardised sheet, contributes to transparency.

All the four directives together address the intelligibility of the information provided. For example, the CCD and MCD demand the provision of *personalised* information.[54] Moreover, with a view to enabling the consumer to make an informed decision, both the CCD and the MCD establish that creditors and credit intermediaries have to provide 'adequate explanations' to the consumer on the proposed credit agreement including the consequences of default in payment, Articles 5(6) CCD and 16 MCD. In a similar vein, the ESIS, on which information for mortgage credit agreements shall be provided, contains simpler language than the legal terms contained in the MCD, acknowledging the difficulty of consumers to understand financial and legal language.[55] The UCP and UCT complete this picture. Articles 5(1) and 7 UCP address the completeness of information by prohibiting misleading omissions of necessary information. In addition, Articles 5(1) and 6 UCP contribute to the transparency of information provided by prohibiting misleading

49 Commission of the European Union (2009), 2, 5–7.
50 Preamble 24 CCD, Article 24 MCD.
51 Article 8(1) CCD.
52 Articles 4, 19 CCD, Articles 11, 17 MCD.
53 Article 11 CCD, 27 MCD
54 For example Preambles 27 CCD and 40 MCD.
55 Preamble (41) MCD.

practices that consist of the provision of false or deceiving information in relation to a list of elements. Similarly, Article 5 UCT requires that standard contractual terms must be 'drafted in plain, intelligible language'. All in all, the pertinent directives contain rather detailed provisions concerning the transparency and completeness of information and thus help to address the problem of limited transparency of information as a possible cause for over-indebtedness. Coupling the information requirements with intelligibility requirements, the directives also address the difficulties of consumers to understand the information provided.

The provision of information as a part of *responsible lending* is supported by the requirements to undertake creditworthiness assessments before granting the credit, with the help of credit bureaus. The aim of the creditworthiness assessment to prevent consumers from the danger of over-indebtedness and insolvency, and more precisely the protection of the consumer from the irresponsible granting of loans that are beyond the financial capacities of the consumers, has recently been underlined by the Court of Justice of the European Union (CJEU).[56] They allow lenders to have a more complete picture of an individual's total debt exposure.[57] It is noteworthy that the MCD elaborates on the criteria of the creditworthiness assessment in the way that it states that the creditworthiness assessment should focus on the consumer's ability to meet the contractual obligations (Preamble 55 and Article 18 (1) MCD) and that therefore the value of the secured property should not generally be a sufficient condition for granting the credit (Preamble 55 and Article 18(3) MCD). This shows that the creditworthiness assessment does not only aim at minimising the risk for the lender, but also at protecting the consumer from the loss of the property acquired with the credit. This has led some commentators to claim that the goal of responsible lending now also comprises the financial stability of the consumer.[58]

In general, creditworthiness assessments are considered a cost-effective tool for preventing over-indebtedness, as the lenders have developed long-standing expertise in screening and monitoring, thus eliminating some of the cognitive biases of consumers when it comes to their borrowing decisions.[59] Furthermore, credit bureaus are considered to contribute to the reduction of over-indebtedness as they help lenders to screen *ex ante* loan applicants and, thus, reduce adverse selection and detect over-committed borrowers.[60] So, in theory, both the provision of transparent, complete and standardised information and creditworthiness assessment are suitable tools to prevent over-indebtedness of consumers.

However, problems remain that could undermine the efficiency of the provisions. Even though standardisation might help to make clearer the information provided, the provision of more or 'better' information does not eliminate the danger of information overload,[61] or the danger of the misuse of information.[62] Moreover, the reliance on credit bureaus as a means to overcome the information asymmetry can be questioned.[63] The use of credit bureaus alone does not ensure responsible lending practices or lending only to consumers who are capable of repaying the debt. Evidence suggests that lenders do not always use their knowledge so as to discourage borrowing. On the contrary, they might even encourage high-risk borrowers to extend their credit.[64]

56 See CJEU Judgment of 27 March 2014, *LCL Le Crédit Lyonnais SA v Fesih Kalhan,* paras 42 and 43.
57 Vandone (2009), 77.
58 For example Rott (2014).
59 Atamer (2011), 199.
60 Chapter 11, this volume.
61 Faure and Luth (2011), 344.
62 Warren (2007), 11.
63 See Rona-Tas, Chapter 11, this volume.
64 Atamer (2011), 199 with further references.

Finally, the efficiency or suitability of a creditworthiness assessment is questionable both in the CCD and MCD. Even though the CCD states in several provisions that creditors should not engage in 'irresponsible lending' practices or give out credit without prior assessment of creditworthiness,[65] it is problematic that the CCD leaves it open to the lender to grant the credit despite a negative outcome of the creditworthiness assessment. There is no obligation to refuse the granting of credit in case of a negative outcome of the assessment.[66] Although the MCD goes further in this regard, by obliging the Member States to ensure that the creditor only makes the credit available to the consumer in case of a positive outcome of the creditworthiness assessment (Article 18(5) lit. a) MCD), implying that credit shall not be granted in case the creditworthiness assessment is negative, it fails to elaborate on precise criteria or methods of that assessment and leaves further guidance to the Member States. It also lacks a provision on the legal consequences of the lender's failure to deny credit in case of a negative creditworthiness assessment.

Responsible Borrowing in the EU Legal Order: The Ability to Understand Information

As the other side of the coin of understanding of *responsible lending* in the EU legal order as being concerned with the transparent provision of information, *responsible borrowing* is mainly equated with the consumer's responsibility and ability to provide and understand all necessary information. Consumers are to contribute to the transparency and completeness of the information provided concerning the financial product. Articles 8(1) CCD and 20(1), for example, mention that the information needed for the creditworthiness assessment shall also come from the consumer. Furthermore, the consumer has to be enabled to understand the information provided to him by the lender. Here, education is supposed to empower consumers and vest them with the capabilities to understand the information provided by the lender. Financial education is considered an efficient tool to ensure the minimum knowledge necessary to make informed choices concerning credit products,[67] as it can improve money management skills as well as the borrower's ability to understand financial decisions and create awareness about the impact of spending decisions.[68] As such, it provides individuals with the necessary knowledge in order to make informed choices when choosing credit services on the market.[69] Understood in this way, financial education of the consumer is symmetrical with the obligation of the lender to provide all relevant information in a transparent way. This symmetry is the reflection of the information paradigm (see below).

For these reasons, financial literacy is a much advocated policy. However, it can be questioned to what extent financial education actually affects the financial decisions of individuals. This issue is difficult, because different studies come to different results. Some research claims that financial education does not have any impact on subsequent financial literacy,[70] while other research has assembled evidence that seminars can foster savings.[71] What is more, it is debatable to what extent this goal is attainable through EU initiatives. Even though, in a rather innovative approach, the MCD specifically mentions the role of education of consumers in relation to responsible

65 Preamble 26, Articles 8 and 9 CCD.

66 In this vein Atamer (2011), 196, 201.

67 See for example Council of Europe, CJ-S-Debt Meeting Report (2006) 6e final, 22.

68 Atamer (2011), 187; Vandone (2009), 78–79.

69 'FINAL ACTIVITY REPORT of the Group of Specialist for Legal Solutions to Debt Problems (CJ-S-DEBT of the Council of Europe' (2007), 22.

70 For financial education in high schools for example, see Mandell and Schmid Klein (2009).

71 With regard to families with low education Lusardi (2004, 2008).

borrowing and debt management,[72] its further development on EU level is hindered by a lack of competence. Article 6 MCD, entitled 'financial education of consumers', addresses the Member States, which 'shall promote' the education of consumers with regard to responsible borrowing and debt management in general and especially in relation to mortgage credit agreements. In turn, the Commission shall be committed to identifying best practices among those Member States' efforts. It remains to be seen to what extent this provision will have an impact on the previous reluctance of Member States to set up country-wide strategies on financial education, define clear competences, include financial topics into school curricula, and the acknowledgement of the need to adapt financial education to different target groups.[73]

Interim Conclusions and Critique of the Underlying Paradigms

Both the CCD and MCD strongly focus on the provision of information and creditworthiness assessment through credit bureaus. Hence, the emphasis of EU law with regard to *responsible lending* is put on the provision of transparent and complete information on the lender's side and on financial education as part of *responsible borrowing*. As such, these two concepts focus on non-rational consumption choices, the limited transparency of and the limited inability of consumers to understand financial information as the causes of over-indebtedness. While EU law also addresses the inability to understand the information provided, it already proves to be weaker in this regard. The CCD and the MCD target the way in which the information is provided to consumers, without putting into a place a strong framework for the financial education of consumers, constrained by a lack of competences.

The UCT and the UCP focus less on the provision of information, but rather on the balance and equilibrium of the negotiation position of the contractual partners and aim at offering compensation in the form of *ex post* control of unfair terms for any imbalance that influences the consumer's decision. Even though the UCT has proven to be of seminal importance for alleviating over-indebtedness situations after the financial crisis – with the *Aziz*[74] case as the most prominent of many cases in point – the *ex officio* control of contract terms with regard to the unfairness, albeit offering some kind of protection to consumers, could also be regarded only as a 'second best' option.[75] Despite the proactive and paternalistic stance of the CJEU in those cases,[76] we have to consider that the protective provisions only apply in circumstances in which there was an element of unfairness.[77] However, over-indebtedness of consumers can arise also without such an element of unfairness, for example through unexpected events that impair the repayment ability of the consumer. What is more, the *ex post* character of this judicial control could be of only limited use to consumers when it comes to the prevention (not alleviation) of over-indebtedness.

The emphasis on the provision of information and control of unfair contract terms, mostly at the time of the contract formation, is very much in line with the prevalent information paradigm and the normative standard of the 'reasonably circumspect and well-informed' consumer, who is supposed to be autonomous, self-reliant and reasonably well-informed. Starting with the *Mars* case – in which the CJEU ruled with regard to markings on Mars ice cream bars packaging that,

72 For example Preamble 29 MCD.

73 These deficiencies are mentioned in the Staff Working Document Review of the initiatives of the European Commission in the area of financial education, 31.03.2011, 1–2.

74 CJEU, Case C-415/11, *Aziz v Catalunyacaixa*, 14 March 2013.

75 Micklitz and Reich (2014), 804, analysing a line of cases adjuticated on the basis of the UCT.

76 Micklitz and Reich (2014), 781 and 804.

77 See Howells (2013), 461.

even though some consumers might be misled, the *reasonably circumspect consumer* must know that 'there is not necessarily a link between the size of publicity markings relating to an increase in a product's quantity and the size of that increase'[78] – the *reasonably circumspect consumer* has become the benchmark for the protective level provided for by EU consumer directives.[79] However, acknowledging that the consumer generally has less knowledge about the product than the professional seller, the starting point of European legislation is the provision of information in order to lift the negotiation position of the consumer on a par with the other contracting party and to increase consumer confidence in the internal market.[80] By providing information to the consumer before concluding a contract, it is argued, the consumer can assess the quality and suitability of the products and services and choose the one that satisfies his needs.

The reliance on the information paradigm leads to a conceptual problem in EU consumer credit and mortgage law when it comes to the prevention of over-indebtedness. Addressing over-indebtedness by means of information disclosure leaves the risk of misunderstanding or misinterpreting the information with the consumer, which eventually emphasises responsible *borrowing* over responsible *lending*.[81] Not many contractual restraints are put on the lender through the concept of responsible lending. Even though the information paradigm does intrude into the substance of private law contracts by imposing certain obligations on the seller, it involves the smallest deviation from the contractual freedom approach[82] and does not touch the substance of the contract. In the end, it emphasises and reinforces contractual freedom. Freedom of contract is the prevalent precept. This has the paradoxical consequence that the consumer is the one 'responsible' for obtaining the 'right' credit in an economic environment in which not only more and more financial products and services are offered, but also more and more political responsibility is put on the consumer with regard to fostering the internal market through cross-border shopping (see above). Measures that would further intrude into the autonomy of the parties and restrict freedom of contract more are neglected. In this way, EU law conceptualises *responsible lending* and *responsible borrowing* in a narrow manner. A number of causes for over-indebtedness remain unaddressed.

A Broader Understanding of Responsible Lending and Responsible Borrowing that Addresses all Risk Factors for Over-Indebtedness

The two concepts of *responsible lending* and *responsible borrowing* could be conceptualised in a broader way than currently in the EU legal order and address further causes of over-indebtedness. The framework for *responsible lending* and *responsible borrowing* could be strengthened with

78 CJEU Case C-470/93 *Verein gegen Unwesen in Handel und Gewerbe Köln eV v Mars GmbH*, 6 July 1995 (*Mars*) [1995] ECR I-1943, para 24.

79 Chapter II of the Directive 2011/83/EU of the European Parliament and of the Council of 25 October 2011 on consumer rights, amending Council Directive 93/13/EEC and Directive 1999/44/EC of the European Parliament and of the Council and repealing Council Directive 85/577/EEC and Directive 97/7/EC of the European Parliament and of the Council, OJ L 304/64, 22.11.2011 (*Consumer Rights Directive 2011/83*) provides for extensive information obligations for sellers.

80 For example the Commission proposal on mortgage credit arrangements based its approach on the fragmentation of mortgage markets on the lack of consumer confidence due to insufficient or bad information, Proposal for a Directive of the European Parliament and of the Council on credit agreements relating to residential property (*Commission Mortgage Credit Proposal*), COM (2011) 142 final, 7.

81 Atamer (2011), 189.

82 Willett (2012), 143, 148.

a view to avoiding the realisation of active over-indebtedness and preventing or reducing the seriousness of passive over-indebtedness. First, the existing framework for the provision and verification of information could be strengthened by sanctions and product regulation. Second, additional tools – deriving from private law – could be put in place in order to address a wider variety of risk factors for over-indebtedness. The inability to understand information as well as over-commitment and irresponsible borrowing choices could be tackled with more policy tools than the promotion of good practices of financial education in the Member States. In addition, adverse events and increased access to credit need to be considered causes of over-indebtedness in the EU legal framework.

Enhancing the Current Framework With Lender Liability and Product Regulation

We have seen that even though the rules on the provision of standardised and personalised information and the creditworthiness assessment in the EU legal framework applicable to consumer and mortgage credit are in place, their value and usefulness for the consumer could be questioned. Tools to enhance the current framework could for example be the liability for irresponsible lending, based on the infringements of the provisions concerning information standards, and product regulation concerned with the quality or standards of financial services for consumers.

The current EU framework under investigation in this chapter does not impose liability on the lender for irresponsible lending. Even though according to Articles 23 CCD and 38 MCD the Member States shall lay down rules on 'effective, proportionate, and dissuasive' penalties and sanctions, respectively, for infringements of the implementing provisions, these articles can be considered weak. The provisions do not specify any sanction or penalty. Instead, the proportionality or dissuasiveness of a sanction are within the realm of Member State competence and can only be questioned through judicial review. Despite the rich case law on this matter that continuously entrenches the procedural autonomy of the Member States through the principles of equivalence and effectiveness and state liability,[83] this *ex post* assessment of the sanction cannot be considered an efficient tool for the *prevention* of over-indebtedness.

In contrast, specific sanctions are already a feature in several jurisdictions, also within the European legal order. For example, the Swiss Federal Law on Consumer Credit (FLCC) imposes clear obligations with regard to the evaluation of the borrower's financial situation. If a creditor 'seriously' violates his obligation to undertake a creditworthiness assessment under acknowledgement of the criteria laid out in Article 28 FLCC, he does not only lose the amount of the credit as well as the interest and charges, but the consumer can also demand repayment of the amounts he has already paid (Article 32(1) FLCC). In case of 'slight' violations, he still loses the interest and the charges (Article 32(2) FLCC). Similar sanctions can be found in South African legislation and French jurisprudence.[84] The use of sanctions in those legal orders implies that the creditor would violate his obligations when he grants a credit to a consumer who, according to this definition, will not be able to repay without burdening his unseizable property. The prospect of losing all claims against the consumers could have a strong deterrent effect, as it, in effect,

83 CJEU cases *C-213/89 The Queen v Secretary of State for Transport*, 19 June 1990 (*Factortame I*), C-271/91 *M. Helen Marshall v Southampton and South-West Hampshire Area Health Authority*, 2 August 1993 (*Marshall*), C-432/05 *Unibet (London) Ltd and Unibet (International) Ltd v Justitiekanslern*, 13 March 2007 (*Unibet*), C-33/76 and C-158/80 *Rewe-Zentralfinanz e.g. and Rewe-Zentral AG v Landwirtschaftskammer für das Saarland*, 16 December 1976 and 7 July 1981 (*REWE I and II*), joined cases C-6/90 and C-9/90 *Andrea Francovich and Danila Bonifaci and others v Italian Republic*, 19 November 1991 (*Francovich*).

84 For further reference see Atamer (2011), 194–196.

strips the contract of any force. In this context, the rationale of the sanction is the fact that credit was granted despite the danger of over-indebtedness – it is not the fact that credit was granted to unfavourable conditions.[85]

In addition to the adoption of sanctions, product regulation could be envisaged for retail financial products. Micklitz, for example, has already argued for a stronger role of the EU in this regard similar to its engagement in the promotion of human rights and environmental protection. He envisages a financial safety directive similar to the one concerning product safety, a prior approval procedure for particularly dangerous financial products, and a general shift from prudential supervision to market surveillance.[86] Also Warren has made the case for such regulation with the prominent toaster-comparison: due to product safety regulation that ensures that tangible products placed on the market do not endanger the health and life of consumers and pricing that cannot be changed, consumers are safer when buying a toaster and other tangible products than when they purchase financial products.[87] Such product regulation in the field of financial services would put into focus the quality of the financial product offered. A regulatory authority could publish further guidelines for consumer disclosure, review financial products for safety, demand modification of risky financial products before placing them onto the market.[88] In this way, financial safety standards would set the floor for all products and make markets more competitive, as they make visible the features of the products.[89] This type of product regulation could even facilitate market access – as one of the main concerns of the EU internal market policy – through a general clause and prior approval procedures.[90] As such, product regulation could be easily made part of the EU legal framework, without changing current preconceptions and ideologies.

Of course, any plan of product regulation has to deal with the objection against outright bans that disadvantage some consumers, who have the financial capacity to engage in risky transactions.[91] Product bans negate the individual dimension of the purchase decision. Indeed, quality standards for financial products would be especially important for low-income consumers, taking account of the fact that high-income consumers of financial products are able to absorb financial shocks through savings and tend to be less affected by such shocks than low-income consumers.[92] However, product regulation does not only mean the banning of certain products, but also the banning of offering certain products just to certain consumers. This is important within the context of belief that some welfare should still be provided by a regulatory power. In this regard, product regulation can be a powerful tool to enhance the transparency of information, reduce complexity, and thus also enhance the protective effect of unfair standard contractual terms legislation.

Additional Measures: Impartial Advisory Services and Safe Financial Inclusion

With a view to strengthening the rather weak answer of the EU to the inability to understand information and irrational consumption choices as causes of over-indebtedness, financial

---

85 Rott (2003).

86 Micklitz in Wilson (2013), 74.

87 Warren (2007), 8.

88 Warren (2007), 17.

89 Warren (2007), 14.

90 Micklitz in Wilson (2013), 75.

91 Financial Services Authority (2010), 42.

92 Warren (2007), 14. Also the country reports in this volume show that low-income consumers are especially 'vulnerable' to over-indebtedness, as reflected in the high numbers of low-income consumers that are affected by the different forms of over-indebtedness.

counselling or debt counselling measures could be put into place. Third-party counselling can provide advice to borrowers concerning the management of household finances and decisions regarding consumption, savings and borrowing.[93] It can also help to overcome cognitive deficits like the optimism bias or the ignorance regarding the complexity of financial products and services.[94] However, this is only the case if advisory services are provided by a third party that is not involved in the financial transactions and has no conflict of interest, because the consumer cannot objectively evaluate the information given, if financial advice is obfuscated by bias, which is oftentimes enhanced by the granting of commission on sales of credit.[95]

The EU legal framework misses a chance to protect consumers better from over-indebtedness, because it does not consider these possibilities. Debt counselling is not specifically mentioned in any of the investigated directives. Even though the CCD and MCD both contain provisions on explanations to be provided on behalf of the lender to the consumer in order to enable the latter to assess whether the credit agreement is 'adapted to his needs and financial situation' (Articles 5(6) CCD and 16(1) MCD), these contract-specific explanations cannot be equated with advice on the management of household finances in general or consumption decisions. As for impartial third-party advisory services, the CCD does not address the issue of conflicts of interests when providing advisory services to the consumer. While the MCD, in Article 6(3) lit. b), speaks of the avoidance of conflicts of interests and sets out standards for financial advice in Article 22, it does not make mandatory the use of non-tied, third advisory parties.

In addition to impartial advisory services, *safer financial inclusion* would be a catchword for addressing *access to easy credit* as a risk factor for over-indebtedness. Here, the difficulty lies in the fact that *financial inclusion* forms part of a larger policy of access to credit.[96] This policy aims at including more and more consumers (citizens) into the financial and therefore also social environment. For example, through access to credit, the consumer will not only contribute to the economy, but is enabled to purchase a house and thus raise his own living standards and be included into a certain social class. At the moment in which measures are put in place to curb such increased marketing and access to credit, these measures must necessarily lead to the exclusion of some consumers from the credit market. On the one hand, this naturally runs counter to the goal of financial inclusion, but could on the other be necessary in order to avoid social exclusion through, for example, bankruptcy or evictions.

If effective prevention of over-indebtedness is to be taken seriously, limitations to the access to credit might be reasonable. Since easy access to credit is inherently connected to the expansion of credit to riskier borrowers, some tools could be put in place to deter lending to high-risk borrowers. For example, interest rate ceilings for lenders can prove to be an efficient tool to discourage lending to high-risk borrowers because the lenders would be deprived of the possibility to mitigate the risk with high interest rates.[97] Another possibility would be to single out high-risk borrowers and include a 'buffer' in their creditworthiness assessments. Already, mortgage credit in the EU shall not be granted in case of a negative creditworthiness assessment (Article 18(5) lit a) MCD), an obligation that clearly restricts access to credit for consumers who do not have the financial means to honour their repayment obligations under the credit agreement. However, even stricter rules are in place in some Member States, in order to exclude high-risk consumers from credit. For example, the Financial Services Authority (FSA) in the UK has proposed to subtract 20 per cent from the

93 Vandone (2009), 77.

94 Atamer (2011), 187.

95 In this regard see Reifner (2011), 88 with reference to the German *Schrottimmobilien* cases.

96 For further reference on this topic see Comparato, Chapter 2, in this volume.

97 As for the description of such interest rate ceilings see Vandone (2009), 78.

current disposable income of a 'credit-impaired' customer in order to allow for arrears on monthly payments up to those 20 per cent.[98] This allows for an additional buffer against financial difficulties arising from unforeseen events and changed circumstances.[99] Some borrowers, who might have merely passed the lender's creditworthiness assessment, might then fall below the threshold when a certain amount is subtracted from their disposable income. This certainly strengthens the idea of excluding certain (mostly low-income) consumers from the credit market in order to prevent their over-indebtedness with all its social adverse repercussions. Even though this approach would diminish the pool of possible borrowers, it would make financial inclusion safer for the ones that pass the enhanced creditworthiness assessment.

Additional Measures: Contract Amendments

Similar to *increased access to credit*, *unexpected events*, as probably the most important cause for over-indebtedness, are difficult to address, given the many different forms they can take. In this chapter, the claim is put forward that contract law is the focal point for addressing unexpected events. The need to put into place arrangements for unforeseen events and conflicts that can arise during the contract period[100] is especially evident when taking into account the long-term character of mortgage loan agreements. So, contracts could be designed in a way that they put the responsibility for action on the side that is best to avoid or mitigate negative events, or, if negative events are beyond control, on the side that can better hedge against external forces.[101] Such an approach is in line with the broad understanding of responsible lending and responsible borrowing, of sharing the responsibility for the repayment ability of the borrower (see above).

One possibility is to take recourse to the traditional private law tool of *frustration of contract*. It is a widely acknowledged principle to adjust or renegotiate contractual commitments to drastically changed circumstances after the contract formation or to terminate the agreement.[102] The rationale of the concept lies in the assumption that, while in case of a foreseeable event the parties can make respective promises to perform even if the event actually occurs, not all contingencies can be spelled out ahead of time. This might be even more so in mortgage credit contracts, which usually cover a long period of time. Considering that the spiral of loss of income, over-indebtedness, default, insolvency, and homelessness and social exclusion can be kicked off by such unforeseen events, the adaption of contractual terms in a long-term agreement can even be considered 'a core necessity'.[103] This rationale is connected to the concept of *social force majeure*, which allows for the mitigation of the consequences of over-indebtedness if it has been caused by unemployment, illness or other similar events.[104] In this vein, providing an exception from the *pacta sunt servanda* principle, the *frustration of contract* doctrine is applied when relief from contractual obligations cannot be derived from the parties' (hypothetical) intentions or from a flaw in the contracting mechanism.[105]

The potential of this concept is neglected by policy makers, jurisprudence and academia alike. On EU level, there is no talk about it, even though many jurisdictions already apply this doctrine – from the *doctrine of frustration* (impossibility), *Wegfall der Geschäftsgrundlage*

98 Financial Services Authority (2010), 27–28.
99 Financial Services Authority (2010), 44.
100 Nogler and Reifner (2014), 3.
101 Rona-Tas in Chapter 11, in this volume.
102 Hondius and Grigoleit (2011), 8, 9.
103 Nogler and Reifner (2014), 43.
104 Wilhelmsson (2004), 730.
105 Hondius and Grigoleit (2011), 6.

(unfulfilled expectations of parties), the *doctrine of assumptions* (unexpected material burden for one party) and *rebus sic stantibus* (extra-ordinary burden or fundamental alteration of contractual obligations) – as well as the *social force majeure* principle.[106] What is more, the country reports in this volume show that national jurisprudence is not ready to accept the financial crisis and the following adverse consequences for the financial capacity of individuals as a possible basis for *frustration of contract*. As for academia, the concept has only just arrived to the debate. With the exception of Nogler and Reifner, who elicit this principle within the private law dimension of life term agreements,[107] most of the academic debate takes place in finance or economics. While Pulgar highlights the importance of the *rebus sic stantibus* principle in terms of the prevention of insolvency of the over-indebted individual,[108] Pistor argues for a modification of contractual obligations with a view to taking account of uncertainty in the future.[109] Within the broader context of financial regulation that acknowledges the interdependencies of financial instruments, intermediaries and markets, she considers this approach part of a legal infrastructure that can enhance efficiency.[110] In economics, Shiller argues for renegotiation of the contractual terms of 'continuous workout mortgages', referring to the continuously adjustable terms of mortgage agreements in response to evidence about the changing ability to repay and changing conditions in housing market.[111] This automatic 'workout' is to be made part already of the initial contract.[112]

Given these suggestions and the existence of the *frustration of contract* principle in various forms in many legal orders, the EU could develop a single approach. Implementing a *frustration of contract* approach into consumer credit and mortgage agreements would have clear advantages, also in comparison with tools already in place. First of all, the possibility of adaptation of contractual clauses to the changed financial situation of the consumer can contribute to the protection of consumers who are at the risk of over-indebtedness, as they could adhere to their – albeit changed – obligations under an existing credit agreement, without being exposed to the choice between exclusion and acceptance of any form of credit.[113] The amendment of contractual provisions would thus make enforcement of the contract unnecessary.[114] Second, the consumer could avoid resorting to bankruptcy proceedings to achieve a possible discharge of debt or to the judicial review of unfair terms in order to alleviate over-indebtedness *ex post*. Even though the control of unfair terms has been of pivotal importance for consumers in the aftermath of the financial crisis (see above), it is limited with regard to *unexpected events* that change the context of the financial obligation after the conclusion of the contract, whether it contains unfair clauses or not. Focussing on the initial design of the contract, the unfair terms regime is not designed to address the change of circumstances.

Of course, problems in the implementation of such concepts into the EU legal order would have to be addressed. There is, for example, the balance between the consumer's interest in adjusting or terminating the now too onerous agreement and the creditor's interest in having struck a deal and his interest in receiving a return on it.[115] Another possible problem to deal with is the bargaining

106 Wilhelmsson (2004), 730–731.
107 Nogler and Reifner (2014).
108 Pulgar (2014), 532.
109 Pistor (2013), 47.
110 Pistor (2013), 47.
111 Shiller (2008), 157.
112 Shiller (2008), 157.
113 In this regard see Reifner, Huls, and Springeneer (2003), 222–223.
114 Implicitly so also Howells (2013), 461.
115 Howells (2013), 461.

power at the time of renegotiation, which would probably be just as unequal as at the time of the conclusion of the first agreement, if not even more unbalanced to the disadvantage of the consumer who is now in financial difficulties. Again, lender liability could mitigate this problem. Furthermore, administrative or judicial guidelines could incentivise a mutually beneficial solution for both contractual parties and encourage them to hold on to the contract by establishing financial obligations for the consumer which he can adhere to under the changed circumstances so that the creditor's interest in receiving a return will not be impaired. Such guidelines would also mitigate the inferior bargaining position of the consumer, who otherwise might be under pressure to accept any form of credit.

Conclusions

Responsible lending and *responsible borrowing* are understood and implemented in a narrow way in the EU legal order. The concepts are strongly related to the provision and understanding of information. The prevention of over-indebtedness is not a prevalent aim of EU legislation in the field of consumer and mortgage credit. On the contrary, European consumers are made responsible for their own financial well-being and supposed to understand the growing amount of and complexity of information concerning financial products in an environment of increasing financialization of the society. EU legislation draws on the balancing of information asymmetries between borrower and lender to a large extent, thus neglecting the potential of *responsible lending* and *responsible borrowing* to prevent over-indebtedness and address its larger socio-economic context.

The analysis above shows that there is room for broadening the understanding of the concepts *responsible lending* and *responsible* lending in the EU legal order so as to address a wider range of causes for over-indebtedness and thus preventing over-indebtedness more effectively. The broad understanding of the two concepts as reflecting a shared responsibility of creditor and debtor for the repayment ability of the debtors could be a useful guideline. On the one hand, debt and financial counselling can enhance the consumer's understanding of financial decision and mitigate behavioural biases in relation to understanding information and possible over-commitment through irrational consumption choices. On the other hand, lender liability and sanctions for a lack or disregard of creditworthiness assessment, together with interest rate ceilings and "buffers" built into the creditworthiness assessment of riskier borrowers in order to allow for some financial margin could discourage lending to risky borrowers. Product regulation laying down safety standards for financial products would be a more paternalistic but clear approach and easily compatible with the current EU approach in other fields. Furthermore, the rules on the creditworthiness assessment under the use of credit bureaus could be strengthened.[116] Legal research has already been done, connecting the economic rationale with the legal framework[117] and pointing at the risks involved,[118] but would need to be integrated into the discussions on how to make creditworthiness assessments more effective and reliable.

The author suggests further research on policy tools to address *unexpected events*. Such events are the most neglected cause of over-indebtedness, even though they are probably the most important one. They have a "kick-off" effect that can turn indebtedness into over-indebtedness if the borrower does not have enough resources to deal with the financial shock entailed. However,

116 See Rona-Tas, Chapter 11, in this volume.

117 Most notably by Ferretti (2008).

118 For example Ferretti (2010).

such unexpected events are problematic from the viewpoint of how deal with uncertainty in contractual relations, especially long-term relations such as mortgage agreements. The problem here is exacerbated because it is difficult to define the unexpected event. It could be the loss of employment, sickness, or divorce, all with possible impacts on the consumer's ability to pay. The advantage of the including the concept of *frustration of contract* into EU consumer and mortgage credit law as means to address *unexpected events* and the subsequent changed circumstances with a view to the ability to repay would be its flexibility. There would be no need for defining *ex ante* such events. The solution would be sought in each individual case. Further research is however indicated with regard to the possibility to introduce this concept into EU consumer credit and mortgage law, also with a view to overcoming the renegotiation barrier and possibly inferior bargaining positions of consumers – now under financial pressure. Inspiration can be sought in the private legal order of the EU Member States and other countries.

The most problematic choice for the EU – if it is to take the prevention of over-indebtedness seriously – lies in the broader policy framework. Building "buffers" into creditworthiness assessments coupled with the sanctioned obligation to not grant credit in case of a negative creditworthiness assessment would entail the exclusion of some borrowers from the credit market, a consequence that runs counter to the clear EU strategy of achieving social inclusion through financial inclusion. Ultimately, this problematic nature of access to credit forms part of the larger question of whether or not the states are still the providers of welfare to their citizens. In the political economy context of the welfare-credit trade-off, it is also problematic to what extent European citizens can exercise their private autonomy while being subjected to the social responsibility vis-à-vis the society as a whole to make arrangements for their and their families' welfare.

References

Atamer, Yesim M. 2011. 'Duty of Responsible Lending: Should the European Union Take Action?' In *Financial Services, Financial Crisis and General European Contract Law*, edited by Stefan Grundmann and Yesim M. Atamer. Alphen aan den Rijn: Wolters Kluwer.

Banks, Erik. 2009. *Risk and Financial Catastrophe*. Basingstoke: Palgrave Macmillan.

Beckert, Jens. 2012. 'Capitalism as a System of Contingent Expectations Toward a Sociological Microfoundation of Political Economy'. 12/4. MPlfG Discussion Paper.

Belvederesi-Kochs, Rebecca. 2012. 'Sparkassen and Consumer Credit in West Germany'. In *The Development of Consumer Credit in Global Perspective*, edited by Jan Logemann, 41–62. New Jersey: Palgrave Macmillan.

Benedict, Jörg. 2008. 'Responsible Lending – Das Europäische Vertragsrecht Zwischen Caveat Emptor Und Caveat Creditor!' *Zeitschrift Für Europäisches Vertragsrecht* 2: 394–410.

Bill, Edgar. 2002. *Access to Housing: Homelessness and Vulnerability in Europe*. Bristol: Bristol Policy Press.

Castles, Francis G. 1998. 'The Really Big Trade-Off: Home Ownership and the Welfare State in the New World and the Old'. *Acta Politica* 33: 5–19.

Commission of the European Union. 2009. 'Summary of Responses to the the Public Consultation on Responsible Lending and Borrowing in the EU'.

Dalton Conley, Brian Gifford. 2006. 'Home Ownership, Social Insurance, and the Welfare State'. *Sociological Forum* 21 (1): 55.

Domurath, Irina. 2013. 'The Case for Vulnerability as the Normative Standard in European Consumer Credit and Mortgage Law – An Inquiry into the Paradigms of Consumer Law'. *Journal of European Consumer and Market Law* 3: 124–137.

Dübel, Achim, Charlotte Duke and Patrice Muller. 2009. 'Study on the Costs and Benefits of the Different Policy Options for Mortgage Credit'. Commissioned by DG Market of the European Commission to LondonEconomics and Finpolconsult, published March 2011.

Dübel, Hans-Joachim and Marc Rothemund. 2011. *A New Mortgage Credit Regime for Europe. CEPS Special Report*. Centre for European Policy Studies/European Credit Research Institute.

Effosse, Sabine. 2012. 'French Consumer Credit Policy in the 1950s and 1960s'. In *The Development of Consumer Credit in Global Perspective: Business, Regulation, and Culture*, edited by Jan Logemann, 183–199. New York: Palgrave Macmillan.

Faure, Michael G. and Hanneke A. Luth. 2011. 'Behavioural Economics in Unfair Contract Terms'. *Journal of Consumer Policy* 34 (3): 337. http://proquest.umi.com/pqdlink?did=2436552051&Fmt=7&clientId=58117&RQT=309&VName=PQD.

Ferretti, Federico. 2008. *The Law and Consumer Credit Information in the European Community – The Regulation of Credit Information Systems*. London and New York: Routledge Cavendish.

Ferretti, Federico. 2010. 'A European Perspective on Consumer Loans and the Role of Credit Registries: The Need to Reconcile Data Protection, Risk Management, Efficiency, Over-Indebtedness, and a Better Prudential Supervision of the Financial System'. *Journal of Consumer Policy* 33 (1): 1–27.

'Financial Activity Report of the Group of Specialist for Legal Solutions to Debt Problems (CJ-S-DEBT of the Council of Europe)'. 2007.

Financial Services Authority. 2010. 'Mortgage Market Review: Responsible Lending'. *Consultation Paper 10/16*, July 2010.

Georgarakos, Dimistris, Adriana Loischova and Melanie Ward-Warmedinger. 2010. 'Mortgage, Indebtedness and Household Financial Distress'. European Central Bank Working Paper Series (No. 1156).

Grundmann, Stefan and Yesim M. Atamer. 2011. '*Financial Services, Financial Crisis and General European Contract Law*. Netherlands: Kluwer Law International BV.

Heuer, Jan, Sylvia Hils and Anika Richter. 2005. 'Überschuldung: Ursachen Und Prävention'. Sehorn Forschungsreihe.

Hondius, Ewoud and Hans Christoph Grigoleit. 2011. *Unexpected Circumstances in European Contract Law*. Cambridge: Cambridge University Press.

Howells, Geraint G. 2013. 'Change of Circumstances in Consumer Credit Contracts – the United Kingdom and a Call for the Maintenance of Sector Specific Rules'. In *Life Time Contracts – Social Long-Term Contracts in Labour, Tenancy and Consumer Credit Law*, edited by Luca Nogler and Udo Reifner. Den Haag: Eleven International Publishing.

Inderst, Roman. 2009. 'Retail Finance: Thoughts on Reshaping Regulation and Consumer Protection after the Financial Crisis'. *European Business Organization Law Review* 10: 455–464.

Korczak, Dieter. 2001. 'Überschuldung in Deutschland Zwischen 1988 Und 1999'. Stuttgart, Berlin, Köln.

Logemann, Jan, ed. 2012. *The Development of Consumer Credit in Global Perspective*. New Jersey: Palgrave Macmillan.

Loos, Marco. 2010. 'Full Harmonisation as a Regulatory Concept and Its Consequences for the National Legal Orders: The Example of the Consumer Rights Directive'. Centre for the Study of European Contract Law Working Paper Series 2010/03. http://ssrn.com/paper=1639436.

Lusardi, Annamaria. 2004. 'Saving and the Effectiveness of Financial Education'. Hanover. http://www.dartmouth.edu/~alusardi/Papers/Financial_Education_2004.pdf.

Lusardi, Annamaria. 2008. 'Household Saving Behaviour: The Role of Financial Literacy, Information, and Financial Eucation Programs'.

MacNeil, Iain G. and Justin O'Brien. 2011. 'Introduction: The Future of Financial Regulation'. In *The Future of Financial Regulation*, edited by Iain G MacNeil and Justin O'Brien. Oxford and Portland: Hart Publishing.

Mandell, Lewis and Linda Schmid Klein. 2009. 'The Impact of Financial Literacy Education on Subsequent Financial Behaviour'. *Journal of Financial Counselling and Planning* 20 (1): 15–21.

Micklitz, Hans-W. and Norbert Reich. 2014. 'The Court and the Sleeping Beauty: The Revival of the Unfair Contract Terms Directive (UCTD)'. *Common Market Law Review* 51: 771–808.

Muir-Watt, Horatia. 2011. 'Private International Law as Global Governance: Beyond the Schize, from Closet to Planet'. http://works.bepress.com/horatia_muir-watt/1/.

Nogler, Luca and Udo Reifner. 2014. 'Introduction: The New Dimension of Life Time in the Law of Contracts and Obligations'. In *Life Time Contracts – Social Long-Term Contracts in Labour, Tenancy and Consumer Credit Law*, edited by Luca Nogler and Udo Reifner. Den Haag: Eleven International Publishing.

Pistor, Katharina. 2013. 'Towards a Legal Theory of Finance'. 196/2013. Law Working Paper.

Poncibó, Cristina. 2007. 'The Challenges of EU Consumer Law'. EUI Working Papers Max Weber Programme MWP 2007/24.

Prasad, Monica. 2012. *The Land of Too Much: American Abundance and the Paradox of Poverty*. Cambridge, MA: Harvard University Press.

Pulgar, Johanna. 2014. 'A Contractual Approach to Over-Indebtedness: Rebus Sic Stantibus Instead of Bankruptcy'. In *Life Time Contracts – Social Long-Term Contracts in Labour, Tenancy and Consumer Credit Law*, edited by Luca Nogler and Udo Reifner, 531–550. Den Haag: Eleven International Publishing.

Ramsay, Iain. 2004. 'From Truth in Lending to Responsible Lending'. http://www.iaclaw.org/Research_papers/Research_papers.html.

Reich, Norbert. 2004. 'The Consumer as Citizen – the Citizen as Consumer – Reflections on the Present State of the Theory of Consumer Law in the EU'. http://www.iaclaw.org/Research_papers/Research_papers.html.

Reifner, Udo. 2011. 'Erfolgsprovisionen Bei Finanzdienstleistungen'. *Verbraucher Und Recht* 3: 83–89.

Reifner, Udo, Nik Huls and Helga Springeneer. 2003. 'Consumer Overindebtedness and Consumer Law in the European Union – Final Report Presented to the Commission of the European Communities, Health and Consumer Protection Directorate-General'. http://www.iaclaw.org/Research_papers/Research_papers.html.

Rott, Peter. 2003. 'Mitverantwortung Des Kreditgebers Bei Der Kreditaufnahme – Warum Eigentlich Nicht?' *Zeitschrift Für Bank- Und Kapitalmarktrecht*: 851–859.

Rott, Peter. 2014. 'Verbraucherschutz durch Prüfung der Kreditwürdigkeit. Bedeutung des EuGH-Urteils vom27 .3.2014- Rs. C-56 sll2,LCL Le Cr6dit Lyonnais fi.ir das deutsche Recht'. *Europäische Zeitschrift für Wirtschafts- und Steuerrecht* 4: 201–204.

Shiller, Robert J. 2008. *The Subprime Solution: How Today's Global Financial Crisis Happened, and What to Do about It. Crisis*. Vol. 1. Princeton: Princeton University Press.

Twigg-Flesner, Christian. 2010. 'Time to Do the Job Properly: The Case for a New Approach to EU Consumer Legislation'. *Journal of Consumer Policy* 33 (4): 355. http://proquest.umi.com/pqdlink?did=2192678181&Fmt=7&clientId=58117&RQT=309&VName=PQD.

Twigg-Flesner, Christian, Deborah Parry, Geraint G. Howells and Annette Nordhausen. 2007. *The Yearbook of Consumer Law 2008 – Markets and the Law*. Aldershot: Ashgate Publishing.

Vandone, Daniela. 2009. *Consumer Credit in Europe – Risks and Opportunities of a Dynamic Industry*. Berlin Heidelberg: Springer Verlag.

Vandone, Daniela. 2012. 'Consumer Credit in Europe. Risks and Opportunities of a Dynamic Industry'. In *The Development of Consumer Credit in Global Perspective*, edited by Jan Logemann. Houndmills and New York: Palgrave Macmillan.

Warren, Elizabeth. 2007. 'Unsafe at Any Rate'. *Democracy*: 8–19.

Weatherill, Stephen. 2005. *EU Consumer Law and Policy*. Cheltenham, UK and Northhampton, MA: Edward Elgar Publishing.

Weatherill, Stephen. 2010. 'Competence and European Private Law'. In *The Cambridge Companion to European Union Private Law*, edited by Christian Twigg-Flesner. Cambridge: Cambridge University Press.

Weatherill, Stephen. 2011. 'Consumer Policy'. In *The Evolution of EU Law*, edited by Paul Craig and Gráinne DeBúrca, 2nd edn, 837–867. Oxford and New York: Oxford University Press.

Wilhelmsson, Thomas. 2004. 'Varieties of Welfarism in European Contract Law'. *European Law Journal* 10 (6): 712–733.

Willett, Chris. 2012. 'Recognising the Limits of Transparency in EU Consumer Law' (with Martin Morgan-Taylor). In *European Consumer Protection: Theory and Practice*, edited by James Devenney and Mel Kenny, 143–216. Cambridge, New York: Cambridge University Press.

Wilson, Therese Ann (ed.). 2013. *International Responses to Issues of Credit and Over-Indebtedness in the Wake of Crisis*". Surrey and Burlington: Ashgate Publishing.

Chapter 11

The Role of Credit Bureaus in Globalised Economies: Why They Matter Less Than We Think and How They Can Matter More

Akos Rona-Tas

Introduction

The number of consumer credit reporting agencies has been growing since the 1990s. International organisations, such as the IFC and the World Bank, and private companies, such as Equifax, Experian and CRIF, have been in the forefront spreading credit bureaus around the globe. In the OECD countries, the only country left without a credit bureau is Luxembourg. Most of these credit bureaus now include positive and negative information, even some of those that started out as black lists, upgraded to a system of full information.

The main arguments for the credit bureaus are familiar. They are built on the Nobel-prize winning literature on information asymmetry[1] that presents the key problem of lending as the strategic use of information by borrowers. The information asymmetry literature takes the lender's perspective, and makes the assumption that the more information the lenders have the more accurately they can price loans and the better credit markets work. Thus, solving the information asymmetry problem requires more information to the lender, and that, in turn, brings better outcomes.

Credit bureaus are the way to increase information and to solve the information asymmetry problem.[2] The virtues of credit bureaus are well known. They help in at least four ways. First, they help *ex ante* screen loan applicants and allow lenders to spot and avoid bad borrowers. This mitigates adverse selection. Second, they help *ex post* by punishing defaulters, thus through deterrence, they decrease moral hazard. Moreover, filing a damning report that prevents bad clients from borrowing in the future from others is cheap, so it is an inexpensive sanction. Third, credit bureaus loosen the information monopoly of lenders over borrowers. By making reputation 'portable' borrowers are not locked in with a bank that through shared past transactions has got to know them. Clients can shop around for credit and approach new lenders 'from the street'. And finally, because lenders can see the entire debt portfolio of an applicant, including obligations elsewhere, they can spot people who are financially overextended. As a result, credit bureaus not only present the whole financial picture of applicants, but they also reduce over-indebtedness.

1 Akerlof 1970, Jaffee and Russell 1976, Stiglitz and Weiss 1981, Sharpe 1990, Dell'Ariccia 2001, von Thadden 2004.

2 Jappelli and Pagano 2002, Barron and Staten 2003.

Indeed, the empirical literature found that credit information sharing increases lending volume,[3] that overall default decreases somewhat after credit bureaus are introduced[4] and credit bureaus do induce borrower turnover.[5]

Because credit bureaus bring results by extending available information to lenders, limiting credit bureaus in their data-gathering ability can be justified only by unrelated but potentially equally important considerations. Data privacy and social justice (the elimination of various forms of discrimination) are two considerations that are thought to be the main obstacles that can limit what credit bureaus may do.

There are two major types of consumer credit bureaus: black lists and full information registries that include both black (negative) and white (positive) information. There are only a handful of countries in the EU that have black lists only: those are Denmark, France, Finland and Malta.[6] The others have full reporting registries.[7]

Of the four blessings of credit bureaus, screening, sanctioning, loosening ties between customers and lenders and reducing over-indebtedness, black lists achieve only the first two. They help in the screening process although not as much as full information registries. They are also good tools of sanctioning. As black lists contain only borrowers proven bad, lenders cannot tell the difference between an applicant who has never borrowed and one that has been a good borrower. Both will be missing from the list. To prove one is a good borrower, one has to build a longer term relationship with a lender, thus black lists will not loosen much the borrower–lender tie. And black lists will not provide information of the overall debt of an applicant. These last two blessings are delivered only by full information registries, which are also equally good at sanctioning and do screening better, hence the predominance of full-reporting registries. Consequently, conventional wisdom posits that the data collected and provided by credit bureaus should be as wide and as deep as possible, not infringing on other societal goals.[8]

Table 11.1 Aims of black lists and full registries

	Black list	Full information registry
Screen	+	++
Sanction	+	+
Loosen borrower–lender tie		+
Reduce over-indebtedness		+

3 Jappelli and Pagano 1999, 2002, Miller 2003, Djankov et al. 2007, de Janvry et al. 2009, McIntosh and Wydick 2009.

4 Jappelli and Pagano 2002, Luoto et al. 2007, de Janvry et al. 2009.

5 Jappelli and Pagano 2002, Cowan and De Gregorio 2003; Miller 2003; Luoto et al. 2007; de Janvry et al. 2009.

6 Until 2011, Hungary belonged to this group.

7 Although the typology seems cut and dry, there are different shades of fullness (or blackness), depending on how a full information registry choose to report the white and black information. For instance, if as in Spain, the threshold of reporting is much higher for reporting white than for black information, the resulting system can be closer to a black list than one where every loan transaction is recorded regardless of value.

8 Barron and Staten 2003, Kiràly 2008.

In this chapter, I would like to raise some doubts about what I take to be the conventional wisdom about credit bureaus. I will not argue that they are useless or pernicious but I will argue that we have to reconsider the way we think about credit reporting.

Our first observation is that there is little empirical evidence that credit bureaus help not just individual lenders but that they result in more stable markets. In fact, some of the countries with the best and most extensive credit reporting, with the longest history of such institutions, such as the US and the UK, are facing a much bigger problem of consumer debt than countries like France or Finland, where consumer registries are just black lists, or countries like the Czech Republic, where the credit bureau is a recent creation. As consumer registries almost never reach across borders, and partially as a consequence, consumer lending rarely happens across state boundaries, this is not an unfair comparison, even if, as we will see, global forces beyond the cognisance of domestic credit bureaus do play an important role in domestic consumer credit markets.

While the conventional wisdom would suggest that better and more powerful credit bureaus would be less likely to result in over-indebtedness, just what over-indebtedness is, is not easy to say. One measure of over-indebtedness is the amount of consumer debt per capita or consumer debt relative to the size of the national economy. We would think that credit bureaus, especially public ones that are unhampered by information constraints, will be less likely to run up a huge overall debt, because borrowers cannot hide their other debts from prospective lenders.

The most indebted countries in the EU, however, are Denmark, the Netherlands, Ireland, Switzerland and the UK. All of these countries have had credit registries for at least four decades and, with the exception of Denmark, they have had full reporting. Yet the countries with the highest debt are not the countries in the biggest trouble. One thing we can observe is that all these countries are rich. Moreover, the overall debt burden masks a very important factor: the distribution of the debt across economic classes and across types of loans. In a country where the poor borrow more and the rich less, and most of the loans are poorly collateralised or uncollateralised, the same overall debt can have a much more detrimental social and economic effect.

Table 11.2 Countries with over-indebtedness problems

Most indebted	Most precarious (household in arrears)	Type of CB/Black list only
Denmark, Netherlands, Ireland, Switzerland, UK, Sweden,	Greece, Cyprus, Romania, Latvia, Bulgaria, Hungary	Finland, France, Denmark, Malta

The countries where default is the biggest problem are not those that are most indebted but those that are poorer. Greece, Cyprus, Romania, Bulgaria, Latvia and Hungary report the most financial stress. The first five have had full reporting consumer registries. Hungary switched from a black list to full reporting in 2011. It is true that these countries have more recent credit bureaus, but their difficulties with consumer debt are not due to the weaknesses of credit reporting.

And if we take Finland, France and Denmark and compare them to countries at the same level of economic development in the EU but with full reporting registries, we don't find them in bigger trouble, in fact, the three are doing better than Italy or Ireland.

So why have credit bureaus been not more helpful during the financial crisis? Why is it that while at the individual level, lenders may be decreasing their exposure to default by using credit bureau data, in the aggregate they don't. We will discuss four sets of reasons: perverse effects, the social construction of data, the relational nature of lending and the endogeneity problem. All four run up against the information asymmetry approach.

Perverse Effects

Learning more about potential borrowers accomplishes not one but four things, which have contradictory consequences. While using credit bureau data decreases the likelihood of default in each case, it also expands lending, increases the number of people applying from the street, and creates overconfidence, which make lending more risky. To some extent, the operation of credit bureaus follow a logic similar to what is referred to as the tragedy of the commons.[9]

As the first positive effect has been the focus of the theoretical literature, we will concentrate on the other three with the negative or perverse effects.[10] Lending expansion means two things. First, borrowers are granted larger and riskier loans, and second, new borrowers enter the market, who are riskier borrowers. This second part is the more important one. Lending usually starts in the higher economic group, where the borrowers are more resilient against external shocks that could result in default. The well-off are less likely to lose their livelihood, or get sick, and if they do, they have savings and other safety mechanisms to avoid loan default. As lenders compete for market share, as they try to take advantage of the economies of scale that comes from the automation of lending, they have to offer loans to people with increasingly vulnerable finances. Expansion, therefore, increases the average risk more – or at least as much as – the additional credit information decreases it. A better selection from a worse pool may not be preferable to worse selection from a better pool. Vulnerable people are not just simply more likely to default, but they are more likely to default when others do, and they do better than expected when others do likewise. When the economy is in the doldrums, worse-off customers will default in droves, and when it is booming they will service their debts as well as the comfortable middle class. Extending lending downward does not just result in an average risk that is higher, but it also creates more volatility.

The other negative effect of credit bureaus is larger turnover. Lenders have more borrowers who are new customers. If one has to judge new customers, using credit bureau data will decrease risk, but, again, those people are riskier than old customers, who the lender not just knows better but has more control over. A client with not just a loan but also with a savings and a checking account with the bank has more to lose in a default. This is another way that a better selection from a riskier pool may result in riskier lending.

There is yet another way that increased information results in worse decisions. More data provides a false sense of security and confidence.[11] The overconfidence is not simply the result of underestimating the uncertainty that still remains in lending. It is also a result of the coverage lenders receive from the accepted practice of relying on credit bureau data and automated, scientific tools of decision-making that prevent mistakes from becoming a liability for the personnel that is interested in selling as many loans as possible.

These three countervailing forces balance better information. Whether the net outcome leans in the positive or the negative direction depends on the empirical importance of each. Just as the

9 Hardin 1968.

10 The term is from Hirschman 1991.

11 McIntosh and Wydick 2009.

tragedy of the commons depends on the parameters of the model, and it may not be a tragedy if the herders' individual gain is greater than the value lost with the depletion of the commons, market expansion, mobility and overconfidence may be a reasonable price to pay for full reporting credit bureaus.

All of what has been argued so far assumes that the credit bureaus are doing their job well and that the assumptions on which they operate, information asymmetry, are essentially correct. In the next segment, we will draw all that into question.

Data Quality: Social Construction of Data

Data is always shaped by the interests of those who produce it. The great advantage of credit bureaus is that it is a closed system that bypasses the borrower. Prospective lenders do not have to ask the borrower about his debts and payment behaviour, other lenders will supply this information. The borrower cannot easily manipulate his own data. As data delivery by the lenders is carefully prescribed in all credit bureaus, neither side seems to have much discretion. Yet some lenders do exercise discretion. They often refrain from reporting late payments as a courtesy to their clients, or sometimes they act punitively, and report infractions that either did not happen or were not the fault of the borrower.

Knowing how the credit bureaus work also allows the borrowers to figure out how to game the registry. This is made easier by the automation of the decision-making process. Automation, once understood, lets people 'manage' their credit record to their own advantage. This is what happened in the US, where borrowers figured out how to raise their credit scores by manipulating their credit bureau records.[12]

Finally, data quality is compromised by simple error. One of the main sources of errors in credit bureaus is that data arrive on transactions, but must be filed under persons. Making this match is the most common source of error.[13]

Data quality is improved by giving people free access to their own records, as it corrects punitive reporting and mismatches. It does nothing to rectify the underreporting of delinquencies and the gaming of the system.

There is an additional problem besetting registries based on voluntary information sharing. Voluntary participation makes enforcement of data quality much harder, especially when the market is highly concentrated. Big players with lots of customers are less interested in sharing data because they have more to give and less to gain. This can lead to large lenders submitting data more selectively and sporadically.[14]

The Relational Nature of Credit

The theory of information asymmetry makes a series of assumptions that while they capture strong intuitions they are ultimately flawed or incomplete. To understand these assumptions is necessary to amplify the beneficial services of credit bureaus.

12 Rona-Tas and Hiss 2010.

13 Rona-Tas 2008.

14 Rona-Tas and Guseva 2014.

The underlying theory, first, assumes that ONLY the lender faces information asymmetry. This is clearly not the case. Anyone who ever had to sign a loan document or read a credit card contract knows that lenders as specialised professionals have an informational advantage in fashioning the contract.[15] In fact, lenders often fully exploit their information advantage. Studies show that transparency is strongly and negatively correlated with price: the more transparent the pre-contractual information the lower the prices are in a country.[16] A stable market requires that both borrowers and lenders find a solution to their own information asymmetry problem. The theory and the practice of credit bureaus assume that this problem exists only on the lender's side because the credit record makes no distinction between loans taken from obfuscating lenders and loans extended by honest creditors.

The second assumption is that the borrower knows more than the lender about his own intentions and capacities. This is true only in a limited way. Loan applicants are often ignorant, overly optimistic or self-deceiving about what they could know, but more importantly, most of the forces that lead to default are causes that are unforeseen by the borrower and beyond his control. Divorce, sickness, loss of employment and a drop in income are the main causes of default.[17] The collapse of the residential property bubble (e.g. Iceland, Spain or the US), bad housing policies (e.g. Hungary), government austerity (e.g. Greece, Portugal, Spain) or unregulated exposure to financial markets (e.g. Greece, Romania, Iceland, Hungary, Spain) were all forces beyond the borrowers' discretion. In fact, the government and the banking sector are far more implicated in these crises than individual borrowers.

As mentioned earlier, the weight of these external factors is growing as the market expands, because being poor means having less financial cushion and being more exposed to economic forces over which one has little command.

The credit bureau model assumes that the borrower is fully or predominantly responsible for non-payment and that the borrower is a knowledgeable, calculating, responsible individual, who knows enough, who is smart enough and who has enough discretion to deliver on his promise of repayment. While it is impossible to build lending without assuming individual responsibility, risk models that essentially make good borrowers pay for the 'sins' of bad ones, do not follow the same moral principles of individual responsibility. As default is already priced in the cost of the loan, it is hard to argue that default is an avoidable sin. This moral ambiguity is reflected in the fact that the garden variety loan default is not a criminal offence anymore but only a civil dispute and, in many countries, defaulters can even ask to discharge their unpaid debt.

The third assumption is that borrowing and repayment is entirely the borrower's business. In fact, any lender knows well that how the loan is made and how it is managed by the lender can be as important for the final outcome as the borrower's capacity, character or external circumstances. Credit bureau records construe the lending transaction as if the lender had no influence over the final outcome. As if the dice were cast once the loan was signed and from then on all the lender could do is to hope that he made the right prediction. Even if we set aside the exogenous forces, whatever is left for human discretion is not completely up to the borrower.

All these point to one fundamental error in the way credit bureaus imagine lending. They built an entire database on the assumption that payment depends solely on the debtor who is intent on exploiting his information advantage. The main corrective insight should be that lending is relational, its success depends on both lender and borrower, and their contract.

15 Bar-Gill and Warren 2008.

16 Van Dijk Management Consultants 2009.

17 Sullivan et al. 2000, Jentzsch and San Jose Riestra 2006.

Therefore if one wants a credit market where borrowers are reliable, attention should be shifted from the debtor's behaviour to the transaction between lender and borrower, and in this respect, regulating the credit contract and the subsequent interaction between lenders and borrowers should take the central place. Each point, the two-sided information asymmetry, the limited agency of the borrower and the considerable agency of the lender, can be addressed by regulators.

There is a large literature on how to improve information flowing towards the customer,[18] but we are not going to discuss this here. The limited agency of the borrowers and the co-responsibility of the lenders should be acknowledged by the structure of the credit contract. There should be two principles that these contracts should honour:

1. The responsibility for action should always be on the side that is best positioned to avoid or mitigate negative events, regardless of who is the proximate cause.
2. If negative events are beyond the control of both lender and borrower, responsibility should go to the side that can better hedge against external forces.

An example of the first principle would be to require lenders of loans with regular installment payments to offer the option of automatic direct payroll deposit,[19] that avoids forgetfulness or error, making that the standard, routine method, but letting people opt out if they want to handle the payments themselves. A large percentage of missed payments can be avoided easily by the lender taking this action, even if the borrower is ultimately at fault if he forgets. For the same reason, increases in borrowing costs that are due to the downgrading of a lender's rating should not be passed on to the borrower.

An example to illustrate the second principle is foreign exchange loans. Households that, unlike banks, cannot hedge against foreign exchange risk (those that have no foreign exchange income of the appropriate amount) should not be given foreign exchange loans. Another example would be to divide the risk of a falling housing market between the lender and the mortgage holder by requiring a cap on the loan-to-value ratio but then also making the mortgage a non-recourse loan.

The problem of two-sided information asymmetry, and the other two problems, are related. Contracts befuddle customers in order to hide the fact that lenders push as much responsibility onto them as they can. Credit relations will be more solid if contracts are more balanced, the market will be more stable and that means lenders will be able to predict the future performance of their loan portfolio better.

Credit bureaus, on the other hand, should require data not just of the type of the loan but also certain elements of the contract (interest rates, penalties, LTV, other collateral, etc., as some credit bureaus do) and also demand data on the loan management practices of the lender (as no credit bureau does now to the best of my knowledge). In sum, contracts should be more regulated so that they are more balanced and uniform, and credit bureaus should gather much more information about loan conditions and management (but less data on other borrower characteristics, as we will see below).

18 Bar-Gill 2004, Sunstein and Thaler 2008, Bar-Gill and Board 2012, Rona-Tas and Guseva 2013.

19 The borrower can also be given the option that after starting direct deposits to temporarily suspend it or suspend it indefinitely or discontinue it altogether.

The Endogeneity Problem

Finally, credit histories do not just reflect past behaviours but they also shape future ones.[20] They are supposed to do that. Credit behaviour is supposed to have consequences even if the borrower is not at fault. Defaulting on a loan will make it harder to get a new one, or will make new loans more expensive. Not being able to finance a loan with another or having to pay high fees and interest will make future default more likely. And it works also in reverse. Good performance makes it easier to perform well on the next loan. This is unavoidable. But because the reputation created by the credit bureau produces a positive feedback, it can easily create vicious (and virtuous) cycles making payment behaviour volatile.[21]

This gets enlarged, if credit history in some shape or form becomes a part of other decisions of financial consequence for the individual. If credit bureau information becomes a factor in calculating someone's insurance premium,[22] or is used in hiring or rental decisions, as is happening in the US, it is not just that any data problem will metastasize and can have enormous consequences for the customer, but it may also create a situation whereby the consequences of a bad record become amplified to a point where they prevent borrowers from correcting mistakes, ultimately punishing the lender. For instance, skipping a few instalments on one's car loan may make it harder to get a job if the employer bases his decision on data from the credit bureau. That, in turn, makes it more difficult to catch up on the car payment. From the perspective of the lender, punishing negligent borrowers is rational only if the punishment does not result in an even bigger loss for the lender by making it impossible for the borrower to make good on his contract.

One difficulty is that what counts as credit is far from cut and dried. Any time when one consumes first and pays later, as it happens with electricity, phone or water, one is taking de facto credit. Therefore, whether, say, utility companies should be participating in credit registries is debatable. That insurance companies should be part of the information exchange is much harder to argue.[23] Nevertheless, limiting the use of credit bureau information is in the interest of not just the borrower but also the lender.

For the same reasons, limiting the data that can be used in credit decisions and therefore can be accepted in credit bureaus is desirable.[24] Credit bureaus should be limited to data on credit behaviour. Taking into consideration adverse events from other areas of life will have the effect of compounding misery creating a self-fulfilling prophecy.

Turning credit bureaus into tools of state administration by linking credit records with various other official registries, or using them as a tool to fight corruption or tax evasion, as is happening in China, opens another set of troubling questions.[25] How government can access individual records should be very carefully circumscribed.

---

20 Rona-Tas and Hiss 2010.

21 The payment behaviour is endogenous with respect to the credit history, because action following from the credit history influences the borrower's ability to pay.

22 American Academy of Actuaries 2002, Hartwig and Wilkinson 2003.

23 It is not a solution to make access of non-lenders contingent on individual consent. People may not be in a position to refuse, for instance, if a prospective employer demands to see their credit record.

24 In the United States, Equifax purchased Talx, a company that manages the payroll of thousands of large and medium-sized companies. Talx has over 100 million employee records, and Equifax seeks to use them to enhance its credit files. This means that a pay cut in principle can reduce one's creditworthiness in 15 days.

25 Jentzsch 2008, Rona-Tas and Guseva 2014.

Conclusion

Credit bureaus, while their international role is quite limited, do play an important role in national consumer credit markets. They help screen and punish customers in markets that are expanding quickly. In fact, if one believes that consumer credit, especially uncollateralised credit, should be available to virtually everyone, credit bureaus should be thought of as indispensable. Yet, in their current forms, they are unlikely to provide serious protection against over-indebtedness and even as a tool to accurately predict how individual borrowers will behave.

In this short chapter, I have expressed scepticism about the conventional wisdom, underpinned by economic theory of information asymmetry, that the central problem of consumer credit markets is the lack of information on the lenders' side, and that the way forward is to offer as much information to lenders as possible. I raised four issues to rethink the role of credit bureaus: perverse effects, the social construction of credit bureau data, the relational nature of lending and the endogeneity problem. The perverse effects call our attention to new risks that market expansion creates and raises the possibility that on balance black lists may be as good as full reporting registries. The social construction of data reminds us that data quality can be kept high only if it is in the interest of both sides and/or if the two sides can keep each other in check. It also suggests that voluntary data sharing relies on low market concentration. The relational nature of lending points to ways to regulate the loan contracts and the need to expand data collected in the credit bureaus. And finally, endogeneity counsels that limiting the gathering and dissemination of credit data is in the interest of both borrowers and lenders. Sometimes less is more.

References

Akerlof, George A. 1970. 'The Market for "Lemons": Quality Uncertainty and the Market Mechanism'. *Quarterly Journal of Economics*, 84(3): 488–500.

American Academy of Actuaries, Risk Classification Subcommittee of the Property/Casualty Products, Pricing, and Market Committee. 2002. 'The Use of Credit History for Personal Lines Insurance: Report to the National Association of Insurance Commissioners'. New York.

Bar-Gill, Oren. 2004. 'Seduction by Plastic', 98 *Northwestern University Law Review* 1373.

Bar-Gill, Oren and Oliver Board. 2012. 'Product Use Information and the Limits of Voluntary Disclosure'. New York University Law and Economics Working Papers. Paper 239.

Bar-Gill, Oren and Elizabeth Warren. 2008. 'Making Credit Safer'. New York University Law and Economics Working Papers. Paper 137. http://lsr.nellco.org/nyu_lewp/137.

Barron, John M. and Michael Staten. 2003. 'The Value of Comprehensive Credit Reports: Lessons from the U.S. Experience', in Margaret J. Miller, ed., *Credit Reporting Systems and the International Economy*. Cambridge, MA: MIT Press, pp. 273–310.

Cowan, Kevin and Jose De Gregorio. 2003. 'Credit Information and Market Performance: The Case of Chile', in Margaret J. Miller, ed., *Credit Reporting Systems and the International Economy*. Cambridge, MA: MIT Press.

de Janvry, Alain, Craig McIntosh and Elizabeth Sadoulet. 2009. 'The Supply and Demand Side Impacts of Credit Market Information'. http://irps.ucsd.edu/faculty/faculty-directory/craigmcintosh.htm.

Dell'Ariccia, Giovanni. 2001. 'Asymmetric Information and the Structure of the Banking Industry'. *European Economic Review*, 45: 1957–1980.

Djankov, Simeon, Caralee McLiesh and Andrei Shleifer. 2007. 'Private Credit in 129 Countries'. *Journal of Financial Economics*, 84(2): 299–329.
Hardin, Garrett. 1968. 'Tragedy of the Commons'. *Science*, 162(1968): 1243–1248.
Hartwig, Robert P. and Claire Wilkinson. 2003. 'The Use of Credit Information in Personal Lines Insurance Underwriting'. Insurance Issues Series, 1 / 2, Insurance Information Institute, New York.
Hirschman, Albert O. 1991. *The Rhetoric of Reaction. Perversity, Futility and Jeopardy*. Cambridge, MA: Harvard University Press.
Jaffee, Dwight M. and Thomas Russell. 1976. 'Imperfect Information, Uncertainty, and Credit Rationing'. *The Quarterly Journal of Economics* 90(4): 651–666.
Jappelli, Tullio and Marco Pagano. 1999. 'Information Sharing in Credit Markets: International Evidence'. Inter-American Development Bank Research Network Working Paper R-371. Washington, DC: Inter-American Development Bank, Research Department.
Jappelli, Tullio and Marco Pagano. 2002. 'Information Sharing, Lending and Defaults: Cross-Country Evidence'. *Journal of Banking and Finance*, 26(10): 2017–2045.
Jentzsch, Nicola. 2008. 'An Economic Analysis of China's Credit Information Monopoly'. *China Economic Review*, 19: 537–550.
Jentzsch, Nicola and Amparo San Jose Riestra. 2006. 'Consumer Credit Markets in the United States and Europe', in Guiseppe Bertola, Richard Disney and Charles Grant, eds, *The Economics of Consumer Credit*. Cambridge, MA: MIT Press, pp. 32–62.
Király, Julia. 2008. 'Jelzálogpiacok Válságban: Kockázatalapú Verseny és Tanulságok' [Mortgage Markets in Crisis: Profit Based Competition and Lessons]. *Hitelintezeti Szemle*, 7(5): 451–480.
Luoto, Jill, Craig McIntosh and Bruce Wydick. 2007. 'Credit Information Systems in Less Developed Countries: A Test with Microfinance in Guatemala'. *Economic Development and Cultural Change*, 55(2): 331–334.
McIntosh, Craig and Bruce Wydick. 2009. 'What Do Credit Bureaus Do? Understanding Screening, Incentive, and Credit Expansion Effects'. Technical report, International Relations and Pacific Studies, University of California, San Diego.
Miller, Margaret J. 2003. *Credit Reporting Systems and the International Economy*. Cambridge, MA: MIT Press.
Rona-Tas, Akos. 2008. Consumer Registries in the United States. Report Prepared for the Hungarian Office of Economic Competition and the Hungarian National Bank.
Rona-Tas, Akos and Alya Guseva. 2013. 'Information and Consumer Credit in Central and Eastern Europe'. *Journal of Comparative Economics*, 41(2): 420–435.
Rona-Tas, Akos and Alya Guseva. 2014. *Plastic Money. Constructing Markets for Credit Cards in Eight Postcommunist Societies*. Stanford, CA: Stanford University Press.
Rona-Tas, Akos and Stefanie Hiss. 2010. 'The Role of Ratings in the Subprime Mortgage Crisis: The Art of Corporate and the Science of Consumer Credit Rating', in M. Lounsbury and P.M. Hirsch, eds, *Markets on Trial: The Economic Sociology of the U.S. Financial Crisis, Part A* (*Research in the Sociology of Organizations* 30: 115–155). Bingley, UK: Emerald Group.
Sharpe, Steven A. 1990. 'Asymmetric Information, Bank Lending, and Implicit Contracts: A Stylized Model of Customer Relationships'. *The Journal of Finance*, 45: 1069–1087.
Stiglitz, Joseph E. and Andrew Weiss. 1981. 'Credit Rationing in Markets with Imperfect Information'. *The American Economic Review*, 71(3): 393–410.
Sullivan, Teresa A., Elizabeth Warren and Jay Lawrence Westbrook. 2000. *The Fragile Middle Class: Americans in Debt*. New Haven: Yale University Press.

Sunstein, Cass R. and Richard Thaler. 2008. *Nudge: Improving Decisions about Health, Wealth, and Happiness*. New Haven: Yale University Press.

Van Dijk Management Consultants. 2009. 'Study on the Data Collection for Prices of Current Accounts provided to Consumers'. http://ec.europa.eu/consumers/strategy/facts_en.htm#Retail 2009.

von Thadden, Ernst-Ludwig. 2004. 'Asymmetric Information, Bank Lending and Implicit Contracts: The Winner's Curse'. *Finance Research Letters*, 1: 11–23.

Chapter 12

Two Cheers for Europe: Austerity, Mortgage Foreclosures and Personal Insolvency Policy in the EU

Iain Ramsay*

Our agenda of structural reform requires a major adjustment effort. It will only work if it is fair and equitable. Because inequality is not sustainable. In some parts of Europe we are seeing a real social emergency. Rising poverty and massive levels of unemployment especially among our young people. That is why we must strengthen social cohesion. It is a feature that distinguishes European society from alternative models. Some say that, because of the crisis, the European Social model is dead. I do not agree. Yes we need to reform our economies and modernize our social protection systems. But an effective social protection system that helps those in need is not an obstacle to prosperity. It is indeed an indispensable part of it. (Manuel Barroso, President EU Commission, State of the Union 2012)

1. Introduction

The Great Recession and subsequent Eurozone crisis placed household debt on the international policy agenda. Over four million homes were foreclosed in the United States. Housing bubbles burst in the UK, Ireland and Spain; problems emerged with foreign currency loans in parts of Central Europe and the Baltic states. Latvia suffered a catastrophic 25 per cent drop in output.[1] The institutionalisation of austerity in Greece, Portugal, Ireland and Spain,[2] after a trial run in Latvia, 'severely depressed growth'[3] with consequent debt problems for consumers.[4] Mortgage foreclosures dominated discussion in some countries, along with problems associated with foreign currency loans.[5]

---

* This chapter is part of a research project 'Personal Insolvency in an Age of Austerity' supported by Research Fellowship RF-2013-193 from the Leverhulme Trust. Thanks to Irina Domurath, Hans-W. Micklitz and Joseph Spooner for comments.

1 See Catriona Pursfield and Christoph Rosenberg, 'Adjustment under a Currency Peg: Estonia, Latvia and Lithuania during the Global Financial Crisis 2008–09' IMF Working Paper 10/2013.

2 Unlike Greece, Portugal and Ireland, the IMF/Troika did not bail out Spain. 'Spain was granted financial support by the European Financial Stability Facility (EFSF), with the Commission monitoring the resolution of banks, and the Fund providing technical assistance on financial sector reform'. Jean Pisani-Ferry, Andre Sapir and Guntram Wolff, *EU-IMF Assistance in Europe: An Early Assessment* (Bruegel 2013) 5.

3 Ibid.

4 This chapter benefited greatly from the individual country reports discussed in Part II and draws on the findings of the report throughout the chapter. See also IMF, *World Economic Outlook* (2012) ch 2; Hans-W. Micklitz, 'Access to and Exclusion of, European Consumers from Financial Markets after the Global Financial Crisis' in Therese Wilson (ed.) *International Responses to Issues of Credit and Over-Indebtedness in the Wake of the Crisis* (Ashgate 2013) ch 3.

5 See e.g. country reports in Part II of this volume.

The IMF reports high levels of household debt within the EU and is concerned that continuing high ratios of household debt to GDP will constrain growth.[6] A swift writing-down of housing debt after a recession following a housing bubble may therefore produce beneficial effects for the overall economy.[7] European data conceal substantial differences between member states in their exposure to debt overhang or 'deleveraging pressures'. A distinction is sometimes drawn between the problems of the 'core' and a minority of 'periphery' states of the EU, for example, Portugal, Ireland, Greece and Spain. This classification is less helpful when applied to debt overhang. One study includes 14 member states in the periphery[8] while DG EC-FIN identifies a significant number of states subject to deleveraging pressures.[9] Middle and lower income consumers[10] are the groups most affected, with occasional wealthy outliers.[11] The European Central Bank identifies 'low income indebted households as particularly vulnerable to economic shocks'.[12] Women are over-represented within this group.[13] Developing appropriate policies for writing-down household debt became a significant aspect of crisis management,[14] and remains a continuing challenge.

This chapter explores EU and member state policy responses to the debt overhang, focusing on mortgage regulation and personal insolvency reforms. These responses involve the regulatory state, the welfare state and the state in crisis. Understanding the responses requires attention to the influence of ideas, both 'deep world views' and technocratic policy assumptions, the role of international, regional and national actors as agents of change, and the institutional settings for change.

---

6 IMF, *Report on the Euro Area* Article IV Consultation 2013 at 10 notes that: 'reduction of debt to GDP ratios has barely started'. See also IMF (n4). For a useful exploration of household debt in the EU see *The Euro System Household Finance and Consumption Survey, Results from the First Wave* ECB Statistics Paper Series No 2 April 2013.

7 This argument is systematically developed in Atif Mian and Amir Sufi, *House of Debt: How They (and You) Caused the Great Recession, and How We Can Prevent it from Happening Again* (Chicago 2014).

8 For example the European Credit Research Institute includes the following states in the periphery: Belgium, Bulgaria, Denmark, Estonia, Greece, Spain, Hungary, Ireland, Lithuania, Latvia, Portugal, Romania, Slovenia, United Kingdom. See Ales Chmelar, 'Household Debt and the European Crisis', ECRI Research Report No 13.

9 See Carlos Cuerpo, Inez Drumond, Julia Lendvai, Peter Pontuch and Rafal Raciborski, 'Indebtedness, Deleveraging Dynamics and Macro-Economic Adjustment' Economic Papers 477 (DG ECFIN 2013). They identify the following countries as 'prone to deleveraging pressures': Cyprus, Denmark, Spain, Ireland, the Netherlands, Portugal, Estonia, Latvia, Slovakia, Sweden and the UK.

10 See chapters in Part II of this volume, e.g. Iceland (middle and lower income) Portugal (middle income) Spain (significant numbers of low-income individuals with high debts), Greece (middle and lower income). Hungary is the exception where it appears that high debt levels are associated with higher income individuals.

11 For example the high-profile (but small in number) Irish bankruptcy tourists. See H. McDonald, 'Irish Dodge Debts through UK "Bankruptcy Tourism"' *Guardian* 27 May 2012.

12 *The Euro System Household Finance and Consumption Survey* (n6) 71.

13 See Francesca Betti, Marcella Corsi, Carlo D'Ippoliti, Antigone Lyberaki, Manuela Samek Lodovici, and Alina Verashchagina, *The Impact of the Economic Crisis on the Situation of Women and Men and on Gender Equality Policies* (DG Justice 2013).

14 See IMF (n 6) 10 'Insolvency regimes need to be made more effective (e.g. by facilitating out of court settlements, reducing time for insolvency proceedings) and provide more flexibility in dealing with personal or corporate bankruptcy'. See Fabian Bornhorst and Marta Arranz, 'Growth and Importance of Sequencing Debt Reductions across Sectors' in Martin Schindler, Helge Berger, Bas B. Bakker and Antonio Spilimbergo (eds) *Jobs and Growth: Supporting the European Recovery* (IMF 2014) ch 2.

Part 2 provides a background to EU credit and over-indebtedness regulation before the crisis of 2008. During this period, personal insolvency and credit regulation were treated as separate spheres, the former part of the social problem of over-indebtedness, the latter an economic aspect of the establishment of a single EU credit market. Part 3 examines the influential discourses which framed the response to the crisis. This part draws on EU Commission and Troika (ECB, IMF) documents and working papers. Household deleveraging is conceptualised as an economic and technical problem which might hamper productivity and growth and have cross-border implications, including through the symbolic 'bankruptcy tourism'.[15] Achieving a balance between maintaining credit discipline and avoiding moral hazard while providing a fresh start are recurring themes. Part 4 focuses on member state regulation of mortgage foreclosure in the wake of the crisis, compares it with the United States and examines the experience in England and Wales, Latvia, Spain and Greece. These latter countries represent neo-liberal and 'Mediterranean' forms of capitalism. Latvia was the pilot for subsequent structural adjustment programmes. In Spain the politics of mortgage and personal insolvency reform involved national, regional and international actors, and its experience stimulated EU Parliamentary amendments to the 2014 EU Mortgage Directive.[16] Greece illustrates the ambiguous influence of the IMF on national insolvency reform. Part 5 analyses the transformation of the EU Mortgage Directive after the crisis through political action by the EU Parliament and examines the emerging EU narrative of promoting entrepreneurialism through personal insolvency. Part 6 concludes by discussing the policy implications of the analysis, linking the emerging EU paradigm of credit, debt and personal insolvency regulation to the competitive social market, financial exclusion and the resilience of neo-liberalism after the crisis.

The European story after the crisis is one of governments acting swiftly to bail out banks but less swiftly to relieve over-indebted consumers and homeowners. Households became the 'shock absorbers'[17] after the crisis in Europe. Several states with mortgage debt problems introduced restrictive and means-tested relief programmes. Spain, for example, responded with limited measures restricted to the most vulnerable and in late 2013 opening a tiny window of possibility for an individual to discharge debts in bankruptcy.[18] Personal insolvency reform in Greece failed initially, basing its reform on the defective German model.[19] Ireland, already in the process of reform when the crisis struck, enacted a complex range of insolvency alternatives which reflect political compromises and international influence by the Troika.[20] England and Wales 'muddled through', resurrecting techniques to protect homeowners from a previous recession. An exception is Iceland, which introduced a battery of restructuring measures including across-the-board write-downs of mortgage debt.[21] The consequences of the crisis shaped Parliamentary amendments to the

15 See below Part 5.

16 Directive 2014/17/EU of the European Parliament and of the Council on credit agreements for consumers relating to residential immovable property OJ L60/34.

17 I use this phrase somewhat ironically. It is taken from a 2005 IMF report which presciently observed that '[T]he household sector has increasingly and more directly become the "shock absorber of last resort" in the financial system', IMF *Global Financial Stability Report* 2005, 5.

18 See Chapter 5, this volume, and see below at 4.2.

19 See Chapter 3, this volume, and below at 4.3.

20 The Insolvency Service of Ireland guide to the alternatives indicates the potential complexity, http://www.isi.gov.i.e./en/ISI/Pages/Possible_Scenarios. See European Commission, DG EC-FIN *Economic Adjustment Programme for Ireland Summer 2012 Review* (Occasional Papers 115). See Joseph Spooner, 'Long Overdue: What the Belated Reform of Irish Personal Insolvency Law tells us about Comparative Consumer Bankruptcy' (2012) 86(2) American Bankruptcy Law Journal 243.

21 See Chapter 7, this volume. The Icelandic solution was praised by the IMF (n4).

EU Mortgage Directive to provide both greater regulation of mortgage lending practices and the development of minimum standards for mortgage foreclosure processes. The crisis also stimulated political change through the CJEU preliminary reference procedure.[22]

International and regional actors lacked a policy script for addressing household debt problems in Europe. Unlike corporate insolvency, best practices for personal insolvency and regulation of mortgage debt foreclosure did not exist. Financial capital opposed measures which would permit individuals to write-down debt,[23] politicians in countries without personal insolvency laws were hesitant to introduce measures which permit individuals to 'not pay their debts', and crises often polarise political positions and result in political gridlock.[24] This may be one explanation for the Spanish outcome. In contrast the IMF/Troika was able to impose substantial reforms to the initial Greek debt adjustment law through the technocratic conditionality process. These reforms will result ultimately in a 'best practices' law in Greece. International actors such as the IMF are often portrayed as imposing unwanted, undemocratic and damaging reforms on countries. The story here is more nuanced. The IMF often cajoled reluctant member states to introduce or reform personal insolvency reforms,[25] and was more aggressive than EU institutions such as the ECB in promoting household deleveraging. The loss of democratic process in conditionality however is disquieting.

But the story is not solely that of the influence of national and international interest groups. Ideas are important. Ordoliberalism, the fear of a financial collapse,[26] technical economic ideas and models, affected responses by national and international actors. The role of these ideas cannot simply be reduced to the strategic actions of groups. The internationalisation of global consumer finance norms by the G20[27] since the Great Recession demonstrates increased convergence of ideas and institutional approaches which influenced the content of the EU Mortgage Directive.[28]

2. Deregulation and the First 'Crises' 1984–2008

The period of the mid-1980s to 2007 in Continental Europe witnessed the introduction of partially effective personal insolvency or debt adjustment laws, which in turn resulted in further reforms and adjustments.[29] Deregulation in the 1980s was followed by a large build-up of debt in some countries and the severe recession of the early 1990s was a rehearsal for the Great Recession. In Scandinavia

22 See discussion of *Aziz* judgement below at note 156.

23 See for example Chapter 8, this volume.

24 See Atif Mian, Amir Sufi and Francesco Trebbi, 'Resolving Debt Overhang: Political Constraints in the Aftermath of Financial Crises' (2012 ssrn) available at http://papers.ssrn.com/sol3/papers.cfm?abstract_id=2002583.

25 For example Spain, Latvia and Lithuania. In Lithuania the IMF convinced the government to introduce a more liberal discharge period.

26 Which of course could be used as an effective argument by financial capital for a bail out.

27 See G-20 *High Level Principles on Consumer Protection* (OECD 2011).

28 Susan Block-Lieb and Terence Halliday argue that a global consensus existed that problems in housing market finance had caused the crisis and therefore it was appropriate to develop international norms of consumer protection to prevent future crises. See Susan Block-Lieb and Terence Halliday, 'The Microeconomics and Macropolitics of Systemic Financial Crisis: Bankruptcy as a Point of Reference' in Jasnica Garasic and Nada Bodiroga-Vukobra (eds) *Sovereign Insolvency – Possible Legal Solutions* (Springer 2014).

29 For accounts of these developments see Iain Ramsay, 'Between NeoLiberalism and the Social Market: Approaches to Debt Adjustment and Insolvency in the EU' (2012) 35(4) Journal of Consumer Policy 421–444: Jason Kilborn, 'Expert Recommendations and the Evolution of European Best Practices

the introduction of debt adjustment systems followed the banking crises in these countries, which threatened middle-class homeowners. As a consequence these laws often permitted homeowners to write-down mortgage debt.

This period might be described as one of 'social learning' as countries often went through cycles of change, learning from mistakes, and identifying anomalies. France, for example, amended its original 1989 law four times between 1989 and 2010. This process continues in states with established systems of debt adjustment or personal insolvency where a major challenge is how to administer at relatively low cost large numbers of individuals with limited ability to finance the process. The great majority of contemporary debtors do not own homes and many have little income and minimal assets. In France the *rétablissement personnel* provides a swift discharge for this group, in England the Debt Relief Order. Germany fails to recognise this group for separate treatment so that the *Nullinsolvenz* (individuals with no repayment capacity) who constitute the majority of insolvencies, must wait out a period of 'good behaviour' before the possibility of a discharge. The growth of this group underlines the vulnerability of low-income households to adverse income shocks. Figure 12.1 indicates substantial increases in personal insolvency in France, Germany and England and Wales (Scotland has a separate system) before the crisis.

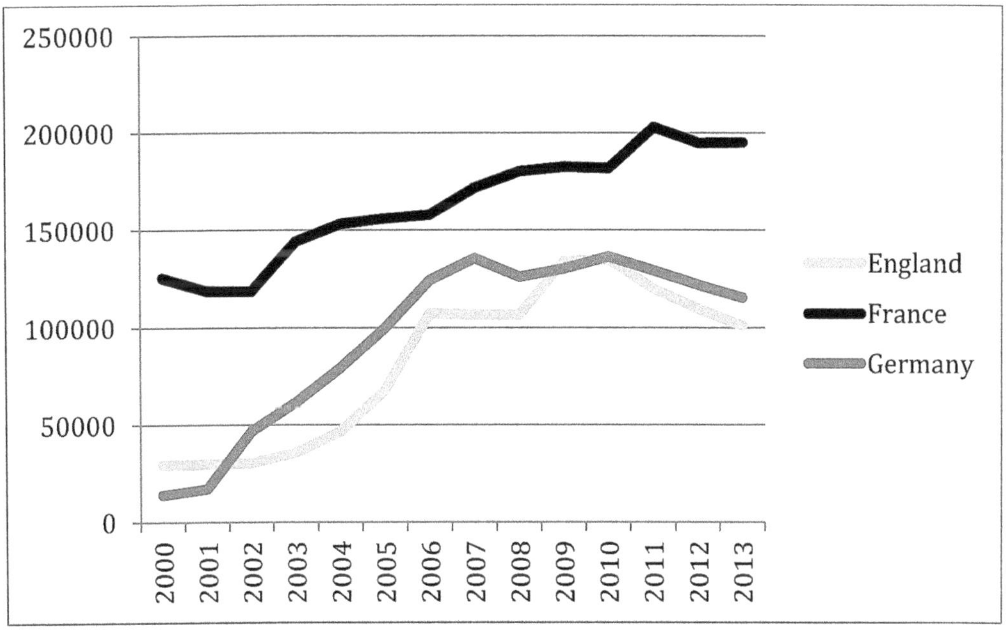

Figure 12.1 Personal insolvency England, France, Germany 2000–2013
Source: England, Insolvency Service Statistics; France, Bank of France; Germany, German Federal Statistics; US Census data

for the Treatment of Overindebtedness, 1984–2010' ssrn http://papers.ssrn.com/sol3/papers.cfm?abstract_id=1663108.

The Great Recession, and the subsequent Eurozone crisis in Europe, accelerated the introduction of new laws in those member states without either an individual insolvency discharge procedure or one that was accessible to individuals.[30] By 2014 almost all member states, except Bulgaria, Hungary and Romania,[31] permitted (under a variety of conditions) individual discharge of debts.

During this initial period, the EU conceptualised the treatment (rather than prevention) of over-indebtedness as a social issue, subject to national cultural, social and political differences.[32] It was an issue primarily for member state regulation. Although EU documents identified the growing European problem of 'over-indebtedness' in 1995,[33] common rules for its treatment were not part of the Commission's plans for establishing the ground rules for a common market for consumer credit. The political costs of introducing European rules which might permit non-payment of debts would, in any event, be high, with opposition from financial institutions and some member states[34] and insolvency law was not conceived as a necessary ground rule for a consumer credit market. This sequencing of credit reform is not uncommon in the development of credit markets. However, as credit markets develop, so do organised creditor groups so that when over-indebtedness becomes a salient issue, these groups will oppose the possibility of debt discharge.[35] Politicians sympathetic to debtors' problems will have difficulties in developing support for the introduction of a personal insolvency law providing for a discharge of debt. As a consequence initial legislative efforts were often cautious and limited access. The relatively liberal bankruptcy discharge of the United States and England existed before the explosion of mass consumer credit and intermediaries, such as lawyers and accountants, were able to 'convert'[36] these laws to consumer insolvency without active political intervention.

Initial EU initiatives on insolvency law, such as the 2000 Insolvency Regulation, focused on corporate and business bankruptcy. In contrast, 'softer' approaches to consumer over-indebtedness were adopted within the Open Method of Co-ordination. This 'framework of cooperation' between members for the achievement of common objectives, uses indicators, peer review, benchmarking

30 In Lithuania, Latvia, Greece, Ireland and Spain. For discussion of Ireland see Joseph Spooner, 'Sympathy for the Debtor? The Modernisation of Irish Personal Insolvency Law' (2012) 25 Insolvency Int 97.

31 See chapters 6 and 8, this volume.

32 In 2001 the head of financial services in DG Sanco noted 'large differences between national social legislation to cope with this phenomenon [over-indebtedness] ... Clearly the objective of a Credit directive cannot be to harmonise social legislation, which remain in the field of the national competences (subsidiarity)'. Thierry Vissol, *Updating and Revising the Consumer Credit Directive* (87/102).

33 'Overindebtedness has become a European problem, irrespective of the Union's volition and powers in the domain'. See *Report on the Operation of Directive 87/102/EEC for the approximation of the laws, regulations and administrative provisions of the Member States concerning consumer credit* COM (95) 117 Final at 93.

34 The 1997 summary of responses to the consultation on reform of the Consumer Credit Directive indicated for example that the UK thought that the Consumer Credit Directive was 'not the appropriate means of promoting wide ranging social policy initiatives' and France indicated that it was a subject falling within national competence. Banking groups also opposed any EU initiative. See *Report on the Operation of Directive 87/102 for the approximation of laws, regulations and administrative provisions of the Member States concerning consumer credit, Summary of Reactions and Comments* COM (97) 465 Final at 17.

35 See discussion in Adam Feibelman, 'Consumer Bankruptcy as Development Policy' (2009) 39 Seton Hall L Rev. 63.

36 See discussion of conversion of laws to new purposes in Jacob Hacker, 'Privatizing Risk without Privatizing the Welfare State: The Hidden Politics of Social Policy Retrenchment in the US' (2004) 98 Am Pol Sci Rev 243.

and 'best practices'.[37] It addresses the limits of EU competence to legislate in many areas of social policy. This soft approach, harnessing states as laboratories,[38] and using peer review as a 'mutual voluntary learning process' produced modest results in the area of debt adjustment.[39] Several academic and expert consultants produced reports for the EU during this period which provide a fairly consistent set of reform ideas[40] for the treatment of over-indebtedness including a repayment plan as a condition for discharge (usually 3–5 years) with the possibility of swift discharge for the 'hopelessly' over-indebted. Open access should be available for good faith debtors.

The Council of Europe proposed in 2007 a wide range of preventive and treatment measures including the possibility of a discharge of debts as 'a residual remedy' if other measures to write-down debt were not possible.[41] These 'moderate' recommendations, with a very cautious endorsement of debt discharge, reflected the composition of the working group which was drawn from states with a residual discharge system.[42] This report characterised over-indebtedness as a human rights issue although references to specific human rights were absent from the document.[43]

---

37 The OMC encourages 'co-operation, promoting exchanges of information and best practices, promoting innovative approaches and evaluating experiences' (art. 153(2)(a)) TFEU.

38 Cf. Brandeis J in *New State Ice Co. v Liebmann* 285 US 262, 311 (1932) ('a single courageous state may, if its citizens choose, serve as a laboratory; try novel social and economic experiments without risk to the rest of the country').

39 The EU also supported NGO networks – such as the European Consumer Debt Network. Attempts were made to analyse best practices. In 2006 the Netherlands put forward its system of debt adjustment for a best practices assessment. The reviewers visited one court in Rotterdam and were provided with some background information. The report is informative and interesting but hardly qualifies as a systematic or critical comparative analysis of the Dutch system. See Dieter Korczak, *Amnesty of Debts: Amicable Agreements and Statutory Solution* (DG Employment, Social Affairs and Equal Opportunities 2006).

40 See e.g. Nick Huls, *Over-Indebtedness of Consumers in the EC Member States: Facts and Search for a Solution* (Story-Scientia 1994), Udo Reifner, Johanna Niemi-Kiesiläinen, Nick Huls and Helga Springeneer *Consumer Overindebtedness and Consumer Law in the European Union: Final Report* (Commission of the European Communities, Health and Consumer Protection Directorate-General 2003); Johanna Niemi and Ann-Sofie Henrikson, *Report on Legal Solutions to Debt Problems in Credit Societies* (Council of Europe 2006).

41 See Council of Europe *Recommendation CM/Rec(2007)8 of the Committee of Ministers to member stateson legal solutions to debt problems*. The document requires: 'that debtors have effective access to impartial advice and to debt adjustment … b. ensuring that payment plans in debt adjustment are reasonable … both in repayment obligations and in duration; c. ensuring that debt adjustment covers all debts, excluding only those covered by special waivers provided under national law; d. establishing mechanisms for extra-judicial settlements and encouraging such settlements between the debtor and creditor; e. effectively limiting the means of creditors to hinder debt settlements unreasonably; f. encouraging effective financial and social inclusion of over-indebted individuals and families, in particular by promoting their access to the labour market; g. encouraging the active participation of the debtor in debt settlement and, where necessary, counselling and advice following the debt settlement; h. allowing partial or total discharge of the debts of individuals and, where applicable, families in cases of over-indebtedness where other measures have proved to be ineffective, with a view to providing them with a new opportunity for engaging in economic and social activities'.

42 See Johanna Niemi, 'Never Too Small to Fail: Insolvency of Consumers as an International Concern' in Wolfram Backert, Susan Block-Lieb and Johanna Niemi (eds) *Contemporary Issues in Consumer Bankruptcy* (Peter Lang 2013) 24.

43 See generally Chrystin Ondersma, 'A Human Rights Framework for Debt Relief' (unpublished paper LSA 2014 on file with author).

The prevention of social exclusion[44] and a respect for human dignity were organising themes. The concept of social exclusion developed initially in France during the 1970s as a substitute for a discourse focused on class inequality and income redistribution. It provided a blueprint for reforms of the welfare state that might appeal to both the right and the centre-left, for example justifying measures to link unemployment benefit to the promotion of active participation in the labour force. Financial inclusion conceptualises social rights as contributing to market objectives – such as greater productivity or participation in the consumption market, rather than permitting an individual to stand outside the market. Financial inclusion is compatible with a range of insolvency regimes including those requiring a period of 'responsibilisation', preparing for re-entry to being a productive citizen.[45] The process of insolvency may itself bring some forms of exclusion, not only through legal rules but non-legal sanctions through credit reports, etc. The balance between responsibilisation (which may involve some exclusion from the market) and facilitating re-entry may be difficult to draw.

Lawyers rather than professional economists authored these documents and they may have had some influence on national reforms, although this is difficult to measure. During this period, the EU Commission was committed to the creation of an integrated retail financial services market with harmonised ground rules.[46] The ability to write-down debt is one of these ground rules but the two pre-crisis Directives on consumer credit regulated primarily the 'front end' of credit. The 2008 Consumer Credit Directive had originally attempted to balance consumer protection with measures intended to expand access, but after substantial lobbying by financial interests, access to an expanding market became the dominant narrative and only a limited concept of responsible lending survived. A rough distinction was drawn between the economic aspects of credit addressed at Community level and social aspects addressed at the national level. The former involved technical expertise to deal with market failures, the latter more messy political and social compromises.[47]

3. Post-Crisis 2008–

The effects of the US subprime mortgage crisis and the Eurozone crisis changed the landscape of EU financial and mortgage regulation. New governance actors emerged such as the European Banking Authority,[48] and the Troika (ECB, IMF and EU Commission), an informal grouping established in

44 This reflects the French influence on the report. French over-indebtedness law is conceptualised in terms of the prevention of social exclusion. See discussion of France in Iain Ramsay, 'A Tale of Two Debtors: Responding to the Shock of Over-Indebtedness in France and England: A Story from the *Trente Piteuses*' (2012) 75 MLR (2) 212–248.

45 Daniel Béland argues that it 'legitimizes modest policy reforms entirely compatible with moderate understandings of economic liberalism and ultimately unable to fight the social evils this idea refers to'. See Daniel Béland, 'The Social Exclusion Discourse: Ideas and Policy Change' (2007) 35 Policy and Politics 123. See e.g the Opinion of the European Economic and Social Committee on Credit and Social Exclusion in an affluent society OJ C 044 16/02/2008 which suggested 'special monitoring of debtors throughout the process of implementing post-bankruptcy payment plans, in order to prevent the same problems re-occurring and help debtors change their patterns of consumption and indebtedness, so that they can make a genuinely fresh start'.

46 For further discussion see Iain Ramsay, 'Changing Policy Paradigms of EU Credit and Debt Regulation' in Stephen Weatherill and Dorota Leczykiewicz (ed.) *The Image of the Consumer in EU Law* (Hart 2015).

47 See e.g. Giandomenico Majone *Regulating Europe* (Routledge 1996).

48 See Regulation 1093/2010/EU establishing a European Supervisory Authority (European Banking Authority) [2010] OJ L331/12. See Article 9: the 'Authority shall take a leading role in promoting transparency,

2010 during the Greece bailout. The EU attained leverage over the domestic policies of countries bailed out through MoUs (conditionality)[49] and the European Semester[50] part of the increased enforcement of the various stability pacts.[51] The IMF became involved in European bailouts in 2007[52] for the first time since 1976. It provided expertise and credibility through its technocratic experience with crisis management and institution-building and it provided an opportunity for the IMF to re-establish its reputation as a global problem solver.

---

simplicity and fairness in the market for consumer financial products and services'. This includes the adoption of guidelines and recommendations for promoting 'convergence of regulatory practice' 9(2), issuing warnings 9(3), achieving a coordinated approach to regulation and supervision of product innovation 9(4); and temporarily prohibiting or restricting activities that 'threaten the orderly functioning and integrity of financial markets or the stability of the whole or part of the financial system in the Union' 9(5).

The EBA Consumer Trends report for 2014 includes 'indebtedness and responsible credit; misselling, household borrowing, and financial literacy' under 'trends and issues'. The EBA monitored the passage of the EU mortgage directive and issued two opinions in 2013 on good practices for responsible mortgage lending and treatment of borrowers in mortgage payment difficulties. The 2014 report indicates that these may be converted into guidelines.

49 Article 136 of the TFEU specifically recognises conditionality. It is not possible in this chapter to discuss the broader implications of these governance changes. Christian Joerges remarks that 'its turn towards a community of austerity' has resulted in 'Europe riding roughshod over considerations of labour and social law' (Joerges, EUI WP 2013/09) with the Troika emblematic of this more autocratic EU. See also e.g. Wolfgang Streeck, 'The Crisis of Democratic Capitalism' (2011) 71 New Left Review 5; Michael Wilkinson, 'The Spectre of Authoritarian Liberalism: Reflections on the Constitutional Crisis of the European Union' (2013) German Law Journal. For an overview of the conditionality programmes see DG Internal Policies, Economic Governance Support Unit (EGOV) *Committee Study on the Troika and Financial Assistance in the Euro Area: Successes and Failures* (February 2014).

50 In June 2013 Spain was instructed to review its insolvency framework for individuals and companies under this procedure. Council of EU 10656/1/13 UEM 207 *Recommendation on Spain's 2013 national reform programme and delivering a Council's opinion on Spain's stability programme.*

51 A good discussion of these developments can be found in Dagmar Schiek (ed.) *The EU Economic and Social Model in the Global Crisis* (Ashgate 2013) ch 1.

52 IMF involvement – Hungary, 2007, Latvia, 2008, Romania, 2009, Greece, 2010, Ireland, 2010, Portugal, 2011. According to Thomas Jost and Franz Seitz the EU request for assistance from the IMF was opposed by the ECB which saw it as a sign of weakness. But 'The EU Commission had no credibility and experience in managing severe financial problems' and the German government insisted on IMF involvement. See 'The Role of the IMF in the European Debt Crisis' (2012) Discussion Paper no 32 9–10 http://www.oth-aw.de/fileadmin/user_upload/Aktuelles/Veroeffentlichungen/WEN-Diskussionspapier/wen_diskussionspapier32.pdf. This article also indicates the large size of the IMF loans in the EU in comparison to contributions to countries such as Korea during the earlier Asian crisis. Ferry et al. (n2) also note 'the exceptionally long durations and exceptionally large size' of the IMF involvement.

For a summary of the contemporary work of the IMF in Europe see IMF factsheet at http://www.imf.org/external/np/exr/facts/europe.htm <http://www.imf.org/external/np/exr/facts/europe.htm.

3.1 Emerging Discourses: Framing the European Response

Deep worldviews may affect how political actors diagnose a problem.[53] The 'long shadow' of German ordoliberalism,[54] a 'productivist' rather than 'consumerist' form of neo-liberalism, framed German approaches to the crisis.[55] Ordoliberalism dominated German post-war economic thought and action, and influenced the structure of the EU.[56] Its philosophy is that the state should establish institutions beyond political control, such as an independent bank which controls inflation as part of wage suppression policies to enhance export competitiveness. Saving rather than credit is subsidised by the state to provide pools of capital for development.[57] '*Erst Sparen dann Kaufen!*' was the motto.[58] To secure political support for this economic constitution, a conservative welfare state was 'bolted on' to the economy[59] with employment status as a basis for differential entitlements. This 'social market state' contrasted with the demand-led consumerist model of the United States where increased access to credit, initially for white males but later extended to all through anti-discrimination laws, was supported as a social goal by a wide cross-section of the political spectrum and consumer credit was constructed as a productive institution permitting individuals to engage in income smoothing and invest in a future upward mobility.[60]

---

53 See Vivien Schmidt, 'Speaking to the Markets or to the People? A Discursive Institutionalist Analysis of the EUs Sovereign Debt Crisis' (2014) 16(1) BJPIR 188.

54 See Sebastian Dullien and Ulrike Guérat, 'The Long Shadow of OrdoLiberalism: Germany's Approach to the Euro Crisis' (European Council on Foreign Relations 2011).

55 James Whitman discusses the distinction between 'producerism' and 'consumerism' using Germany as a paradigm of producerism. See James Whitman, 'Consumerism versus Producerism: An Essay in Comparative Law' (2007) 117 Yale L.J. 340.

56 See the discussion by Mark Blyth in *Austerity: The History of a Dangerous Idea* (Oxford 2013) who argues that these German ideas have carried over to the EU, with 'the centrality of competitiveness' and the role of the ECB in controlling inflation. See Blyth at 141–143.

57 See Jan Logemann, *Trams or Tailfins? Public and Private Prosperity in Postwar Germany and the United States* (University of Chicago Press 2012) and 'Americanization through Credit? Consumer Credit in Germany 1860s to 1960s' (2001) 85 Business History Review 529. Logemann concludes that although there is increased convergence between the US model and Germany, 'Differences continue to exist in the public perception of consumption, in the role of saving and consumer credit for household spending, and in retailing and consumer housing choices. The mortgage and credit crisis that began in 2007 was felt less acutely by German than American consumers ... only in the wake of the crisis of 2007–08, amid mortgage defaults and personal bankruptcies has the American consumption model received renewed attention'. Ibid. at 225.

58 'First Save, then Spend' quoted in Blyth (n56) at 135. Logemann argues that 'consumer goods were more likely financed through household savings. Saving rather than spending defined Bürgerlichkeit or middle-class status in the eyes of many West Germans, separating them from the working class' (ibid. 10).

59 Blyth (n56) at 137. Logemann, 'The German social security state retained a rather "conservative" character with little social levelling' (n57,53). See also Monica Prasad, *The Land of too Much: American Abundance and the Paradox of Poverty* (Harvard 2012) at 34–35. The German reforms of 2002–2005 did modify the 'Bismarckian' model. See Bruno Palier (ed.) *A Long Goodbye to Bismarck? The Politics of Welfare Reforms in Continental Europe* (Amsterdam University Press 2010); Bruno Palier and Kathleen Thelen, 'Institutionalizing Dualism: Complementarities and Change in France and Germany' (2010) 38(1) Politics and Society 119–148.

60 See e.g. Louis Hyman, *Debtor Nation: The History of America in Red Ink* (Princeton 2011); Gunnar Trumbull, 'Credit Access and Social Welfare: The Rise of Consumer Lending in the United States and France' (2012) 40 Politics and Society (1) 9–34; Gunnar Trumbull, *Consumer Lending in France and America: Credit and Welfare* (Cambridge 2014); Lizabeth Cohen, *A Consumers' Republic: The Politics of Mass Consumption in Post War America* (Knopf 2003).

Ordoliberalism developed as a reaction to the National Socialist interventionist state and the hyperinflation of the 1920s, favouring austerity to purge public debt which would create investor confidence in the long run. The Eurozone crisis was, on this view, created by profligate and irresponsible spending by countries and these countries must, hence, submit to austerity measures from which they would benefit in the long run. These ideas fitted with the more technical economic idea of 'expansionary fiscal contraction',[61] which argued that contracting the state would create investor confidence in the long run future of an economy. These ideas became embedded in the EU through the various pacts and fiscal compacts of 2010 and 2011 and justified the draconian remedies applied in Latvia, its testing ground in European structural adjustment. 'Expansionary fiscal contraction' is however contested within the economics literature and some IMF economists express reservations about its validity.[62] It translates into a simple political slogan that 'we must all tighten our belts' in the short run to benefit from long run prosperity. It resonated with the idea that the crisis was caused by profligate spending rather than reckless lending by German and French banks. The image was therefore that of a 'sober creditor EU North addressing the problems of the profligate debtor South'.[63]

The contrast between producerist and consumerist neo-liberalism is of course stylised. A variety of capitalisms exist within the EU.[64] However, the strict rule-based German personal insolvency law[65] with its obligation on the bankrupt to search for work, and long period of 'good behaviour', which has become an influential European model,[66] represents a state that 'establishes both the freedom and responsibility of the citizens'.[67] Although there is no direct connection between

61 Fransesco Giavazzi and Marco Pagano, 'Can Severe Fiscal Contractions Be Expansionary? Tales of Two Small European Countries' (1990) NBER Macroeconomics Annual 5: 75–111.

62 See Jaime Guajardo Daniel Leigh and Andrea Pescatori, 'Expansionary Austerity: New International Evidence' IMF Working Paper WP/11/158. See also the criticism in Blyth (n56) at 204–212.

63 See Philippe Legrain, 'Euro-Zone Fiscal Colonialism' *New York Times* 21 April 2014, http://www.nytimes.com/2014/04/22/opinion/euro-zone-fiscal-colonialism.html?_r=2, 'European Union institutions have become instruments for creditors to impose their will on debtors, subordinating Europe's southern "periphery" to the Northern "core"'.

64 See Peter Hall and David Soskice, *Varieties of Capitalism: The Institutional Foundations of Comparative Advantage* (Oxford 2001) and subsequent literature. Only modest analysis exists of the role of houschold credit within these distinct capitalisms. See e.g. Colin Crouch, 'Employment, Consumption, Debt and European Industrial Relations Systems' (2012) 51 Industrial Relations 389.

65 For criticisms of the German law see e.g. Wolfram Backert, Ditmar Brock, Gotz Lechner and Katja Maischatz, 'Bankruptcy in Germany: Filing Rates and the People behind the Numbers' in Johanna Niemi, Iain Ramsay and William Whitford (eds) *Consumer Credit Debt and Bankruptcy: Comparative and International Perspectives* (Hart 2009) 288. After noting that many debtors have no repayment capacity, 'It has to be questioned whether there is much sense in a six year long period of good conduct before discharge from remaining debts is allowed. Why should people be kept under financial probation when there is no recognizable output for creditors and there is evidence of poor quality of life for debtors'. Even with the 2013 German reforms few debtors will be able to take advantage of the three-year discharge period which requires an individual to pay 35 per cent of her debts. See the useful summary of these reforms by Jason Kilborn in credit slips http://www.creditslips.org/credilips/2013/07/earlier-discharge-for-german-debtors-but-not-many.html#more.

66 For example, Austria, Greece and Portugal.

67 Ludwig Erhard, quoted by Michel Foucault, *The Birth of Bio Politics, Lectures at the Collège de France 1978–79* (Palgrave 2008) at 81. Jan-Ocko Heuer describes the German system as a paradigm liability model emphasising the debtor's responsibility for repayment. Jan Ocko-Heuer, 'Social Exclusion in European Consumer Bankruptcy Systems' (on file with author).

ordoliberalism and the German law, all groups involved in the enactment of the law 'emphasized the need for debtors to demonstrate worthiness for relief'.[68] The new law would 'demand much more' than the 'debtor-friendly' US model. If the crisis was caused by a surfeit of 'easy credit'[69] then a liberal US-style bankruptcy law linked to a 'democratised' credit market, which facilitates individuals pressing the 'reset' button for more consumer credit, is not an attractive option. England and Wales has the only personal insolvency law in Europe resembling the US model and the liberal English consumer discharge provisions are a sidewind of the promotion of entrepreneurialism. A modified German approach seems to be an important reference point for international agencies. Personal responsibility for biographical risks is a central aspect of neo-liberalism so that a waiting period for discharge links with contemporary neo-liberal approaches to insolvency.

Economic discourse was influential in affecting the sequencing of policy responses. Atif Mian and Amir Sufi argue[70] that the 'bank lending' view dominated responses to the crisis. This posits that the most important task for government after a bank crisis is to get the banks lending again by ensuring their stability, for example through recapitalisation. Reducing an overhang of consumer debt is a secondary objective. Aggressive deleveraging of household debt might threaten the banks' capitalisation and promote moral hazard. This bank lending view has strong support among economic technocrats and policymakers in Europe and constrained write-downs of mortgage debt.

3.2 International Discourse on Household Deleveraging

Neither the EU nor the IMF had experience with programmes of household debt deleveraging. Standardised international or regional reform scripts did not exist. The UNCITRAL legislative guide, used by the World Bank and IMF in evaluating countries' business bankruptcy systems and for the purpose of loan conditionality,[71] was limited in its application to consumer and individual bankruptcy. No influential national model such as the US Chapter 11 existed for consumer insolvency. Powerful professional groups were not promoting particular models of personal insolvency. Nor was there a *Doing Business* project for consumer debt. The older European states in the EU only introduced discharge systems for personal insolvency towards the end of the twentieth century and a variety of approaches existed. Limited systematic analysis existed of their operation. The treatment of mortgage debt was a key issue but best practices here – for example whether to deal with secured debt within insolvency law – did not exist, and indeed this issue continues to pose a challenge for policymakers. There was therefore no Washington or Brussels consensus on how to proceed.

---

68 Jason Kilborn, 'The Innovative German Approach to Consumer Debt Relief: Revolutionary Changes in German Law and Surprising Lessons for the United States' (2006) 24 Nw J Int'l L&Bus 257, 271–272.

69 Lack of international consensus as to diagnosis of crisis limited the development of international standards on personal insolvency. See Susan Block-Lieb and Terence Halliday (n28).

70 Mian and Sufi (n7) ch 9.

71 UNCITRAL 'managed to leverage its norms by linking them to institutions with the power to persuade and enforce'. Terence Halliday and Bruce Carruthers, *Bankrupt: Global Lawmaking and Systemic Financial Crisis* (Stanford 2010) 165. The UNCITRAL legislative guide on insolvency outlines 'the core issues that it would be desirable to address in that law with recommendations providing specific guidance on how certain legislative provisions might be drafted' (para 2). The guide has specific recommendations where there appears to be a 'high degree of consensus', while others outline alternatives (ibid. at 158–159). The US and expert professional groups led by Americans were influential in developing this consensus along with the IMF.

The World Bank Report on the Treatment of the Insolvency of Natural Persons[72] makes an economic case for the introduction of a personal insolvency discharge, in terms of reducing externalities from debt default (such as lost productivity, costs to family and communities), creating incentives for responsible lending and accounting practices, and allocating losses to those in the best position to spread them.[73] It does not, however, identify best practices, which would give effect to these ideas because personal insolvency is 'intertwined with social, political and cultural issues that present too many differences to be treated uniformly'.[74]

Analysis of the publications of the Troika and IMF on personal insolvency reform in Europe (primarily Ireland, Greece, Portugal, Latvia, Lithuania, Spain) reveals ideas developed through experience, and informed by textbook economic concepts and underlying ideas about government 'intervention'. The IMF appears more aggressive in promoting household deleveraging than European institutions such as DG-ECFIN[75] and (not surprisingly) the European Central Bank, which focuses on moral hazard, 'credit discipline' and threats to the banking system,[76] grudgingly admitting in 2009 that increases in bankruptcy filings may be caused by over-indebtedness related to adverse income shocks, in addition to opportunistic behaviour by individuals.[77] These European interventions do not generally refer to empirical studies of consumer bankruptcy systems and propose solutions at times inconsistent with dominant insolvency opinion.[78]

An early IMF paper by Luc Laeven and Thomas Laryea in 2009[79] noted that governments might develop household debt restructuring based on 'social considerations' but 'the design of … debt restructuring programs should be based on sound economic principles'.[80] This seems to reflect a fear of populism distorting political decision-making in a crisis. Governments might be tempted to respond to public concern by overreacting and introducing widespread schemes of debt write-down which damage the economy. The paper also highlighted the issue of moral hazard created by debt relief programmes – a theme reiterated in many subsequent documents.

The IMF in its 2012 World Economic Outlook concluded that recessions triggered by household debt could result in a slower recovery than those triggered by other events.[81] An economic case existed beyond simply relief of hardship for 'intervention' by governments to facilitate 'the writing

72 See World Bank *Report on the Treatment of the Insolvency of Natural Persons* (World Bank 2013) (the author was a drafter of this report).

73 See also José Garrido, 'The Role of Personal Insolvency Law in Economic Development: An Introduction to the World Bank Report on the Treatment of the Insolvency of Natural Persons' (2013) 5 World Bank Law Review 111.

74 World Bank (n72) para. 12.

75 See e.g. DG ECFIN, Economic Adjustment Programme for Ireland Summer 2012 Review at 28–29 (concern for 'opportunistic behavior' and demanding 'additional safeguards against moral hazard').

76 The ECB opinions are available at https://www.ecb.europa.eu/ecb/legal/opinions/html/index.en.html.

77 'Aside from the effects of opportunistic behavior of individuals taking advantage of debtor friendly legislation by filing for bankruptcy in response to financial distress, this trend is mainly due to excessive indebtedness and adverse income shocks'. ECB, *Housing Finance in the Euro Area* Occasional Paper No 101 (2009) 72.

78 For example proposing a privilege for tax authorities (see DG ECFIN (n75) at 29), which has increasingly been viewed as inappropriate by most modern insolvency systems.

79 Luc Laeven and Thomas Laryea, 'Principles of Household Debt Restructuring' (2009) IMF Staff Position Note SPN/09/15.

80 Ibid. at 3.

81 'Household busts preceded by larger run-ups in gross household debts are associated with significantly larger contractions in economic activity'. IMF, *World Economic Outlook* 2012, 91 (IMF 2012).

down of household debt', and the prevention of foreclosures. Measures should target those 'with the highest marginal propensity to consume', generally average to lower income consumers who would drive a recovery. However, moral hazard by borrowers and lenders and the need to control strategic defaults must also be considered. In addition, the distributional conflict in the establishment of these programmes might result in 'social friction' leading to an ineffective policy or political gridlock. The IMF analysed historical and contemporary case studies on responses to household debt overhangs: the United States in the 1930s, Colombia in 1999, Hungary and Iceland in the Great Recession and the Nordic countries in the early 1990s. They concluded that 'bold household debt restructuring programs, such as those implemented in the United States in the 1930s and in Iceland today'[82] could prevent recurring cycles of declining prices and aggregate demand.[83] Those conclusions were generally not followed by European states after the Eurozone crisis.

The IMF conclusion that household debt was a problem for the overall economy made it a higher priority on the policymaking agenda.[84] In 2013 an IMF lawyer and economist reflected on their experience in advising and convincing EU governments (e.g. Greece, Latvia, Lithuania, Spain) to introduce or modify personal insolvency systems.[85] They conclude that the introduction of debt-restructuring mechanisms posed several challenges: the absence of international best practices; the design of the law 'inevitably' being driven by 'social policy considerations';[86] the need to keep an appropriate balance between 'maintaining credit discipline' and 'affording financially responsible debtors a fresh start; the need for an adequate institutional infrastructure'. The politics of reform was messy since 'reform may be resisted by vested interests and individual creditors and debtors defend the status quo of leaving high debt unresolved'.[87]

Household debt with its 'social policy' and 'political dimension' is less amenable to technocratic solutions than corporate restructuring.[88] However the authors outline certain 'basic design features' which emerged from their work on personal insolvency in Europe:

- a fresh start for *financially responsible* individuals from the liabilities at the end of the insolvency proceedings (*typically after 3–5 years*);
- establish *appropriate* filing criteria to make insolvency procedures accessible to individual debtors *while minimizing abuse*;

82 Ibid. at 114.

83 The IMF suggested combining standardized rules with individual discretion and having a clear time framework for writing down debt. Ibid. 114–115. Chapter 7 in this volume outlines the various measures adopted.

84 This theme is referenced in subsequent central bank Financial Stability reports.

85 Yan Liu and Christoph Rosenberg, 'Dealing with Private Debt Distress in the Wake of the European Financial Crisis, A Review of the Economic and Legal Toolbox' IMF WP/13/44. See also Michael Erbenova, Yan Liu and Magnus Saxegaard, 'Corporate and Household Debt Distress in Latvia: Strengthening the Incentives for a Market-Based approach to Debt Resolution' IMF WP/11/85. This document describes the 2010 Latvian law in the following manner (at 18): 'The new law provides financially responsible individual debtors a fresh start at the end of the insolvency period by discharging their remaining liabilities after the sale of non-exempt assets and meeting the specified repayments requirements.'

86 These include: 'to reinvigorate the individual productive potential' and 'reduce the social costs of leaving debtors in a state of perpetual debt distress'.

87 Liu and Rosenberg (n85) 6 and 13.

88 The introduction of corporate restructuring is also not a purely technocratic exercise. See generally Terence Halliday and Bruce Carruthers, *Bankrupt: Global Lawmaking and Systemic Financial Crisis* (Stanford 2010).

- impose *automatic and temporary stay on enforcement actions* with adequate safeguards of creditor interests;
- set *repayment terms that accurately reflect the debtor's capacity to repay* to ensure an effective fresh start;
- and recognize foreign proceedings and enable cross-border co-operation to *avoid bankruptcy tourism*.[89]

Most of these principles are open-textured, permitting a variety of solutions, which might claim to have 'appropriately' balanced the various considerations. Given the absence of detailed empirical studies of different personal insolvency systems in the EU and with the possibility always of the argument that 'social conditions are different here', these factors provide a starting point for political argument. The limits of 'expertise' and the absence of best practices reduce the leverage of the international experts, whose influence will depend on the nature of their relationship to a state – ranging from the strong influence exercised in conditionality, through technical advice and the annual Article IV monitoring. Success in introducing or modifying measures might depend on the ability to build support within a country, including groups and experts favourable to reform.

The need to provide intellectual scaffolding (even if *ex post*) for the work of the Troika was taken up by EU economists in DG EC-FIN, who attempted to initially identify those member states likely to experience deleveraging pressures as a preliminary to assessing the role of personal insolvency in promoting an 'orderly and co-ordinated deleveraging process'.[90] As part of this learning process, EC-FIN brought together experts from the IMF, BISS, DG Market, Enterprise, Sanco and the ECB as well as representatives of member states of vulnerable countries (Latvia, Greece, Ireland, Portugal) with recent reforms. DG EC-FIN continues its research on this topic. But substantial empirical uncertainty continues to exist as to how to balance bank stability and debt deleveraging.[91]

These EU and international documents might support the following consensus on 'high level principles' of European personal insolvency law: a 'balance' of maintaining credit discipline, avoiding moral hazard and providing a fresh start for the financially responsible debtors.[92] Central concepts such as moral hazard are rarely explored in any depth, so that it is not clear what are the specific techniques, which might be successful in preventing moral hazard by debtors and creditors.[93] The emerging European consensus on a discharge period of three to five years is less 'debtor friendly' to consumers and entrepreneurs than the English (or US and Canadian) discharge period.[94] The evidence base for this 'European' discharge period is limited since few systematic

89 Liu and Rosenberg 15 (n87) (my italics). In its staff report on Spain in 2013 the IMF suggests also that 'provision should be made for those with no repayment capacity'. IMF Country Report, Staff Document Selected Issues 13/245 (July 2013) at 25.

90 See Cuerpo et al. (n9) 41.

91 The IMF in its 2012 Report notes that 'Overall there is no accepted wisdom about whether and how gross debt may restrain economic activity' (n81) 89.

92 See e.g. ECB, 'Opinion of the European Central Bank of 14 September 2012 on measures relating to personal insolvency' CON/2012/70, available at www.ecb.europa.eu/ecb/legal/pdf/en_con_2012_70_f.pdf (accessed February 6, 2013).

93 For a careful analysis of moral hazard in the context of an existing insolvency system see Joseph Spooner, *Personal Insolvency Law in the Modern Consumer Credit Society: English and Comparative Perspectives* (PhD Thesis, University College London, 2013) 189 et seq.

94 The European position will provide leverage to those groups in England currently proposing an extension of the discharge period from one to three years. See R3 (The Association of Turnaround Professionals)

empirical studies exist of European personal insolvency and debt adjustment systems. However, this EU model is not only an attempt at understanding the problem of over-indebtedness but its repetition by experts may also *constitute* the world of debt deleveraging as politicians act on the assumption that 'moral hazard' exists and explains particular patterns of behaviour.

4. Household Debt, Losing the Home and Mortgage Foreclosure

> This middle class of wealth … [W]ithin this vast group … a key role is often played by ownership of a primary residence and the way it is acquired and paid for.[95]

Home ownership is an important economic and social institution in the EU with high levels of home ownership in many countries (see Table 12.1).[96]

Table 12.1 Housing tenure 2012 EU

	Owner outright or mortgage	Tenant at market price	Tenant reduced price or free
Romania	96.6	0.8	2.6
Lithuania	91.9	1.4	6.7
Hungary	90.5	2.8	6.7
Slovakia	90.4	7.8	1.8
Croatia	89.5	1.6	8.9
Bulgaria	87.4	1.3	11.3
Norway	84.8	9.1	6.1
Estonia	83.5	3.0	14.7
Poland	82.1	4.0	13.6
Malta	81.8	2.1	15.8
Latvia	81.5	7.8	10.7
Czech Rep	80.4	13.2	6.4
Spain	78.9	12.7	8.3
Iceland	77.3	13	9.7
Slovenia	76.2	5.5	18.3
Greece	75.9	18.2	5.9
Portugal	74.5	10.9	14.5

The Personal Insolvency Landscape: A Way Forward for Formal Debt Relief, http://www.r3.org.uk/media/documents/policy/policy_papers/personal_insolvency/R3_Personal_Insolvency_Landscape_Jan_2014.pdf; R3 Redressing the Balance Strengthening the Bankruptcy Process and Recognising Prior Behaviour, http://www.r3.org.uk/media/documents/policy/policy_papers/personal_insolvency/Redressing_the_balance.pdf .

95 Thomas Piketty, *Capitalism in the Twentieth Century* (Harvard University Press 2014) 260.

96 Lorna Fox Mahoney identifies the many meanings of home – as financial investment, as territory, as identity and as a social and cultural signifier. See Lorna Fox O'Mahony, 'Meanings of Home', in Susan Smith (ed.) *The International Encyclopaedia of Housing and Home* (Elsevier 2011).

	Owner outright or mortgage	Tenant at market price	Tenant reduced price or free
Italy	74.1	13.3	12.6
Finland	73.9	10.5	15.6
Cyprus	73.2	11.5	15.3
Belgium	72.3	18.5	9.2
Luxembourg	70.8	24.6	4.6
EU	**70.4**	**19.1**	**11.5**
Sweden	70.1	29.7	0.2
Ireland	69.6	15.4	15.0
Netherlands	67.5	32.1	0.4
UK	66.7	15.9	17.5
US	**64.4**	…	…
Denmark	64.3	35.4	0.3
France	63.7	19.5	16.8
Austria	57.5	26.1	16.4
Germany	53.3	38.6	8.1

Source: Eurostat silc http://appsso.eurostat.ec.europa.eu/nui/show.do?dataset=ilc_lvho02&lang=en.

Germany is the outlier. Many of the countries bailed out had limited alternative forms of housing tenure for individuals facing foreclosures.[97] Table 12.2 indicates the change in home-ownership levels between 2007 and 2012 in selected countries. Ireland, the UK, Greece and Iceland experienced a significant contraction in home ownership during this period. Home ownership constitutes a form of asset-based welfare, and may be linked to social mobility and individual identity.

Table 12.2 Change in housing tenure 2007–2012 selected countries

Owner including with mortgage	2007	2012
Ireland	78.1	69.6
UK	73.3	66.7
Spain	80.6	78.9
Greece	75.6	69.66
Portugal	74.2	74.5
Romania	96.1	96.6
Hungary	88.5	90.5
Latvia	86.0	81.5
Iceland	86.4	77.3
United States	68.9 (2006)	64.4

Source: Eurostat silc, US Census Data.

97 See e.g. chapters 3, 4, 5, 6 and 8, this volume.

Article 8 of the ECHR may provide a level of human rights protection against the loss of a home.[98] Housing markets are constituted, regulated and shaped[99] by many forms of private and public regulation. Markets may be encouraged through state insurance (Fannie Mac and Mae in the United States), tax deductions on interest payments (United States, Sweden) and absence of taxation on capital gains. Regulation affects the risks of home ownership. Before deregulation of mortgage markets in the 1980s, the UK had a 'safe' housing market with a low repossession rate because access to mortgage finance was limited, particularly for 'non-standard' individuals such as the self-employed or those with less secure employment.[100] A consequence of the changes since the 1980s is a market with greater risk. The UK example was re-enacted in more dramatic form in Iceland where deregulation in the early 2000s triggered a 'massive credit boom',[101] and in countries of Central and Eastern Europe.[102] In contrast, the French system of financing home ownership, including maximum loan-to-income ratios, continues the model of a 'safe' housing market which has the effect of limiting access to younger individuals and those not in secure jobs. The consequence is a default rate lower than in the UK.[103] The Great Recession appears to have had a modest effect in France on housing defaults. The more risky English homeownership market with liberal access needs effective safety nets for individuals in an economy prone to periodic housing bubbles.

Foreclosures cause significant distress and dislocation to an individual and her family. In countries with limited alternative rental markets it may increase homelessness. Foreclosures on a large scale can devastate neighbourhoods and communities. Although it may be in the interests of both financial institutions and debtors to renegotiate mortgages, financial institutions may adopt a tough bargaining position from a desire to sort out the 'genuinely' needy debtor from individuals who might be acting strategically. Negotiation costs may also be high where mortgage debt has been securitised and mortgage servicers rather than the original lender are involved. The structure of the servicers' incentives may reduce their willingness to negotiate.

Default and foreclosure rates in the EU were generally lower than in the United States, but were a significant political issue in states where housing bubbles burst (Ireland, Spain, UK, Iceland) and foreign currency mortgages became unmanageable (Hungary, Romania, Latvia, Iceland). Mortgage foreclosure laws in the EU differ substantially[104] but unlike the United States the ability to 'walk away' from a mortgage is limited by the absence of non-recourse mortgages and the

---

98 See Susan Nield and Nicholas Hopkins, 'Human Rights and Mortgage Repossession: Beyond Property Law using Article 8' (2013) 33 Legal Studies 431.

99 See the discussion in Waltraud Schelkle, 'A Crisis of What? Mortgage Credit Markets and the Social Policy of Promoting Homeownership in the US and Europe' (2012) 40 Politics & Society 59.

100 See discussion in Mark Stephens, 'Mortgage Market Deregulation and its Consequences' (2007) 22 Housing Studies 1.

101 Iceland Central Bank quoted in Chapter 7, this volume.

102 See e.g. Chapter 6, this volume.

103 Waltraud Schelkle (n99) argues that both France and the UK had bigger housing bubbles than the United States but that the impact of the crisis was less severe in the UK and France. She attributes this to more pre-contract controls in France and post-default interventions in the UK.

104 For an outline of differences in European Housing Markets see European Central Bank, *Housing Finance in the Euro Area* Occasional Paper 101 (2009). A summary of national approaches to foreclosures can be found in the Commission Staff Working Paper, *National Measures and practices to avoid foreclosure procedures for residential mortgage loans, Accompanying document to the proposal for a Directive of the European Parliament and of the Council on credit agreements relating to residential property* SEC (2011) 357 final, http://ec.europa.eu/internal_market/finservices-retail/docs/credit/mortgage/sec_2011_357_en.pdf. Substantial differences exist in the average time for foreclosures within the EU. The average in 2009 was two years with substantial variations (e.g. claimed to be a few months in the UK). Most of this time was for court

difficulty in some countries of writing-off a deficiency on the forced sale of a home in bankruptcy.[105] In addition states in Europe do not have 'homestead exemptions'.

The post-crisis EU provides a laboratory of experiments in addressing mortgage debt through a mixture of regulation and subsidies. These included: (1) temporary or permanent moratoria on foreclosures; (2) foreclosure to be used a last resort; (3) protocols for identifying and treating consumers in arrears on mortgage debt;[106] (4) possibilities for restructuring mortgages and foreign currency loans; (5) writing-down of the principal; (6) buy-backs by local governments or agencies with the debtor becoming a tenant; (7) state transfer payments (subsidies) for mortgage interest payments. These techniques included both hard and soft law, such as the 'protocol' on foreclosure in England or the code of practice of Spanish banks to restructure mortgages. Table 12.3 provides a rough guide to these techniques broken down by different countries. Hungary, Romania and Latvia provided little protection, although financial institutions may have instituted voluntary procedures for renegotiation. Hungary provided a limited programme for individuals with foreign currency loans to repay the loans but the requirement of full repayment benefited primarily better off consumers. Spain seems to provide significant relief but its programme has very restrictive access criteria.

Table 12.3 State responses to mortgage crisis

	Moratoria	Write down principal?	Write off deficiency	State buys and rents	Restructure mortgage debt in insolvency	Targeted relief (grace periods, extensions)	State subsidy for mortgage
Hungary				x		x	
Greece	x	x	x		x	x	
Spain	x	x	x			x	*
Romania							
Portugal						x	
Iceland	x	x	x			x	
England				x	x	x	x
Latvia							

Notes: Targeted relief = possibility of refinancing, extending maturity.
* Spain has a social fund for renting for individuals rendered homeless through foreclosure
Source: country reports in Part II of this volume.

hearings. See European Central Bank, *Household Finance in the EU* (2009) at 72, https://www.ecb.europa.eu/pub/pdf/other/housingfinanceeur. area0309en.pdf.

105 Gabrielle Steinhauser and Mathew Dalton, 'Lingering Bad Debts Stifle Europe Recovery' *Wall Street Journal* 31 January 2013. For an international overview of this issue see Lienne Steyn, 'Treatment of a Debtor's Home in Insolvency: Comparative Perspectives and Potential Developments in South Africa' (2013) 22 Int'l Insolvency Review 144–170.

106 See e.g. Portugal law no 58/2012 providing mortgage protection for those in 'a harsh economic situation' and Decree law 227/2012 which requires banks to establish an action plan to monitor its clients and prevent default. The UK FSA requires financial institutions to 'treat customers fairly' and has detailed rules on the fair treatment of customers in arrears. See FSA MCOB 13.

Almost all countries provided relief outside of the insolvency system through special measures. Only England and Wales provides direct assistance through the state welfare system. Those states under the tutelage of austerity plans would have faced difficulties in justifying the introduction of subsidies for mortgage repayments.

Establishing effective deleveraging programmes in a crisis faces several challenges. First, not enough individuals may take up the programme. Writing-down debt or applying for a social benefit may carry a stigma and individuals may strive to pay down their debt slowly without defaulting, notwithstanding the economic benefits of a faster write-down. Many homeowners who are in negative equity do not default on their mortgages but may be living under stressful conditions.[107] Many mortgage rescue programmes resemble means-tested welfare programmes. Studies of benefits programmes demonstrate that many individuals do not take up benefits[108] because of the high costs of claiming, the difficulties in obtaining information on programmes, and stigma. These factors may be particularly relevant during a crisis when accurate information on government programmes may be costly to provide and access. The effect of stigma on claiming is supported by US studies which indicate that a substantially larger percentage of the population could benefit from bankruptcy if they applied a rational cost–benefit calculus to the benefits of bankruptcy.[109]

Second, too many individuals may take up a programme, the so-called problem of opportunistic or strategic default. In a situation where political and economic institutions have lost legitimacy there may be a cascade effect of non-payment. Little evidence of this phenomenon exists in Europe.[110] However, the fear of over-inclusive plans which may harm bank stability will often be exploited by financial institutions who generally oppose across-the-board moratoria. The influence of the 'bank lending' approach to crises will also caution against general moratoria.

Ensuring that a programme is neither over- or under-inclusive is 'politically and technically, one of the most challenging tasks facing us'.[111] Across-the-board moratoria benefit all homeowners whether or not they need protection. However, 'targeting' vulnerable consumers may result in complex and restrictive programmes with a small take-up. The evidence suggests that programmes were often highly targeted as occurred in both Spain and Portugal with the consequence (predictable from the literature on take-up) that few consumers benefited.

The US experience after the crisis is relevant. Many writers argue that the Obama administration's response to the foreclosure crisis was inadequate.[112] Mian and Sufi are trenchant

107 See Mian et al. (n24) 11. Currently over half a million UK homeowners are in negative equity. BBC News 1 March 2014, http://www.bbc.co.uk/news/business-26389009.

108 See e.g. Manos Matsaganis, Alari Paulus and Holly Sutherland, 'The Take Up of Social Benefits' Research Note (2008).

109 See Michelle White, 'Why it Pays to File for Bankruptcy: A Critical Look at Incentives under US Bankruptcy Laws and a Proposal for Change' (1998) University of Chicago L Rev 65.

110 Claudia Abreu-Lopes and Catarina Frade discuss these issues in the context of Portugal, noting a rather modest increase (in international terms) in the use of bankruptcy. See 'The Way into Bankruptcy: Market Anomie and Sacrifice among Portuguese Consumers' (2012) 35 Journal of Consumer Policy 477.

111 '"Greece Needs New Targeted Measures" says IMF's Poul Thomsen', interview by Greek newspaper *Kathimerini* with IMF Mission Chief for Greece Poul Thomsen, 24 November 2013, available at http://www.imf.org/external/np/vc/2013/112413.htm.

112 For an overview of some of the reasons for the absence of success see David Dayen, 'The Government Program that Failed Homeowners, the Hamp Program, Supposed to Help Homeowners Save their Houses, May have Led them Deeper into a Bureaucratic Swamp' *Guardian* 30 March 2014 at http://

in their criticism, commenting that 'despite the biggest housing collapse in post-Great Depression American history, indebted home owners were left drowning underwater with only minimal assistance by government'.[113] The Home Affordable Modification Programme (HAMP) provided the possibility of mortgage principal modification but only a modest percentage achieved this goal, significant numbers of individuals re-defaulted and the programme never came close to meeting its target of assisting four million homeowners. One reason for the failure included securitisation which prevented effective negotiation. However the Obama administration was from 2009 driven by two ideological concerns: 'contract sanctity and moral hazard'[114] which limited the nature of the programmes. The government would only use taxpayers' money to support 'responsible' homeowners and broad scale principal write-down was rejected as encouraging opportunism. The US programme muddled through with some modifications in 2011. The IMF judged the US programme in 2012 to be relatively ineffective, comparing it with the more aggressive deleveraging programmes in response to the 1930s depression.[115]

An early question in the US handling of the crisis was whether to address mortgage debt primarily within bankruptcy procedures, by amending Chapter 13 of the US Bankruptcy Code to permit write-down of the principal on residential mortgage debt ('cram-down'),[116] or to establish separate (and often temporary) programmes. Adam Levitin argued that the well-established US Chapter 13 bankruptcy procedure administered by the US bankruptcy courts was the most effective and fair method of addressing housing debt overhang at no cost to the taxpayer.[117] The ability to write-down principal under Chapter 13 would also create incentives for more informal agreements between lenders and borrowers. The bankruptcy system could distinguish those genuinely in need of a write-down from opportunists. Moral hazard would be unlikely since lenders would be sanctioned for bad borrowing decisions and debtors required to live on a three- to five-year Chapter 13 programme before being discharged. Variations on this cram-down approach were proposed with the objective of creating incentives for borrowers to stay in their home (for example by relating the cram-down to declines in property prices in the relevant ZIP code) and conferring on lenders a right to receive a percentage of any appreciation in value.[118] One limitation of these proposals is that the continuing stigma of bankruptcy might result in a less than optimal take-up.

A Congressional Bill to permit cram-down failed to be enacted in 2009 because of political opposition, supported by lobbying by financial institutions. Commentators also argue that the Obama administration did not support this option out of concern for the financial health of the

www.theguardian.com/money/2014/mar/30/government-program-save-homes-mortgages-failure-banks. 'Obama's HAMP Initiative Struggling To Help Homeowners' *Huffington Post* 24 July 2013 http://www.huffingtonpost.com/2013/07/24/obama-hamp-mortgage_n_3644187.html.

113 Mian and Sufi (n7) 135.

114 Kristin Roberts and Stacy Kaper, 'Out of their Depth' *National Journal* 22 March 2012. This article provides a 'blow by blow' insider account of the administration of the debt programme.

115 IMF (n81) 110–113, and see IMF 'Concluding Statement of the 2012 Article IV Mission to the United States of America' 3 July 2012.

116 Chapter 13 does permit cram-down on security over automobiles and vacation homes. It is also possible to cure arrears on a first mortgage in a Chapter 13. But it is not possible to write-down the mortgage principal of a primary residence.

117 Adam Levitin, 'Resolving the Foreclosure Crisis: Modification of Mortgages in Bankruptcy' (2009) Wisc L Rev 565. See also Michelle White and Ning Zhu, 'Saving Your Home in Chapter 13 Bankruptcy' (2010) 39 Journal of Legal Studies 33–61.

118 See Eric Posner and Luigi Zingales, 'A Loan Modification Approach to the Housing Crisis' (2009) American Law and Economics Review 575.

banks and private investors in mortgage-backed bonds. A subsequent study by Alan White and Carolina Reid concludes that greater success was achieved through specific loan modification programmes than through existing Chapter 13 bankruptcy procedures (without principal write-down) which delayed rather than stopped the foreclosure process.[119]

The Scandinavian states had experienced widespread mortgage default during the severe recession of the early 1990s which overwhelmed the capacity of the welfare state. Norway instituted a programme of principal write-down after the banking crisis of the early 1990s.[120] This intervention recognised the limits of traditional welfare state instruments such as unemployment insurance in protecting individuals against market volatility. Iceland introduced a similar programme after the crisis and received praise from the IMF for having introduced an integrated set of procedures, which combined standardised methods for mortgage renegotiation with targeted relief of principal write-down for those with negative equity. These European examples are however exceptions to the general unwillingness of states to permit the adjustment of mortgage principal.

Some European states (e.g. England) use transfer payments to support homeownership either through higher unemployment benefits or specific payments for mortgage interest. England and Wales has a volatile housing market and by the early 2000s mortgages were available to an increasingly risky group of borrowers subject to employment and income volatility. Mortgage repossessions were already increasing before the recession and subsequently increased 54 per cent between 2007 and 2008, creating a fear that they would reach the high levels of the early 1990s crisis.[121]

Cutting interest rates was a factor in reducing the impact of the recession on English homeowners.[122] England's 'safety net' for homeowners after the Great Recession represented a mixture of subsidies and regulation, namely: (1) state support for mortgage interest payments; (2) a mortgage rescue scheme; (3) homeowner mortgage support; (4) regulation of the foreclosure process so that it was used as a last resort. These measures targeted vulnerable consumers and underline the overlap of regulatory and social welfare measures in compensating for market problems.[123] The Support for Mortgage Interest (SMI) programme is targeted at the unemployed and low-income individuals with a time limit of two years for those on Jobseeker's Allowance (formerly unemployment insurance), underlining the temporary nature of the relief and providing an incentive 'for people to return to work'.[124] During the 1990s the government had attempted to encourage the private insurance market to substitute for SMI but failures in that market and

119 See Alan White and Carolina Reid, 'Saving Homes? Bankruptcies and Loan Modifications in the Foreclosure Crisis' (2013) 65 Fla L Rev 1713.

120 Thus a home purchased for €300,000 and now worth €100,000 would result in a debtor paying interest on €110,000 for five years and the €190,000 treated as unsecured and written off after five years. See discussion in Legislating for Personal Insolvency in Ireland: The Norwegian Experience http://www.flac.i.e./download/pdf/egilrokhqaug_paper_flacconf19apr2012.pdf.

121 See Alison Wallace and Janet Ford, 'Limiting Possession? Managing Mortgage Arrears in a New Era' (2010) 10(2) International Journal of Housing Policy 133.

122 See Resolution Foundation, *Hangover Cure: Dealing with the Household Debt Overhang as Interest Rates Rise* (2014).

123 See discussion in Schelkle (n103) and see Deborah Mabbett, 'The Regulatory Rescue of the Welfare State' in David Levi-Faur (ed.) *Handbook on the Politics of Regulation* (Elgar 2012) ch 15.

124 See discussion in Steve Wilcox and Peter Williams, *Building an Effective Safety Net for Homeowners and the Housing Market* (Rowntree 2013) at 27. During the repossession crisis of the early 1990s (15,000 repossessions in 1989 escalating to 70,000 in 1991) government support for mortgage interest was paid directly to lenders in exchange for lenders developing forbearance schemes and mortgage-to-rent schemes.

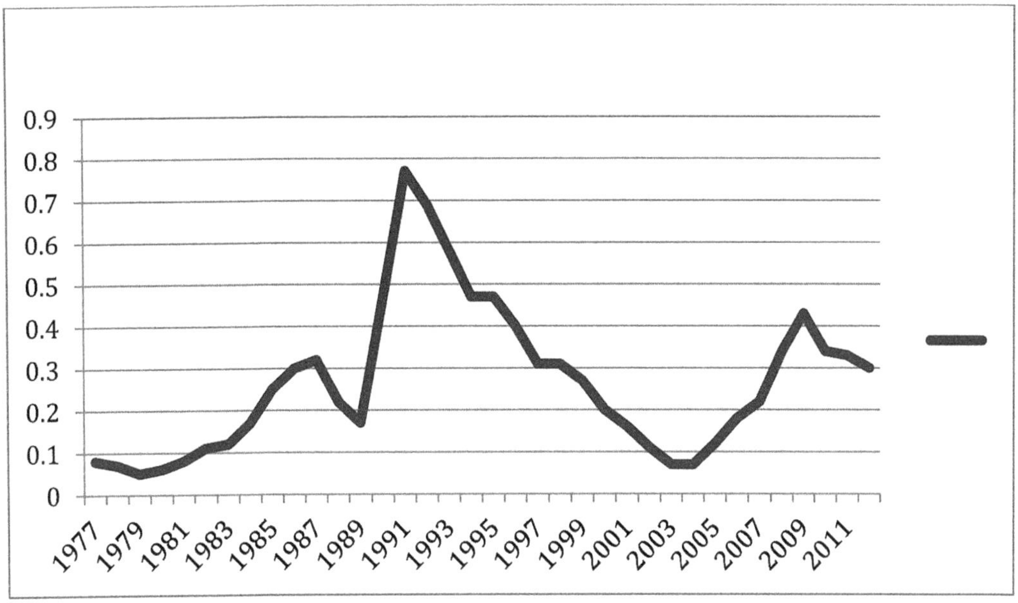

Figure 12.2 Mortgage repossessions England and Wales as a percentage of mortgages 1977–2011
Source: Council of Mortgage Lenders.

misselling resulted in a poor take-up. SMI was made more accessible in 2009 after the crisis and in early 2013, 230,000 households received SMI representing an expenditure of £359 million.[125] The interest is paid directly to the lender by the state.

A highly targeted[126] mortgage rescue scheme was introduced in 2009 which offered either the possibility of a shared equity or mortgage to rent option. The scheme delivered 2,600 completed rescues over two years, the majority being a mortgage to rent option.[127] The National Audit Office assessed the programme as 'poorly planned and executed'. The Homeowner Mortgage support scheme provided for the deferral of mortgage interest for a period of up to two years.[128] Between 2009 and 2010, 32 borrowers were assisted under this scheme compared with over 30,000 who

125 SMI will help pay the interest on a mortgage up to £200,000 (increased from £100,000 in 2009). The waiting period was reduced in 2009 by 'temporary measures' introduced by the Labour government in response to the crisis. 93,000 users are pensioners. The average amount paid is £30 per week. House of Commons, Standard Note, Steven Kennedy, *Support for Mortgage Interest Scheme* (2013). The payment of interest uses a standard rate based on the average mortgage rate published by the Bank of England.

126 Only available to individuals who had exhausted all possibilities and would be deemed to be 'statutory homeless' individuals with a consequent local state obligation to house. See National Audit Office, Mortgage Rescue Scheme (HC 1030 2011) at 16.

127 Ibid. 5.

128 The Treasury requirements for the Homeowner Mortgage Support Scheme were that a borrower will:

'* have suffered a loss of income from employment or self-employment of a scale which now makes full mortgage payments difficult, but which is not expected to be a permanent loss of income;

entered on lenders' own forbearance schemes.[129] Debt advisors were ambivalent about this scheme because individuals would end up owing more at the end of the deferral period, which was unlikely therefore to lead to sustainable ownership. A small repossession prevention fund was made available to local authorities. Regulation of debt collection and foreclosure procedure was tightened. A pre-court action protocol[130] was agreed with lenders so that other alternatives were considered before repossession, and the FSA sanctioned several firms for not 'treating customers fairly' in their approach to collections and repossession policy.[131]

English insolvency law provides some protection for the homeowner through the Individual Voluntary Arrangement, a form of insolvency.[132] This arrangement involves individuals repaying a percentage of their unsecured debts, usually over five years, but it cannot affect the rights of secured creditors without their consent. However, an individual may remain in the home provided she can pay the mortgage (and usually make a contribution from any equity in the home at the end of the repayment plan) while making partial repayments of unsecured debts such as credit card debt. Homeowners represent about 30 per cent of IVAs but there is little evidence on the success of homeowners in completing a plan: about 30 per cent of plans fail. Mortgage cram-down was never raised as a policy option in the UK. Housing debt was treated as *sui generis* distinct from personal insolvency reform notwithstanding the evidence that individuals whose homes are repossessed often file for bankruptcy to discharge any deficiency after the sale of the home.[133]

---

* have been in dialogue with their lender, including over the use of existing forbearance policies, and have been making some level of regular payment;

* have taken out a mortgage of up to £400k;

* have savings below £16,000 (which is the same as for the existing Support for Mortgage Interest scheme (SMI));

* apply for assistance as owner-occupier – the programme will not apply to people with second homes or buy-to-let properties;

* not be in receipt of SMI or mortgage rescue assistance;

* have been assessed as being able to pay a certain monthly amount on an ongoing basis;

* have received financial advice from a party other than their lender to determine their eligibility for the scheme, including testing the long-term sustainability of their financial position, and their ability to resume full payments once their income increases; and

* have fallen into arrears for a number of months during which the lender has exercised forbearance.'

See House of Commons Library Standard Note SN/SP/4769 (Wendy Wilson) *Mortgage Arrears and Repossessions* (2014) at 12–13. The scheme was closed in 2011.

129 Ibid. 13.

130 See http://www.justice.gov.uk/courts/procedure-rules/civil/pro'tocol/prot_mha. Note article 1.2, 'The protocol does not alter the parties rights' and obligations'.

131 See ch 4 of *FSA Mortgage Market Review: Responsible Lending* FSA10/16 (2010) at 45–57 for discussion of the development of its rules, and its action against GMAC for unfairness in arrears practices resulting in fines and redress. The case is discussed at 476–481 of Iain Ramsay, *Consumer Law and Policy* (3rd edn, Hart 2012). See also Financial Conduct Authority, *Mortgage Lenders Arrears Management and Forbearance* TR14/3 (2014) 3–4. The rules on arrears and repossession can be found in MCOB 13. MCOB 13.3.2a (6) states that a lender shall 'not repossess the property unless all other reasonable attempts to resolve the position have failed'. For a criticism of the effectiveness of these measures see Lisa Whitehouse, 'A Longitudinal Analysis of the Mortgage Repossession Process 1985–2010: Stability Regulation and Reform' (ssrn).

132 See Part VIII Insolvency Act 1986.

133 See Janet Ford, Joanne Bretherton, Anwen Jones and David Rhodes, *Giving Up Home Ownership: A Qualitative Study of Voluntary Possession and Selling because of Financial Difficulties* (Department of Communities and Local Government 2010) at 9 ('Over two thirds of households interviewed who gave

4.1 Latvia: The Pilot – 'Toughing it Out'

Latvia became a model for subsequent structural adjustment in Southern Europe and is regarded as a 'success story' by the IMF.[134] Mark Blyth tells a different story, in *Austerity: The History of a Dangerous Idea*, of a growth model based on massive foreign investment in non-export based industries such as housing fuelled by a banking system which was foreign owned so that the subsequent bailout was essential to save the foreign banks.[135] Latvia certainly embraced deregulation and price and trade liberalisation after the fall of Communism, suffered severe setbacks during the 1990s with waves of bank failures and experienced a subsequent boom in the early 2000s after joining the EU. Bank lending grew during this period primarily through subsidiaries of Swedish banks 'eager to gain market share'.[136] The 2008 crash in Latvia was the deepest in the world at the time[137] with a drop of 25 per cent in output. Non-performing loans represented almost 20 per cent of loans in 2010,[138] and over 15 per cent of mortgages were in default. In 2008 Latvia sought support from the IMF, the World Bank, the EU and Nordic countries. The great majority of loans to business and individuals were in euros, with the Latvian currency pegged to it at a fixed exchange rate. The government refused to devalue the currency as a solution to the crisis and an 'internal devaluation' occurred through a combination of fiscal limits, and reduction in wages. This internal devaluation was 'unprecedented by historical and international standards'.[139]

Reforms to social security only partly addressed the problems caused by the crisis and indeed led to reduced trust in the state, and increases in the shadow economy. Latvia also experienced substantial emigration.[140] Before 2008 Latvia did not have a personal insolvency law which permitted a discharge of debts. The 2008 law, a clone of the German law, with an initial seven-year payment plan as a condition of discharge, and high access costs, was in practice unavailable for many individuals. Latvia agreed to reform both its corporate and individual insolvency law as a condition of IMF aid.[141] The 2010 law makes it possible to obtain a discharge of unsecured debts

---

voluntary possession were households where one or more person, was, or was in the process of being declared bankrupt or had an Individual Voluntary Arrangement').

134 See Andrew Higgins, 'Used to Hardship, Latvia Accepts Austerity, and Its Pain Eases' *New York Times* 1 January 2013, noting that Christine Lagarde celebrated the success of Latvia. '"We are here to celebrate your achievements", Christine Lagarde, the chief of the International Monetary Fund, told a conference in Riga'. But see the response by Paul Krugman, 'Latvia Once Again' *New York Times* 2 January 2013, 'So we're looking at a Depression-level slump, and 5 years later only a partial bounceback; unemployment is down but still very high, and the decline has a lot to do with emigration. It's not what you'd call a triumphant success story.'

135 'A set of patently unsustainable and unstable economies financed by foreign credit bubbles blew up, quite predictably, the minute there was a shock to these economies. These countries are now supposed to be the role models for the rest of the world?' Blyth (n56) 221.

136 See discussion of Latvia in Catriona Pursfield and Christoph Rosenberg, 'Adjustment under a Currency Peg: Estonia, Latvia and Lithuania during the Global Financial Crisis 2008–09' IMF Working Paper 10/213 4.

137 See Erbenova et al. (n85).

138 Ibid. 3.

139 Ibid.

140 See Signe Dobelniece and Tana Lace, 'Global Economic Crisis in Latvia: Social Policy and Individuals' Responses' (2012) 23(2) Filosofija Sociologiija 111–118.

141 Republic of Latvia: Request for Stand-By Arrangement – Staff Report; Staff Supplement; Press Release on the Executive Board Discussion; and Statement by the Executive Director for the Republic of Latvia (2009) at 13.

after a maximum of 3.5 years with the possibility of two years for an individual with limited assets and income. The IMF has collaborated on increased judicial training to upgrade the institutional infrastructure. The use of personal insolvency has increased substantially since 2010 when over 12 per cent of loans were in 'workout' (bank is in process of foreclosing on collateral, invoking guarantees, or has initiated legal proceedings). The typical insolvency cases are individuals who had guaranteed businesses and individuals left with a deficiency payment on a mortgage.[142]

Table 12.4 Latvian personal insolvency

2008	2009	2010	2011	2012	2013
1	153	199	845	1,354	2,000+

Source: Latvian Insolvency Statistics.

The importance of mortgage debt in insolvency did not, however, result in any special provisions for mortgage write-downs in Latvia. These were strongly opposed by the banks.[143] It was also claimed (but never substantiated) that mortgages are primarily held by higher-income individuals and protection would be distributionally regressive. In 2014 Latvia promised the IMF that it would oppose Parliamentary amendments to limit liability to mortgage collateral.[144] The banks continue to oppose the more 'liberalised personal insolvency regime'.[145] Latvians constitute one of the groups of bankruptcy 'tourists' to England, seeking discharge under the more liberal English law. Ironically the recent liberalisation of Latvian insolvency may result in more bankruptcy tourism to Latvia from neighbouring states.[146]

4. 2 Spain: The Politics of Reform[147]

Spain provides a case study of national, regional and international influences on Spanish reform and in turn Spanish influence on EU law through provisions in the Mortgage Directive. Spain has a high level of home ownership. The apparently 'undeveloped' rental market could provide little

142 Email communication Laila Medlin, Latvian Ministry of Justice, 6 October 2013 (on file with author).

143 Erbenova et al. (n85)16.

144 See IMF (2014) 'Staff Report Latvia Article IV Consultation', 9. Referring to this proposal 'staff warned against the hasty passage of recent legislative proposals that could act as a drag on new lending … The authorities confirmed that they will not support the measure, which is likely to drive down the supply and raise the cost of new mortgage lending if enacted'.

145 The EBRD comment in October 2011 that the law 'has been very controversial and was criticized by the banking community as being too debtor friendly and detrimental to the lending business'. European Bank for Reconstruction and Development, *Commercial Laws of Latvia: An Assessment by the EBRD* at 2, http://www.ebrd.com/downloads/sector/legal/latvia.pdf.

146 'Latvia Could Become an Area of Bankrupt Tourism', http://bnn-news.com/latvia-area-bankrupt-tourism-86580.

147 The following account benefited greatly from Chapter 5, this volume, and by the papers by Fr Javier Arias Varona on credit slips see e.g. http://www.creditslips.org/creditslips/2014/03/what-happened-to-mortgage-debtors.html#more, his unpublished paper at the LSA 2013, and correspondence and discussion with Javier.

cushion for individuals unable to sustain home ownership.[148] Governments in the era leading up to the crisis had provided tax and other incentives to promote home ownership and Spain represented a paradigm of 'privatised Keynesianism' where states rely on private debt to fuel increased asset prices in the housing market, which in turn promotes increased consumption.[149] It also promotes housing bubbles as asset prices outstrip income growth.

Spain entered the crisis without a personal insolvency law which permitted an individual to discharge debts, and a creditor-friendly foreclosure system. Business insolvency was the focus of the 2003 bankruptcy law reforms and during this period of optimistic prosperity, reform of individual insolvency to provide a discharge was too politically controversial and perhaps deemed unnecessary during a period of prosperity. Attempts to introduce parliamentary amendments permitting an individual insolvency discharge failed. Federal/provincial division of competencies allocated consumer competence to provinces and this complicated any Federal attempt to regulate consumer insolvency.

After the crisis, the collapse of the housing bubble, and the doubling of unemployment rates, many individuals faced significant repayment difficulties. Immigrants were disproportionately affected.[150] Reliable data are difficult to locate on foreclosures in Spain[151] but mortgage foreclosure reform became a significant political and social issue. The politics of Spanish reform include many sites of change, from grassroots civil society action, provincial, national and EU litigation and regulation, and pressure from the IMF and EU European Semester. Public demonstrations took place against the distress caused by the high levels of foreclosures; some bailiffs refused to enforce foreclosures. The Platform of Mortgage Victims (*Plataforma de Afectados por la Hipoteca*), a grassroots social movement,[152] mobilised a citizens' legislative initiative requiring the Spanish Parliament to consider reform. International attention focused on the apparent Spanish tragedy. The *New York Times* published in 2010 a dramatic critique of the crisis.[153]

Litigation also became a site for stimulating change. Some 'low law' judges delivered radical judgments such as refusing to permit a deficiency claim (to be ultimately quashed by 'high law' courts). The preliminary reference procedure to the CJEU, used primarily by those 'interested in judicial politics'[154] wishing to bring about changes in national law, confers some power on diffuse interests such as consumers to pursue reform.[155] In the Spanish crisis it provided the opportunity for public interest groups and lower courts to sidestep the higher national courts. The *Aziz* judgment[156] by the CJEU in 2013 forced amendments to Spanish mortgage foreclosure law and stimulated

148 See IMF, 'Spain Country Report Selected Issues' no 09/129 (2009), http://www.imf.org/external/pubs/ft/scr/2009/cr09129.pdf.

149 See discussion of this in relation to Spain in Isidro Lopez and Emmanuel Rodriguez, 'The Spanish Case' (2011) 69 New Left Review 5; on mortgage Keynesianism see Colin Crouch, *The Strange Non-Death of NeoLiberalism* (Polity 2011) ch 5.

150 See Human Rights Watch, *Shattered Dreams Impact of Spain's Housing Crisis on Vulnerable Groups* (2014) at 3.

151 See Chapter 5, this volume. The data in the report suggest that the number of home foreclosures in 2012 was 0.53 of total mortgages outstanding (32,490). The UK rate was 0.3 in 2012.

152 Formed in 2009 in Barcelona.

153 See Suzanne Daley, 'In Spain Homes are Taken but Debt Stays', *New York Times* 27 October 2010, http://www.nytimes.com/2010/10/28/world/europe/28spain.html?pagewanted=all&_r=0.

154 Damian Chalmers, Gareth Davies and Gioirgio Monti, *European Union Law* (2nd edn, 2010) 179.

155 See discussion by Hans-W. Micklitz in 'Judicial Activism of the ECJ and the Development of the European Social Mode in Anti Discrimination and Consumer Law' EUI Working Paper 2009.

156 See *Mohamed Aziz v Caixa d'Estalvis de Catalunya* Case C-415–11 (2013). This case concerned foreclosure against a Moroccan citizen.

further litigation challenging consumer credit terms.[157] The government introduced in 2012 a targeted code of practice permitting a moratorium and restructuring of the debt, including the possibility of a principal write-down and giving up a home without any deficiency liability.[158] These provisions drew arbitrary distinctions between different groups. Many banks found difficulties in justifying these distinctions to consumers and provided more broadly based protections. A further law in 2012 permitted those who had given up their homes to stay on as renters.[159]

Initial attempts after the crisis, in 2009–2010, to float a bankruptcy discharge procedure for individuals were met by arguments of moral hazard, and the limitation on court capacity to process large numbers of debtors. Although Spain was not subject to the formal conditionality of the structural adjustment measures imposed on Portugal, Ireland and Greece, both the EU[160] and IMF[161] recommended that Spain should introduce a personal insolvency regime. The Spanish government was reluctant to introduce such a measure, which may have reflected lobbying by Spanish financial institutions or a genuine fear of its impact on consumers' willingness to repay. IMF Staff documents on Spain (2013) attempted to sweeten the pill by recommending 'strict entry requirements' for 'clearly insolvent people' in order to maintain the strong 'Spanish payment culture' and avoid 'strategic defaults'.[162] The Spanish government however deemed existing measure to protect homeowners to be adequate and raised concerns that 'a personal insolvency regime that include[d] a different solution for mortgages would overburden the courts, could lead to strategic defaults, and jeopardize Spain's strong payment culture'.[163]

The insolvency law enacted in October 2013 provides relief for 'entrepreneurs' with an extremely limited possibility for individuals to discharge their debts. It is almost a symbolic gesture. However several provisions in the personal insolvency law will require judicial interpretation opening up the possibility for creative interpretations. Such a provision is typical of political gridlock with responsibility passed to the judiciary to sort out the legislative disorder.

The reference by both the IMF and Spanish government to the concept of 'payment culture' refers possibly to the hypothesis that in some European countries a debtor's family and social networks may assist individuals in difficulties, preventing formal defaults.[164] 'National culture' is also a useful tool for states to 'foil' attempts by international agencies to impose reforms.[165] Culture

---

157 See the cases cited in Chapter 5, this volume. A recent example is *Barclays Bank v Sara Sanchez Garcia* (Case C-280/13) (request from the Court of First Instance of Palma Mallorca) (case challenging deficiency judgement)

158 Royal Decree-Law 6/2012.

159 Royal Decree-Law 27/2012.

160 See EU Council of the European Union, Council Recommendation on the National Reform Programme 2013 of Spain and delivering a Council Opinion on the Stability Programme of Spain 2012–2016 11212/13 at 18.

161 The IMF documents are more insistent on the introduction of an effective personal insolvency regime. See Article IV Consultation 2013 Staff Report: 'Going forward … a more comprehensive approach that includes an effective personal insolvency regime'.

162 See IMF Country Report no 13/244. Staff Report at 15–16. IMF Country Report, Staff Document, Selected Issues 13/245 July 2013.

163 See IMF 2013 Country Report 13/244 para 19 'Authorities views'. In a later press release the IMF noted that 'Directors stressed the importance of facilitating private sector deleveraging. The insolvency regime should continue to be improved. A number of Directors encouraged the authorities to consider in the future introducing a personal insolvency regime'. Press Release, 'IMF Concludes 2013 Article IV Consultation with Spain'.

164 See discussion in Lopes and Frade (n110).

165 See on 'foiling' Halliday and Carruthers (n71) 28–30.

functions here as a strategic weapon in political debates.[166] Whatever the validity of this hypothesis one might worry about a policy which distributes the burdens of austerity to the families of a debtor and where immigrants 'appear to be disproportionately represented among those who have faced foreclosure and eviction'.[167]

The Spanish experience informed provisions of the EU Mortgage Credit Directive in 2014. The Spanish rapporteur in the European Parliament proposed standards for foreclosure proceedings, regulation of default interest and the possibility of member states introducing *datio in solutum* (the possibility of giving up a home in full settlement of the loan). It also highlighted the human rights aspect of over-indebtedness where foreclosure in a country with limited housing alternative could mean homelessness. The right to adequate housing defined as the 'right to live somewhere in security, peace and dignity',[168] may be threatened by foreclosure proceedings which are not used a last resort.

4.3 Greece: If at First You Don't Succeed ...[169]

Both international institutions and consumer groups conclude that the 2010 Greek personal insolvency law was a failure.[170] The period of the early 2000s represented an unprecedented growth in household debt-to-income and between 2003 and 2008 an increase from 6 to 15 per cent in the consumer loan to GDP ratio. Although the overall household debt-to-income ratio is lower than the EU average, and there was not a housing bubble in Greece, the sudden retrenchment caused by austerity created financial difficulties for many middle and lower income individuals. The 2010 'debt adjustment' law transplanted many aspects of the defective German personal insolvency model including the requirement of an attempt at out-of-court settlement before the possibility of a judicial settlement, and a repayment period of three to five years before the possibility of a discharge. The law added the possibility of restructuring a home mortgage as part of the insolvency process. An individual could repay over a period of 20–30 years an amount up to 80 per cent of the value of the home.[171] Since the mortgage would often exceed the depressed value of the home, this represented principal write-down. In addition a general moratorium on foreclosures was enacted through a prohibition on auctions of repossessed properties.

The absence of an adequate institutional structure of courts and advisors as well as defects in the framing of the law resulted in a failure of the 2010 law. The pre-judicial settlement-phase rarely resulted in an agreement (under 1 per cent), merely adding further costs and time to the process. Consumer groups attributed this to the intransigence of credit institutions but it is also possible that

166 The Romanian government refused to introduce a personal insolvency bill claiming that the IMF supported this opposition. The refusal was based on the particular 'cultural' characteristics of Romania. See also London Economics, *Study on Means to Protect Consumers in Financial Difficulty: Personal Bankruptcy, Datio in Solutum of Mortgages, and Restrictions on Debt Collection Abusive Practices* (2012) 84–85.

167 Human Rights Watch (n150) 29. 'Immigrants appear to be disproportionately affected, with the PAH estimating that they represent one-third of those who have faced foreclosure and eviction, well out of proportion to their 12 per cent share of the population'.

168 Ibid. at 7.

169 Chapter 3, this volume, was extremely helpful in writing this section.

170 See Law 3869/2010. For the IMF view see e.g. Greece Third Review – under the extended fund facility – Staff Report Country Report No13/153. The views of the Greek consumer group Ekpizo can be found in the London Economics Report (n166) at 55. See generally Chapter 3, this volume.

171 Chapter 3, this volume, 29–45.

limited specialist advice existed for consumers[172] and there were no guidelines on negotiations. Court applications were made to the local Magistrates' Courts which were ill-equipped and under-resourced to address the issues. Free legal advice was not available. The courts are overloaded with applications with hearings being delayed for years. A debtor did not have the benefit of an automatic stay on enforcement after filing but had to file a separate procedure to prevent continuing creditor action. Guidelines did not exist for establishing the amount of income left to an individual. Courts were criticised for setting unrealistically low levels of exemption from seizure. These problems are not unique to Greece. A similar process occurred in France in the early implementation of the *loi Neiertz* with uncooperative creditors, long court delays, and unsympathetic judges.[173] The out-of-court settlement procedure in Germany was recognised as a failure in terms of achieving negotiated settlements. Sweden abolished its required out-of-court procedure in 2007 three years before the introduction of the Greek law. The repetition of these failures in Greece suggests an absence of social learning in the transplantation of legal institutions.[174]

The IMF concluded that the Greek insolvency regime was a failure, claiming that it did not help 'distressed borrowers in need of temporary forbearance, while imposing very high costs on banks'.[175] It instructed Greece to reform its procedures to 'safeguard the payment culture while providing relief to over-indebted households' by providing a targeted moratorium procedure, and more standardised processing of cases. The IMF claimed that the broad mortgage enforcement moratorium resulted in a rise in strategic defaults. Greece agreed to review its insolvency framework in consultation with the Troika ensuring that the framework preserved 'bank discipline, avoids the use of fiscal resources to protect private borrowers and minimizes moral hazard by targeting borrowers that are in real need'.[176] It added that 'we will refrain from supporting any initiative that may undermine the payment culture in Greece'.[177]

In 2013 regulations rendered the pre-judicial settlement procedure optional, changed the payment period to 3–5 years, introduced targeted protection for vulnerable homeowners, required minimum debt payments in the period between filing of a petition and a court hearing, and abolished the general moratorium on foreclosures (from 2014). In July 2013 the Greek government indicated to the IMF that it would adopt more standardised definitions of 'acceptable living expenses' as guidance for the judiciary and the banks.[178] By 2014 a government council was created[179] in consultation with the Troika to 'coordinate legal .and institutional reforms to enhance … personal

172 See Melina Mouzouraki, 'Adopting and Implementing the Law on Debt Adjustment and Debt Relief in Greece at the Time of the Economic Crisis' (2012) (unpublished paper on file with author).

173 See Ramsay (n44) 228.

174 See World Bank Report (n72) para 130 '[E]xperience in many existing systems, however, has revealed that the merits of voluntary settlements are often illusory'.

175 IMF Country Report no 13/153 (2013) 17: 'The existing framework for dealing with household debt – centered around a case-by-case approach applied by the banks, and ineffective insolvency law, and two blanket moratoria on auctions of repossessed assets (de facto preventing property foreclosures) is deficient. It does not help distressed borrowers in need of temporary forbearance, while imposing very high costs on banks.'

176 Greece, *Letter of Intent, MoU*, December 2012 14–15. https://www.imf.org/external/np/loi/2012/grc/122112.pdf.

177 Ibid. 15

178 Greece, *Letter of Intent, MoU*, 17 July 2013. http://www.imf.org/external/np/loi/2013/grc/071713.pdf.

179 See Law 4224/2013 – Government Council for the management of Private Debt, Institution for Growth in Greece and other provisions.

debt resolution frameworks'.[180] This includes establishing benchmarks for in-court insolvency procedures, creating a profession of insolvency administrators in 'line with best practice in the EU', launching an awareness campaign among debtors of their options, developing 'a coherent plan for a means-tested social safety net for vulnerable home owners', and introducing better monitoring of the effectiveness of the 2013 reforms.

Greek personal insolvency law has been rewritten and reformed under the tutelage of the IMF. Authoritative accounts of the Greek story of insolvency reform remain to be written. The belief that there was widespread opportunism by debtors under the 2010 law to demand unreasonable modifications from their creditors is a theme in IMF and Greek government documents. Supporting data for the opportunism argument have not been produced. However the institutional failures, common to the establishment of debt relief systems in Europe, were repeated in Greece and the banks were unprepared to deal with the new law. The construction of the Greek experience in terms of moral hazard and credit discipline may not be difficult for those looking at the world through economic models of insolvency. The reality may be more complex.

5. EU Credit Regulation After the Crisis: The Mortgage Lending Directive

We might expect EU consumer credit law and its implementation to be skewed towards the interests of finance capital which represents a relatively well-organised and concentrated industry in comparison with the diffuse consumer interest where individuals may have cross-cutting interests as debtors and potential borrowers.[181] Financial interests often exploit this distinction by arguing that liberal relief for debtors will result in higher credit prices. This narrative is even more compelling when accompanied by a dominant construction of those seeking relief as likely to take advantage of the system if provided the opportunity. The technical complexity of credit law – where the devil is often in the detail – would also seem to favour financial interests' ability to influence policy. However, concentrated interests may be vulnerable (because they are concentrated and visible) and therefore regarded as less legitimate than those representing diffuse groups.[182] Crises provide potential opportunities to political entrepreneurs who can galvanise public opinion and associate their campaign with widely shared values.[183] However long-term change will depend on the ability of groups to monitor the process of reform and its implementation.

Consumer financial protection had a higher public salience after the crisis (if measured by media coverage) which provided an opportunity for civil society groups to influence the agenda of reform and the content of the G20 principles on consumer financial protection.[184] The high-

180 Greece Letter of Intent, 14 May 2014.

181 See generally on EU interest representation Simon Hix and Bjørn Høyland, *The Political System of the European Union* (3rd edn, Palgrave 2011) at 162–186.

Simon Wren Lewis documents several studies demonstrating the power of the banking lobby in the US and the UK in 'The Banks And Austerity: A Simple Story Of The Last Ten Years', http://www.social-europe.eu/2014/04/banks-and-austerity/.

182 Gunnar Trumbull, *Strength in Numbers: The Power of Weak Interests* (Harvard 2012).

183 David Vogel explains the differences in EU and US food and safety policies in terms of the higher political salience of risks (after scandals such as BSE etc.) in the EU and changes in the policy preferences of key decision-makers. David Vogel, *The Politics of Precaution* (Princeton 2012).

184 For a useful discussion of the role of international civil society groups in this process of reform see Lisa Kastner, '"Much Ado about Nothing?" Transnational Civil Society. Consumer Protection and Financial Regulatory Reform' (2014) 21(6) Review of International Political Economy 1313. See also Toni Williams,

level G20 principles are 'voluntary' but the document requests that all G20 members 'and other interested economies should assess their national frameworks for financial consumer protection in the light of these principles'. Key principles include a duty on lenders to treat consumers fairly throughout the transaction and to adopt responsible lending principles.

The EU Commission, through DG Market, had worked for several years on preparatory work on mortgage regulation. DG Market was viewed by consumer groups as closer to financial interests than DG Sanco. Early work on harmonising mortgage regulation embraced the market goals of improving competitiveness, product diversity and choice and more efficient enforcement of mortgages, reflecting a 'lubricant' model of credit.[185] These goals were modified in the White Paper of 2007, just after the first reverberations of the subprime mortgage crisis.[186] While continuing to emphasise the integration of the EU mortgage market to the efficient functioning of the EU financial system the paper recognised the potential dangers of product innovation and the need to regain consumer confidence by sanctioning irresponsible lending. The Commission also established an expert group on credit histories, initiated a consultation on responsible lending and borrowing, published a communication on financial education, and sponsored studies on interest rate ceilings.[187] The initial draft of the Directive in 2011 outlined the objectives as twofold: creating an efficient and competitive single market with a high level of protection and promoting financial stability by ensuring that mortgage credit markets operate responsibly.[188]

The policy diagnosis now was that reform was necessary because of 'irresponsible lending and borrowing caused by market and regulatory failure, the general economic climate and low levels of financial literacy'.[189] The proposal was accompanied by a Staff Working Paper on national measures to avoid foreclosure procedures documenting several 'lessons to be learned' from the crisis. These were that 'foreclosures should constitute a measure of last resort', and the full economic situation of the debtor should be taken into account. It concluded by noting that 'losing the family home after having lost one's job has intolerable social and human implications for both borrowers and their families'.[190] The report was intended to 'provide inspiration' for member states rather than a benchmark. The Commission claimed that it would continue to monitor closely default rates (but

---

'Continuity not Rupture: The Persistence of Neo Liberalism in the Internationalization of Consumer Finance Regulation' in Therese Wilson (ed.) *International Responses to Issues of Credit and Over-Inebtedness in the Wake of the Crisis* (Ashgate 2013).

185 See Green Paper: 'Mortgage Credit in the European Union' (2005) COM/2005/0327 final.

186 See 'Integration of Mortgage Credit Markets' (White Paper) COM 2007/807 final para 45. See also DG Internal Market and Services 'Towards more Responsibility and Competitiveness in the European Financial Services Sector' (2010) available at http://ec.europa.eu/internal_market/finances/docs/leaflet/financial_services_en.pdf.

187 Many of these documents are available at http://ec.europa.eu/internal_market/finservices-retail/archive/mortgage_en.htm.

188 'Proposal for a Directive of the European Parliament and of the Council on credit agreements relating to residential property' COM(2011) 142 final – COD 2011/0062 'The mortgage credit directive has to be seen in the context of efforts to create an internal market for mortgage credit and against the background of the financial crisis … addressing irresponsible lending and borrowing is therefore an important element in financial reform efforts', http://eur-lex.europa.eu/legal-content/EN/TXT/?uri=CELEX:52011PC0142.

189 Recital 4.

190 See Commission Staff Working Paper, 'National Measures and practices to avoid foreclosure procedures for residential mortgage loans Accompanying document to the Proposal for a Directive of the European Parliament and of the Council on credit agreements relating to residential property', SEC 2011 357 Final 11.

has apparently failed to carry through on this promise). No specific measures on foreclosure were contained in the initial draft proposal.

The EU Parliamentary Committee which reviewed the legislation, under the leadership of its Spanish rapporteur, widened the scope of the Mortgage Directive to include issues of financial education, and post-contractual relations and arrears. It also strengthened existing provisions on responsible lending in the Directive. Consistency with the FSB international principles was added as an objective with references in specific recitals.[191] The final version, developed through the 'trilogue' procedure,[192] contains responsible lending provisions, an obligation on states to support financial literacy, and increased regulation of foreign currency loans. States are exhorted to require creditors to exercise reasonable forbearance before foreclosure proceedings are initiated, to cap default charges and ensure best efforts by creditors in achieving a fair price from foreclosure sales.[193]

The final draft of the Mortgage Credit Directive illustrates a more protective orientation in the wake of the crisis. The Commission now hails it as a measure demonstrating that the EU is a 'citizen's Europe' close to the problems of everyday life and that the Directive 'required to meet the commitments made in the G20' places 'the EU at the forefront of global mortgage legislation'.[194] Although many of the proposals are vague and hortatory (e.g. on foreclosure) the EBA may promote greater convergence in supervisory practices, with guidelines on responsible lending and foreclosure practices.

6. EU Personal Insolvency after the Crisis: Entrepreneurs, Tourists and the Precariat

Personal insolvency includes both consumption and production debt. The EU, however, traditionally separated these spheres. DG Sanco addresses consumer issues and conceptualised the problem as consumer over-indebtedness. This had the benefit of widening the frame to include both prevention and treatment of over-indebtedness, but in practice not much attention was paid to the role of insolvency law. DG Market did not view insolvency as related to its work on mortgage credit. The Financial Services Users Group[195] however commissioned an extensive report on personal insolvency and has urged the EU to adopt harmonised provisions in this area. Since the Eurozone crisis, DG Justice has increased its interest in insolvency as part of the European Semester programme and in the context of revision of the Insolvency Regulation. Bankruptcy reform is a

191 For example Recital 3, 'Union's regulatory framework … robust, consistent with international principles' 55 'member states … should be encouraged to implement the Financial Stability Board's Principles for Sound Residential Mortgage Underwriting Practices'.

192 This is a small group of the Commission, Parliament and Council which attempts to achieve agreement on differences. See Joint Declaration on Practical Arrangements for the [Ordinary Legislative] Procedure 2007 OJ C 145/2. Chalmers et al. raise concerns about the transparency of this process, suggesting that 'only very well connected actors have the opportunity to lobby these informal processes because they can know where they are taking place or who is important within them'. Chalmers et al. (n154) 109.

193 Art. 28.

194 'Nous avons donc avec ce texte un des exemples – auxquels je tiens comme vous, Mesdames et Messieurs les députés – de cette Europe concrète, de cette Europe citoyenne proche des gens, de leurs problèmes, de leurs difficultés ou de leurs éléments de leur vie quotidienne.' Michel Barnier Commissioner DG Market, Debates European Parliament, http://www.europarl.europa.eu/sides/getDoc.do?pubRef=-//EP//NONSGML+CRE+20130910+SIT+DOC+PDF+V0//EN&language=EN.

195 A group established by the EU in 2010 to increase the effectiveness of existing consumer and user representation. See Commission Decision of 20 July 2010 setting up a Financial Services User Group. 2010/C 199/02 http://eur-lex.europa.eu/legal-content/EN/TXT/?uri=uriserv:OJ.C_.2010.199.01.0012.01.ENG.

key part of the entrepreneurialism agenda with the 2020 vision[196] promoting both restructuring and liberal non-stigmatising bankruptcy provisions with a discharge period of three years or less to facilitate risk-taking by small businesses. The most recent Commission 'recommendation' (a form of soft model law[197]) from DG Justice proposes a 'second chance' for honest entrepreneurs with an automatic discharge after three years.[198] Although the recommendations are aimed at entrepreneurs (no definition is proposed), member states might apply relevant (i.e. discharge) provisions to consumers.[199] This narrative of 'entrepreneurship' drove insolvency reform in England in 2002 and the shortening of the discharge period in Germany from six to three years (taking effect in 2014) for individuals able to pay a portion of their debts (the cynical assumption being that only entrepreneurs will be able to take advantage of this provision).[200]

Econometric studies cited to support this 'entrepreneurial narrative' indicate a correlation between the length of discharge periods and levels of self-employment.[201] However, these studies equate self-employment with entrepreneurship and do not comment on the quality or innovative nature of the self-employment. One study suggests no connection between insolvency and innovative entrepreneurship.[202] Self-employment may simply describe individuals who were formerly employed and are often in precarious positions with low incomes and few social protections. It is a category which ranges from the 'very self-sufficient to extremely vulnerable'.[203]

196 'The Entrepreneurship Action Plan is a blueprint for decisive action to unleash Europe's entrepreneurial potential, to remove existing obstacles and to revolutionise the culture of entrepreneurship in Europe'. See Entrepreneurship Action Plan, Re-Igniting the Entrepreneurial Spirit in Europe (COM (2012) 795 Final) at 17–18. Principle 2 of the 'Small Business Act' refers to ensuring that 'honest entrepreneurs who have faced bankruptcy quickly get a second chance'. Communication from the Commission to the Council, the European Parliament, the European Economic and Social Committee and the Committee of the Regions 'Think Small First' A Small Business Act for Europe SEC(2008) 2101.

197 See Art. 288 TFEU. For a summary of this form of soft law see Chalmers et al. (n154) 102.

198 See Commission Recommendation on a New Approach to Business Failure and insolvency C(2014) 1500.

199 See Recital 15.

200 Frank Fossen quotes the German Minister of Justice who states that the 'reform of insolvency law is one of the most important projects in business law' and that 'those who exhibit the entrepreneurial spirit deserve legal protection that encourages them in their decision to depart into self-employment'. F. Fossen, 'Personal Bankruptcy Law, Wealth, and Entrepreneurship – Evidence from the Introduction of a "Fresh Start" Policy' (2013) 16(1) Am Law Econ Rev 269, 274 quoting Leutheusser-Schnarrenberger.

201 See e.g. John Armour and Douglas Cumming, 'Bankruptcy and Entrepreneurship' (2008) 10 (2) American Law and Economics Review 303.

202 David Primo and William Green, 'Bankruptcy Law and Entrepreneurship' (2011) Entrepreneurship Research Journal 1(2) Issue 5. The socio-legal literature suggests that many entrepreneurs do not 'bounce back' from bankruptcy. See Robert Lawless, 'Striking Out on their Own; The Self-Employed in Bankruptcy' in Katherine Porter (ed.) *Broke: How Debt Bankrupts the Middle Class* (Stanford 2012) ch 6.

203 Mies Westerveld, 'The "New" Self-Employed: An Issue for Social Policy' (2012) 14(3) European Journal of Social Security 15, 19, referring to the analysis by Martine D'Amours and Stephane Crespo, 'The Dimensions of Heterogeneity Among Own Account Self-Employed: Elements for a Typology' (2009) 59(3) Industrial Relations 459. The OECD defines entrepreneurs for the purpose of the OECD-Eurostat Entrepreneurship Indicators Programme as 'those persons (business owners) who seek to generate value, through the creation or expansion of economic activity, by identifying and exploiting new processes or markets', *The Missing Entrepreneurs: Policies for Inclusive Entrepreneurship in Europe* OECD/EU (2013) 18. See Guy Standing, *The Precariat: The New Dangerous Class* (Bloomsbury 2011).

In some cases governments encourage self-employment to massage the unemployment statistics.[204] The 'consumption/production debt' distinction is also blurred when an individual uses consumer credit to invest in education or training which in theory may produce higher future returns or when homes are used to guarantee business debts or credit cards used to finance a business.

Having sketched earlier in Part 3 the increased convergence of high level ideas on personal insolvency it must be stated that significant differences remain between European systems, notwithstanding the convergence of high level principles.[205] These differences include entry requirements (e.g. compare the UK to Sweden and France), the institutional process (role of courts, agencies, different types of intermediaries), the balance of private and public financing of the system, the length of the discharge period, the nature of debts discharged, and the ability to impose a plan on creditors. These differences result in different treatment for individuals in countries such as Sweden, France, the UK and Germany, encouraging 'bankruptcy tourism' for debtors where individuals in strict bankruptcy regimes move their COMI (Centre of Main Interests) to a more liberal regime (generally England).[206] Bankruptcy tourism, although of symbolic significance rather than representing a widespread phenomenon, documents the impact of freedom of movement on national systems[207] and generates arguments of unfairness not only to local creditors, but also to other consumers since only affluent debtors are often able to take advantage of the freedom of movement to access a more liberal discharge procedure. Addressing bankruptcy tourism became a significant part of negotiations on reform of the EC Insolvency Regulation.

---

204 See Ian Jack, *Guardian* 10 May 2014. Westerveld (n203) notes that self-employment accounts for almost 15 per cent of total employment in the EU contrasting with 8.4 per cent 'independent contractors' in 2005. The OECD statistics on self-employment indicate that 'Self-employment may be seen either as a survival strategy for those who cannot find any other means of earning an income or as evidence of entrepreneurial spirit and a desire to be one's own boss. The self-employment rates shown here reflect these various motives'. OECD, 'Self-employment', in OECD Factbook 2014 Economic, Environmental and Social Statistics 138 (2014) http://www.oecd-ilibrary.org/docserver/download/3013081ec055.pdf?expires=1423242927&id=id&accname=guest&checksum=78126CDF816D9002C054C8ADEAA0600D.

205 See discussion in Ramsay (n29) for further discussion.

206 Bankruptcy jurisdiction within the EU is determined by an individual's COMI at the time of the opening of the proceedings under the EU Council regulation (EC) No 1346/2000 of 29 May 2000 on insolvency proceedings OJ/ L160. A new reformed regulation will take effect in 2017. See discussion in Irene Lynch Fannon, 'Bankruptcy Tourism in the UK: Why and How?' (2013) 26 Insolvency Intelligence 6. The extent of bankruptcy tourism in England and Wales is limited. The English Insolvency Service collects data on insolvencies where 'The debtor is a foreign national who appears to have been resident in the UK for a period of less than 12 months, and all or most of the debts disclosed are owed to creditors based outside the UK'. In 2013 the following nationalities were represented within this category: Germany (63); Austria (2); Ireland (34); Poland (9); Latvia (9); Lithuania (10); Spain (2). A very small percentage of these bankruptcies will be annulled (Freedom of Information Request, Insolvency Service June 2014): see also Heinz Vallender, Hildegard Allemand, Stephen Baister, Pawel Kuglanz, Hans Mahijsen, Barry O'Neill, Eugene Collins and Stathis Potamitis, 'A Minimum Standard for Debt Discharge in Europe' (2013) Insolvency Intelligence 97, footnote 2.

207 The CJEU has favoured the principle of freedom of movement over residency requirements for bankruptcy. See *Ulf Kazimierz Radziejewski v Kronofogdemyndighten i Stockholm* Case C-461/11. In this case the debtor's business went bankrupt in 1996. He had been subject to an earning attachment order by the KFM since 1997(!). He worked in Belgium for a Swedish employer and in 2011 applied to KFM for debt relief and was refused because he did not have a registered residence in Sweden. The ECJ held the Swedish residence requirement to infringe his right to freedom of movement under art 45 TFEU.

The few empirical studies of European personal insolvency systems[208] suggest that many individuals have no repayment capacity. They represent those using the *rétablissement personnel* in France, the large numbers of *Nullinsolvenz* in Germany or bankrupts and *DROs* in England and Wales. The great majority of this group are renters not homeowners. French data suggest that this group is at risk of social exclusion.[209] European policymaking has been less interested in the plight of this group. A European model based on the German approach seems inappropriate for this group.

7. Conclusion

Middle and lower income households were primary casualties of the crisis. This group generally holds few financial assets apart from a home.[210] The housing crisis also seriously affected low-income households. Women are over-represented within this group.[211] 'Vulnerability' here for these groups is primarily structural – related to exogenous economic shocks, changes in the employment market, and more limited career opportunities. Writers describe the 'new insecure' in society which includes not merely the excluded but also large sections of the 'middle' of society. A recent document refers to the 5/75/20 society.[212] Governments were generally reluctant to provide relief for these groups beyond targeted means-tested programmes. Governments in Europe and the United States were initially concerned with protecting bank capital, reflecting the importance which policymakers attributed to the economic idea that the banks must be protected (i.e. bailed out) 'at all costs' in order to sustain lending. When policymakers turn to protection of indebted individuals the concept of moral hazard, with its undertones of individual irresponsibility, recurs as a continuing theme, notwithstanding the limited evidence to substantiate this phenomenon.

Addressing the vulnerability of the 'new insecure' and excluded groups extends far beyond traditional consumer protection and personal insolvency. However the Spanish case study indicates the significant role of private law litigation as part of political conflict and the mortgage crisis emphasised the importance of the private law ground rules of mortgage markets. The crisis exposed the consequences of different approaches to establishing the ground rules of these markets, and the need to provide appropriate safety nets for home ownership. The difficulties in achieving successful *ex post* interventions in the market suggest that *ex ante* approaches – planning ahead

208 See review in Ramsay (n29).

209 See Ramsay (n44).

210 See discussion in Piketty (n95) 257–262.

211 See Francesca Betti, Marcella Corsi, Carlo D'ippoliti, Antigone Lyberaki, Manuela Samek Lodovici and Alina Verashchagina, 'The Impact of the Economic Crisis on the Situation of Women and Men and on Gender Equality Policies' (DG Justice 2013).

212 Policy Exchange, 'How Social Democracy Can Survive in the 5./75/20 Society' at http://www.policy-network.net/pno_detail.aspx?ID=4627&title=-How-social-democracy-can-triumph-in-the-5–75–20-society. 'Roughly 5 per cent who are enjoying "runaway" rewards at the top, as asset prices and returns to wealth soar – a group largely composed of professionals working in finance and property, the corporate elite and successful entrepreneurs, as well as those who inherit significant wealth.

Seventy-five per cent in the middle who are either in work or have a retirement income, but are relatively insecure and often anxious about the future. Large parts of this group consists not only of "blue-collar" industrial workers threatened by outsourcing to Asia, but also groups of middle-class professionals who fear their jobs will be next as the emerging "MINT" economies move up the economic value-chain ... And the 20 per cent at the "bottom" of society who struggle in a vicious cycle of low-wage, irregular work, unemployment and limited access to welfare and are arguably "outsiders" in the labour market and struck down by entrenched social immobility'.

for potential trouble – might be adopted. The Mortgage Credit Directive embraces responsible lending but this may have limits in protection against future change of circumstances. It has also the disadvantage of potentially limiting access at the margins. Private insurance could protect individuals but this also has limitations in availability and has been associated with misselling. Mian and Sufi suggest greater risk sharing of downside risk in debt contracts so that they resemble equity contracts (similar to Islamic finance). This shared responsibility mortgage would offer downside protection to the borrower through reduced mortgage payments, if the value of a home decreased, while the lender would take 5 per cent of any capital gain. This would produce an automatic stabiliser during recessions through reduced payments. Other proposals include a shared responsibility (government, lender, borrower) insurance against risks.[213]

Most Federal states locate bankruptcy law within the Federal power. The EU is not a Federal state but phenomena such as bankruptcy tourism, the promotion of entrepreneurialism and the work of the Troika have driven greater convergence of personal insolvency law, at least at the level of general principles. A modified German model, where an individual obtains an 'earned start' rather than a 'fresh start', is influential and national variations on this theme might be predicted.[214] Lisa Quaglia argues that the outcomes of EU policy represent (a) a battle of the systems; (b) the Commission as the core actor; or (c) the influence of transnational capital.[215] Neither the Commission nor transnational capital are likely to promote the more liberal 'Anglo' insolvency discharge for consumers at the EU level and, given the reluctant acceptance in England of the liberal discharge for consumers, the UK will not promote this option for Europe.

The development of personal insolvency norms should be set within the framework of achieving a 'competitive social market economy' including combating social and financial exclusion. Many authors point to the resilience of neo-liberalism after the crisis and its threat to the European social model – a somewhat amorphous ideal[216] – embraced in the introductory quotation by Manuel Barroso.

The emerging credit paradigm in the EU envisages competition driven by responsibilised (confident) consumers in a market where toxic products[217] and systematic misselling are minimised by effective public regulation and *ex ante* obligations of responsible lending.[218] Suitably upskilled and responsible borrowers will drive competition. Insolvency law will provide a re-entry to the market for the responsible consumer – who must usually wait 3–5 years for this re-entry.[219] This model could be described as neo-liberal because the ultimate goal is market expansion and growth. Personal insolvency within this paradigm seems therefore partly a disciplining or responsibilising approach consistent with other approaches which condition the availability of social entitlements

213 See also Steve Wilcox and Peter Williams (n124).

214 Bankruptcy statistics in England and Wales note the continuing increase in IVAs (which are similar to European discharge plans) and a reduction in straight bankruptcies. See Insolvency Service Insolvency Statistics, https://www.gov.uk/government/publications/insolvency-statistics-january-to-march-2014.

215 See Lisa Quaglia, 'The "Old" and "New" Politics of Financial Services Regulation in the European Union' (2012) 17(4) New Political Economy 515.

216 See discussion in Schiek (n51).

217 Note difficulties of defining 'toxic product'.

218 Thus the Mortgage Credit Directive diagnoses a need for reform in 'irresponsible lending and borrowing caused by market and regulatory failure the general economic climate and low levels of financial literacy'. Recital 4.

219 Almost all member states of the EU now have insolvency or debt adjustment laws which permit a discharge of debts for individuals. The conditions for granting the discharge vary significantly between countries

on an individual's behaviour. Increased resort to personal insolvency may also be a conscious government decision to attempt to reduce public costs. The introduction of personal insolvency regimes in some countries was linked to getting individuals back into the market so that they would not continue to live on social security.[220]

Governments are however unwilling to commit significant resources to personal insolvency systems. Cost-saving mechanisms (e.g. promotion of out-of-court settlements) are encouraged but are often not effective or require further regulation. These difficulties evoke David Harvey's paradox of the role of the state in neo-liberalism where there are continuing pressures to intervene 'in a world where the state is not supposed to be interventionist'.[221] Personal insolvency in the EU addresses financial and social exclusion from the market by providing 'not a hand out but a hand up', without necessarily solving the long-term problems of insolvents.[222]

Finally, credit and debt relations are about power, and the imposition of austerity within the EU is a contested political issue. History is replete with political conflicts over debt. David Graeber has produced *un bric* on the historical connections between debt and political conflict.[223] Marxism characterises the basic conflict in society as that of labour and capital. A defining characteristic of contemporary societies is however the relationship of creditor and debtor, from sovereign debt to individual consumers. Maurizio Lazzarrato argues that in contemporary society with fewer traditional 'sites of discipline' such as the factory, we have moved to a society of control[224] and that the creditor–debtor relationship is central to contemporary capitalism. Susanne Soederberg has coined the term 'debtfare state'[225] to describe the contemporary United States where the facilitation of high cost credit extends worker exploitation, legitimating it through the ideologies of the 'democratisation of credit' and 'consumer protection' which represents an individualised conception of protection, with an underlying assumption of market equality which can be redressed through empowered consumers. US bankruptcy law, with its attempt to push more consumers towards repayment plans rather than an immediate discharge, represents an increasingly coercive disciplining measure.

These approaches should make us reflect on the future role of personal insolvency in a contemporary capitalism characterised by declining growth, increasing inequality and rising indebtedness in many countries.[226] Personal insolvency can act as a 'safety valve' to reduce

220 See e.g. Nick Huls 'American Influences on European Consumer Bankrutpcy Law Reform' (1992) 15(2) Journal of Consumer Policy 125. Current reforms in Sweden are concerned about getting 'perpetual debtors' back into productive activity by encouraging them to access the debt settlement process.

221 David Harvey, *A Brief History of NeoLiberalism* (Oxford 2005) 65–66.

222 See Lopes and Frade (n110) 'the improvement of the insolvency procedures will not resolve the situation of financial distress if the structural causes persist, such as unemployment and deterioration of salaries and cuts in social benefits'. See also Charlotte O'Brien, 'From Safety Nets and Carrots to Trampolines and Sticks; National use of the EU as both Menace and Model to Help Neoliberalize Welfare Policy' in Schiek (n51) ch 5.

223 David Graeber, *Debt the First 5000 Years* (Melville House 2012). He states for example at 8 that in 'the ancient world all revolutionary movements had a single program: "cancel the debts and redistribute the land"'. Teresa Sullivan, Elizabeth Warren and Jay Westbrook make a similar comment in their 1989 study of US bankruptcy – 'Debt is social dynamite and always has been'. See Teresa Sullivan, Elizabeth Warren and Jay Westbrook, *As We Forgive our Debtors* (Oxford University Press 1989) 334.

224 See Gilles Deleuze, 'Postscript on the Societies of Control' Pourparlers no 1.

225 Susanne Soederberg, 'The Debtfare State and the Credit Card Industry: Forging Spaces of Dispossession (2013) 45(2) Antipode 493.

226 See Wolfgang Streeck, 'How Will Capitalism End' (2014) NLR 87.

mass political protest and dissent.[227] However, policies which might seem progressive such as the introduction of insolvency and debt relief programmes may be depoliticising because of their individualising tendencies and their focus on the 'vulnerable' and deserving debtor. Insolvency may be a second-best solution for individuals who are in marginal or insecure jobs. Highlighting these aspects of contemporary insolvency in Europe indicates the potential politicising role of insolvency research. Just as progressives criticise contemporary bankruptcy relief in the United States as 'an enormously wasteful, efficient and incapable means of providing economic security to those who most need it',[228] so we might conclude by raising 'two cheers' for European personal insolvency.

227 See discussion of institutions as a response to political backlash in Mark Roe, Backlash (1998) 98 Colum LRev 217.

228 Jacob Hacker, 'The Middle Class at Risk' in K. Porter (n202) ch 12.

Chapter 13

Conclusions: Consumer Over-Indebtedness and Consumer Insolvency – from Micro to Macro

Hans-W. Micklitz

In the late 1970s and early 1980s Norbert Reich,[1] Udo Reifner[2] and Günter Hörmann[3] discovered consumer credit legislation in Germany as a prominent field of research. Each Member State has its own pioneers, as documented in the series on Consumer Protection Legislation edited by Norbert Reich and published by van Nostrand Reynolds.[4] A significant number of the founding fathers of consumer credit dedicated their academic lives to this ever-growing field of consumer law.[5] The general discussion in legal scholarship at this time focussed on access to credit, opening the credit market to all consumers, and allowing consumers to use credit as part of their income in order to participate in consumer society. Consequently, much attention was also paid to combating opaque and overpriced credit agreements or agreements which left consumers in debt even after the good that had been bought using consumer credit (usually a car or similarly expensive good) had been repossessed. Whilst this is not the place to recount the history of consumer credit,[6] it is nevertheless important to emphasise that it took some time before the dark side of the consumer credit society and the potential negative consequences of credit became clear.

1 Konsumentenkredit, Luchterhand 1979.

2 Alternatives Wirtschaftsrecht am Beispiel der Verbraucherverschuldung, Luchterhand 1979.

3 Knut Holzscheck, Günter Hörmann and Jürgen Daviter, Praxis des Konsumentenkredits, eine empirische Untersuchung zur Rechtssoziologie und Ökonomie des Konsumentenkredits, Bundesanzeiger Verlag 1982.

4 The whole project was initiated by Ludwig Krämer, at the time responsible for Consumer Protection at the European Commission, and was comprised of nine country reports from the then nine Member States, Belgium, Denmark, France, Germany, Ireland, Italy, Luxemburg, Netherlands, United Kingdom. As author N. Reich and H.-W. Micklitz, Verbraucherschutzrecht in der BRD, 1980, 410 pages; the same, Consumer Legislation in the Federal Republic of Germany, 1981, 383 pages; the same Verbraucherschutzrecht in den E.G.-Staaten – Eine vergleichende Analyse, 1980, 235 pages, in English, Consumer Legislation in the EC Countries – A Comparative Analy-sis, 206 pages; the same in French, Le Droit de la Consommation dans les Pays Membres de la CEE – Une Analyse Comparative, 1981, 231 pages.

5 Iain Ramsay and Udo Reifner spring to mind.

6 Udo Reifner, Kreditrecht – Handbuch zum Konsum- und Hypothekenkreditrecht, C.H.Beck 1991 (2nd edition in preparation) (Credit Law – Handbook on Consumer Credit and Mortgage Law); David Graeber, Debt, The First 5.000 Years, Melville House 2012.

Subjective versus Objective Reasons for Consumer Insolvency

Consumer insolvency only began to attract academic interest after a significant period of time, and when it did, it was in a rather distorted form. The first study on consumer insolvency was published in the 1980s.[7] For more than two decades the search for reasons for consumer insolvency split the discussion into two camps. On the one hand were those who identified individual failure of the consumer as the major reason; an explanation very much in line with the dominant ideology of Western democratic and capitalist societies at this time. Up until 2002 the German Civil Code contained a rule in Article 279 which in essence stated that 'Geld muss man haben' – 'the debtor has to have money' – when they enter into a financial commitment. If the debtor fails to honour their commitment, it is their responsibility. The debtor has to bear the consequences in the form of a life-long obligation: there is no other way out. Only businesses had the chance to declare bankruptcy and to earn the chance of a fresh start. The German Konkursordnung dates back to 1877. It took roughly 100 years before consumers were offered a similar option.

On the other hand, there were those who argued and provided evidence that any failure to honour credit obligations could be attributed to objective factors such as the debtor losing their job or going through a divorce. It took decades and endless research before the undeniable relationship between credit failure and unemployment or separation of families yielded political and legal results. The United States, where consumer credit became an integral part of consumer society, was the first to recognise the consequences of such factors and the first to introduce a procedure for insolvency.[8] European countries gradually followed suit[9] and the economic crisis that followed the collapse of Lehman Brothers served to expedite this development. However, even today not all European Member States have enacted insolvency legislation. Spain, one of the countries which was hit hardest by the crisis, is one such country that has not enacted any insolvency legislation.

National insolvency legislation attempts to strike a delicate balance. To elaborate, whilst individual responsibility, in line with Protestant ethics, requires an element of punishment in order to ensure that the debtor feels some guilt for their personal failure, a more objective approach underpins the necessity for the possibility of a fresh start to reintegrate the consumer into the consumption process. Not least due to different cultures in different states, insolvency procedures vary significantly, adopting more or less subjective or more or less objective models in terms of how bankrupt consumers are relieved of their debts. However, there is a certain tendency to downplay the 'guilt' and the ethical dimension of having debt and to promote the need for a fair insolvency procedure, which implies the right to a second chance.

One thing that both camps have in common is that they focus by and large on the micro perspective. Analytical and political attention tends to focus on the individual consumer. However, there are significant differences in points of view. Those who stress individual responsibility will not accept that the consumer is a victim of the consumer society, but will argue that the consumer is in some way a 'wrongdoer' who entered into credit commitments beyond their means and who ought to only in exceptional circumstances be discharged of these obligations after a period of pain and suffering. In contrast, those who stress objective reasons tend to downplay individual

7 Günter Hörmann (Hrsg./Editor), Consumer Credit and Consumer Insolvency, Perspectives for Legal Policy from Europe and the USA, Bremen 1982 (published by Zentrum für Europäische Rechtspolitik, Centre for European Legal Policy).

8 David Caplovitz, The Poor Pay More, Consumer Practices of Low-Income Families, Sage Publications 1967.

9 Hans-W. Micklitz (special editor), The Regulation of Over-Indebtedness of Consumers in Europe, Special Issue Journal of Consumer Policy 35(4), December 2012.

responsibility in highlighting 'social force majeure',[10] which is inherent in the two key events – unemployment and breakdown of the family unit. However, both are united in what could be called a contractual approach; a focus on the different types of contracts the consumer concluded and an attempt to weigh and rank the contracts in relation to the type of creditor and the type of obligations. Universal services,[11] which each and every consumer needs for their daily lives, such as water, electricity, public transport, telephones for instance, prevail over less important obligations resulting from luxury consumption decisions.

Therefore the predominant perspective of insolvency legislation is micro management, organising support and advice for the over-indebted or bankrupt consumer, finding mechanisms to reduce and even discharge the debt after a maximum period of one to five years. Setting the moral and the ethical dimension of debt relief aside, consumer insolvency procedures where they exist may not explicitly aim at, but ultimately promote, the reintegration of the failed consumer back into the market. The connection between individual insolvency and the economy, if any, remains rather loose, via so-called objective reasons such as unforeseen unemployment and the breakdown of family relations.

The Game Changer

The 2008 economic crisis led to a dramatic change. The six country studies in Part II, as well as the contributions of Elaine Kempson and Iain Ramsay (chapters 9 and 12), clearly document that consumer debt has reached levels which are potentially dangerous for the economy. However, action taken so far as been directed towards bailing out banks and stabilising the economy rather than helping the individual consumer. Despite tremendous intellectual investment in consumer credit research attempting to introduce a collective or societal dimension to consumer credit through the concept of social force majeure, this did not materialise.[12] In fact, it was not the social dimension but the economic dimension behind consumer credit which smashed the genuine individual and individualistic concept of consumer credit and consumer insolvency.

The most visible sign is the change of language; 'individual' consumer debt was upgraded to 'common' household debt. Now and to a growing extent the importance of household debt for the economy as a whole was perceived. It is no longer the fate of the over-indebted or bankrupt consumer which attracts attention but the impact of the total amount of household debt on the economy. It is here where the World Bank comes in. Its mandate is not to look after individual consumers but to look after the broader economic and social dimension of household debt. This might explain why the World Bank has turned into the most important player in the analysis of household debt worldwide.[13] It has even bypassed the European Union, or more specifically the

10 Thomas Wilhelmsson, Critical Studies in Private Law, Kluwer International 1992

11 This concept has been introduced by the European Commission, in line with its policy to liberalise and privatise former public services, such as telecommunications, postal services, energy, transport and to some extent financial services. From the abundant literature see Marise Cremona (ed.), Market Integration and Public Services in the European Union, OUP 2011.

12 See Iain Ramsay and Tony Williams, The Crash that Launched a Thousand Fixes: Regulation of Consumer Credit after the Lending Revolution and the Credit Crunch, in K. Alexander and Niamh Moloney, Law Reforms and Financial Markets, Edward Elgar 2011, 221 et seq

13 See World Bank, Good Practices For Financial Consumer Protection [2012] available at: http://siteresources.worldbank.org/EXTFINANCIALSECTOR/Resources/Good_Practices_for_Financial_CP.pdf; World Bank, Global Survey on Consumer Protection and Financial Literacy: Oversight Frameworks and

European Commission, which has been limited to making policy recommendations, as Guido Comparato has clearly shown in Chapter 2, not least due to limits on competence.

However, it is highly likely that the European Central Bank will at least use its mandate under the establishment of the Banking Union to standardise the criteria on how to measure over-indebtedness and insolvency of consumers in order to obtain a sound overview of the reach and importance of household debt across the European Union – the Euro Member States and those who are ready to join in.[14] This would allow the European Central Bank and necessarily the EU to take household debt into consideration when implementing the Banking Union. This overview may lead to a revision of the role and function of consumer credit bureaus in the Banking Union – a point that Akos Rona-Tas makes in Chapter 11. However, the regulatory technique of the European Central Bank remains problematic as political solutions are disguised as technical ones.[15] An open political debate in public forums on the use and usefulness of common criteria for measuring over-indebtedness, on the role and importance of household debt not only for the economy but also for the society would appear to be about to be circumvented, or even downplayed and de-politicised. This highly political issue is again turned into a mere technocratic issue, providing grist for the mill to critics of the EU's democratic legitimacy.[16]

The well-known *Aziz*[17] case demonstrates how the transformation of consumer debt into household debt yields new alliances. In the case at issue the European Commission and the Spanish government together argued that EU consumer law does not provide for remedies to protect bankrupt consumers against the establishment of a self-executing title via standard contract terms, eliminating each and every possibility for over-indebted and bankrupt consumers to contest the legality of the mortgage contract in this regard. Why is or why could that be so?

The deeper non-legal socio-economic reasons behind the position of the Spanish government are relatively easy to understand. The Caixa Bank, the key player in the Spanish housing bubble, was bailed out and subsequently bought by the Spanish government. Accepting responsibility for evicted consumers would have been a costly enterprise which would have worsened the financial situation of the bank and therefore of Spain. The political measures taken in the aftermath of the

Practices in 114 Economies" [2013]; http://www.worldbank.org/en/results/2014/04/07/consumer-protection-in-banking-and-microfinance.

14 Confidential information given to the author by the consumer credit bureaus. It seems that the ECB is regarding the development of common criteria as a mere technical issue which lies within its competences. Whether this is true whether such an approach must be regarded as legal regulation which requires an explicit competence remains to be seen.

15 There is abundant literature, the link to Carl Schmitt is particularly interesting, see Ch. Joerges, Europa a Großraum? Shifting Legal Conceptualisations of the Integration Project, in Christian Joerges and Navray Singh Galeigh (eds), Darker Legacies of Law in Europe, The Shadow of National Socialism and Fascism over Europe and its Legal Traditions, Hart Publishing 2003, 133.

16 Fritz Scharpf, Monetary Union, Fiscal Crisis and the Preemption of Democracy. MPIfG Discussion Paper 11/11. New source: Zeitschrift für Staats- und Europawissenschaften 9(2), 2011, 163–198; Legitimacy Intermediation in the Multilevel European Polity and Its Collapse in the Euro Crisis. MPIfG Discussion Paper 12/6.

17 CJEU, Case C-415/11 – Mohamed Aziz ECR 2013 I- nyr; thereto H.-W. Micklitz, Unfair Contract Terms – Public Interest Litigation before European Courts Case C-415/11 Mohamed Aziz, in V. Colaert and E. Terryn (eds), Landmark Cases of EU Consumer Law – in Honour of Jules Stuyck, Intersentia 2013, 615–634; same author, Mohamed Aziz, Sympathetic and Activist – did the Court get it Wrong? in A. Sodersten and J.H.H. Weiler (eds), Where the Court Gets it Wrong, forthcoming.

Aziz judgment, which did not accept the Spanish argument, are now subject to a whole series of new references to the CJEU.[18]

It is much harder to understand the position of the European Commission. The conflict at issue concerns one of the key successes of European consumer policy, the adoption of Directive 93/13/EEC on unfair contract terms and its interpretation through the CJEU.[19] There is only one reason which might explain why the European Commission is not standing side by side with Mr Mohamed Aziz, and why the European Commission is not invoking the Charter of Fundamental Rights to save Mr Aziz's home. The European Commission has given the financial recovery in Spain precedence over the fate of the thousands of Spanish homeowners who have been evicted in the aftermath of the financial crisis.

Were the CJEU to alter its position, the European Commission might be prompted to rethink its position. It will be interesting to see how the European Commission argues in the pending cases. More importantly this would put pressure on the Spanish government not to regard Spanish homeowners as a social *quantité négligeable* or even more drastically as a form of collateral damage to be accepted. However, this is not all there is. The *Aziz* case led to a revision of the division of responsibilities between the executive and the judiciary, between politics and courts. The European Commission and the Spanish government seem to be caught in their technocratic bailout policy, which looks at the macro effects of household debts on the economy, but sets aside the social individual side including the potential effects of the over-indebtedness on Spanish citizens as human beings, thereby reducing politics to saving banks. The CJEU stepped in as a policy maker and social engineer, compensating for the deficiencies of the Spanish government and the European Commission. The actions of the CJEU in this way themselves raise far-reaching questions on the consequences and the legitimacy of a court taking over from politics. [20]

Contract Governance

The shift from *micro* to *macro*, from *individual* consumer insolvency to *collective* household debt, from *social* concerns to *economic* concerns, entails consequences for contract law and private law. Consumer credit and consumer insolvency are regarded as bilateral relationships where the parties have reciprocal rights and obligations and where it falls to the parties to solve payment difficulties, fallouts and possible insolvency. The risk of not recouping the money loaned or the risk 'Haus und Hof zu verlieren' – 'to lose the roof over one's head' – lies with the parties. Courts and agencies might step in to solve problems, but their involvement does not and did not change the genuine bilateral character of the creditor/debtor relationship.

Mr Mohamed Aziz and the thousands of Spanish homeowners who stand behind the *Aziz*-case highlight the macro-economic dimension of household debt in our economies. It is no longer possible to understand consumer insolvency as an individual problem which can be solved to the benefit or the detriment of the bankrupt consumer. Each and every individual insolvency must be

18 For the pending cases see C-116/13 Banco de Valencia, C-602/13, Banco Bilbao Vizcaya Argentaria, referred the 25.11.2013; C-8/14, BBVA, referred on 10/1/2014; C-90/14, Banco Grupo Cajatres, referred on 24.2.2014; C-93/14, Zurbano Belaza and Artieda Soria, referred on 26.2.2014; C-122/14, Aktiv Kapital Portfolio Investment, referred on 14.3.2014.

19 Hans-W. Micklitz and Norbert Reich, The Court and the Sleeping Beauty: The Revival of the Unfair Contract Terms Directive (UCTD) 771–808 CMLR 51 (2014).

20 Daniel Keleman, The Transformation of Law and Regulation in the European Union, Harvard University Press 2012.

understood and reconstructed in its macro-economic context. The collective dimension challenges the bilateral understanding of contract law, and requires links to be built between the micro and the macro level. 'Beyond privity' has become the domain of 'contract governance', a concept which enshrines and combines older discussions on linked contracts and networks.[21] The discussion is still at the early stages theoretically and doctrinally (theoretically in coming to grips with what contract governance in the various phenomena that are subsumed under this broad category, doctrinally in finding a balance between extending contracts beyond bilateral relations without making contracts as a concept meaningless).

Grundmann, Möslein and Riesenhuber, who are trailblazers in this field,[22] distinguish between four modes of contract governance:[23] governance of contract law (the framework in which the rules are elaborated, public/private, national/European/international – EU credit law versus national insolvency law), governance of contract (study of good order in a market society versus private law society – the deeper question of the embeddedness of private law/credit law in the market economy), governance with the means of contract law (regulation through contract law, combination of different policy objectives – social protection of the insolvent consumers versus protection of the banks against potential fallouts) and governance through contract (supplementing the framework via autonomous rules – standard terms in consumer credit).

I think the four categories can be merged into two. The first two concern the *structural* level of governance (the institutional framework, in my case of consumer credit and consumer insolvency), the second two deal with the *substantive* level, the interplay of regulation and autonomy (what I call 'regulated autonomy'[24] and what Irina Domurath enshrines in the formula of responsible lending and responsible lending). What is missing in the proposed fourfold distinction, even when condensed into two as I propose, is the *procedural* dimension of governance (accountability, transparency, legitimacy) which connects the *structural* to the *content* level. Again there is something to learn from the *Aziz* case and the way in which the ECJ handled this case. The judges invented a new remedy, injunctive relief, in order to connect the declaratory to the enforcement proceedings. This new remedy builds a bridge between two different legal worlds – autonomous contract making via standard terms which allows for self-execution of the contract – and the almost macro-institutional level of enforcement that brings politics, but not necessarily economics, back in. It shows that there are ways and means even in legal doctrine to break down the bilateral relationship via procedural means, not via substantive means.

---

21 Notably, see Marc Amstutz and Gunther Teubner (eds), Networks: Legal Issues of Multilateral Cooperation, Hart 2009; Gunther Teubner, Networks as Connected Contracts, Hart 2011 (translated by Michelle Everson, and with an exceptionally helpful introduction by Hugh Collins); Fabrizio Cafaggi (ed.), Contractual Networks, Inter-Firm Cooperation and Economic Growth, Edward Elgar 2011; and Stefan Grundmann, Fabrizio Cafaggi and Giuseppe Vettori (eds), The Organizational Contract: From Exchange to Long-Term Network Cooperation in European Contract Law, Ashgate 2013.

22 For European private law see Fabrizo Cafaggi and Horatia Muir-Watt (eds), Making European Private Law: Governance Design, Edward Elgar 2008.

23 Karl Riesenhuber and Florian Möslein, Contract Governance – Skizze eines Forschungsprojekts, in the same (eds), Perspektiven eines Europäischen Schuldvertragsrechts, De Gruyter Recht 2008, 4; F. Möslein, Contract Governance and Corporate Governance im Zusammenspiel (2010), Juristenzeitung 72; Stefan Grundmann, Florian Möslein and Karl Riesenhuber (eds), Contract Governance – Dimensions in Law and Interdisciplinary Research, Oxford University Press 2015.

24 Guido Comparato and Hans-W. Micklitz, Regulated Autonomy between Market Freedoms and Fundamental Rights in the Case Law of the CJEU, in Ulf Bernitz, Xavier Groussot and Felix Schulyok (eds), General Principles of EU Law and European Private Law, Ashgate 2013, 121–154

However, what is needed is to understand contract governance not only as the domain of private parties and courts, but to integrate the competent agencies into the analysis. The CJEU is not in a position to solve the issue behind the *Aziz* case, it might not even be competent to help Mr Aziz himself, let alone the many *Aziz* behind him. Here an interaction between European and national courts, between the national government and national courts, is needed to find a solution which strikes a balance between the micro and the macro level.

Perspectives

This is not the place to go deeper into the *Aziz* case in exploiting the idea of injunctive relief as a means to link structures and content. It remains for separate research to study the potential and the limits of contract governance as a possible answer to link the micro to the macro. One point that must be highlighted, however, is the change in perspective of over-indebtedness and consumer insolvency from micro to macro – from individual destinies of failed consumers to failed banks and not least to sovereign default. Consumer insolvency or, better, household insolvency has finally attracted attention at the macro level. Whilst this change in perspective also opens new avenues and new perspectives for contract law, it should not be forgotten that at the very end of the latter there are always those like Mohamed Aziz who risk losing their homes, most often due to a combination of subjective and objective reasons, of (ir)responsible lending and (ir)responsible borrowing.

Index

For Product Safety Concerns and Information please contact our EU
representative GPSR@taylorandfrancis.com
Taylor & Francis Verlag GmbH, Kaufingerstraße 24, 80331 München, Germany

www.ingramcontent.com/pod-product-compliance
Ingram Content Group UK Ltd.
Pitfield, Milton Keynes, MK11 3LW, UK
UKHW050753180926
475701UK00007B/1022
* 9 7 8 1 0 3 2 0 9 8 5 3 1 *